"No other guide h[...]
a pleasure to read [...]

". . . Excellently organized for the casual traveler who is looking for a mix of recreation and cultural insight."
Washington Post

★ ★ ★ ★ ★ (5-star rating) "Crisply written and remarkably personable. Cleverly organized so you can pluck out the minutest fact in a moment. Satisfyingly thorough."
Réalités

"The information they offer is up-to-date, crisply presented but far from exhaustive, the judgments knowledgeable but not opinionated."   *New York Times*

"The individual volumes are compact, the prose succinct, and the coverage up-to-date and knowledgeable . . . The format is portable and the index admirably detailed."
John Barkham Syndicate

". . . An abundance of excellent directions, diversions, and facts, including perspectives and getting-ready-to-go advice — succinct, detailed, and well organized in an easy-to-follow style."   *Los Angeles Times*

"They contain an amount of information that is truly staggering, besides being surprisingly current."
Detroit News

"These guides address themselves to the needs of the modern traveler demanding precise, qualitative information . . . Upbeat, slick, and well put together."
Dallas Morning News

". . . Attractive to look at, refreshingly easy to read, and generously packed with information."   *Miami Herald*

"These guides are as good as any published, and much better than most."   *Louisville* (Kentucky) *Times*

Stephen Birnbaum Travel Guides

Acapulco
Bahamas, Turks & Caicos
Barcelona
Bermuda
Boston
Canada
Cancun, Cozumel, and Isla Mujeres
Caribbean
Chicago
Disneyland
Eastern Europe
Europe
Europe for Business Travelers
Florence
France
Great Britain
Hawaii
Ireland
Italy
Ixtapa & Zihuatanejo
London
Los Angeles
Mexico
Miami
New York
Paris
Portugal
Rome
San Francisco
South America
Spain
United States
USA for Business Travelers
Venice
Walt Disney World
Western Europe

CONTRIBUTING EDITORS

Frederick H. Brengelman
Patricia Canole
Wendy Luft
Thérèse Margolis
Eileen Morin
Melinda Tang
Carol Zaiser

MAPS   B. Andrew Mudryck
SYMBOLS   Gloria McKeown

A Stephen Birnbaum Travel Guide

Birnbaum's
CANCUN,
COZUMEL, AND
ISLA MUJERES
1992

Stephen Birnbaum
Alexandra Mayes Birnbaum
EDITORS

Lois Spritzer
EXECUTIVE EDITOR

Laura L. Brengelman
Managing Editor

Mary Callahan
Ann-Rebecca Laschever
Julie Quick
Beth Schlau
Dana Margaret Schwartz
Associate Editors

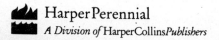 HarperPerennial
A Division of HarperCollins*Publishers*

BIRNBAUM'S CANCUN, COZUMEL, AND ISLA MUJERES. Copyright © 1991 by
HarperCollins Publishers. All rights reserved. Printed in the United States of
America. No part of this book may be used or reproduced in any manner
whatsoever without written permission except in the case of brief quotations
embodied in critical articles and reviews. For information address
HarperCollins*Publishers,* 10 East 53rd Street, New York, NY 10022.

FIRST EDITION

ISSN: 0749-2561 (Stephen Birnbaum Travel Guides)
ISSN: 1055-5641 (Cancun, Cozumel, and Isla Mujeres)
ISBN: 0-06-278003-4 (pbk.)

91 93 94 95 96 CC/WP 10 9 8 7 6 5 4 3 2 1

Contents

GETTING READY TO GO

All the practical travel data you need to plan your Mexican vacation to the final detail.

When and How to Go

Preparing

On the Road

Sources and Resources

USEFUL WORDS AND PHRASES

THE ISLANDS

A thorough, qualitative guide to Mexico's three most often visited resort islands. This is a comprehensive report on the most compelling attractions and amenities, designed to be used on the spot.

DIVERSIONS

A selective guide to more than 15 active and/or cerebral theme vacations, including the best places in Mexico to pursue them.

For the Experience

For the Body

For the Mind

DIRECTIONS

The Yucatán's major driving routes, leading from the country's most beautiful beaches to it's farthest jungles.

A Word from the Editor

I don't normally find myself particularly receptive to resorts designated by computer. Yet even I have to admit — however grudgingly — that the computer knew exactly what it was doing when it determined that Cancún, the ancient playground of the Maya, would make an equally appealing place in the sun for today's holidaymakers. If anything, Cancún — and the neighboring islands of Cozumel and Isla Mujeres — have suffered from the intense popularity spawned by the reliability of the local weather and the lure of wonderful sand beaches and irresistible Caribbean waters, so much so that there are those who now consider the region's national bird to be the construction crane.

Spectacular sand and sun notwithstanding, the last couple of years have been especially confusing for travelers heading for Mexico. The recent roller-coaster ride that has characterized Mexico's political, personal, financial, and industrial relationships with other North American countries — and the rest of the world, for that matter — has been mirrored by severe swings in currency relationships that have made an accurate estimation of the cost of a visit to Mexico very difficult. Clearly, there has never been a time when an up-to-date guide to Cancún, Cozumel, and Isla Mujeres was a more useful travel tool.

What's more, the broadening sophistication of contemporary travelers has made it essential that guidebooks evolve in very fundamental ways in order to keep pace with their readers. That's why we've tried to create a guide to these resort islands adjacent to Mexico's Yucatán Peninsula that's specifically organized, written, and edited for this more demanding, modern traveler headed to this increasingly popular country. This is a traveler for whom qualitative information is infinitely more desirable than mere quantities of unappraised data. We think that this book, along with the other guides in our series, represents a new generation of travel guides — one that is especially responsive to modern needs and interests.

For years, dating back as far as Herr Baedeker, travel guides have tended to be encyclopedic, seemingly much more concerned with demonstrating expertise in geography and history than with any real analysis of the sorts of things that genuinely concern a typical tourist. But today, when it is hardly necessary to tell a traveler where Mexico's Caribbean Coast is located (in many cases, the traveler has been to that area nearly as often as the guidebook editors), it becomes the responsibility of those editors to provide new perceptions and to suggest new directions to make a guide genuinely valuable.

That's exactly what we've tried to do in this series. I think you'll notice a different, more contemporary tone to the text, as well as an organization and focus that are distinctive and more functional. And even a random reading of what follows will demonstrate a substantial departure from the standard guidebook orientation, for we've not only attempted to provide information of a different sort, but we also have tried to present it in a format that makes it particularly accessible.

Needless to say, it's difficult to decide what to include in a guidebook — and what to omit. Early on, we realized that giving up the encyclopedic approach precluded the inclusion of every single route and restaurant, a realization that helped define our overall editorial focus. Similarly, when we discussed the possibility of presenting certain information in other than strict geographical order, we found that the new format enabled us to arrange data in a way that we feel best answers the questions travelers typically ask.

Large numbers of specific questions have provided the real editorial skeleton for this book. The volume of mail I regularly receive seems to emphasize that modern travelers want very precise information, so we've tried to organize our material in the most responsive way possible. Readers who want to know the best restaurant in Cancún or the most fascinating place to dive off Cozumel will have no trouble whatever extracting that data from this guide.

Travel guides are, above all, reflections of personal taste, and putting one's name on a title page obviously puts one's preferences on the line. But I think I ought to amplify just exactly what "personal" means. I don't believe in the sort of personal guidebook that's a palpable misrepresentation on its face. It is, for example, hardly possible for any single writer to visit thousands of restaurants (and nearly as many hotels) in any given year and provide accurate appraisals of each one. And even if it *were* possible for one human being to survive such an itinerary, it would of necessity have to be done at a dead sprint and the perceptions derived therefrom would probably be less valid than those of any other intelligent individual visiting the same establishments. It is, therefore, impossible (especially in an annually revised and updated guidebook *series* such as we offer) to have only one person provide all the data on the entire world.

I also happen to think that such individual orientation is of substantially less value to readers. Visiting a single hotel for just one night or eating one hasty meal in a random restaurant hardly equips anyone to provide appraisals that are of more than passing interest. No amount of doggedly alliterative or oppressively onomatopoeic text can camouflage a technique that is essentially specious. We have, therefore, chosen what I like to describe as the "thee and me" approach to restaurant and hotel evaluation and, to a somewhat more limited degree, to the sites and sights we have included in the other sections of our text. What this really reflects is personal sampling tempered by intelligent counsel from informed local sources, and these additional friends-of-the-editors are almost always residents of the city and/or area about which they have been consulted.

Despite the presence of several editors, writers, researchers, and local correspondents, very precise editing and tailoring keep our text fiercely subjective. So what follows is the gospel according to the Birnbaums, and it represents as much of our own tastes and instincts as we can manage. It is probable, therefore, that if you prefer chili peppers that leave the roof of your mouth largely intact, can't stand canned fruit juices, and won't tolerate fresh fish that is relentlessly overcooked, then we're likely to have a long and meaningful relationship. Readers with dissimilar tastes may be less enraptured.

I should also point out something about the person to whom this guidebook is directed. Above all, he or she is a "visitor." This means that such elements as restaurants have been specifically picked to provide the visitor with a representative, enlightening, stimulating, and, above all, pleasant experience. Since so many extraneous considerations can affect the reception and service accorded a regular restaurant patron, our choices can in no way be construed as an exhaustive guide to resident dining. We think we've listed all the best places in various price ranges, but they were chosen with a visitor's enjoyment in mind.

Other evidence of how we've tried to tailor our text to reflect modern travel habits is most apparent in the section we call DIVERSIONS. Where once it was common for travelers to spend a visit to Mexico's resorts simply lying beside some pool or beachfront, the emphasis today is more likely to be directed toward pursuing some favorite activity while visiting this unique turf. So we've selected every activity we could reasonably evaluate and organized the material in a way that is especially accessible to activists of either athletic or cerebral bent. It is no longer necessary, therefore, to wade through a pound or two of superfluous prose just to find the most challenging dive spot or Maya ceremonial center within a reasonable distance of your hotel.

Although the sheer beauty of the Mexican Caribbean is reason enough to want to visit, there also are a number of added bonuses once you arrive. The entire adjacent Yucatán Peninsula offers a veritable cornucopia of activities to challenge the imagination of any visitor. Deep in the tropical jungles of the region lie archaeological treasures from one of the richest civilizations in human history. Naturalists also will find the region an ideal setting for studying flamingos, manatees, and even sharks in their natural habitats.

If there is one single thing that characterizes the revolution in and evolution of current holiday habits, it is that most travelers now consider travel a right rather than a privilege. Travel today translates as the enthusiastic desire to sample all of the world's opportunities, to find that elusive quality of experience that is not only enriching, but comfortable. For that reason, we've tried to make what follows not only helpful and enlightening, but the sort of welcome companion of which every traveler dreams.

Finally, I should point out that every good travel guide is a living enterprise; that is, no part of this text is carved in stone. In our annual revisions, we refine, expand, and further hone all our material to serve your travel needs even better. To this end, no contribution is of greater value to us than your personal reaction to what we have written, as well as information reflecting your own experiences while using the book. We earnestly and enthusiastically solicit your comments about this book *and* your opinions and perceptions about places you have recently visited. In this way, we will be able to provide the most current information — including the actual experiences of real travelers — and to make those experiences more readily available to others. So please write to us at 60 E. 42nd St., New York, NY 10165.

We sincerely hope to hear from you.

STEVE BIRNBAUM.

How to Use This Guide

? A great deal of care has gone into the special organization of this guidebook, and we believe it represents a real breakthrough in the presentation of travel information. Our aim is to create a new, more modern generation of travel books, and to make this guide the most useful and practical travel tool available today.

Our text is divided into five basic sections in order to present information in the most useful way on every possible aspect of a vacation to Mexico's Caribbean Coast. This organization itself should alert you to the vast and varied opportunities available, as well as indicating all the specific data necessary to plan a successful trip. You won't find much of the conventional "swaying palms and shimmering sands" type of text in this guide; we've chosen instead to deliver more useful and practical information. Prospective itineraries tend to speak for themselves, and with so many diverse travel opportunities, we feel our main job is to highlight what's where and to provide basic details — how, when, where, how much, and what's best (and what's not) — to assist you to make the most intelligent choices possible.

Here is a brief summary of the five sections of this book, and what you can expect to find in each. We believe that you will find both your travel planning and en route enjoyment enhanced by having this book at your side.

GETTING READY TO GO

This mini-encyclopedia of practical travel facts is meant to be a sort of know-it-all companion, with all the precise information necessary to create a journey to and through Cancún, Cozumel, and Isla Mujeres, and along the Yucatán Peninsula. There are entries on more than 25 separate topics, including how to get where you're going, what the trip is likely to cost, and how to avoid prospective problems. The individual entries are specific, realistic, and, where appropriate, cost-oriented.

We expect you to use this section most in the course of planning your trip, for its ideas and suggestions are intended to simplify this often confusing period. Entries are intentionally concise, in an effort to get to the meat of the matter. These entries are augmented by extensive lists of specific sources from which to obtain even more detailed data, plus some suggestions for obtaining travel information on your own.

USEFUL WORDS AND PHRASES

Though most resorts in Cancún, Cozumel, and Isla Mujeres have English-speaking staff, at smaller establishments and on most stops along the Yucatán trail, a little knowledge of Spanish will go a long way. This collection of often-used words and phrases will help you to make a hotel or dinner reservation, order a meal, mail a letter — and even buy toothpaste.

THE ISLANDS

The individual reports on Cancún, Cozumel, and Isla Mujeres have been created with the assistance of researchers, contributors, professional journalists, and experts who live on the islands. Although useful at the planning stage, THE ISLANDS is really designed to be taken along and used on the spot. The reports offer a short-stay guide, including an essay introducing each island as a historic entity and as a contemporary place to visit. *At-a-Glance* material is actually a site-by-site survey of the most important, interesting (and sometimes most eclectic) sights to see and things to do. *Sources and Resources* is a concise listing of pertinent tourist information meant to answer a range of potentially pressing questions as they arise — from something simple like the address of the tourist office, how to get around, which sightseeing tours to take, when special events and holidays occur, to something more difficult like where to find the best nightspot, which are the shops that have the finest merchandise and/or the most irresistible bargains, and where the best golf, tennis, fishing, and swimming are to be found. *Best in Town* is our collection of cost-and-quality choices of the best places to eat and sleep on a variety of budgets.

DIVERSIONS

This very selective guide is designed to help travelers find the very best place in which to pursue a wide range of physical and cerebral activities, without having to wade through pages of unrelated text. With a host of activities, DIVERSIONS provides a guide to the special place where the quality of experience is likely to be highest. Whether you opt for golf or tennis, scuba or surfing, bullfights or ancient ruins, each category is the equivalent of a comprehensive checklist of the absolute best in the area.

DIRECTIONS

Here are 4 day trips from Cancún's superb beaches, plus 2 extended driving itineraries for exploring Maya relics on the Yucatán Peninsula. The itineraries can be "connected" for longer drives or used individually for short, intensive explorations.

Each entry includes a guide to sightseeing highlights; a cost-and-quality guide to accommodations along the road (small inns, clean and comfortable motels, country hotels, campgrounds, and detours to off-the-main-road discoveries); hints and suggestions for activities; and detailed driving maps of the route, noting points of interest described in the text.

Although each of the book's sections has a distinct format and a special function, they have been designed to be used together to provide a complete inventory of travel information. To use this book to full advantage, take a few minutes to read the table of contents and random entries in each section to give you an idea of how it all fits together.

Pick and choose needed information from different sections. Assume, for example, that your idea of a dream vacation has always been to golf or just bask on a beach on Cancún, go scuba diving off the coast of Cozumel, and explore the major ruins on the Yucatán Peninsula — Chichén Itzá, Uxmal, and Tulum — but you never really knew how to put such a trip together. Since your vacation will include driving, start by reading the short, informative section on traveling by car in GETTING READY TO GO. This will provide all the factual information needed to organize and prepare a road trip. It will alert you to insurance needs (and direct you to the insurance chapter in the same section of the book) and other equally detailed potential problems and pleasures of a driving vacation. But where to go and what to see? Turn to DIVERSIONS, *Scuba and Skin Diving,* for the best dive spots in the waters around Cozumel; *Good Golf* for information on Cancún's *Pok-Ta-Pok* golf course; *The Yucatán's Magnificent Archaeological Heritage,* for descriptions of the most compelling archaeological sites and sights in the area. Then turn to DIRECTIONS for an explicit guide to our suggested driving routes from Cancún to the various destinations along the Yucatán Peninsula.

In other words, the sections of this book are building blocks to help you put together the best possible trip. Use them selectively as a tool, a source of ideas, a reference work for accurate facts, and a guide to the best buys, the most exciting sights and sites, the most pleasant accommodations, and the tastiest food — *the best travel experience* that you can have.

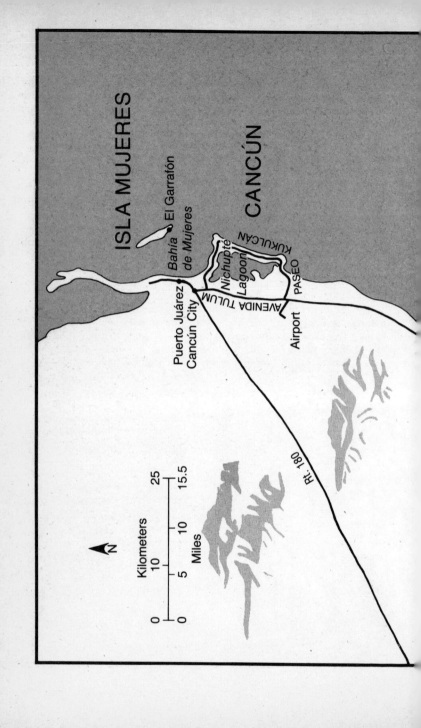

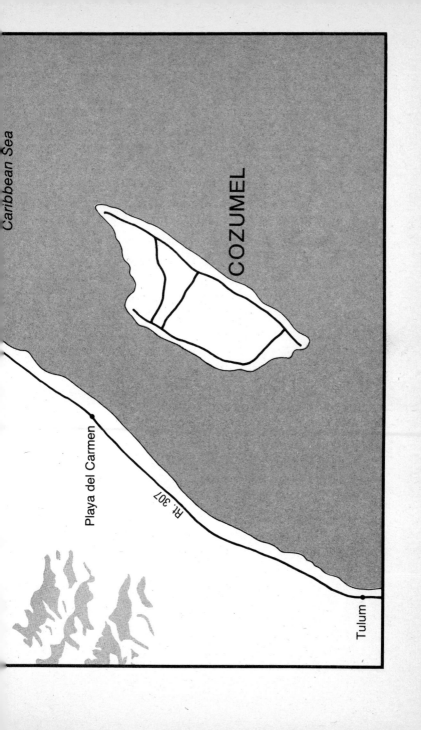

GETTING READY TO GO

When and How to Go

What's Where

There are three resort islands where the Caribbean Sea meets the Gulf of Mexico. The best known of these is **Cancún**, which was developed into a resort after the Mexican government conducted a series of computerized feasibility studies. Less posh, but very popular with scuba divers and snorkelers, is **Cozumel**, a few miles south of Cancún. At **Isla Mujeres**, just 6 miles (10 km) north of Cancún, it's great fun to swim among huge schools of rainbow-colored fish and ride giant sea turtles.

These islands lie just off Mexico's **Yucatán Peninsula**, a hook of land at the southeastern end of the mainland. The peninsula consists of three states: **Campeche, Yucatán,** and **Quintana Roo.** Mostly *plano* jungle, steamy and very hot throughout most of the year, this is the province of the contemporary Maya, whose forebears left incredibly intricate fortresses, pyramids, temples, and cities dotting the jungles of the peninsula. The most famous of these ruins, **Chichén Itzá**, contains sacrificial wells and altars which the Toltec built after they took over the Maya city. The capital of Yucatán state, Mérida, is 33 miles inland from the port of Progreso.

When to Go

Most people associate Cancún, Cozumel, and Isla Mujeres with winter suntans and beautiful seaside resorts. They aren't wrong. Mexico's Caribbean Coast is one of the all-time favorite escapes for Americans trapped in snow and icy slush. (The winter season begins on December 15, when Mexicans traditionally take their annual 2-week, year-end vacation. It ends around the middle of April, after *Easter.*)

The destinations covered in this book are blessed with year-round tourism seasons, so there really isn't a "best" time to visit them. But it is important to emphasize that more and more travelers are enjoying the substantial advantages of off-season travel; that is, late spring, summer, and fall at most of the coastal resorts. Getting there and staying there are less expensive during the off-season as airfares, hotel rooms, and car rental rates go down, and less expensive package tours become available; the independent traveler can go farther on less, too. What's more, major tourist attractions, beaches, and other facilities tend to be less crowded, and — throughout Mexico — life proceeds at a more leisurely pace.

It should also be noted that what the travel industry refers to as shoulder seasons — the 1½ to 2 months before and after the peak seasons — often are sought out because they offer fair weather and somewhat smaller crowds. But be aware that very near high-season prices still can prevail.

CLIMATE AND CLOTHES: Chamber of Commerce types claim that Cancún and its sister islands have some of the best weather in the Caribbean, with 200 rain-free days each year. Temperatures usually are in the 90s between May and October and in the mid-80s from October through April, although it can be chilly at night. It also may be cooler and windy at times, and the rainy season, which lasts from June through September, drops a couple of hours of refreshing rain in the afternoons. Danger from hurricanes is historically most severe in September. On Cancún, dress is elegant but informal; jackets are seldom worn and there's never a need for a tie. On Cozumel and Isla Mujeres, fashions are somewhat more casual than Cancún.

Travelers can get current readings and 3-day Accu-Weather forecasts through *American Express Travel Related Services'* Worldwide Weather Report number. By dialing 1-900-WEATHER and punching in CAN for Cancún, you will hear an up-to-date recording of the current temperature, sky conditions, wind speed and direction, heat index, relative humidity, local time, and beach and boating report. This 24-hour service can be accessed from any Touch-Tone phone in the US and costs 75¢ per minute. The charge will show up on your phone bill. For a listing of other areas covered and the corresponding access codes, send a self-addressed, stamped envelope to *1-900-WEATHER*, 261 Central Ave., Farmingdale, NY 11735.

Traveling by Plane

The quickest, most efficient way to get to Cancún is by air. Among the airlines offering flights to Mexico, almost all sell seats at a variety of prices under a vast spectrum of requirements and restrictions. You probably will spend more for your airfare than for any other single item in your travel budget. In order to take advantage of the lowest available fare, you should know what kinds of flights are available, the rules and regulations pertaining to air travel, and all the special package options.

SCHEDULED FLIGHTS: Leading airlines offering regularly scheduled flights to Cancún from the US, many on a daily basis, include *Aerocancun, Aerocaribe, Aeroméxico, American, Continental, Mexicana, Northwest,* and *United. Aerocancun, Aerocaribe, Aeroméxico, American, Continental,* and *Mexicana* also offer frequent flights to Cozumel. As of this writing, direct flights — with no change of plane between the originating and terminating cities — to Cancún depart from Chicago, Dallas, Miami, New York, and Washington, DC. Direct flights to Cozumel depart from Dallas, Miami, and New York.

Regional airlines serve specialized domestic routes. For information, consult *Aeroméxico* (phone: 800-237-6639), *Aeromar* (phone: 800-950-0747), *Aero California* (phone: 800-258-3311), or *Mexicana* (phone: 800-531-7921).

Tickets – A full-fare ticket provides maximum travel flexibility (although at considerable expense) because there are no advance booking requirements. This "open reservation" system means that a prospective passenger can buy a ticket for a flight right up to the minute of takeoff — if a seat is available. If your ticket is for a round trip, you can make the return reservation any time you wish and you can cancel your flight at any time without penalty. These tickets are good for a year, but can be renewed if not used. However, while it is true that this category of ticket can be purchased at the last minute, it is advisable to reserve well in advance during popular vacation periods and around holiday times.

Fares – Perhaps the most common misconception about fares on scheduled airlines is that the cost of the ticket determines how much service will be provided on the flight. This is true only to a certain extent. A far more realistic rule of thumb is that the less you pay for your ticket, the more restrictions and qualifications are likely to come into play *before* you board the plane (as well as after you get off). These qualifying aspects relate to the months (and the days of the week) during which you must travel, how far in advance you must purchase your ticket, the minimum and maximum amount of time you may or must remain away, your willingness to decide on a return date at the time of booking — and your ability to stick to that date. It is not uncommon for passengers sitting side by side on the same wide-body jet to have paid fares varying by hundreds of dollars, and all too often the traveler paying more would have been equally willing (and able) to accept the terms of the less expensive ticket.

In general, the great variety of fares to Cancún and Cozumel can be reduced to four basic categories, including first class, coach (also called economy or tourist class), and excursion or discount fares. A fourth category, called business class, has been added by many airlines in recent years.

A **first class** ticket is your admission to the special section of the aircraft — larger seats, more legroom, sleeperette seating on some wide-body aircraft, better (or more elaborately served) food, free drinks and headsets for movies and music channels, and, above all, personal attention. First class fares are about twice those of full-fare economy, although both first class passengers and those paying full-fare economy fares are entitled to reserve seats and are sold tickets on an open reservation system.

Not too long ago, there were only two classes of air travel, first class and all the rest, usually called economy or tourist. Then **business class** came into being. Business class passengers usually sit in a separate cabin or cabins toward the front of the plane. While standards of comfort and service are not as high as in first class, they represent a considerable improvement over conditions in the rear of the plane, with roomier seats, more leg and shoulder space between passengers, and fewer seats abreast. Free liquor and headsets, a choice of meal entrées, and a separate counter for speedier check-in are other inducements. As in first class, business class passengers are sold seats on an open reservation system, and neither booking restrictions nor cancellation penalties apply. Note that airlines often have their own names for their business class services — such as *Aeroméxico*'s Premier Class, which is offered on nonstop flights between New York and Cancún.

The terms of the **coach** or **economy** fare may vary slightly from airline to airline, and, in fact, from time to time airlines may be selling more than one type of economy fare. Coach or economy passengers sit more snugly, as many as 10 in a single row on a wide-body jet, behind the first class and business class sections. Normally, alcoholic drinks are not free, nor are the headsets. If there are two economy fares on the books, one (often called "regular economy") still may include free stopovers. The other, less expensive (often called "special economy"), may limit stopovers to one or two, usually with a charge for each one. Like first class, there are no advance booking requirements, no minimum or maximum stay requirements, and no cancellation penalties; tickets are sold on an open reservation system. The cost of economy and business class tickets on flights between the US and Mexican island and coastal resort areas generally varies from a basic (low-season) price in effect most of the year to a peak (high-season) price in winter.

Excursion and other **discount** fares are the airlines' equivalent of a special sale and usually apply to round-trip bookings only. These fares generally differ according to the season and the number of travel days permitted. They are only a bit less flexible than full-fare economy tickets and are, therefore, often useful for both holiday and business travelers. Most round-trip excursion tickets include strict minimum and maximum stay requirements — generally a minimum of 3 to 7 days and a maximum of 2 months. Reservations can be changed only within the prescribed time limits. So don't count on extending a ticket beyond the prescribed time of return or staying less time than required. The ticket must be purchased a certain number of days — usually no fewer than 7 or 14 days — in advance of departure, and the return reservation usually has to be made at the time of the original ticketing and cannot be changed later than a certain number of days (again, usually 7 or 14) before the return flight. If events force a passenger to change the return reservation to a date less than the minimum stay or more than the maximum stay, the difference between the round-trip excursion rate and the round-trip coach rate probably will have to be paid. Last, cancellation penalties of up to 50% of the full price of the ticket have been assessed — check the specific penalty in effect when you purchase your discount/excursion ticket.

The availability of these reduced-rate seats is most limited at busy times, such as holidays. Discount or excursion fare ticket holders sit with the coach passengers and, for all intents and purposes, are indistinguishable from them. They receive all the same basic services, even though they may have paid anywhere between 30% and 55% less for the trip. Obviously, it's wise to plan early enough to qualify for this less expensive transportation, if possible.

Of even greater risk — and bearing the lowest price of all the current discount fares — is the ticket where no change at all in departure and/or return flights is permitted, and where the ticket price is totally nonrefundable. If you do buy a non-refundable ticket, you should be aware that for a fee — set by the airline and payable at the airport when checking in — you *may* be able to change the time or date of a return flight on a nonrefundable ticket. However, if the nonrefundable ticket price for the replacement flight is higher than that of the original (as is generally the case when trading in a weekday for a weekend flight), you will have to pay the difference. Any such change must be made a certain number of days in advance — in some cases as little as 2 days — of either the original or the replacement flight, whichever is earlier; restrictions are set by the individual carrier. (Travelers holding a nonrefundable or other restricted ticket who must change their plans due to a family emergency should know that some carriers may make special allowances in such situations; for further information, see *Medical and Legal Aid and Consular Services,* in this section.)

Standby fares, at one time the rock-bottom price at which a traveler could fly, recently have become rather elusive. While the definition of standby varies somewhat from airline to airline, it generally means that you make yourself available to buy a ticket for a flight (usually no sooner than the day of departure), then literally stand by on the chance that a seat will be empty. Once aboard, however, a standby passenger has the same meal service and frills (or lack of them) enjoyed by others in the economy class compartment.

Something else to check is the availability of a **GIT** (Group Inclusive Travel) fare, which requires that a specified dollar amount of ground arrangements be purchased, in advance, along with the ticket. The requirements vary as to the number of travel days and stopovers permitted, and the minimum number of passengers in a group. (The last can be as few as two full fares.) The actual fares also vary, but the cost will be spelled out in brochures distributed by the tour operators handling the ground arrangements. In the past, GIT fares typically were among the least expensive in the fare schedules of the established carriers. But although very attractive group fares may still appear from time to time, the advent of discount fares has caused group fares to all but disappear from some air routes, or their price tags have become the equivalent of all the other discount fares. Travelers reading brochures on group package tours to Cancún or Cozumel will find that, in almost all cases, the applicable airfare given as a sample (to be added to the price of the land package to obtain the total tour price) is the same discount fare available to the independent traveler.

The major airlines serving Cancún and Cozumel from the US sometimes also offer individual fare excursion rates similar to GIT fares, which are sold in conjunction with ground accommodation packages. Previously called ITX, these fares generally are offered as part of "air/hotel/car transfer packages," and can reduce the cost of an economy fare by more than a third. They are booked for a specific amount of time, with return dates specified; rescheduling and cancellation restrictions and penalties vary from carrier to carrier. These fares usually are offered to Cancún and Cozumel, sometimes including a stopover of day or more in Mexico City. (For further information on fly/drive packages, see *Package Tours,* in this section.)

Travelers looking for the least expensive airfares possible should, finally, scan the pages of their hometown newspapers (especially the Sunday travel sections) for announcements of special promotional fares. Most airlines traditionally have offered their most attractive special fares to encourage travel in slow seasons, and to inaugurate and publicize new routes. Even if none of these factors apply, prospective passengers can be fairly sure that the number of discount seats per flight at the lowest price is strictly limited, or that the fare offering includes a set expiration date — which means it's absolutely necessary to move fast to obtain the lowest possible price.

Among other special airline promotional deals for which you should be on the lookout are discount or upgrade coupons sometimes offered by the major carriers. They are good for either a percentage discount or an upgrade on domestic and international airline tickets — including flights to Mexico. There are usually some minimum airfare restrictions before the coupon is redeemable, but in general these are worthwhile offers. Restrictions often include certain blackout days (when the coupon cannot be used at all), usually imposed during peak travel periods. These coupons are particularly valuable to business travelers who tend to buy full-fare tickets, and while the coupons are issued in the buyer's name, they can be used by others who are traveling on the same itinerary.

It's always wise to ask about discount or promotional fares and about any conditions that might restrict booking, payment, cancellation, or changes in plans. Check the prices from other neighboring cities. A special rate may be offered in a nearby city but not in yours, and it may be enough of a bargain to warrant your leaving from that city. Ask if there is a difference in price for midweek versus weekend travel, or if there is a further discount for traveling early in the morning or late at night. Also be sure to investigate package deals, which are offered by virtually every airline. These may include car rentals, accommodations, and dining and/or sightseeing features in addition to the basic airfare, and the combined cost of packaged elements usually is considerably less than the cost of the exact same elements when purchased separately.

If in the course of your research you come across a deal that seems too good to be true, keep in mind that logic may not be a component of deeply discounted airfares — there's not always any sane relationship between miles to be flown and the price to get there. More often than not, the level of competition on a given route dictates the degree of discount, and don't be dissuaded from accepting an offer that sounds irresistible just because it also sounds illogical. Better to buy that inexpensive fare while it's being offered and worry about the sense — or absence thereof — while you're flying to your desired destination.

When you're satisfied that you've found the lowest possible price for which you can conveniently qualify (you may have to call the airline more than once, because different airline reservation clerks have been known to quote different prices), make your booking. Then, to protect yourself against fare increases, purchase and pay for your ticket as soon as possible after you've received a confirmed reservation. Airlines generally will honor their tickets, even if the operative price at the time of your flight is higher than the price you paid; if fares go up between the time you *reserve* a flight and the time you *pay* for it, you likely will be out of luck. Finally, with excursion or discount fares, it is important to remember that when a reservation clerk says that you must purchase a ticket by a specific date, this is an absolute deadline. Miss it and the airline may automatically cancel your reservation without telling you.

■ **Note:** Another wrinkle in the airfare scene is that if the fares go *down* after you purchase your ticket, you *may* be entitled to a refund of the difference. However, this is possible only in certain situations — availability and advance purchase restrictions pertaining to the lower rate are set by the airline. If you suspect that you may be able to qualify for such a refund, check with your travel agent or the airline.

Frequent Flyers – Most of the leading carriers serving Cancún and Cozumel offer a bonus system to frequent travelers. After the first 10,000 miles, for example, a passenger might be eligible for a first class seat for the coach fare; after another 10,000 miles he or she might receive a discount on his or her next ticket purchase. The value of the bonuses continues to increase as more miles are logged.

Bonus miles also may be earned by patronizing affiliated car rental companies or hotel chains, or by using one of the credit cards that now offers this reward. In deciding whether to accept such a credit card from one of the issuing organizations that tempt you with frequent flyer mileage bonuses on a specific airline, first determine whether the interest rate charged on the unpaid balance is the same as (or less than) possible alternate credit cards, and whether the annual "membership" fee is also equal or lower. If these charges are slightly higher than those of competing cards, weigh the difference against the potential value in airfare savings. Also ask about any bonus miles awarded just for signing up — 1,000 is common, 5,000 generally the maximum.

For the most up-to-date information on frequent flyer bonus options, you may want to send for the monthly newsletter *Frequent.* Issued by Frequent Publications, it provides current information about frequent flyer plans in general, as well as specific data about promotions, awards, and combination deals to help you keep track of the profusion — and confusion — of current and upcoming availabilities. For a year's subscription, send $33 to Frequent Publications, 4715-C Town Center Dr., Colorado Springs, CO 80916 (phone: 800-333-5937).

There also is a monthly magazine called *Frequent Flyer,* but unlike the newsletter mentioned above, its focus is primarily on newsy articles of interest to business travelers and other frequent flyers. Published by Official Airline Guides (PO Box 58543, Boulder, CO 80322-8543; phone: 800-323-3537), *Frequent Flyer* is available for $24 for a 1-year subscription.

Taxes and Other Fees – Travelers who have shopped for the best possible flight at the lowest possible price should be warned that a number of extras will be added to that price and collected by the airline or travel agent who issues the ticket. There is also a $6 International Air Transportation Tax — a departure tax paid by all passengers flying from the US to a foreign destination.

Still another fee is charged by some airlines to cover more stringent security procedures, prompted by recent terrorist incidents. The 8% federal US Transportation Tax, which applies to travel within the US or US territories (such as the US Virgin Islands or Puerto Rico), is already included in advertised fares and in the prices quoted by reservations clerks. It does not apply to passengers flying between US cities or territories en route to a foreign destination, unless the trip includes a stopover of more than 12 hours at a US point. Someone flying from Denver to Cancún and stopping in Chicago for more than 12 hours before boarding a flight to Cancún, for instance, would pay the 8% tax on the domestic portion of the trip.

Reservations – For those who don't have the time or patience to investigate personally all possible air departures and connections for a proposed trip, a travel agent can be of inestimable help. A good agent should have all the information on which flights go where and when, and which categories of tickets are available on each. Most have computerized reservation links with the major carriers, so that a seat can be reserved and confirmed in minutes. An increasing number of agents also possess fare-comparison computer programs, so they often are very reliable sources of detailed competitive price data. (For more information, see *How to Use a Travel Agent,* in this section.)

When making plane reservations through a travel agent, ask the agent to give the airline your home phone number as well as your daytime business phone number. All too often the agent uses the agency number as the official contact for changes in flight plans. Airlines are fairly reliable about getting information about drastically delayed flights to passengers if they can reach them; diligence does little good at 10 PM if the airline has only the agency's or an office number.

Reconfirmation is strongly recommended for all international flights. Some (though increasingly fewer) reservations to and from international destinations are automatically canceled after a required reconfirmation period (typically 72 hours) has passed — even if you have a confirmed, fully paid ticket in hand. It is always a good idea to call ahead to make sure that the airline did not slip up in entering your original reservations, or in registering any changes you may have made since, and that it has your seat reservation and/or special meal request in the computer. Although policies vary from carrier to carrier, some recommend that you reconfirm your return flight 48 to 72 hours in advance. If you look at the printed information on your ticket, you'll see the airline's reconfirmation policy stated explicitly. Don't be lulled into a false sense of security by the "OK" on your ticket next to the number and time of the return flight. It only means that a reservation has been entered; a reconfirmation still may be necessary. If in doubt — call.

If you plan not to take a flight on which you hold a confirmed reservation, by all means inform the airline. Because the problem of "no-shows" is a constant expense for airlines, they are allowed to overbook flights, a practice that often contributes to the threat of denied boarding for a certain number of passengers (see "Getting Bumped," below).

Seating – For most types of tickets, airline seats are usually assigned on a first-come, first-served basis at check-in, although some airlines make it possible to reserve a seat at the time of ticket purchase. Always check in early for your flight, even with advance seat assignments. A good rule of thumb for international flights is to arrive at the airport *at least* 2 hours before the scheduled departure to give yourself plenty of time in case there are long lines.

Most airlines furnish seating charts, which make choosing a seat much easier, but in general, there are only a few basics to consider. You must decide whether you prefer a window, aisle, or middle seat. On flights where smoking is permitted, you should also indicate if you prefer the smoking or nonsmoking section.

There is a quarterly publication called the *Airline Seating Guide* that publishes seating charts for most major US airlines and many foreign carriers as well. Your travel agent should have a copy, or you can buy the US edition for $39.95 per year and the international edition for $44.95. Order from Carlson Publishing Co., Box 888, Los Alamitos, CA 90720 (phone: 800-728-4877 or 213-493-4877).

Simply reserving an airline seat in advance, however, may actually guarantee very little. Most airlines require that passengers arrive at the departure gate at least 1 hour (sometimes more) ahead of time to hold a seat reservation, and *ask* travelers to check in at least 2 hours before international flights. It pays to read the fine print on your ticket carefully and plan ahead.

A far better strategy is to visit an airline ticket office (or one of a select group of travel agents) to secure an actual boarding pass for your specific flight. Once this has been issued, airline computers show you as checked in, and you effectively own the seat you have selected (although some carriers may not honor boarding passes of passengers arriving at the gate less than 10 minutes before departure). This is also good — but not foolproof — insurance against getting bumped from an overbooked flight and is, therefore, an especially valuable tactic at peak travel times.

Smoking – One decision regarding choosing a seat has been taken out of the hands of many travelers who smoke. Effective February 25, 1990, the US government imposed a restrictive airline smoking ban that prohibits smoking on all flights scheduled for 5 hours or less within the US and its territories. The regulation applies to both domestic and international carriers serving these routes.

In the case of flights to Cancún or Cozumel, these rules do not apply to nonstop flights flying directly from the US to Cancún or Cozumel or those with a continuous flight time of over 5 hours between stops in the US or its territories. Smoking is not permitted on segments of international flights where the flight time between US landings is under 5 hours — for instance, flights that include a stopover (even with no change of plane) or connecting flights.

On those flights that do permit smoking, the US Department of Transportation has determined that nonsmoking sections must be enlarged to accommodate all passengers who wish to sit in one. The airline does not, however, have to shift seating to accommodate nonsmokers who arrive late for a flight. Cigar and pipe smoking are prohibited on all flights, even in the smoking sections.

For a wallet-size guide that notes in detail the rights of nonsmokers according to these regulations, send a self-addressed, stamped envelope to ASH (Action on Smoking and Health), Airline Card, 2013 H St. NW, Washington, DC 20006 (phone: 202-659-4310).

Meals – If you have specific diet requirements, be sure to let the airlines know well before departure time. The available meals include vegetarian, seafood, kosher, Muslim, Hindu, high-protein, low-calorie, low-cholesterol, low-fat, low-sodium, diabetic, bland, and children's menus. There is no extra charge for this option. It usually is necessary to request special meals when you make your reservations — check-in time is too late. It's also wise to reconfirm that your request for a special meal has made its way into the airline's computer — the time to do this is 24 hours before departure.

Baggage – Travelers from the US face two different kinds of rules. When you fly on a US airline or on a major international carrier, US baggage regulations will be in effect. Though airline baggage allowances vary slightly, in general all passengers are allowed to carry on board, without charge, one piece of luggage that will fit easily under a seat of the plane or in an overhead bin, and whose combined dimensions (length, width, and depth) do not exceed 45 inches. (Most airlines will allow you to check this bag in the hold if you prefer not to carry it with you.) A reasonable amount of reading material, camera equipment, and a handbag are also allowed. In addition, all passengers are allowed to check two bags in the cargo hold: one usually not to exceed 62 inches when length, width, and depth are combined, the other not to exceed 55 inches in combined dimensions. Generally, no single bag may weigh more than 70 pounds.

On domestic Mexican flights (aboard such carriers as *Aeroméxico* and *Mexicana*), baggage allowances may be subject to a different weight determination, under which each economy cabin passenger is allowed only a total of 55 pounds (or less) of luggage without additional charge. First class or business class passengers may be allowed a total of 66 pounds. (If you are flying from the US to Mexico and connecting to a domestic flight, you generally will be allowed the same amount of baggage as on the international flight. If you break your trip and then take a domestic flight, the local carrier's weight restrictions apply.)

Charges for additional, oversize, or overweight bags usually are made at a flat rate; the actual dollar amount varies from carrier to carrier. If you plan to travel with any special equipment or sporting gear, be sure to check with the airline beforehand. Most have specific procedures for handling such baggage, and you may have to pay for transport regardless of how much other baggage you have checked. Golf clubs may be checked through as luggage (most airlines are accustomed to handling them), but tennis rackets should be carried onto the plane. Aqualung tanks, depressurized and appropriately packed with padding, and surfboards (minus the fin and padded) also may go as baggage. Snorkeling gear should be packed in a suitcase, duffel, or tote bag. Some airlines require that bicycles be partially dismantled and packaged.

Airline policies regarding baggage allowances for children vary and are usually based on the percentage of full adult fare paid. Although on many US carriers children who are ticket holders are entitled to the same baggage allowance as a full-fare passenger, some carriers allow only one bag per child. Often there is no luggage allowance for a child traveling on an adult's lap or in a bassinet. Particularly for international carriers, it's wise to check ahead. (For more information on flying with children, see *Hints for Traveling with Children,* in this section.)

To reduce the chances of your luggage going astray, remove all airline tags from previous trips, label each bag inside and out — with your business address rather than your home address on the outside, to prevent thieves from knowing whose house might be unguarded. Lock everything and double-check the tag that the airline attaches to make sure that it is coded correctly for your destination: CUN for Cancún and CZM for Cozumel.

If your bags are not in the baggage claim area after your flight, or if they're damaged, report the problem to airline personnel immediately. Keep in mind that policies regarding the specific time limit within which you have to make your claim vary from carrier to carrier. Fill out a report form on your lost or damaged luggage and keep a copy of it and your original baggage claim check. If you must surrender the check to claim a damaged bag, get a receipt for it to prove that you did, indeed, check your baggage on the flight. If luggage is missing, be sure to give the airline your destination and/or a telephone number where you can be reached. Also take the name and number of the person in charge of recovering lost luggage.

Most airlines have emergency funds for passengers stranded away from home without their luggage, but if it turns out that your bags are truly lost and not simply delayed, do not then and there sign any paper indicating you'll accept an offered settlement. Since the airline is responsible for the value of your bags within certain statutory limits ($1,250 per passenger for lost baggage on a US domestic flight; $9.07 per pound or $20 per kilo for checked baggage and up to $400 per passenger for unchecked baggage on an international flight), you should take some time to assess the extent of your loss (see *Insurance,* in this section). It's a good idea to keep records indicating the value of the contents of your luggage. A wise alternative is to take a Polaroid picture of the most valuable of your packed items just after putting them in your suitcase.

Be aware that airport security is increasingly an issue in countries worldwide including Mexico, and is taken very seriously. Police patrol the airports, and unattended luggage of any description may be confiscated and quickly destroyed. Passengers checking in at an airport may undergo at least two separate inspections of their tickets, passports, and luggage by courteous, but serious, airline personnel — who ask passengers if their baggage has been out of their possession between packing and the airport, or if they have been given gifts or other items to transport — before checked items are accepted.

Airline Clubs – US carriers often have clubs for travelers who pay for membership. These clubs are not solely for first class passengers, although a first class ticket *may* entitle a passenger to lounge privileges. Membership (which, by law, requires a fee) entitles the traveler to use the private lounges at airports along their route, to refreshments served in these lounges, and to check-cashing privileges at most of their counters. Extras include special telephone numbers for individual reservations, embossed luggage tags, and a membership card for identification. Airlines that offer membership in such clubs include the following:

> *American:* The *Admiral's Club.* Single yearly membership $175 for the first year; $125 yearly thereafter; spouse an additional $70 per year.
> *Continental:* The President's Club. Single yearly membership $140 for the first year; $90 yearly thereafter; spouse an additional $50 per year.
> *Northwest:* The *World Club.* Single yearly membership $150 (plus a one-time $25 initiation fee); spouse an additional $45 per year; 3-year and lifetime memberships also available.

United: The *Red Carpet Club.* $200 to join; $100 yearly thereafter; spouse an additional $50; 3-year and lifetime memberships also available.

Note that such companies do not have club facilities in all airports; other airlines also offer a variety of special services in many airports.

Getting Bumped – A special air travel problem is the possibility that an airline will accept more reservations (and sell more tickets) than there are seats on a given flight. This is entirely legal and is done to make up for "no-shows," passengers who don't show up for a flight for which they have made reservations and bought tickets. If the airline has oversold the flight and everyone does show up, there simply aren't enough seats. When this happens, the airline is subject to stringent rules designed to protect travelers.

In such cases, the airline first seeks ticket holders willing to give up their seats voluntarily in return for a negotiable sum of money or some other inducement, such as an offer of upgraded seating on the next flight or a voucher for a free trip at some other time. If there are not enough volunteers, the airline may bump passengers against their wishes.

Anyone inconvenienced in this way, however, is entitled to an explanation of the criteria used to determine who does or does not get on the flight, as well as compensation if the resulting delay exceeds certain limits. If the airline can put the bumped passengers on an alternate flight that is *scheduled to arrive* at their original destination within 1 hour of their originally scheduled arrival time, no compensation is owed. If the delay is more than 1 hour — but less than 2 hours on a domestic US flight or less than 4 hours on an international flight — they must be paid denied-boarding compensation equivalent to the one-way fare to their destination (but not more than $200). If the delay is more than 2 hours after the original arrival time on a domestic flight or more than 4 hours on an international flight, the compensation must be doubled (but not more than $400). The airline may also offer bumped travelers a voucher for a free flight instead of the denied-boarding compensation. The passenger may be given the choice of either money or the voucher, the dollar value of which may be no less than the monetary compensation to which the passenger would be entitled. The voucher is not a substitute for the bumped passenger's original ticket; the airline continues to honor that as well. Keep in mind that the above regulations and policies are for flights leaving the US only and do *not* apply to charters or to inbound flights from Cancún or Cozumel, even on US carriers.

To protect yourself as best you can against getting bumped, arrive at the airport extra early. If the flight is oversold, ask immediately for the written statement explaining the airline's policy on denied-boarding compensation and its boarding priorities. If the airline refuses to give you this information, or if you feel it has not handled the situation properly, file a complaint with both the airline and the appropriate government agency (see "Consumer Protection," below).

Delays and Cancellations – The above compensation rules also do not apply if the flight is canceled or delayed, or if a smaller aircraft is substituted because of mechanical problems. Each airline has its own policy for assisting passengers whose flights are delayed or canceled or who must wait for another flight because their original one was overbooked. Most airline personnel will make new travel arrangements if necessary. If the delay is longer than 4 hours, the airline may pay for a phone call or telegram, a meal, and in some cases, a hotel room and transportation to it.

■**Caution:** If you are bumped or miss a flight, be sure to ask the airline to notify other airlines on which you have reservations or connecting flights. When your name is taken off the passenger list of your initial flight, the computer automatically cancels all of your reservations unless *you* take steps to preserve them.

CHARTER FLIGHTS: By booking a block of seats on a specially arranged flight, charter operators offer travelers air transportation for a substantial reduction over the full coach or economy fare. These operators may offer air-only charters (selling trans-

portation alone) or charter packages (the flight plus a combination of land arrangements such as accommodations, meals, tours, or car rental). Charters are especially
attractive to people living in smaller cities or out-of-the-way places, because they
frequently leave from nearby airports, saving travelers the inconvenience and expense
of getting to a major gateway.

From the consumer's standpoint, charters differ from scheduled airlines in two main
respects: You generally need to book and pay in advance, and you can't change the
itinerary or the departure and return dates once you've booked the flight. In practice,
however, these restrictions don't always apply. Today, most of the charter flights to
Mexico have the most popular resort areas, such as Cancún, as their prime destinations,
and although most still require advance reservations, some permit last-minute bookings
(when there are unsold seats available), and some even offer seats on a standby basis.

Though charters almost always are round-trip, and it is unlikely that you would be
sold a one-way seat on a round-trip flight, on rare occasion one-way tickets on charters
are offered. Although it may be possible to book a one-way charter in the US, giving
you more flexibility in scheduling your return, note that US regulations pertaining to
charters may be more permissive than the charter laws of other countries. For example,
if you want to book a one-way charter back to the US, you may find advance booking
rules in force.

Some things to keep in mind about the charter game:

1. If you are forced to cancel your trip, you can lose much (and possibly all) of your
   money unless you have cancellation insurance, which is a must (see *Insurance,* in
   this section). Frequently, if the cancellation occurs far enough in advance (often
   6 weeks or more), you may forfeit only a $25 or $50 penalty. If you cancel only
   2 or 3 weeks before the flight, there may be no refund at all unless you or the
   operator can provide a substitute passenger.
2. Charter flights may be canceled by the operator up to 10 days before departure
   for any reason, usually underbooking. Your money is returned in this event, but
   there may be too little time to make new arrangements.
3. Most charters have little of the flexibility of regularly scheduled flights regarding
   refunds and the changing of flight dates; if you book a return flight, you must be
   on it or lose your money.
4. Charter operators are permitted to assess a surcharge, if fuel or other costs warrant
   it, of up to 10% of the airfare up to 10 days before departure.
5. Because of the economics of charter flights, your plane almost always will be full,
   so you will be crowded, though not necessarily uncomfortable. (There is, however,
   a new movement among charter airlines to provide flight accommodations that are
   comfort-oriented, so this situation may change in the near future.)

To avoid problems, *always* choose charter flights with care. When you consider a
charter, ask your travel agent who runs it and carefully check the company. The Better
Business Bureau in the company's home city can report on how many complaints, if
any, have been lodged against it in the past. Protect yourself with trip cancellation and
interruption insurance, which can help safeguard your investment if you or a traveling
companion is unable to make the trip and must cancel too late to receive a full refund
from the company providing your travel services. (This is advisable whether you're
buying a charter flight alone or a tour package for which the airfare is provided by
charter or scheduled flight.)

Bookings – If you do fly on a charter, read the contract's fine print carefully and
pay particular attention to the following:

Instructions concerning payment. To ensure that the charter company can't spend
your money until your flight has safely returned, make out your check to the company's
escrow account. By law, the name of the depository bank and the account number must
appear on the operator-participant contract (all too often on the back, in minuscule

print). Write the details of the charter, including the destination and dates, on the face of the check; on the back, print "For Deposit Only." Your travel agent may prefer that you make out your check to the agency, saying that it will then pay the tour operator the fee minus commission. It is perfectly legal to write the check as we suggest, however, and if your agent objects too vociferously (he or she should trust the tour operator to send the proper commission), consider taking your business elsewhere. If you don't make your check out to the escrow account, you lose the protection of that escrow. Furthermore, even the protection of escrow may not be enough to safeguard your investment, and trip cancellation insurance is strongly advised. Payment by credit card has become popular, since it offers some additional safeguards.

Specific stipulations and penalties for cancellations. Most charters allow you to cancel up to 45 days in advance without major penalty, but some cancellation dates are 50 to 60 days before departure.

Stipulations regarding cancellation and major changes made by the charterer. US rules say that charter flights may not be canceled within 10 days of departure except when circumstances — such as natural disasters or political upheavals — make it physically impossible to fly. Charterers may make "major changes," however, such as in the date or place of departure or return, but you are entitled to cancel and receive a full refund if you don't wish to accept these changes. A price increase of more than 10% at any time up to 10 days before departure is considered a major change; no price increase at all is allowed during the last 10 days immediately before departure. The charter company should be bonded (usually by an insurance company), and if you want to file a claim against it, the claim should be sent to the bonding agent. The contract will set a time limit within which a claim must be filed.

At the time of this writing, the following companies regularly offered charter flights to Cancún and Cozumel. As indicated, some of these companies sell charter flights directly to clients, while others are wholesalers and must be contacted through a travel agent.

Amber Tours (7337 W. Washington St., Indianapolis, IN 46251; phone: 800-225-9920). Retails to the general public.

Apple Vacations East (7 Campus Blvd., Newtown Sq., PA 19073; phone: 800-727-3400). This agency is a wholesaler, so use a travel agent.

Apple Vacations West (25 NW Point Blvd., Elk Grove Village, IL 60007; phone: 800-365-2775). This agency is a wholesaler, so use a travel agent.

Club America Vacations (3379 Peachtree Rd., Suite 625, Atlanta, GA 30326; phone: 800-221-2931). This agency is a wholesaler, so use a travel agent.

Club de Vacaciones (775 Park Ave., Suite 200, Huntington, NY 11743; phone: 516-424-9600 in New York State; 800-648-0404 elsewhere in the US). This agency is a wholesaler, so use a travel agent.

Funway Holidays (PO Box 1460, Milwaukee, WI 53201-1460; phone: 800-558-3050). This agency is a wholesaler, so use a travel agent.

GWV International (300 First Ave., Needham, MA 02194; phone: 800-225-5498). This agency is a wholesaler, so use a travel agent.

MLT Vacations (5130 Hwy. 101, Minnetonka, MN 55345; phone: 800-328-0025). This agency is a wholesaler, so use a travel agent.

Morris Air Service (260 E. Morris Ave., Salt Lake City, UT 84115-3200; phone: 800-444-5660). Retails to the general public.

Suntrips (2350 Paragon Dr., San Jose, CA 95131; phone: 800-444-7866 in California; 800-937-0747 elsewhere in the US). Retails to the general public.

Travel Charter (1120 E. Longlake Rd., Detroit, MI 48098; phone: 313-528-3570). This agency is a wholesaler, so use a travel agent.

For the most current information on charter flight options, the travel newsletter *Jax Fax* regularly features a list of charter companies and packagers offering seats on charter flights. For a year's subscription send a check or money order for $12 to *Jax Fax* (397 Post Rd., Darien, CT 06820; phone: 203-655-8746).

DISCOUNTS ON SCHEDULED FLIGHTS: Promotional fares often are called discount fares because they cost less than what used to be the standard airline fare — full-fare economy. Nevertheless, they cost the traveler the same whether they are bought through a travel agent or directly from the airline. Tickets that cost less if bought from some outlet other than the airline do exist, however. While it is likely that the vast majority of travelers flying to Mexico in the near future will be doing so on a promotional fare or charter rather than on a "discount" air ticket of this sort, it still is a good idea for cost-conscious consumers to be aware of the latest developments in the budget airfare scene. Note that the following discussion makes clear-cut distinctions among the types of discounts available based on how they reach the consumer; in actual practice, the distinctions are not nearly so precise.

Net Fare Sources – The newest notion for reducing the costs of travel services comes from travel agents who offer individual travelers "net" fares. Defined simply, a net fare is the bare minimum amount at which an airline or tour operator will carry a prospective traveler. It doesn't include the amount that normally would be paid to the travel agent as a commission. Traditionally, such commissions amount to about 10% on domestic fares and 8% to 20% on international fares — not counting significant additions to these commission levels that are payable retroactively when agents sell more than a specific volume of tickets or trips for a single supplier. At press time, at least one travel agency in the US was offering travelers the opportunity to purchase tickets and/or tours for a net price. Instead of making its income from individual commissions, this agency assesses a fixed fee that may or may not provide a bargain for travelers; it requires a little arithmetic to determine whether to use the services of a net travel agent or those of one who accepts conventional commissions. One of the potential drawbacks of buying from agencies selling travel services at net fares is that some airlines refuse to do business with them, thus possibly limiting your flight options.

Travel Avenue is a formula fee-based agency that rebates its ordinary agency commission to the customer. For domestic flights, an agent will find the lowest retail fare, then rebate 7% to 10% (depending on the airline) of that price minus a $10 ticket-writing charge. The rebate percentage for international flights varies from 5% to 16% (again, depending on the airline), and the ticket-writing fee is $25. The ticket-writing charge is imposed per ticket; if the ticket includes more than eight separate flights, an additional $10 or $25 fee is charged. Customers using free flight coupons pay the ticket-writing charge, plus an additional $5 coupon-processing fee.

Travel Avenue will rebate its commissions on all tickets, including heavily discounted fares and senior citizen passes. Available 7 days a week, reservations should be made far enough in advance to allow the tickets to be sent by first class mail, since extra charges accrue for special handling. It's possible to economize further by making your own airline reservation, then asking *Travel Avenue* only to write/issue your ticket. For travelers outside the Chicago area, business may be transacted by phone and purchases charged to a credit card. For information, contact *Travel Avenue* at 641 W. Lake, Suite 201, Chicago, IL 60606-1012 (phone: 312-876-1116 in Illinois; 800-333-3335 elsewhere in the US).

Consolidators and Bucket Shops – Other vendors of travel services can afford to sell tickets to their customers at an even greater discount because the airline has sold the tickets to them at a substantial discount (usually accomplished by sharply increasing commissions to that vendor), a practice in which many airlines indulge, albeit discreetly, preferring that the general public not know they are undercutting their own "list" prices. Airlines anticipating a slow period on a particular route sometimes sell off a certain portion of their capacity to a wholesaler, or consolidator. The wholesaler sometimes is a charter operator who resells the seats to the public as though they were charter seats, which is why prospective travelers perusing the brochures of charter operators with large programs frequently see a number of flights designated as "scheduled service." As often as not, however, the consolidator, in turn, sells the seats to a travel agency specializing in discounting. Airlines can also sell seats directly to such an agency, which thus acts as its own consolidator. The airline offers the seats either at a net wholesale price, but without the volume-purchase requirement that would be difficult for a modest retail travel agency to fulfill, or at the standard price, but with a commission override large enough (as high as 50%) to allow both a profit and a price reduction to the public.

Travel agencies specializing in discounting sometimes are called "bucket shops," a term once fraught with connotations of unreliability in this country. But in today's highly competitive travel marketplace, more and more conventional travel agencies are selling consolidator-supplied tickets, and the old bucket shop's image is becoming respectable. Agencies that specialize in discounted tickets exist in most large cities, and usually can be found by studying the smaller ads in the travel sections of Sunday newspapers.

Before buying a discounted ticket, whether from a bucket shop or a conventional, full-service travel agency, keep the following considerations in mind: To be in a position to judge how much you'll be saving, first find out the "list" prices of tickets to your destination. Then do some comparison shopping among agencies. Also bear in mind that a ticket that may not differ much in price from one available directly from the airline may, however, allow the circumvention of such things as the advance purchase requirement. If your plans are less than final, be sure to find out about any other restrictions, such as penalties for canceling a flight or changing a reservation. Most discount tickets are non-endorsable, meaning that they can be used only on the airline that issued them, and they usually are marked "nonrefundable" to prevent their being cashed for a list price refund.

A great many bucket shops are small businesses operating on a thin margin, so it's a good idea to check the local Better Business Bureau for any complaints registered against the one with which you're dealing — before parting with any money. If you still do not feel reassured, consider buying discounted tickets only through a conventional travel agency, which can be expected to have found its own reliable source of consolidator tickets — some of the largest consolidators, in fact, sell only to travel agencies.

A few bucket shops require payment in cash or by certified check or money order, but if credit cards are accepted, use that option. Note, however, if buying from a charter operator selling seats for both scheduled and charter flights, that the scheduled seats are not protected by the regulations — including use of escrow accounts — governing the charter seats. Well-established charter operators, nevertheless, may extend the same protections to their scheduled flights, and when this is the case consumers should be sure that the payment option selected directs their money into the escrow account.

Listed below are some of the consolidators frequently offering discount fares to Cancún and Cozumel:

> *Maharaja Consumer Wholesale* (393 5th Ave., New York, NY 10016; phone: 212-213-2020 in New York; 800-223-6862 elsewhere in the US).
>
> *TFI Tours International* (34 W. 37th St., 12th Floor, New York, NY 10001; phone: 212-736-1140).
>
> *25 West Tours* (2490 Coral Way, Miami, FL 33145; phone: 305-856-0810; 800-423-6954 in Florida; 800-252-5025 elsewhere in the US).
>
> ■**Note:** Although rebating and discounting are becoming increasingly common,

there is some legal ambiguity concerning them. Strictly speaking, it is legal to discount domestic tickets but not international tickets. On the other hand, the law that prohibits discounting, the Federal Aviation Act of 1958, is consistently ignored these days, in part because consumers benefit from the practice and in part because many illegal arrangements are indistinguishable from legal ones. Since the line separating the two is so fine that even the authorities can't always tell the difference, it is unlikely that most consumers would be able to do so, and in fact it is not illegal to *buy* a discounted ticket. If the issue of legality bothers you, ask the agency whether any ticket you're about to buy would be permissible under the above-mentioned act.

OTHER DISCOUNT TRAVEL SOURCES: An excellent source of information on economical travel opportunities is the *Consumer Reports Travel Letter,* published monthly by Consumers Union. It keeps abreast of the scene on a wide variety of fronts, including package tours, rental cars, insurance, and more, but it is especially helpful for its comprehensive coverage of airfares, offering guidance on all the options from scheduled flights on major or low-fare airlines to charters and discount sources. For a year's subscription, send $37 ($57 for 2 years) to *Consumer Reports Travel Letter,* PO Box 53629, Boulder, CO 80322-3629 (phone: 800-999-7959).

Another source is *Travel Smart,* a monthly newsletter with information on a wide variety of trips and additional discount travel services available to subscribers. For a year's subscription, send $37 to Communications House, 40 Beechdale Rd., Dobbs Ferry, NY 10522 (phone: 914-693-8300 in New York; 800-327-3633 elsewhere in the US). For information on other travel newsletters, see *Sources and Resources,* in this section.

Last-Minute Travel Clubs – Still another way to take advantage of bargain airfares is open to those who have a flexible schedule. A number of organizations, usually set up as last-minute travel clubs and functioning on a membership basis, routinely keep in touch with travel suppliers to help them dispose of unsold inventory at discounts of between 5% and 50%. A great deal of the inventory consists of complete tour packages and cruises, but some clubs offer air-only charter seats and, occasionally, seats on scheduled flights.

Members pay an annual fee and receive a toll-free hotline number to call for information on imminent trips. In some cases, they also receive periodic mailings with information on bargain travel opportunities for which there is more advance notice. Despite the suggestive names of the clubs providing these services, last-minute travel does not necessarily mean that you cannot make plans until literally the last minute. Trips can be announced as little as a few days or as much as 2 months before departure, but the average is from 1 to 4 weeks' notice.

Among such organizations offering discounted travel opportunities to Cancún and Cozumel are the following:

Discount Club of America (61-33 Woodhaven Blvd., Rego Park, NY 11374; phone: 800-321-9587 or 718-335-9612). Annual fee: $39 per family.

Discount Travel International (Ives Building, 114 Forrest Ave., Suite 205, Narberth, PA 19072; phone: 215-668-7184 in Pennsylvania; 800-543-0110 elsewhere in the US). Annual fee: $45 per household.

Encore Short Notice (4501 Forbes Blvd., Lanham, MD 20706; phone: 301-459-8020; 800-638-0930 for customer service). Annual fee: $48 per family.

Last-Minute Travel (1249 Boylston St., Boston, MA 02215; phone: 800-LAST-MIN or 617-267-9800). No fee.

Moment's Notice (425 Madison Ave., New York, NY 10017; phone: 212-486-0503). Tours offered to Cancún, but not Cozumel. Annual fee: $19.95 per family.

Spur-of-the-Moment Tours and Cruises (10780 Jefferson Blvd., Culver City, 90230; phone: 213-839-2418 in California; 800-343-1991 elsewhere in the US). No fee.

Traveler's Advantage (3033 S. Parker Rd., Suite 1000, Aurora, CO 80014; phone: 800-548-1116). Annual fee: $49 per family.

Vacations to Go (2411 Fountain View, Suite 201, Houston, TX 77057; phone: 800-338-4962). Annual fee: $19.95 per family.

Worldwide Discount Travel Club (1674 Meridian Ave., Miami Beach, FL 33139; phone: 305-534-2082). Annual fee: $40 per person; $50 per family.

Generic Air Travel – Organizations that apply the same flexible-schedule idea to air travel only and sell tickets at literally the last minute also exist. The service they provide sometimes is known as "generic" air travel, and it operates somewhat like an ordinary airline standby service, except that the organizations running it offer seats on not one but several scheduled and charter airlines.

One pioneer of generic flights is *Airhitch* (2790 Broadway, Suite 100, New York, NY 10025; phone: 212-864-2000), which arranges flights to Cancún and Cozumel from various US cities at relatively low prices. Prospective travelers register by paying a fee (applicable toward the fare) and stipulate a range of acceptable departure dates and their desired destination, along with alternate choices. The week before the date range begins, they are notified of at least two flights that will be available during the time period, agree on one, and remit the balance of the fare to the company. If they do not accept any of the suggested flights, they lose their deposit; if, through no fault of their own, they do not ultimately get on any agreed-on flight, all of their money is refunded. Return flights are arranged the same way. The company's Sunhitch program is available for week-long stays on Cancún and Cozumel from December through April. Their slightly more expensive Target program offers greater certainty regarding destinations and is available throughout the year.

Bartered Travel Sources – Suppose a hotel buys advertising space in a newspaper, as payment, the hotel gives the publishing company a number of hotel rooms in lieu of cash. This is barter, a common means of exchange among hotels, airlines, car rental companies, cruise lines, tour operators, restaurants, and other travel service companies. When a bartering company finds itself with empty airline seats (or excess hotel rooms or cruise ship cabin space, and so on) and offers them to the public, considerable savings can be enjoyed.

Bartered-travel clubs often offer discounts of up to 50% to members who pay an annual fee (approximately $50 at press time) which entitles them to select the flights, cruises, hotel rooms, or other travel services that the club obtained by barter. Members usually present a voucher, club credit card, or scrip (a dollar-denomination voucher negotiable only for the bartered product) to the hotel, which in turn subtracts the dollar amount from the bartering company's account.

Selling bartered travel is a perfectly legitimate means of retailing. One advantage to club members is that they don't have to wait until the last minute to obtain flight or room reservations.

Among the companies specializing in bartered service, several that frequently offer members travel services to Cancún and Cozumel include the following:

IGT (In Good Taste) Services (1111 Lincoln Road, 4th Floor, Miami Beach, FL 33139; phone: 800-444-8872 or 305-531-6300). Annual fee: $48 per family.

The Travel Guild (18210 Redmond Way, Redmond, WA 98052; phone: 206-885-1213). Annual fee: $48 per family.

Travel World Leisure Club (225 W. 34th St., Suite 2203, New York, NY 10122; phone: 800-444-TWLC or 212-239-4855). Annual fee: $50 per family.

CONSUMER PROTECTION: Consumers who feel that they have not been dealt with fairly by an airline should make their complaints known. Begin with the customer service representative at the airport where the problem occurs. If he or she cannot resolve your complaint to your satisfaction, write to the airline's consumer office. In a businesslike, typed letter, explain what reservations you held, what happened, the names of the employees involved, and what you expect the airline to do to remedy the situation. Send copies (never the originals) of the tickets, receipts, and other documents that back your claims. Ideally, all correspondence should be sent via certified mail, return receipt requested. This provides proof that your complaint was received.

Passengers with consumer complaints — lost baggage, compensation for getting bumped, smoking and nonsmoking rules, deceptive practices by an airline, charter regulations — who are not satisfied with the airline's response should contact the US Department of Transportation (DOT), Consumer Affairs Division (400 Seventh St. SW, Washington, DC 20590; phone: 202-366-2220). DOT personnel stress, however, that consumers should initially direct their complaints to the airline that provoked them.

Travelers with an unresolved complaint involving a foreign carrier also can contact the US Department of Transportation. DOT personnel will do what they can to help resolve all such complaints, although their influence may be limited.

Although Mexico does not have a specific government bureau that deals with airline complaints, consumers with complaints against other travel-related services can contact the tourist office in Mexico, or write to Lic. Gilberto Calderón Romo, Director General de Auxilio Turístico, Presidente Masaryk No. 172, 2nd Floor, Ler. Nivel., México, DF.

To avoid more serious problems, *always* choose charter flights and tour packages with care. When you consider a charter, ask your travel agent who runs it and carefully check out the company. The Better Business Bureau in the company's home city can report on how many complaints, if any, have been lodged against it in the past. As emphasized above, protect yourself with trip cancellation and interruption insurance, which can help safeguard your investment in case you or a traveling companion is unable to make the trip and must cancel too late to receive a full refund from the company providing your travel services. (This is advisable whether you're buying a charter flight alone or a tour package for which the airfare is provided by charter or scheduled flight.) Some travel insurance policies have an additional feature, covering the possibility of default or bankruptcy on the part of the tour operator or airline, charter or scheduled.

Remember, too, that the federal Fair Credit Billing Act permits purchasers to refuse to pay charges if they do not receive the travel services for which they've been billed, so the onus of dealing with the receiver for a bankrupt airline falls on the credit card company. Do not rely on another airline to honor the ticket you're holding, since the days when virtually all major carriers subscribed to a default protection program that bound them to do so are long gone. Some airlines may voluntarily step forward to accommodate the stranded passengers of a fellow carrier, but this is now an entirely altruistic act.

The deregulation of US airlines has meant that travelers must find out for themselves what they are entitled to receive. The Department of Transportation's informative consumer booklet *Fly Rights* is a good place to start. To receive a copy, send $1 to the Superintendent of Documents, US Government Printing Office (Washington, DC 20402-9325; phone: 202-783-3238). Specify its stock number, 050-000-00513-5, and allow 3 to 4 weeks for delivery.

■ **Note:** Those who tend to experience discomfort due to the change in air pressure while flying may be interested in the free pamphlet *Ears, Altitude and Airplane Travel;* for a copy send a self-addressed, stamped, business-size envelope to the *American Academy of Otolaryngology* (One Prince St., Alexandria, VA 22314; phone: 703-836-4444). And for when you land, *Overcoming Jet Lag* offers some helpful tips on minimizing post-flight stress; it is available from Berkeley Publishing Group (PO Box 506, Mail Order Dept., East Rutherford, NJ 07073; phone: 800-631-8571) for $6.95, plus shipping and handling.

Traveling by Ship

There was a time when traveling by ship was extraordinarily expensive, time consuming, utterly elegant, and utilized almost exclusively for getting from one point to another. No longer primarily pure transportation, cruising is riding a new wave of popularity as a leisure activity in its own right.

Among the destinations favored by cruise ship passengers, Mexico, with stops at Cancún or Cozumel, ranks extremely high. From eastern US ports, cruises to Mexico most often head for Cozumel and Playa del Carmen (on the Yucatán Peninsula), or sail through the Panama Canal and call at popular resorts along Mexico's west coast. Sailings from West Coast docks reverse the trans-canal route, and may run from Los Angeles down the west coast of Mexico through the Panama Canal, and then continue on to Caribbean ports such as Cancún and Cozumel before returning to the US.

Many modern-day cruise ships seem much more like motels-at-sea than the classic liners of a couple of generations ago, but they are consistently comfortable and passengers are often pampered. Cruise prices can be quite reasonable, since the single cruise price covers all the major items in a typical vacation — transportation, accommodations, all meals, entertainment, a full range of social activities, sports, and recreation — a traveler need not fear any unexpected assaults on the family travel budget.

Generally, people take a cruise ship to Mexico for the sheer pleasure of being at sea, because it's part of a far broader itinerary, or because of a special interest in a particular area that is best visited by ship. Cruise lines promote sailings to Mexico as "get away from it all" vacations. But the prospective cruise ship passenger will find that the variety of cruises is tremendous, and the quality, while generally high, varies depending on shipboard services, the tone of shipboard life, the cost of the cruise, and operative itineraries. Although there are less expensive ways to see Mexico, the romance and enjoyment of a sea voyage remain irresistible for some. Such sojourners should find out as much as possible before signing on for a seagoing vacation (after all, it's hard to get off in mid-ocean).

CRUISES TO MEXICO: Several cruise lines include Mexican ports as part of their itineraries. These lines either sail directly to Mexico or offer passengers the option of joining a leg of longer cruises or positioning cruises with stopovers in Mexico. Prices vary greatly in the cruise ship category, depending on levels of luxury, accommodations, and length of the journey.

Below is a list of cruise lines and ships sailing to Mexico from the US.

Bermuda Star Line (1086 Teaneck Rd., Teaneck, NJ 07666; phone: 800-237-5361). It offers a 15-day cruise sailing from New Orleans to New York. Ports of call include Cozumel and some Caribbean islands.

Carnival Cruise Lines (3655 NW 87th Ave., Miami, FL 33178; phone: 800-327-7373). The *Holiday* makes 7-day cruises from Miami every Saturday. Ports of call include Playa del Carmen, Cozumel, and other ports in the Caribbean.

Chandris Fantasy Cruises (200 Blue Lagoon Dr., Miami, FL 33126; phone: 800-621-3446). The *SS Britanis* makes 5-day sailings from Miami to Cozumel and Playa del Carmen.

Commodore Cruise Line (800 Douglas Rd., Suite 700, Coral Gables, FL 33134; phone: 800-237-5361). The *Caribe* and *Enchanted Seas* both offer 7-day itineraries sailing from Miami and New Orleans respectively, and calling at Caribbean and Mexican ports.

Costa Cruises (World Trade Center Building, 80 SW 8th St., Miami, FL 33130-3097; phone: 800-462-6782). The *Costa Riviera* sails from Ft. Lauderdale to Cancún and Cozumel on a 7-day cruise. The *Costa Classica,* to be launched in February of this year, will offer the same itinerary.

Dolphin Cruise Line (901 S. American Way, Miami, FL 33132; phone: 800-222-1003). The *Sea Breeze* makes 7-day sailings from Miami that include stops in Cozumel and Playa del Carmen, as well as a number of other Caribbean ports of call.

Princess Cruises (10100 Santa Monica Blvd., Santa Monica, CA 90067; phone: 800-421-0522). This is it, folks, the "Love Boat" — or perhaps we should say the Love Boats — in person. Its offerings include a 7-day cruise aboard the *Crown Princess,* bringing its passengers from Ft. Lauderdale to Cozumel, and calling at several Caribbean ports. The *Royal Princess* makes an 11-day trans-canal cruise sailing from Acapulco to Ft. Lauderdale. Ports of call include Playa del Carmen, Cozumel, and other Caribbean islands.

Royal Caribbean Cruise Lines (1050 Caribbean Way, Miami, FL 33132; phone: 800-327-6700). The *Song of America* makes a 7-day sailing from Miami, calling at Cozumel and several Caribbean islands.

Royal Viking Lines (95 Merrick Way, Coral Gables, FL 33134; phone: 800-422-8000). The *Royal Viking Sky* offers a 13-day cruise from Ft. Lauderdale to Acapulco; ports of call include Cozumel.

Special Expeditions (720 Fifth Ave., New York, NY 10019; phone: 212-765-7740 in New York; 800-762-0003 elsewhere in the US). The M.S. *Polaris* offers an 8-day sailing from Cozumel that explores the Maya coast, including historic ruins, and calls at Belize and South American ports.

A monthly newsletter that may be of interest to those planning to cruise Mexican waters is *Ocean and Cruise News,* which offers comprehensive coverage of the latest on the cruise ship scene. A year's subscription costs $24. Contact *Ocean and Cruise News,* PO Box 92, Stamford, CT 06904 (phone: 203-329-2787).

■**A final note on picking a cruise:** A "cruise-only" travel agency can best help you choose a cruise ship and itinerary. Cruise-only agents are best equipped to tell you about a particular ship's "personality," the kind of person with whom you'll likely be traveling on a particular ship, what dress is appropriate (it varies from ship to ship), and much more. Travel agencies that specialize in booking cruises usually are members of the *National Association of Cruise Only Agencies (NACOA).* For a listing of the agencies in your area (requests are limited to three states), send a self-addressed, stamped envelope to *NACOA,* PO Box 7209, Freeport, NY 11520, or call 516-378-8006.

Touring by Car

Driving is the best way to explore out-of-the-way regions of Mexico on the way to or from your visit on Cancún or Cozumel. The privacy, comfort, and convenience of touring by car can't be matched by any other form of transportation. A car provides maximum flexibility, allowing visitors to cover large amounts of territory, to visit major cities and sites, or to move from one small town to the next while exploring the countryside.

Mexico's highways and roads are renowned for their scenery. Sudden, unexpected glimpses of tropical flowers, desert plants, pine trees, mountains, and aquamarine waters form the moving backdrop of the road as you drive. The distances between cities and towns are usually reasonable, and a visitor can use a car's flexibility to maximum advantage.

When planning your route, be realistic in calculating the amount of ground you can cover, and make plans on the conservative side when you have any doubts. Road incidents involving assaults and robberies of tourists, though relatively infrequent, are on the rise, and usually befall ill-advised travelers who have underestimated the distances between towns — or the time it takes to cover these distances. Try to avoid driving after dark, and *never* stop and spend the night in the car or on some deserted stretch of beachfront. Our choices of the most interesting driving itineraries, described in DIRECTIONS, include approximate distances to help in your calculations.

Most roads are well surfaced, but you will find few of the multi-lane highways found in the US, except around the larger cities. In general, secondary and lesser roads also are kept in reasonably good condition, although this may not always be the case, particularly during the rainy season. If you are planning to explore off the beaten track, consider renting a four-wheel-drive vehicle. Either way, there is plenty to see en route.

As the only road often goes through the middle of the town or resort area, be prepared to slow down as you pass through busy, populated centers. The speed limit on the best highways is 110 kilometers per hour (approximately 69 miles per hour). Speeds always are given in kilometers per hour and distances in kilometers (a kilometer is equal to approximately .62 miles); major highway signs use international symbols, which are quite easy to understand.

License – Any valid US driver's license is acceptable in Mexico. You do not need an International Driving Permit. If you are driving from the United States, remember that a driver's license cannot be used as proof of citizenship. Bring a passport, naturalization certificate (if applicable), a voter's registration card, or a certified birth certificate. A notarized affidavit attesting to US citizenship is also acceptable. The same regulations apply to Canadian citizens.

Maps – Consult road maps. A number of the automobile clubs listed below offer their members (and members of affiliated clubs) free or inexpensive maps. Maps also are available at service stations on both sides of the border.

A company with more than half a century of experience in publishing maps of Mexico City and other areas of Mexico is *Guía Roji* (31 J. Moran, México, DF 11850; phone: 5-277-2307). *Guía Roji* also sells road maps of all Mexican states and wall maps of several Mexican cities. The company's newest publication is a road atlas called *Atlas de Carreteras;* it costs about $2.65 and is extremely useful for the motorist. It also is available from several US offices of *Sanborn's Mexican Insurance Service* (2009 S. 10th St., McAllen, TX 78502; phone: 512-686-7011; and 2212 Santa Ursula, Laredo, TX 78040-3122; phone: 512-722-0931).

Another wall map, the *Rand McNally Cosmopolitan Map of Mexico* ($2.95), indicates each Mexican state in a different color. All major highways are indicated, and there is no problem figuring out what is near what. For use on the road, the *Rand McNally Road Atlas: US, Canada and Mexico* ($7.95 paperback; $11.95 hardcover) is excellent. Both of these books may be found in bookstores or can be ordered directly from *Rand McNally* (150 E. 52nd St., New York, NY 10022; phone: 212-758-7488); call for information on charges for postage and handling.

An up-to-date road map of Mexico, published by the Mexican Ministry of Tourism, is available free from its offices (see *Mexican Consulates and Tourist Offices in the US,* in this section). Perhaps the most detailed series of maps available from the Mexican government are those published by Mexico's *Dirección General de Geografía* (a department similar to the US National Ocean Service). A broad selection of maps of Mexico is available, with the emphasis ranging from topography to tourism. Numerous bookstores in Mexican cities carry these maps. A variety of Mexican maps also is available by writing to the *Servicio Meteorológico Nacional* (192 Av. Observatorio, Tacubaya, México, DF 11860).

A good source for most of the maps listed above, and just about any other kind of map of just about anywhere in the world, including Mexico, is *Map Link* (25 E. Mason St., Suite 201, Santa Barbara, CA 93101; phone: 805-965-4402). They also carry the particularly useful *International Travel Maps (ITM)* series, which covers much of Mexico. If they don't stock a map of the area in which you are interested, they will do their best to get it for you.

Automobile Clubs – Most Mexican automobile clubs offer emergency service to any breakdown victim, whether a club member or not; however, only members of these clubs or affiliated clubs may have access to certain information services and receive discounted or free towing and repair services.

Members of the *American Automobile Association (AAA)* often are entitled automatically to a number of services from foreign clubs. With over 31 million members in chapters throughout the US and Canada, the *AAA* is the largest automobile club in North America. *AAA* affiliates throughout the US provide a variety of travel services to members, including a travel agency, trip planning, fee-free traveler's checks at some locations, and roadside assistance. They will help plan an itinerary, send a map with clear routing directions, and even make hotel reservations; these services apply to traveling in both the US and Mexico. Although *AAA* members receive maps and other brochures for no charge or at a discount (depending on the publication and branch), non-members also can order from an extensive selection of highway and topographical maps. You can join the *AAA* through local chapters (listed in the telephone book under *AAA*) or contact the national office, 1000 AAA Dr., Heathrow, FL 32746-5063 (phone: 407-444-8544).

The *American Automobile Association* also is affiliated with a Mexican automobile association, the *Asociación Mexicana Automovilística (AMA;* Mexican Automobile Association), with branches in the metropolitan Mexico City area, Cuernavaca, and Puebla. *AMA*'s main office in Mexico City is at 7 Calle Orizaba, México, DF 06700 (phone: 5-209-8329 or 5-511-6285). The association provides a variety of maps in English at no charge and, in some parts of Mexico, *AAA* members can call the *AMA* for emergency service.

The *Asociación Nacional Automovilística (ANA),* perhaps the most widely based in Mexico, also can be helpful to *AAA* members, as well as members of other automobile associations belonging to the *International Federation of Automobile Associations* (ask if a club is a member before joining). The association also sells a useful road map for about 50¢. The main offices are in Mexico City at 140 Calle Miguel E. Schultz, México, DF 06470 (phone: 5-705-0258).

Breakdowns – If you break down on the road, immediate emergency procedure is to get the car off the road. Major highways and other two-lane roads tend to have narrower shoulders than you're used to, so make sure you get all the way off, even if you have to hang off the shoulder a bit. Raise the hood as a signal that help is needed, and tie a white rag to the door handle or radio antenna. Don't leave the car unattended, and don't try any major repairs on the road.

The major Mexican highways are patrolled by the government's **Green Angel** fleet of emergency service trucks. They are manned by English-speaking crews and carry equipment for a modest range of on-the-road repairs. (Don't expect miracles, just an adequate, average repair job for a common emergency.) The Green Angels know how to change tires, give first aid, and take care of minor problems. They also carry gasoline and oil and provide information on road conditions. Except for parts and fuel, the service is free. That's why they're called "angels" — they literally cruise the main highways looking for motorists to rescue. Sooner or later, if you break down on a main road, one of the Green Angels will get to you, as crews patrol every day (from 8 AM to 8 PM). Supplementing their efforts are the following hotline emergency numbers for tourists needing guidance or help: 915-250-4817 (24 hours), 915-250-0123, 915-250-8601, 915-250-8419, or 915-250-8221. (When calling within the Mexico City area, do *not* dial 915.)

Gasoline – *Pemex* (an acronym for *Petróleos Mexicanos*) is the only brand of gasoline and oil sold in Mexico since the petroleum industry was nationalized. Gasoline is sold in liters (approximately 3.7 liters equal 1 gallon), and two grades of gas are available: Nova (or regular) from the blue pump, and higher-priced Extra (or premium) from the silver pump (though Extra often is difficult if not impossible to find). Both grades come in leaded and unleaded varieties; ask the gas station attendant for *"con plomo"* if you want *leaded* gas or *"sin plomo"* for *unleaded*.

Gas prices everywhere rise and fall, depending on the world supply of oil, even in oil-producing nations such as Mexico. US visitors generally will find gasoline to be slightly less expensive than they are accustomed to paying in the US. Be prepared to pay for gas in cash (American oil company credit cards aren't accepted by *Pemex*). And if you request the attendants to check your oil and water or coolant in your radiator, or wipe your windshield, be sure to tip them between 500 and 1,000 pesos. We recommend tipping gas station attendants even if you are only filling up.

Particularly when traveling in rural areas, fill up whenever you come to a gas station. It may be a long way to the next station. You *don't* want to get stranded on an isolated stretch — so it is a good idea to bring along an extra few gallons in a steel container. Also note that in rural areas, gasoline may be diluted with water or kerosene. So if the car stops after you have just filled up, it could be due to impure gasoline.

Also note that rental cars usually are delivered with a full tank of gas (this is not always the case, however, so check the gas gauge when picking up the car, and have the amount of gas noted on your rental agreement if the tank is not full). Refill the tank before you return the car or you will have to pay to have the rental company fill it, and gasoline at the car rental company's pump always is much more expensive than at a service station. This policy may vary for smaller local and regional companies; ask when picking up the vehicle.

RENTING A CAR: Most visitors who want to drive in Mexico rent a car through a travel agent or international rental firm before leaving home, or from a local company once in Mexico. Another possibility, also arranged before departure, is to rent the car as part of a larger package of travel services.

Renting is not inexpensive, but it is possible to economize by determining your own needs and then shopping around among the car rental companies until you find the best deal. As you comparison shop, keep in mind that rates vary considerably, not only from city to city, but also from location to location within the same city. For instance, it might be less expensive to rent a car from an office in the center of a city rather than at the airport. Ask about special rates or promotional deals, such as weekend or weekly rates, bonus coupons for airline tickets, or 24-hour rates that include gas and unlimited mileage. It also should be noted that the general condition of rental cars in Mexico — even the most expensive ones — is tangibly worse than similar cars in most other parts of the world.

Rental car companies operating in Mexico can be divided into three basic categories: large national or international companies, regional companies, and local companies. Because of aggressive local competition, the cost of renting a car can be less expensive once a traveler arrives in Mexico, compared to the prices quoted in advance from the US. Local companies usually are less expensive than the international giants (although travelers who do not speak fluent Spanish may have to rule out smaller local companies that rent primarily to natives).

Given this situation, it's tempting to wait until arriving to scout out the lowest-priced rental from the company located the farthest from the airport high-rent district and offering no pick-up services. But if your arrival coincides with a holiday or peak travel period, you may be disappointed to find that even the most expensive car in town was spoken for months ago. Whenever possible, it is best to reserve in advance, anywhere from a few days in slack periods to a month or more during the busier seasons.

If you can read and speak Spanish, and decide to wait until after you arrive in Mexico and let your fingers do the walking through the local phone books, you'll often find a surprising number of small companies listed. Often the best guide to sorting through the options is the local tourist board, which usually can provide recommendations and a list of reputable firms.

Travel agents can arrange rentals for clients, but it is just as easy to call and rent a car yourself. Listed below are several national Mexican rental companies, as well as the major international rental companies represented on Cancún, Cozumel, and the Yucatán Peninsula:

> *Alpri Rent a Car* (phone: 5-564-2543 or 5-564-5076 for the main office in Mexico City). Has 1 location on Cancún.
>
> *Auto Europe* (phone: 800-223-5555). Has 3 locations on Cancún, 1 on Cozumel, and 3 in Mérida.
>
> *Avis Rent-A-Car* (phone: 800-331-1212). Has 3 locations on Cancún, 3 on Cozumel, 1 in Chetumal, and 3 in Mérida.
>
> *Budget Rent-A-Car* (phone: 800-472-3325). Has 7 locations on Cancún, 2 on Cozumel, and 3 in Mérida.
>
> *Dollar Rent-A-Car* (phone: 800-800-4000). Has 5 locations on Cancún, 2 on Cozumel, and 2 in Mérida.
>
> *Economovil Rent* (phone: 5-604-5960 or 5-604-2118 for the main office in Mexico City). Has 2 locations on Cancún.
>
> *Hertz* (phone: 800-654-3001). Rents cars at over 60 locations throughout Mexico. Has 10 locations on Cancún, 2 on Cozumel, and 1 in Mérida.
>
> *National Car Rental* (phone: 800-CAR-EUROPE). Has 3 locations on Cancún and 2 in Mérida.
>
> *Thrifty Rent-A-Car* (phone: 800-367-2277). Has 5 locations on Cancún, 3 on Cozumel, and 2 in Mérida.

For further information on local car rental companies, see *Sources and Resources,* THE ISLANDS.

Requirements – Whether you decide to rent a car in advance from a large international rental company with Mexican branches or wait to rent from a local company, you should know that renting a car is rarely as simple as signing on the dotted line and roaring off into the night. If you are renting for personal use, you must have a valid driver's license and will have to convince the renting agency that (1) you are personally credit-worthy; and (2) you will bring the car back at the stated time. This will be easy if you have a major credit card; most rental companies accept credit cards in lieu of a cash deposit, as well as for payment of your final bill. If you prefer to pay in cash, leave your credit card imprint as a "deposit," then pay your bill in cash when you return the car.

If you are planning to rent a car once in Mexico, *Avis, Budget, Hertz,* and other US rental companies usually will rent to travelers paying in cash and leaving either a credit card imprint or a substantial amount of cash as a deposit. This is not necessarily standard policy, however, as some of the other international chains, and a number of regional and local Mexican companies, will *not* rent to an individual who doesn't have a valid credit card. In this case, you may have to call around to find a company that accepts cash.

Also keep in mind that although the minimum age to drive a car in Mexico is 18 years, the minimum age to rent a car is set by the rental company. Many firms have a minimum age requirement of 21 years, some raise that to 24 or 25 years, and for some models of cars it rises to 30 years. The upper age limit at many companies is between 69 and 75; others have no age limit or may make drivers above a certain age subject to special conditions.

Costs – Finding the most economical car rental will require some telephone shopping on your part. As a *general* rule, expect to hear lower prices quoted by the smaller, strictly local companies than by the well-known international names, with those of the national Mexican companies falling somewhere between the two. Comparison shopping always is advisable, however, because the company that has the least expensive rentals in one city may not have the least expensive cars in another, and even the international giants offer discount plans whose conditions are easy for most travelers to fulfill.

If driving short distances for only a day or two, the best deal may be per-day, per-mile (or per-kilometer) rate: You pay a flat fee for each day you keep the car (which can be as low as $25), plus a per-mile charge of 12¢ to 40¢ (or 7¢ to 25¢ per kilometer) or more. An increasingly common alternative is to be granted a certain number of free miles or kilometers each day and then be charged on a per-mile or per-kilometer basis over that number.

A better alternative for Mexican touring is a flat per-day rate with unlimited free mileage; this is certainly the most economical rate if you plan to drive over 100 miles. (*Note:* When renting a car in Mexico, the term "mileage" may refer to either miles or kilometers.) Make sure that the low, flat daily rate that catches your eye, however, is indeed a per-day rate: Often the lowest price advertised by a company turns out to be available only with a minimum 3-day rental — fine if you want the car that long, but not the bargain it appears if you really intend to use it no more than 24 hours. Flat weekly rates also are available, as well as some flat monthly rates that represent a further saving over the daily rate.

Another factor influencing cost is the type of car you rent. Rentals generally are based on a tiered price system, with different sizes of cars — variations of budget, economy, regular, and luxury. Charges may increase by only a few dollars a day through several classes of subcompact and compact cars — where most of the competition is — then increase by great leaps through the remaining classes of full-size and luxury cars and passenger vans. The larger the car, the more it costs to rent and more gas it consumes, but for some people the greater comfort and extra luggage space of a larger car (in which bags and sporting gear can be safely locked out of sight) may make it worth the additional expense.

Electing to pay for collision damage waiver (CDW) protection also will add to the cost of renting a car; however, buying the offered coverage (for about $11 to $13 a day) will relieve you of responsibility for the value of the vehicle being rented. Before making any decisions about optional collision damage waivers, first determine if you already are adequately covered by your personal automobile insurance policy or by a credit card company if you charge the rental to that card. (For further information, see *Insurance,* in this section.)

Another cost to be added to the price tag is drop-off charges or one-way service fees. The lowest price quoted by any given company may apply only to a car that is returned to the same location from which it was rented. A slightly higher rate may be charged if the car is to be returned to a different location.

Fly/Drive – Airlines, charter companies, car rental companies, and tour operators have been offering fly/drive packages for years, and even though the basic components of the package have changed somewhat — return airfare, a car waiting at the airport, and perhaps a night's lodging all for one inclusive price used to be the rule — the idea remains the same. You rent a car *here* for use *there* by booking it along with other arrangements for the trip. These days, the very minimum arrangement possible is the result of a tie-in between a car rental company and an airline, which entitles customers to a rental car for less than the company's usual rates, provided they show proof of having booked a flight on that airline. For information on available packages, check with the airline or your travel agent.

Package Tours

 If the mere thought of buying a package for travel to Mexico conjures up visions of a trip spent marching in lockstep with a horde of frazzled fellow travelers, remember that packages have come a long way. For one thing, not all packages necessarily are escorted tours, and the one you buy does not have to include any organized touring at all — nor will it necessarily include traveling companions. If it does, however, you'll find that people of all sorts — many just like yourself — are taking advantage of packages today because they are economical and convenient, save you an immense amount of planning time, and exist in such variety that it's virtually impossible not to find one that fits at least the majority of your travel preferences. Given the high cost of travel these days, packages have emerged as a particularly wise buy.

In essence, a package is just an amalgam of travel services that can be purchased in a single transaction. A package (tour or otherwise) to or around Mexico may include any or all of the following: transportation from your home to Mexico, local transportation (and/or car rentals), accommodations, some or all meals, sightseeing, entertainment, transfers to and from the hotel at each destination, taxes, tips, escort service, and a variety of incidental features that might be offered as options at additional cost. In other words, a package can be any combination of travel elements, from a fully escorted tour offered at an all-inclusive price to a simple fly/drive booking allowing you to move about totally on your own. Its principal advantage is that it saves money: The cost of the combined arrangements invariably is well below the price of all of the same elements if bought separately. A package provides more than economy and convenience: It releases the traveler from having to make individual arrangements for each separate element of a trip.

Tour programs generally can be divided into two categories — "escorted" (or locally hosted) and independent. An escorted tour means that a guide will accompany the group from the beginning of the tour through to the return flight; a locally hosted tour means that the group will be met upon your arrival by a local host. On independent tours, there generally is a choice of hotels, meal plans, and sightseeing trips, as well as a variety of special excursions. The independent plan is for travelers who do not want a totally set itinerary, but who do prefer confirmed hotel reservations. Whether choosing an escorted or independent tour, always bring along complete contact information for your tour operator in case a problem arises, although tour operators often have local affiliates who can give additional assistance or make other arrangements on the spot.

To determine whether a package — or, more specifically, *which* package — fits your travel plans, start by evaluating your interests and needs, deciding how much and what you want to spend, see, and do. Gather whatever package tour information is available for your schedule. Be sure that you take the time to read the brochure *carefully* to determine precisely what is included. Keep in mind that travel brochures are written to entice you into signing up for a package tour. Often the language is deceptive and devious. For example, a brochure may quote the lowest prices for a package tour based on facilities that are unavailable during the off-season, undesirable at any season, or just plain nonexistent. Information such as "breakfast included" or "plus tax" (which can add up) should be taken into account. Note, too, that prices quoted in brochures almost always are based on double occupancy: The rate listed is for each of two people sharing a double room, and if you travel alone the supplement for single accommodations can raise the price considerably (see *Hints for Single Travelers,* in this section).

In this age of erratic airfares, the brochure most often will *not* include the price of an airline ticket in the price of the package, though sample fares from various gateway cities usually will be listed separately, to be added to the price of the ground arrangements. Before figuring your actual cost, check the latest fares with the airlines, because the samples invariably are out of date by the time you read them. If the brochure gives more than one category of sample fares per gateway city — such as an individual tour-basing fare, a group fare, an excursion, or other discount ticket — your travel agent or airline tour desk will be able to tell you which one applies to the package you choose, depending on when you travel, how far in advance you book, and other factors. When the brochure does include round-trip transportation in the package price, don't forget to add the cost of round-trip transportation from your home to the departure city to come up with the total cost of the package.

Finally, read the general information regarding terms and conditions and the responsibility clause (usually in fine print at the end of the descriptive literature) to determine the precise elements for which the tour operator is — and is not — liable. Here the tour operator frequently expresses the right to change services or schedules as long as equivalent arrangements are offered. This clause also absolves the operator of responsibility for circumstances beyond human control, such as hurricanes or floods, or injury to you or your property. While reading, ask the following questions:

1. Does the tour include airfare or other transportation, sightseeing, meals, transfers, taxes, baggage handling, tips, or any other services? Do you want all these services?
2. If the brochure indicates that "some meals" are included, does this mean a welcoming and farewell dinner, two breakfasts, or every evening meal?
3. What classes of hotels are offered? If you will be traveling alone, what is the single supplement?
4. Does the tour itinerary or price vary according to the season?
5. Are the prices guaranteed; that is, if costs increase between the time you book and the time you depart, can surcharges unilaterally be added?
6. Do you get a full refund if you cancel? If not, be sure to obtain cancellation insurance.
7. Can the operator cancel if too few people join? At what point?

One of the consumer's biggest problems is finding enough information to judge the reliability of a tour packager, since individual travelers seldom have direct contact with the firm putting the package together. Usually, a retail travel agent is interposed between customer and tour operator, and much depends on his or her candor and cooperation. So ask a number of questions about the tour you are considering. For example:

- Has the agent ever used a package provided by this tour operator?
- How long has the tour operator been in business? Check the Better Business Bureau in the area where the tour operator is based to see if any complaints have been filed against it.
- Is the tour operator a member of the *United States Tour Operators Association* (*USTOA*, 211 E. 51st St., Suite 12B, New York, NY 10022; phone: 212-944-5727) The *USTOA* will provide a list of its members upon request; it also offers a useful brochure, *How to Select a Package Tour.*

- How many and which companies are involved in the package?
- If air travel is by charter flight, is there an escrow account in which deposits will be held; if so, what is the name of the bank?

This last question is very important. US law requires that tour operators place every charter passenger's deposit and subsequent payment in a proper escrow account, and money paid into such an account cannot legally be used except to pay for the costs of a particular package or as a refund if the trip is canceled. To protect your investment, you should either make your check payable to the escrow account or use a credit card. (As this procedure follows the same guidelines as payments for charter flights, see our discussion in *Traveling by Plane.*)

■ **A word of advice:** Purchasers of vacation packages who feel they're not getting their money's worth are more likely to get a refund if they complain in writing to the operator — and bail out of the whole package immediately. Alert the tour operator or resort manager to the fact that you are dissatisfied, that you will be leaving for home as soon as transportation can be arranged, and that you expect a refund. They may have forms to fill out detailing your complaint; otherwise, state your case in a letter. Even if the availability of transportation home detains you, your dated, written complaint should help in procuring a refund from the operator.

Following is a list of many of the major US operators who provide escorted or independent tours to Cancún, Cozumel, Isla Mujeres, and the Yucatán Peninsula. Most tour operators offer several departure dates, depending on the length of the tour and areas visited. As indicated, some operators are wholesalers only, and will deal only with a travel agent.

American Express Travel Related Services (300 Pinnacle Way, Norcross, GA 30071; phone: 800-327-7737 or 404-368-5100). Offers escorted and independent package tours to Cancún and Cozumel. The tour operator is a wholesaler, so use a travel agent.

Arrow to the Sun Bicycle Touring (PO Box 115, Taylorsville, CA 95983; phone: 800-634-0492 or 916-284-6263). Offers a 12-day biking trip in December from Cancún to Mérida.

Asti Tours (21 East 40th St., New York, NY 10016; phone: 800-535-3711 in New York; 800-223-7728 elsewhere in the US). Offers air/hotel package to Cancún.

Caiman Expeditions (3449 E. River Rd., Tucson, AZ 85718; phone: 800-365-ADVE or 602-299-1047). Packages 10-day trips on the Yucatán Peninsula which include rafting and camping.

Fishing International (4010 Montecito Ave., PO Box 2132, Santa Rosa, CA 95405; phone: 800-950-4242). This fishing and hunting specialist offers packages to Cancún and Cozumel. Also books customized packages.

Fling Vacations (999 Postal Rd., Allentown, PA 18103; phone: 800-523-9624). Offers several 7-day packages on Cancún. The tour operator is a wholesaler, so use a travel agent.

Frontiers International (PO Box 959, 100 Logan Rd., Wexford, PA 15090; phone: 412-935-1577 in Pennsylvania; 800-245-1950 elsewhere in the US). They offer 7-day fishing and hunting packages to Cancún.

GoGo Tours (contact the central office for the nearest location: 69 Spring St., Ramsey, NJ 07446-0507; phone: 201-934-3860). It offers 3-, 5- or 7-day air/hotel packages to Cancún and Cozumel. This operator is a wholesaler, so use a travel agent.

Journeys (3516 NE 155th St., Seattle, WA 98155; phone: 206-365-0686 in Washington; 800-345-4453 elsewhere in the US). It offers a 16-day hiking trip, exploring the Yucatán's Maya ruins.

Liberty Travel (contact the central office for the nearest location: 69 Spring St., Ramsey, NJ 07446; phone: 201-934-3500). Offers air/hotel packages to Cancún and Cozumel.

Maya Route Tours (Box 1948, Murray Hill Station, New York, NY 10156; phone: 212-683-2136). This agency packages the Yucatán Peninsula tours of several Mexican tour operators.

Mountain Travel (6420 Fairmont Ave., El Cerrito, CA 94530; phone: 800-227-2384 or 415-527-8100). This adventure package specialist offers a number of trips to the Yucatán Peninsula.

MTA International (1717 N. Highland Ave., Los Angeles, CA 90028; phone: 213-462-6444 in California; 800-876-6824 elsewhere in the US). Offers several package to Cancún and Cozumel. The tour operator is a wholesaler, so use a travel agent.

Nature Expeditions International (PO Box 11496, Eugene, OR 97440; phone: 503-484-6529). Offers 16-day cultural and historical tours studying the ancient temples and Maya ruins of the Yucatán Peninsula.

Olson-Travelworld (100 N. Sepulveda Blvd., Suite 1010, El Segundo, CA 90245; phone: 800-421-5785 or 213-605-0711 in California; 800-421-2255 elsewhere in the US). Offers deluxe, all-inclusive, and fully escorted tours throughout Mexico, including Cancún and Cozumel. The tour operator is a wholesaler, so use a travel agent.

Outback Expeditions (Box 16343, Seattle, WA 98116; phone: 206-932-7012). Their 10-day packages explore the Maya ruins on the Yucatán Peninsula.

Trans National Travel (2 Charlesgate W., Boston, MA 02215; phone: 800-262-0123). Offers 3- to 7-day packages to Cancún and Cozumel.

Travel Impressions (465 Smith St., Farmingdale, NY 11735; phone: 800-284-0077 in the Southeast, Midwest, and Western US; 800-284-0044 or 800-284-0055 in the Northeast and elsewhere in the US). Offers a wide range of packages to Cancún and Cozumel. The tour operator is a wholesaler, so use a travel agent.

Trek America (PO Box 1138, Gardena, CA 90249; phone: 800-221-0596). Offers a 25-day leisurely hiking trip on the Yucatán Peninsula.

Two Worlds Travel (PO Box 3636, Humble, TX 77347-3636; phone: 800-446-2166). Offers 1-week diving vacations to Cancún every year during September and October.

Wilderness: Alaska/Mexico (1231 Sundance Loop, Fairbanks, AK 99709; phone: 907-457-8907 or 907-452-1821). Their Mexican hiking and kayaking itineraries include packages to the Yucatán Peninsula.

Preparing

Calculating Costs

$ **DETERMINING A BUDGET:** A realistic appraisal of travel expenses is the most crucial bit of planning required before any trip. It is also, unfortunately, one for which it is most difficult to give precise, practical advice.

In Mexico, estimating travel expenses depends on the mode of transportation you choose, how long you will stay, and, in some cases, what time of year you plan to travel. In addition to the basics of transportation, hotels, meals, and sightseeing, you have to take into account seasonal price changes.

When calculating costs, start with the basics, the major expenses being transportation, accommodations, and food. However, don't forget such extras as local transportation, shopping, and such miscellaneous items as laundry and tips. Package programs can reduce the price of a vacation in Mexico, because the rates obtained by the tour packager are usually lower than the tariffs for someone traveling on a free-lance basis; that is, paying for each element — airfare, meals, car rental — separately. And keep in mind, particularly when calculating the major expenses, that costs vary according to fluctuations in the exchange rate — that is, how much of a given foreign currency the dollar will buy.

Other expenses, such as the cost of local sightseeing tours and other excursions, will vary depending on the tour and the guide you select. The tourist information office and most of the better hotels will have someone at the front desk to provide a rundown on the cost of local tours and full-day excursions in and out of the city. Travel agents also can provide this information.

In planning a travel budget, it also is wise to allow a realistic amount for both entertainment and recreation. Are you planning to spend time sightseeing and visiting local tourist attractions? Do you intend to rent a sailboat or take parasailing lessons? Is daily golf or tennis a part of your plan? Finally, don't forget that if haunting discotheques or other nightspots is an essential part of your vacation or you feel that one dinner show may not be enough, allow for the extra cost of nightlife. This one item alone can add a great deal to your daily expenditures.

If at any point in the planning process it appears impossible to estimate expenses, consider this suggestion: The easiest way to put a ceiling on the price of all these elements is to buy a package tour. A totally planned and escorted tour, with almost all transportation, rooms, meals, sightseeing, local travel, tips, and a dinner show or two included and prepaid, provides a pretty exact total of what the trip will cost beforehand, and the only surprise will be the one you spring on yourself by succumbing to some irresistible, expensive souvenir.

■ **Note:** The combination of rapid peso devaluation and Mexico's inflation rate has led the government to authorize increases in hotel rates of as much as 35% from time to time. Between the time you originally make your hotel reservations and your arrival, the price in US dollars may vary substantially from the price originally quoted. To avoid paying more than you expected, it's wise to confirm rates by writing directly to hotels or by calling their representatives in the US.

Planning a Trip

123 Travelers fall into two categories: those who make lists and those who do not. Some people prefer to plot the course of their trip to the finest detail, with contingency plans and alternatives at the ready. For others, the joy of a voyage is its spontaneity; exhaustive planning only lessens the thrill of anticipation and the sense of freedom.

For most travelers, any week-plus trip to Cancún or Cozumel can be too expensive for an "I'll take my chances" type of attitude. Even perennial gypsies and anarchistic wanderers have to take into account the time-consuming logistics of getting around, and even with minimal baggage, they need to think about packing. Hence at least some planning is crucial.

This is not to suggest that you work out your itinerary in minute detail before you go; but it's still wise to decide certain basics at the very start: where to go, what to do, and how much to spend. These decisions require a certain amount of consideration. So before rigorously planning specific details, you might want to establish your general travel objectives:

1. How much time will you have for the entire trip, and how much of it are you willing to spend getting where you're going?
2. What interests and/or activities do you want to pursue while on vacation? Do you want to visit one, a few, or several different places?
3. At what time of year do you want to go?
4. Do you want peace and privacy or lots of activity and company?
5. How much money can you afford to spend for the entire vacation?

There is an abundance of travel information on Mexico, including Cancún and Cozumel. You can seek the assistance of travel agents, turn to travel clubs such as *AAA* and other motoring organizations, or use general travel sources such as guidebooks, brochures, and maps. Mexican tourist offices in ths US and Mexico have brochures and extensive material on all parts of Mexico, and there's a 24-hour information hotline in Mexico City (phone: 5-250-0123, 5-250-0493, 5-250-0151, or 5-250-0589). The US Department of State's brochure *Travel to Mexico* is another source of general information to the country. It can be obtained free from the Washington Passport Agency, 1425 K St. NW, Washington, DC 20524 (phone: 202-647-0518).

. You now can make almost all of your own travel arrangements if you have time to follow through with hotels, airlines, tour operators, and so on. But you'll probably save considerable time and energy if you have a travel agent make arrangements for you. The agent also should be able to advise you of alternative arrangements of which you may not be aware. Only rarely will a travel agent's services cost a traveler any money, and they may even save you some (see *How to Use a Travel Agent*, below).

If you are traveling by plane and want to benefit from savings offered by a charter flight to Cancún or Cozumel (see *Traveling by Plane*, in this section), you may need reservations as much as 3 months in advance. In the high season, hotel reservations also are required months in advance. Many hotels on Cancún and Cozumel require deposits before they will guarantee reservations, and this most often is the case during peak travel periods. (Be sure to request a receipt for any deposit.) Travel during *Easter Week*, the *Christmas/New Year* period, and local festival and holiday times also requires reservations well in advance.

Make a list of any valuable items you are carrying with you, including credit card numbers and the serial numbers of your traveler's checks. Put copies in your purse or pocket and leave other copies at home. Put a label with your name and home address on the inside of your luggage for identification in case of loss. Put your name and business address — *never your home address* — on a label on the outside of your luggage. (Those who run businesses from home should use the office address of a friend or relative.)

Review your travel documents. If you are traveling by air, check to see that your ticket has been filled in correctly. The left side of the ticket should have a list of each stop you will make (even if you are only stopping to change planes), beginning with your departure point. Be sure that the list is correct, and count the number of copies to see that you have one for each plane you will take. If you have confirmed reservations, be sure that the column marked "status" says "OK" beside each flight. Have in hand vouchers or proof of payment for any reservation for which you've paid in advance; this includes hotels, transfers to and from the airport, sightseeing tours, car rentals, and special events. Although policies vary from carrier to carrier, it's still smart to reconfirm your flight 48 to 72 hours before departure, both going and returning.

Finally, you always should bear in mind that despite the most careful plans, things do not always occur on schedule — especially in Mexico, where *ahora* ("now") means anytime between today and tomorrow, and *ahorita* ("right now") means anytime within the next few hours. If you maintain a flexible attitude and try to accept minor disruptions as less than cataclysmic, you will enjoy yourself a lot more.

How to Use a Travel Agent

 A reliable travel agent remains your best source of service and information for planning a trip abroad, whether you have a specific itinerary and require an agent only to make reservations or you need extensive help in sorting through the maze of airfares, tour offerings, hotel packages, and the scores of other arrangements that may be involved in a trip to Cancún or Cozumel.

Know what you want from a travel agent so that you can evaluate what you are getting. It is perfectly reasonable to expect your agent to be a thoroughly knowledgeable travel specialist, with information about your destination and, even more crucial, a command of current airfares, ground arrangements, and other wrinkles in the travel scene.

Most travel agents work through computer reservations systems (CRS). These are used to assess the availability and cost of flights, hotels, and car rental firms, and through them they can book reservations. Despite reports of "computer bias," in which a computer may favor one airline over another, the CRS should provide agents with the entire spectrum of flights available to a given destination, as well as the complete range of fares in considerably less time than it takes to telephone the airlines individually — and at no extra charge to the client.

Make the most intelligent use of a travel agent's time and expertise; understand the economics of the industry. As a client, traditionally you pay nothing for the agent's services; with few exceptions, it's all free, from hotel bookings to advice on package tours. Any money the travel agent makes on the time spent arranging your itinerary — booking hotels, resorts, or flights, or suggesting activities — comes from commissions paid by the suppliers of these services — the airlines, hotels, and so on. These commissions generally run from 10% to 15% of the total cost of the service, although suppliers often reward agencies that sell their services in volume with an increased commission, called an override. In most instances, you'll find that travel agent make their time and experience available to you at no charge, and you do not pay more for an airline ticket, package tour, or other product bought from a travel agent than you would for the same product bought directly from the supplier.

Exceptions to the general rule of free service by a travel agency are the agencies

beginning to practice net pricing. In essence, such agencies return their commissions and overrides to their customers and make their income by charging a flat fee per transaction instead (thus adding a charge after a reduction for the commission has been made). Net fares and fees are a growing practice, though hardly widespread.

Even a conventional travel agent sometimes may charge a fee for special services. These chargeable items may include long-distance telephone or cable costs incurred in making a booking, for reserving a room in a place that does not pay a commission (such as a small, out-of-the-way hotel), or for special attention such as planning a highly personalized itinerary. A fee also may be assessed in instances of deeply discounted airfares.

Choose a travel agent with the same care with which you would choose a doctor or lawyer. You will be spending a good deal of money on the basis of the agent's judgment, so you have a right to expect that judgment to be mature, informed, and interested. At the moment, unfortunately, there aren't many standards within the travel agent industry to help you gauge competence, and the quality of individual agents varies enormously.

At present, only nine states have registration, licensing, or other form of travel agent–related legislation on their books. Rhode Island licenses travel agents; Florida, Hawaii, Iowa, and Ohio register them; and California, Illinois, Oregon, and Washington have laws governing the sale of transportation or related services. While state licensing of agents cannot absolutely guarantee competence, it can at least ensure that an agent has met some minimum requirements.

Perhaps the best-prepared agents are those who have completed the CTC Travel Management program offered by the *Institute of Certified Travel Agents (ICTA)* and carry the initials CTC (Certified Travel Counselor) after their names. This indicates a relatively high level of expertise. For a free list of CTCs in your area, send a self-addressed, stamped, #10 envelope to *ICTA,* 148 Linden St., Box 82-56, Wellesley, MA 02181 (phone: 617-237-0280 in Massachusetts; 800-542-4282 elsewhere in the US).

An agent's membership in the *American Society of Travel Agents (ASTA)* can be a useful guideline in making a selection. But keep in mind that *ASTA* is an industry organization, requiring only that its members be licensed in those states where required; be accredited to represent the suppliers whose products they sell, including airline and cruise tickets; and adhere to its Principles of Professional Conduct and Ethics code. *ASTA* does not guarantee the competence, ethics, or financial soundness of its members, but it does offer some recourse if you feel you have been dealt with unfairly. Complaints may be registered with *ASTA* (Consumer Affairs Dept., PO Box 23992, Washington, DC 20026-3992; phone: 703-739-2782). First try to resolve the complaint directly with the supplier. For a list of *ASTA* members in your area, send a self-addressed, stamped, #10 envelope to *ASTA,* Public Relations Dept., at the address above.

There also is the *Association of Retail Travel Agents (ARTA),* a smaller but highly respected trade organization similar to *ASTA.* Its member agencies and agents similarly agree to abide by a code of ethics, and complaints about a member can be made to *ARTA*'s Grievance Committee, 1745 Jeff Davis Hwy., Arlington, VA 22202-3402 (phone: 800-969-6069 or 703-553-7777).

Perhaps the best way to find a travel agent is by word of mouth. If the agent (or agency) has done a good job for your friends over a period of time, it probably indicates a certain level of commitment and competence. Always ask not only for the name of the company, but for the name of the specific agent with whom your friends dealt, for it is that individual who will serve you, and quality can vary widely within a single agency. There are some superb travel agents in the business, and they can facilitate vacation or business arrangements.

You may decide to use a travel agent within Mexico to set up tours for the duration or for portions of your stay. Among the leading travel agencies that have offices on Cancún or Cozumel are the following:

American Express Travel Related Services: In Cancún City: in the lobby of *America Hotel* at the corner of Av. Tulum and Calle Brisa (phone: 988-41999).

Aviamex Tours de México: In Cancún City: Plaza Tropical, 192 Av. Tulum, Suite 47 (phone: 988-48053 or 988-48031); on Cozumel: 27 Av. Rafael E. Melgar (phone: 987-20831 or 987-20974).

Garza Travel: On Cancún: Plaza Quetzal, Suite 10, Kukulcán Blvd., hotel zone (phone: 988-30161); on Cozumel: in the *Cantarell Hotel,* San Juan Beach (phone: 987-20144).

Turismo Caleta: On Cancún: Plaza Quetzal, Kukulcán Blvd., Suite 11, hotel zone (phone: 988-32538 or 988-31659).

Viajes Parmac: In Cancún City: in the *Plaza del Sol Hotel,* 36 Av. Yaxchilan (phone: 988-40058).

Wagons-lits Mexicana: On Cancún: in the *Camino Real Hotel,* Kukulcán Blvd., Punta Cancún, hotel zone (phone: 988-30824); and the *Calinda Cancún Beach Hotel,* Kukulcán Blvd., Lote C-1 (phone: 988-30847).

Entry Requirements and Documents

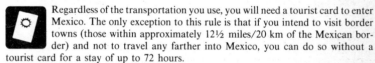

Regardless of the transportation you use, you will need a tourist card to enter Mexico. The only exception to this rule is that if you intend to visit border towns (those within approximately 12½ miles/20 km of the Mexican border) and not to travel any farther into Mexico, you can do so without a tourist card for a stay of up to 72 hours.

In order to obtain a tourist card, you must have proof of your US citizenship. This proof may consist of an original or certified copy of a birth certificate, a voter's registration certificate, or a valid passport. A driver's license, credit card, or military papers will not suffice. A naturalized citizen must present at least one of the following documents: naturalization papers, a US passport, or an affidavit of citizenship.

A tourist card can be obtained from a number of sources, including any Mexican Ministry of Tourism office or Mexican consulate in the US; the Mexican government border offices at any port of entry; and some travel agencies. Regardless of where you obtain the card, when you cross the border you must sign it in the presence of the Mexican immigration official, who also may ask to see proof of your citizenship. For those arriving by plane, the card can be obtained from any airline ticket office. It also must be presented along with proof of citizenship when you land in Mexico. The tourist card allows you to stay in Mexico for a specified number of days; if you request one for 90 days — the maximum is 6 months — you don't have to stay that long but you are covered for that period of time.

In order to be issued a tourist card, minors under 18 who are traveling alone must present a passport or a notarized copy of a letter signed by a parent or guardian and indicating permission. If the minor is traveling with only one parent, an individual passport or a letter signed by the other parent or legal guardian will be needed.

During your stay in Mexico, you always should carry your tourist card with you, although you aren't likely to be asked for it after the border crossing. If you happen to lose your card, you should report it immediately to the nearest office of the Secretaría de Gobernación. They should be able to replace it for you.

US citizens will not need any vaccination certificates in order to enter Mexico for a short period of time. There are, however, a number of vaccinations that travelers to

Mexico would be well advised to have before leaving and medicines that should be brought along, particularly if traveling in jungle areas. (See *Staying Healthy*, in this section, for our recommendations and other information on health concerns and precautions.)

Although other forms of identification (such as those cited above) will suffice, a valid passport is the best identification and proof of US citizenship to carry when traveling through Mexico. While abroad, you should carry your passport with you at all times, and if you lose it, immediately report the loss to the nearest US consulate or embassy (for locations in Mexico, see *Medical and Legal Aid and Consular Services*, in this section). It's likely to speed up the replacement process if you have a record of your passport number and the place and date of its issue (a photocopy of the first page of your passport is perfect). Keep this information separate from your passport — you might want to give it to a traveling companion to hold.

DUTY AND CUSTOMS: As a general rule, the requirements for bringing the majority of items *into Mexico* is that they must be quantities small enough not to imply commercial import.

If you are accustomed to certain American brands of bourbon or whiskey (although imported brands are increasingly available, they are very costly), you are allowed to bring 3 liters of liquor into Mexico duty-free — any amount over this will be taxed. And if you prefer American cigarettes, be advised that the limit is 1 carton (20 packs). Each person also may bring in one still and one video camera, plus 12 rolls of film and 3 video cartridge tapes. For further information on Mexican customs regulations, contact the Mexican Ministry of Tourism offices or Mexican consulates in the US (see *Sources and Resources*, in this section, for addresses).

If you are bringing along a computer, camera, or other electronic equipment for your own use that you will be taking back to the US, you should register it with the US Customs Service in order to avoid being asked to pay duty both entering and returning from Mexico. (Also see *Customs and Returning to the US*, in this section.) For information on this procedure, as well as for a variety of informative pamphlets on US Customs regulations, contact the local office of the US Customs Service or the central office, PO Box 7407, Washington, DC 20044 (phone: 202-566-8195).

■ **One rule to follow:** When passing through customs, it is illegal not to declare dutiable items; penalties range from stiff fines and seizure of the goods to prison terms. So don't try to sneak anything through — it just isn't worth it.

Insurance

 It is unfortunate that most decisions to buy travel insurance are impulsive and usually made without any real consideration of the traveler's existing policies. Therefore, the first person with whom you should discuss travel insurance is your own insurance broker, not a travel agent or the clerk behind the airport insurance counter. You may discover that the insurance you already carry protects you adequately while you travel or that you need no more than excess value insurance for baggage, or trip cancellation insurance.

TYPES OF INSURANCE: To make insurance decisions intelligently, however, you first should understand the basic categories of travel insurance and what they cover. Then you can decide what you should have in the broader context of your personal insurance needs, and you can choose the most economical way of getting the desired protection: through riders on existing policies; with onetime short-term policies; through a special program put together for the frequent traveler; through coverage that's part of a travel club's benefits; or with a combination policy sold by insurance companies through brokers, automobile clubs, tour operators, and travel agents.

There are seven basic categories of travel insurance:

1. Baggage and personal effects insurance
2. Personal accident and sickness insurance
3. Trip cancellation and interruption insurance
4. Default and/or bankruptcy insurance
5. Flight insurance (to cover injury or death)
6. Automobile insurance (for driving your own or a rented car)
7. Combination policies

Baggage and Personal Effects Insurance – Ask your insurance agent if baggage and personal effects are included in your current homeowner's policy, or if you will need a special floater to cover you for the duration of a trip. The object is to protect your bags and their contents in case of damage or theft anytime during your travels, not just while you're in flight and covered by the airline's policy. Furthermore, only limited protection is provided by the airline (see *Traveling by Plane,* in this section).

If you are carrying goods worth more than the maximum protection offered by the airline, consider excess value insurance. Additional coverage is available from the airlines at an average, currently, of $1 to $2 per $100 worth of coverage, up to a maximum of $5,000. This insurance can be purchased at the airline counter when you check in, though you should arrive early to fill out the necessary forms and to avoid holding up other passengers.

Major credit card companies also provide coverage for lost or delayed baggage — and this coverage often also is over and above what the airline will pay. The basic coverage is automatic for all cardholders who use the credit card to purchase tickets, but to qualify for additional coverage, cardholders generally must enroll in advance.

> *American Express:* Provides $500 coverage for checked baggage; $1,250 for carry-on baggage; and $250 for valuables, such as cameras and jewelry.
> *Carte Blanche and Diners Club:* Each provides $1,250 worth of free insurance for checked or carry-on baggage that's lost or damaged.
> *Discover Card:* Offers $500 insurance for checked baggage and $1,250 for carry-on baggage — but to qualify for this coverage, cardholders first must purchase additional flight insurance (see "Flight Insurance," below).
> *MasterCard and Visa:* Baggage insurance coverage is set by the issuing institution.

Additional baggage and personal effects insurance also is included in certain of the combination travel insurance policies discussed below.

■ **A note of warning:** Be sure to read the fine print of any excess value insurance policy; there often are specific exclusions, such as cash, tickets, furs, gold and silver objects, art, and antiques. And remember that insurance companies ordinarily will pay only the depreciated value of the goods rather than their replacement value. The best way to protect the items you're carrying in your luggage is to take photos of your valuables and keep a record of the serial numbers of such items as cameras, laptops, radios, and so on. This will establish that you do, indeed, own the objects. If your luggage disappears or is damaged en route, deal with the situation immediately.

Personal Accident and Sickness Insurance – This covers you in case of illness during your trip or death in an accident. Most policies insure you for hospital and doctor's expenses, lost income, and so on. In most cases, it is a standard part of existing health insurance policies, though you should check with your insurance broker to be sure that your policy will pay for any medical expenses incurred abroad. If not, take out a separate vacation accident policy or an entire vacation insurance policy that includes health and life coverage.

One company offering such comprehensive health and life insurance policies is *Wallach & Co.* Both their HealthCare Global and HealthCare Abroad programs may be bought in combination with trip cancellation and baggage insurance at extra cost. For information, write to *Wallach & Co.*, 243 Church St. NW, Suite 100-D, Vienna, VA 22180 (phone: 703-281-9500 in Virginia; 800-237-6615 elsewhere in the US).

Trip Cancellation and Interruption Insurance – Most charter and package tour passengers pay for their travel well before departure. The disappointment of having to miss a vacation because of illness or any other reason pales before the awful prospect that not all (and sometimes none) of the money paid in advance might be returned. So cancellation insurance for any package tour is a must.

Although cancellation penalties vary (they are listed in the fine print in every tour brochure, and before you purchase a package tour you should know exactly what they are), rarely will a passenger get more than 50% of this money back if forced to cancel within a few weeks of scheduled departure. Therefore, if you book a package tour or charter flight, you should have trip cancellation insurance to guarantee full reimbursement or refund should you, a traveling companion, or a member of your immediate family get sick, forcing you to cancel your trip or *return home early.*

The key here is *not* to buy just enough insurance to guarantee full reimbursement for the cost of the package or charter in case of cancellation. The proper amount of coverage should be sufficient to reimburse you for the cost of having to catch up with a tour after its departure or having to travel home at the full economy airfare (from the farthest destination on your itinerary) if you have to forgo your return flight of your charter. There is usually quite a discrepancy between a charter fare and the amount necessary to travel the same distance on a regularly scheduled flight at full economy fare. Before you decide on a policy, also be sure to check the fine print for stipulations concerning "family members" and "pre-existing medical conditions," as well as allowances for living expenses if you must delay your return due to bodily injury or illness.

Trip cancellation insurance is available from travel agents and tour operators in two forms: as part of a short-term, all-purpose travel insurance package (sold by the travel agent); or as specific cancellation insurance designed by the tour operator for a specific charter tour. Generally, tour operators' policies are less expensive, but also less inclusive. Cancellation insurance also is available directly from insurance companies or their agents as part of a short-term, all-inclusive travel insurance policy.

Default and/or Bankruptcy Insurance – Although trip cancellation insurance usually protects you if *you* are unable to complete — or begin — your trip, a fairly recent innovation is coverage in the event of default and/or bankruptcy on the part of the tour operator, airline, or other travel supplier. In some travel insurance packages, this contingency is included in the trip cancellation portion of the coverage; in others, it is a separate feature. Either way, it is becoming increasingly important. While default/bankruptcy insurance will not ordinarily result in reimbursement in time to pay for new arrangements, it can ensure that you will get your money back, and even independent travelers buying no more than an airplane ticket may want to consider it.

Flight Insurance – Airlines have carefully established limits of liability for injury to or the death of passengers for international flights. For international flights to, from, or with a stopover in the US, all carriers are liable for up to $75,000 per passenger. For all other international flights, the liability is based on where you purchase the ticket: If booked in advance in the US, the maximum liability is $75,000; if arrangements are made abroad, the liability is $10,000. But remember, these liabilities are not the same thing as insurance policies; every penny that an airline eventually pays in the case of injury or death will likely be subject to a legal battle.

But before you buy last-minute flight insurance from an airport vending machine, consider the purchase in light of your total existing insurance coverage. A careful review of your current policies may reveal that you already are amply covered for accidental death, sometimes up to three times the amount provided for by the flight insurance you're buying at the airport.

Be aware that airport insurance, the kind typically bought at a counter or from a vending machine, is among the most expensive forms of life insurance coverage, and that even within a single airport, rates for approximately the same coverage vary widely. Often policies sold in vending machines are more expensive than those sold over the counter, even when they are with the same national company.

If you buy your plane ticket with a major credit card, you generally receive automatic insurance coverage at no extra cost. Additional coverage usually can be obtained at extremely reasonable prices, but a cardholder must sign up for it in advance. (Note that rates vary slightly for residents of some states.) As we went to press, the travel accident and life insurance policies of these major credit cards were as follows:

American Express: Automatically provides $100,000 in insurance to its *Green, Gold,* and *Optima* cardholders, and $500,000 to *Platinum* cardholders. With *American Express,* $4 per ticket buys an additional $250,000 worth of flight insurance; $6.50 buys $500,000 worth; and $13 provides an added $1 million worth of coverage.

Carte Blanche: Automatically provides $150,000 flight insurance. An additional $250,000 worth of insurance is available for $4; $500,000 costs $6.50.

Diners Club: Provides $350,000 free flight insurance. An additional $250,000 worth of insurance is available for $4; $500,000 costs $6.50.

Discover Card: Provides $500,000 free flight insurance. An additional $250,000 worth of insurance is available for $4; $500,000 costs $6.50.

MasterCard and Visa: Insurance coverage for each is set by the issuing institution.

Automobile Insurance – When you rent a car, the rental company is required to offer you insurance. In your car rental contract, you'll see that for about $11 to $13 a day, you may buy optional collision damage waiver (CDW) coverage, which relieves you of all responsibility for damage to the rental car. If you do not accept this coverage, you may be liable for the full retail cost of the car.

Before agreeing to this coverage, however, ask your insurance agent if your personal automobile insurance policy covers rented vehicles — it very well may cover your entire liability exposure without any additional cost. Be aware, too, that increasing numbers of credit cards automatically provide CDW coverage if the car rental is charged to the appropriate credit card. As the specific terms of such coverage differ sharply among individual credit card companies, contact the issuing institution for information on the nature and amount of coverage provided. (Business travelers should be aware that, at the time of this writing, *American Express* had withdrawn its automatic CDW coverage from some corporate *Green* card accounts — watch for similar cutbacks by other companies.)

You also should know that an increasing number of the major international car rental companies are including the cost of the CDW in their quoted prices. This does not mean that they are absorbing this cost and you are receiving free coverage — total car rental prices have increased to include this coverage. The disadvantage of this inclusion is that you may not have the option to refuse this coverage, and will end up paying the added charge — even if you already are adequately covered by your own insurance policy or through a credit card company.

Combination Policies – Short-term insurance policies, which may include any combination of any or all of the types of insurance discussed above, are available through retail insurance agencies, automobile clubs, and many travel agents. These combination policies are designed to cover you for the duration of a single trip.

Companies offering policies of this type include the following:

Access America (600 Third Ave., PO Box 807, New York, NY 10163; phone: 800-284-8300 or 212-490-5345).

Carefree Travel Insurance (Arm Coverage, PO Box 310, Mineola, NY 11501; phone: 800-645-2424 or 516-294-0220).

Near (1900 N. MacArthur Blvd., Suite 210, Oklahoma City, OK 73127; phone: 800-654-6700 or 405-949-2500).

Tele-Trip (PO Box 31685, 3201 Farnam St., Omaha, NE 68131; phone: 402-345-2400 in Nebraska; 800-228-9792 elsewhere in the US).

Travel Assistance International (1133 15th St. NW, Suite 400, Washington, DC 20005; phone: 202-347-2025 in Washington, DC; 800-821-2828 elsewhere in the US).

Travel Guard International (1145 Clark St., Stevens Point, WI 54481; phone: 715-345-0505 in Wisconsin; 800-826-1300 elsewhere in the US).

The Travelers Company (Ticket and Travel Plans, One Tower Sq., Hartford, CT 06183-5040; phone: 203-277-2319 in Connecticut; 800-243-3174 elsewhere in the US).

WorldCare Travel Assistance Association (605 Market St., Suite 1300, San Francisco, CA 94105; phone: 800-666-4993 or 415-541-4991).

Hints for Handicapped Travelers

From 40 to 50 million people in the US alone have some sort of disability, and over half this number are physically handicapped. Like everyone else today, they — and the uncounted disabled millions around the world — are on the move. More than ever before, they are demanding facilities they can use comfortably, and they are being heard.

Those who have chosen to visit Mexico are in luck, because more and more disabled travelers are returning from this most luscious of destinations bearing tales of ramped sidewalks, a style of warm-weather architecture that erects fewer barriers between the indoors and the outdoors, and sightseeing tours designed especially for them. Also, in recent years, a series of imaginative, inter-American programs aimed at improving facilities and services for the handicapped in Mexico and Latin America have been initiated. Chief among these is *Partners of the Americas,* with chapters based in 45 states, which coordinates joint projects with these states working in various Mexican and Latin American areas. *Partners of the Americas* also maintains an extensive library with information on programs for the handicapped throughout Mexico, as well as Central and South America, and they often can put disabled travelers in touch with self-help organizations of disabled persons in these locations. For more information, contact the central office of *Partners of the Americas,* 1424 K St., NW, Suite 700, Washington, DC 20005 (phone: 800-322-7844 or 202-628-3300).

Despite this effort to develop special facilities for the disabled, however, handicapped travelers face pretty much the same problems in Mexico as in most other parts of the world. Rural areas have no facilities. Cities have some, but there is no consistency.

PLANNING: Collect as much information as you can about your specific disability and facilities for the disabled in Mexico; make your travel arrangements well in advance, and specify to all services involved the exact nature of your condition or restricted mobility to ensure accommodations and facilities to suit your needs. The best way to find out if your intended destination can accommodate a handicapped traveler is to write or call the local tourist authority or hotel and ask specific questions. If you require a corridor of a certain width to maneuver a wheelchair or if you need handles on the bathroom wall for support, ask the hotel manager (some large hotels have rooms designed for the handicapped). A travel agent or an organization that deals with your particular disability — for example, the *American Foundation for the Blind* — will supply the most up-to-date information on the subject. The following organizations offer general information on access:

ACCENT on Living (PO Box 700, Bloomington, IL 61702; phone: 309-378-2961). This information service for persons with disabilities provides a free list of travel agencies specializing in trips for the disabled, as well as a wide range of publications, including a quarterly magazine ($8 per year; $14 for 2 years).

Information Center for Individuals with Disabilities (Fort Point Pl., 1st Floor, 27-43 Wormwood St., Boston, MA 02210; phone: 800-462-5015 in Massachusetts; 617-727-5540/1 elsewhere in the US; both numbers provide voice and TDD — telecommunications device for the deaf). The center offers information and referral services on disability-related issues, publishes fact sheets on travel resources, and can help you research your trip.

Mobility International USA (*MIUSA;* PO Box 3551, Eugene, OR 97403; phone: 503-343-1284; both voice and TDD). This US branch of *Mobility International,* a nonprofit British organization with affiliates worldwide, offers members advice and assistance, information on travel services, and various publications, including a comprehensive sourcebook, *A World of Options for the 90s: A Guide to International Education Exchange, Community Service and Travel for Persons with Disabilities* ($14 for members; $16 for non-members) and a quarterly newsletter (included in the $20 yearly membership fee; $10 a year for non-members).

National Rehabilitation Information Center (8455 Colesville Rd., Suite 935, Silver Spring, MD 20910; phone: 301-588-9284). A general information, resource, research, and referral service.

Paralyzed Veterans of America (*PVA;* PVA/ATTS Program, 801 18th St. NW, Washington, DC 20006; phone: 202-416-7708 in Washington, DC; 800-424-8200 elsewhere in the US). The members of this national service organization all are veterans who have suffered spinal cord injuries, but it offers advocacy services and information to all disabled persons. *PVA* also sponsors *Access to the Skies,* a program that coordinates the efforts of the air travel industry in increasing accessibility. Members receive several helpful publications and notification of conferences of interest to disabled travelers.

Royal Association for Disability and Rehabilitation (*RADAR;* 25 Mortimer St., London W1N 8AB, England; phone: 44-71-637-5400). Offers a number of useful publications, including a comprehensive guide to international travel, *Holidays and Travel Abroad 1991/1992 — A Guide for Disabled People* (just over £6 as we went to press; payment must be sent in British pounds).

Society for the Advancement of Travel for the Handicapped (*SATH;* 26 Court St., Penthouse, Brooklyn, NY 11242; phone: 718-858-5483). Members of this nonprofit organization include consumers and travel service professionals. For an annual fee of $45 ($25 for students and travelers 65 and older), members receive a quarterly newsletter and have access to information and referral services. Also offers two useful publications: *Travel Tips for the Handicapped* (a series of informative fact sheets) and *The United States Welcomes Handicapped Visitors* (a 48-page guide that includes hints for disabled travelers abroad).

Travel Information Service (Moss Rehabilitation Hospital, 1200 W. Tabor Rd., Philadelphia, PA 19141-3099; phone: 215-456-9600 for voice; 215-456-9602 for TDD). This service assists physically handicapped people in planning trips and supplies detailed information on accessibility for a nominal fee.

Blind travelers should contact the *American Foundation for the Blind* (15 W. 16th St., New York, NY 10011; phone: 212-620-2147 in New York State; 800-232-5463 elsewhere in the US) and *The Seeing Eye* (Box 375, Morristown, NJ 07963-0375; phone: 201-539-4425); both provide useful information on resources for the visually impaired. *Note:* Seeing Eye dogs arriving in Mexico must be accompanied by a certificate of inoculation against rabies, hepatitis, and distemper, as well as a certificate of health, issued within the previous 3 months. Both must be authorized by a Mexican consul (for a fee of $20 at press time). *The American Society for the Prevention of Cruelty to Animals (ASPCA*, Education Dept., 441 E. 92 St., New York, NY 10128; phone: 212-876-7700) offers a useful booklet, *Traveling With Your Pet* ($5, postpaid), which lists inoculation and other requirements by country.

In addition, there are a number of publications — from travel guides to magazines — of interest to handicapped travelers. Among these are the following:

Access to the World, by Louise Weiss, offers sound tips for the disabled traveler ($16.95; Facts on File, 460 Park Ave. S., New York, NY 10016; phone: 212-683-2244 in New York State; 800-322-8755 elsewhere in the US; 800-443-8323 in Canada).

The Diabetic Traveler is a useful quarterly newsletter that focuses on resources and hints for diabetic travelers. To subscribe, send $15 ($4 per back issue) to PO Box 8223 RW, Stamford, CT 06905 (phone: 203-327-5832).

Guide to Traveling with Arthritis, a free brochure available by writing to the Upjohn Company (PO Box 307-B, Coventry, CT 06238), provides commonsense tips on trip planning and comfort while traveling.

Handicapped Travel Newsletter is a bimonthly publication edited by wheelchair-bound Vietnam veteran and world traveler Michael Quigley. To subscribe, send $10 to PO Box 269, Athens, TX 75751 (phone: 214-677-1260).

Handi-Travel: A Resource Book for Disabled and Elderly Travellers, by Cinnie Noble, is full of practical tips for those with disabilities affecting mobility, hearing, or sight. To order, send $12.95, plus postage, to the *Canadian Rehabilitation Council for the Disabled*, 45 Sheppard Ave. E., Suite 801, Toronto, Ontario M2N 5W9, Canada (phone: 416-250-7490; both voice and TDD).

The Itinerary, a bimonthly travel magazine for people with disabilities, includes information on accessibility, tours, adaptive devices and aids, special services, and travel hints. To subscribe, send $10 to PO Box 2012, Bayonne, NJ 07002-2012 (phone: 201-858-3400).

The Physically Disabled Traveler's Guide, by Rod W. Durgin and Norene Lindsay, rates accessibility and includes a list of organizations specializing in travel for the disabled. It is available for $9.95, plus shipping and handling, from *Resource Directories*, 3361 Executive Pkwy., Suite 302, Toledo, OH 43606 (phone: 419-536-5353 in the Toledo area; 800-274-8515 elsewhere in the US).

Ticket to Safe Travel offers useful information for diabetic travelers. This reprint of an article is available from the *American Diabetes Association;* for the nearest local chapter, contact the central office at 505 Eighth Ave., 21st Floor, New York, NY 10018 (phone: 212-947-9707 in New York State; 800-232-3472 elsewhere in the US).

Travel for the Patient with Chronic Obstructive Pulmonary Disease, a publication of the George Washington University Medical Center, provides practical suggestions for those with asthma, bronchitis, or other lung ailments. To order, send $2 to Dr. Harold Silver, 1601 18th St. NW, Washington, DC 20009 (phone: 202-667-0134).

Traveling Like Everybody Else: A Practical Guide for Disabled Travelers, by Jacqueline Freedman and Susan Gersten, offers travel tips and resources, including lists of accessible accommodations and tour operators specializing in tours for disabled travelers. To order, send $11.95, plus postage, to Modan Publishing, PO Box 1202, Bellmore, NY 11710 (phone: 516-679-1380).

Travel Tips for Hearing Impaired People, a free pamphlet for deaf and hearing-impaired travelers, is available by sending a self-addressed, stamped, business-size envelope to the *American Academy of Otolaryngology,* One Prince St., Alexandria, VA 22314 (phone: 703-836-4444).

Travel Tips for People with Arthritis, a free 31-page booklet, provides helpful information regarding transportation, trip planning, medical considerations, and conserving your energy while traveling. It also includes listings of helpful resources for disabled travelers. For a copy, contact your local *Arthritis Foundation* chapter, or write to the national office, PO Box 19000, Atlanta, GA 30326 (phone: 404-872-7100).

The Wheelchair Traveler lists accessible accommodations and restaurants in Mexico, including Cancún. To order a copy, and for current pricing, contact the author, Douglass R. Annand, 123 Ball Hill Rd., Milford, NH 03055 (phone: 603-673-4539).

A few more basic resources to look for are *Travel for the Disabled* ($9.95) and *Directory of Travel Agencies for the Disabled* ($19.95), both by Helen Hecker, and *Wheelchair Vagabond* (hardcover, $14.95; paperback, $9.95), by John G. Nelson. All three are published by Twin Peaks Press, PO Box 129, Vancouver, WA 98666 (phone: 800-637-CALM or 206-694-2462).

PLANE: Disabled passengers always should make reservations well in advance. Provide the airline with all relevant details of your condition, including information on mobility and equipment that you will need the airline to supply — such as a wheelchair for boarding or portable oxygen for in-flight use. Be sure that the person to whom you speak fully understands your needs, and on the day before the flight call back to make sure that all arrangements have been prepared. Arrive early for your flight so that you can board before the rest of the passengers.

Because most airports have jetways (corridors connecting the terminal with the door of the plane), a disabled passenger usually can be taken as far as the plane, and sometimes right onto it, in a wheelchair. If not, a narrow boarding chair may be used to take you to your seat. Your own wheelchair, which will be folded and put in the baggage compartment, should be tagged as escort luggage to assure that it's available at planeside upon landing rather than in the baggage claim area. (If your wheelchair is battery-operated, it might not be accepted on board unless it has non-spillable batteries, or is specially packaged for the flight; check with the airline ahead of time.) Usually people in wheelchairs are asked to wait until other passengers have disembarked. If you are making a tight connection, be sure to tell the attendant.

Passengers who use oxygen may not use their personal supply in the cabin, though it may be carried on the plane as cargo when properly packed and labeled. If you will need oxygen during the flight, the airline will supply it to you (there is a charge) provided you have given advance notice — 24 hours to a few days, depending on the carrier.

Among the airlines flying to Cancún and Cozumel, TDD toll-free lines for the hearing-impaired are provided by *American* (phone: 800-582-1573 in Ohio; 800-543-1586 elsewhere in the US) and *United* (phone: 800-942-8819 in Ohio; 800-323-1070 elsewhere in the US).

Useful information on every stage of air travel, from planning to arrival, is provided in the booklet *Incapacitated Passengers Air Travel Guide.* To receive a free copy, write to the International Air Transport Association (Publications Sales Department, 2000 Peel St., Montreal, Quebec H3A 2R4, Canada; phone: 514-844-6311). Another helpful publication is *Air Transportation of Handicapped Persons,* which explains the general guidelines that govern air carrier policies. For a copy of this free booklet, write to the US Department of Transportation (Distribution Unit, Publications Section, M-443-2, Washington, DC 20590) and ask for "Free Advisory Circular #AC-120-32."

SHIP: Check with your travel agent or cruise line when making reservations, as some cruise ships cannot accommodate handicapped travelers because of their many sets of narrow steps, which are less convenient than wide ramps.

For those in wheelchairs or with limited mobility, one of the best sources for evaluating a ship's accessibility is the free chart issued by the *Cruise Lines International Association* (500 Fifth Ave., Suite 1407, New York, NY 10110; phone: 212-921-0066). The chart lists accessible ships and indicates whether they accommodate standard-size or only narrow wheelchairs, have ramps, wide doors, low or no doorsills, handrails in the rooms, and so on. (For further information on ships cruising Mexican waters, see *Traveling by Ship,* in this section.)

GROUND TRANSPORTATION: Perhaps the simplest solution to getting around is to travel with an able-bodied companion who can drive. Another alternative in Mexico is to hire a driver/translator with a car — be sure to get a recommendation from a reputable source. The organizations listed above may be able to help you make arrangements — another source is your hotel concierge.

If you are accustomed to driving your own hand-controlled car and determined to rent one in Mexico, you may have to do some extensive research. If agencies do provide hand-controlled cars, they are apt to be offered only on a limited basis and usually are in high demand. The best course is to contact the major car rental companies listed in *Touring by Car,* in this section, well before your departure.

The *American Automobile Association (AAA)* publishes a helpful booklet, *The Handicapped Driver's Mobility Guide.* Contact the central office of your local *AAA* club for availability and pricing, which may vary in different branch offices.

TOURS: Programs designed for the physically impaired are run by specialists who have researched hotels, restaurants, and sites to be sure they present no insurmountable obstacles. The following travel agencies or tour operators specialize in making group or individual arrangements for travelers with physical or other disabilities:

> *Access: The Foundation for Accessibility by the Disabled* (PO Box 356, Malverne, NY 11565; phone: 516-887-5798). A travelers' referral service that acts as an intermediary with tour operators and agents worldwide, and provides information on accessibility.
>
> *Accessible Journeys* (412 S. 45th St., Philadelphia, PA 19104; phone: 215-747-0171). This company offers cruises and tours for people with special needs and can arrange for medical professional traveling companions.
>
> *Accessible Tours/Directions Unlimited* (720 N. Bedford Rd., Bedford Hills, NY 10507; phone: 914-241-1700 in Westchester County, NY; 800-533-5343 elsewhere in the continental US). Arranges group or individual tours for disabled persons traveling in the company of able-bodied friends or family members. Accepts the unaccompanied traveler if completely self-sufficient.
>
> *Dialysis at Sea Cruises* (611 Barry Place, Indian Rocks Beach, FL 34635; phone: 813-596-7604 or 800-544-7604 throughout the US and Canada). Offers cruises for dialysis patients that include full medical services, including a nephrologist (a specialist in kidney disease) and dialysis nurses. Although family and companions are welcome, the number of patients usually is limited to roughly ten travelers per trip.
>
> *Evergreen Travel Service* (4114-198th St. SW, Suite 13, Lynnwood, WA 98036-6742; phone: 206-776-1184 or 800-435-2288 throughout the continental US and

Canada). Offers tours and cruises for the disabled (Wings on Wheels Tours), sight impaired/blind (White Cane Tours), and hearing impaired/deaf (Flying Fingers Tours). Most programs are first class and escorted.

Flying Wheels Travel (143 W. Bridge St., Box 382, Owatonna, MN 55060; phone: 507-451-5005; 800-535-6790 throughout the US and Canada). Handles both tours and individual arrangements.

The Guided Tour (555 Ashbourne Rd., Elkins Park, PA 19117; phone: 215-782-1370). Arranges tours for people with developmental and learning disabilities, and those who are physically disabled or who need a slower pace.

Handi-Travel (First National Travel Limited, Thornhill Sq., 300 John St., Suite 405, Thornhill, Ontario L3T 5W4, Canada; phone: 416-731-4714). Handles tours and individual arrangements.

USTS Travel Horizons (11 E. 44th St., New York, NY 10017; phone: 800-487-8787 or 212-687-5121). Travel agent and registered nurse Mary Ann Hamm makes all arrangements for travelers requiring kidney dialysis.

Whole Person Tours (PO Box 1084, Bayonne, NJ 07002-1084; phone: 201-858-3400). Owner Bob Zywicki travels the world with his wheelchair and offers a lineup of escorted tours (many conducted by himself) for the disabled. *Whole Person Tours* also publishes *The Itinerary* (see above).

Travelers who would benefit from being accompanied by a nurse or physical therapist also can hire a companion through *Traveling Nurses' Network,* a service provided by Twin Peaks Press (PO Box 129, Vancouver, WA 98666; phone: 800-637-CALM or 206-694-2462). For $10, the client receives the names of three nurses, whom he or she can then contact directly; for $125, the agency will do the screening and hiring. Travel arrangements also may be made in some cases.

A similar service is offered by *MedEscort International* (ABE International Airport, PO Box 8766, Allentown, PA 18105; phone: 800-255-7182 in the continental US; elsewhere call 215-791-3111). The potential companions include nurses, paramedics, respiratory therapists, and physicians. Fees are based on the disabled traveler's needs, and *MedEscort* also can assist in making travel arrangements.

Hints for Single Travelers

Just about the last trip in human history on which the participants were neatly paired was the voyage of Noah's Ark. Ever since, passenger lists and tour groups have reflected the same kind of asymmetry that occurs in real life, as countless individuals set forth to see the world unaccompanied (or unencumbered, depending on your outlook) by spouse, lover, friend, or relative. Unfortunately, traveling alone also can turn a traveler into a second class citizen.

The truth is that the travel industry is not very fair to people who vacation by themselves. People traveling alone almost invariably end up paying more than individuals traveling in pairs. Most travel bargains, including package tours, accommodations, resort packages, and cruises, are based on *double occupancy* rates. This means that the per-person price is offered on the basis of two people traveling together and sharing a double room (which means they each will spend a good deal more on meals and extras). The single traveler will have to pay a surcharge, called a single supplement, for exactly the same package. In extreme cases, this can add as much as 30% to 55% to the basic per-person rate.

Don't despair, however. Throughout Mexico, there are scores of smaller hotels and other hostelries where, in addition to a cozier atmosphere, prices still are quite reasonable for the single traveler. And some ship lines have begun to offer special cruises for singles.

The obvious, most effective alternative is to find a traveling companion. Even special "singles' tours" that promise no supplements are based on people sharing double rooms. Perhaps the most recent innovation along these lines is the creation of organizations that "introduce" the single traveler to other single travelers (somewhat like a dating service) in order to match compatible travel mates. Among these organizations are the following:

Jane's International (2603 Bath Ave., Brooklyn, NY 11214; phone: 718-266-2045). This service puts potential traveling companions in touch with one another. No age limit, no fee.

Partners-in-Travel (PO Box 491145, Los Angeles, CA 90049; phone: 213-476-4869). Members receive a list of singles seeking traveling companions; prospective companions make contact through the agency. The membership fee is $40 per year and includes a chatty newsletter (6 issues per year).

Singleworld (401 Theodore Fremd Ave., Rye, NY 10580; phone: 914-967-3334 or 800-223-6490 in the continental US). For a yearly fee of $25, this club books members on tours and cruises, and arranges shared accommodations, allowing individual travelers to avoid the single supplement charge; members also receive a quarterly newsletter. *Singleworld* also offers its own package tours for singles with departures categorized by age group.

Travel Companion Exchange (PO Box 833, Amityville, NY 11701; phone: 516-454-0880). This group publishes a newsletter for singles and a directory of individuals looking for travel companions. On joining, members fill out a lengthy questionnaire and write a small listing (much like an ad in a personal column). Based on these listings, members can request copies of profiles and contact prospective traveling companions. It is wise to join well in advance of your planned vacation so that there's enough time to determine compatibility and plan a joint trip. Membership fees, including the newsletter, are $6 a month for a single-sex listing and $11 a month for a complete listing; the minimum enrollment period is 6 months. Subscription to the newsletter alone costs $24 for 6 months or $36 per year.

In addition, a number of tour packagers cater to single travelers. These companies offer packages designed for individuals interested in vacationing with a group of single travelers or in being matched with a traveling companion. Among the better established of these agencies are the following: *Grand Circle Travel* (347 Congress St., Boston, MA 02210; phone: 800-221-2610 or 617-350-7500). Arranges extended vacations, escorted tours and cruises for the over-50 traveler, including singles. Membership, which is automatic when you book a trip through *Grand Circle,* includes travel discounts and other extras, such as a Pen Pals service for singles seeking traveling companions. *Saga International Holidays* (120 Boylston St., Boston MA 02116; phone: 617-451-6808 or 800-343-0273). A subsidiary of a British company specializing in older travelers, many of them single, *Saga* offers a broad selection of packages for people age 60 and over, or those 50 to 59 traveling with someone 60 or older. *Singles in Motion* (545 W. 236th St., Suite 1D, Riverdale, NY 10463; phone: 212-884-4464). Offers a number of packages for single travelers, including tours, cruises, and excursions focusing on outdoor activities such as hiking and biking. *STI* (8619 Reseda Blvd., Suite 103, Northridge, CA 91324; phone: 800-525-0525 throughout the US). Specializes in travel for 18- to 30-year-olds; their broad tour program includes packages to Cancún and Cozumel. *Travel in Two's* (239 N. Broadway, Suite 3, N. Tarrytown, NY 10591; phone: 914-631-8409). This company books solo travelers on packages offered by a number of companies (at no extra cost to clients), offers its own tours, and matches singles with traveling companions. Many offerings are listed in their quarterly *Singles Vacation Newsletter,* which costs $7.50 per issue or $20 per year.

A good book for single travelers is *Traveling On Your Own,* by Eleanor Berman, which offers tips on traveling solo and includes information on trips for singles, ranging from outdoor adventures to educational programs. Available in bookstores, it also can be ordered by sending $12.95, plus postage and handling, to Random House, Order Dept., 400 Hahn Rd., Westminster, MD 21157 (phone: 800-733-3000).

Single travelers also may want to subscribe to *Going Solo,* a newsletter that offers helpful information on going on your own. Issued eight times a year, a subscription costs $36; contact Doerfer Communications, PO Box 1035, Cambridge, MA 02238 (phone: 617-876-2764).

An attractive alternative for the single traveler is *Club Med,* which operates scores of resorts in more than 37 countries worldwide and caters to the single traveler, as well as couples and families. Though the clientele often is under 30, there is a considerable age mix; the average age is 37. *Club Med* has five Mexican resorts — including one on Cancún — and offers single travelers package vacations that include airfare, food, wine, lodging, entertainment, and athletic facilities. The atmosphere is relaxed, the dress is informal, and the price reasonable. For information, contact *Club Med* (3 E. 54th St., New York, NY 10022; phone: 800-CLUB-MED). For further information on accommodations options suitable for singles, see our discussions in *On the Road,* in this section.

Hints for Older Travelers

Special discounts and more free time are just two factors that have given Americans over age 65 a chance to see the world at affordable prices. Senior citizens make up an ever-growing segment of the travel population, and the trend among them is to travel more frequently and for longer periods of time.

PLANNING: When planning a vacation, prepare your itinerary with one eye on your own physical condition and the other on a topographical map. Keep in mind variations in climate, terrain, and altitudes, which may pose some danger for anyone with heart or breathing problems.

Older travelers may find the following publications of interest:

The Discount Guide for Travelers Over 55, by Caroline and Walter Weintz, is an excellent book for budget-conscious older travelers. It is available by sending $7.95, plus shipping and handling, to Penguin USA (Att. Cash Sales, 120 Woodbine St., Bergenfield, NJ 07621); when ordering specify the ISBN number: 0-525-48358-6.

The International Health Guide for Senior Citizen Travelers, by Dr. W. Robert Lange, covers a variety of topics. It also includes a list of resource organizations that provide medical assistance for travelers. It is available for $4.95 postpaid from Pilot Books, 103 Cooper St., Babylon, NY 11702 (phone: 516-422-2225).

The Mature Traveler is a monthly newsletter that provides information on travel discounts, places of interest, and useful tips for travelers 49 and up. To subscribe, send $21.95 to GEM Publishing Group, PO Box 50820, Reno, NV 89513 (phone: 702-786-7419).

Travel Easy: The Practical Guide for People Over 50, by Rosalind Massow, discusses a wide range of travel-related subjects. It's available for $6.50 (plus postage) to members of the *American Association of Retired Persons (AARP),* and for $8.95 (plus postage) to non-members. Order from AARP Books, c/o Customer Service, Scott, Foresman & Company, 1900 E. Lake Ave., Glenview, IL 60025 (phone: 708-729-3000).

Travel Tips for Older Americans is a useful booklet with general advice. To order send a check or money order for $1 to the Superintendent of Documents (US Government Printing Office, Washington, DC 20402) or call 202-783-3238 for credit card orders; request stock number 044-000-02270-2.

Unbelievably Good Deals & Great Adventures That You Absolutely Can't Get Unless You're Over 50, by Joan Rattner Heilman, offers travel tips for older travelers, including discounts on accommodations and transportation, as well as a list of organizations for seniors. It is available for $7.95, plus shipping and handling, from Contemporary Books, 180 N. Michigan Ave., Chicago, IL 60601 (phone: 312-782-9181).

HEALTH: Health facilities in Mexico generally are good; however, an inability to speak the language can pose a problem. For information on organizations that help travelers avoid or deal with medical emergencies abroad, see *Medical and Legal Aid and Consular Services,* in this section.

Pre-trip medical and dental checkups are strongly recommended for older travelers. Prepare a personal medical kit to take abroad, which should include vital medical information, enough of any medication you need to last for the duration of your trip, and some basic first-aid ingredients (for further information, see *Staying Healthy,* in this section).

DISCOUNTS AND PACKAGES: Although guidelines change from place to place, many hotel and motel chains, airlines, car rental companies, and other travel suppliers offer discounts to older travelers. In order to take advantage of these discounts, you should carry proof of your age (or eligibility). A driver's license, membership card in a recognized senior citizens' organization, or a Medicare card should be adequate.

Some of these discounts, however, are extended only to bona fide members of certain senior citizens organizations. Because the same organizations frequently offer package tours, the benefits of membership are twofold: Those who join can take advantage of discounts as individual travelers and also reap the savings that group travel affords. In addition, because the age requirements for some of these organizations are quite low (or nonexistent), the benefits can begin to accrue early. Among the organizations dedicated to helping older travelers see the world are the following:

American Association of Retired Persons (*AARP;* 1909 K St. NW, Washington, DC 20049; phone: 202-872-4700). The largest and best known of these organizations. Membership is open to anyone 50 or over, whether retired or not; dues are $5 a year, $12.50 for 3 years, or $35 for 10 years, and include spouse. The *AARP* Travel Experience program, available through *American Express Travel Related Services,* offers members tours, cruises, and other travel programs designed exclusively for older travelers that cover the globe. Members can book these services by calling *American Express* at 800-927-0111 for land and air travel, or 800-745-4567 for cruises.

Mature Outlook (Customer Service Center, 6001 N. Clark St., Chicago, IL 60660; phone: 800-336-6330). Through its *TravelAlert,* tours, cruises, and other vacation packages are available to members at special savings. Hotel and car rental discounts and travel accident insurance also are available. Membership is open to anyone 50 years of age or older, costs $9.95 a year, and includes a bimonthly newsletter and magazine.

National Council of Senior Citizens (925 15th St. NW, Washington, DC 20005; phone: 202-347-8800). Here, too, the emphasis is on keeping costs low. This nonprofit organization offers members a different roster of package tours each year, as well as individual arrangements through its affiliated travel service

(Vantage Travel Service). Although most members are over 50, membership is open to anyone (regardless of age) for an annual fee of $12 per person or couple. Lifetime membership costs $150.

Certain travel agencies and tour operators offer special trips geared to older travelers. Among them are the following:

Evergreen Travel Service (4114-198th St. SW, Suite 13, Lynnwood, WA 98036-6742; phone: 206-776-1184 or 800-435-2288 throughout the continental US and Canada). This specialist in trips for persons with disabilities recently introduced Lazybones Tours, a program offering leisurely tours for older travelers.

Gadabout Tours (700 E. Tahquitz Way, Palm Springs, CA 92262; phone: 619-325-5556 or 800-521-7309 in California; 800-952-5068 elsewhere in the US). Offers seniors escorted tours to a number of destinations, including the Yucatán Peninsula.

Grand Circle Travel (347 Congress St., Boston, MA 02210; phone: 800-221-2610 or 617-350-7500). Caters exclusively to the over-50 traveler and packages a large variety of escorted tours, cruises, and extended vacations. Membership, which is automatic when you book a trip through *Grand Circle,* includes discount certificates on future trips and other extras, including a helpful free booklet, *Going Abroad: 101 Tips for Mature Travelers.*

Saga International Holidays (120 Boylston St., Boston MA 02116; phone: 617-451-6808 or 800-343-0273). Offers a broad selection of packages for people age 60 and over or those 50 to 59 traveling with someone 60 or older. Although anyone can book a *Saga* trip, a $15 club membership includes a subscription to their newsletter, as well as other publications and travel services.

Many travel agencies, particularly the larger ones, are delighted to make presentations to help a group of senior citizens select destinations. A local chamber of commerce should be able to provide the names of such agencies. Once a time and place are determined, an organization member or travel agent can obtain group quotations for transportation, accommodations, meal plans, and sightseeing. Larger groups usually get the best breaks.

Hints for Traveling with Children

What better way to encounter the world's variety than in the company of the young, wide-eyed members of your family? Their presence does not have to be a burden or an excessive expense. The current generation of discounts for children and family package deals can make a trip together quite reasonable.

A family trip will be an investment in your children's future, making geography and history come alive to them, and leaving a sure memory that will be among the fondest you will share with them someday. Their insights will be refreshing to you; their impulses may take you to unexpected places with unexpected dividends. The experience will be invaluable to them at any age.

PLANNING: Here are several hints for making a trip with children easy and fun:

1. Children, like everyone else, will derive more pleasure from a trip if they know something about their destination before they arrive. Begin their education about a month before you leave. Using maps, travel magazines, and books gives children a clear idea of where you are going and how far away it is.
2. Children should help to plan the itinerary, and where you go and what you do

should reflect some of their ideas. If they already know something about the sites they'll visit, they will have the excitement of recognition when they arrive.

3. Children also will enjoy learning some Spanish phrases — a few basics like "hola!" (hello), "adiós" (good-bye), and "gracias" (thanks).
4. Familiarize the children with *pesos*. Give them an allowance for the trip, and be sure they understand just how far it will or won't go.
5. Give children specific responsibilities: The job of carrying their own flight bags and looking after their personal things, along with some other light travel chores, will give them a stake in the journey.
6. Give each child a travel diary or scrapbook to take along.

One useful resource to which you may want to refer is the *Berlitz Jr. Spanish* instructional series for children. The series combines an illustrated storybook with a lively 60-minute audiocassette; the set is available for $19.95, plus shipping and handling, from Macmillan Publishing Company, Front and Brown Sts., Riverside, NJ 08075 (phone: 800-257-5755).

For parents, *Travel With Your Children* (*TWYCH;* 80 Eighth Ave., New York, NY 10011; phone: 212-206-0688) publishes a newsletter, *Family Travel Times,* that focuses on families with young travelers and offers helpful hints. An annual subscription (10 issues) is $35 and includes a copy of the "Airline Guide" issue (updated every other year), which focuses on the subject of flying with children. This special issue is available separately for $10.

Another newsletter devoted to family travel is *Getaways.* This quarterly publication provides reviews of family-oriented literature, activities, and useful travel tips. To subscribe, send $25 to *Getaways,* att. Ms. Brooke Kane, PO Box 11511, Washington, DC 20008 (phone: 703-534-8747).

Also of interest to parents traveling with their children is *How to Take Great Trips With Your Kids,* by psychologist Sanford Portnoy and his wife, Joan Flynn Portnoy. The book includes helpful tips from fellow family travelers, a chapter on child development relating to travel, tips on economical accommodations and touring by car, as well as over 50 games to play with your children en route. It is available for $8.95, plus shipping and handling, from Harvard Common Press, 535 Albany St., Boston, MA 02118 (phone: 617-423-5803).

Another book on family travel, *Travel with Children* by Maureen Wheeler, offers a wide range of practical tips on traveling with children. It is available for $10.95, plus shipping and handling, from Lonely Planet Publications, Embarcadero West, 112 Linden St., Oakland, CA 94607 (phone: 415-893-8555).

Parents arranging a trip with their children may want to deal with an agency specializing in family travel, such as *Let's Take the Kids* (1268 Devon Ave., Los Angeles, CA 90064; phone: 800-726-4349 or 213-274-7088). In addition to arranging and booking trips for individual families, this group occasionally organizes trips for single-parent families traveling together. They also offer a "parent travel network," whereby parents who have been to a particular destination can evaluate it for others.

GETTING THERE AND GETTING AROUND: Begin early to investigate all available family discount and charter flights, as well as any package deals and special rates offered by the major airlines.

Plane – When you make your reservations, tell the airline that you are traveling with a child. Children ages 2 through 12 generally travel at about half to two-thirds of an adult economy fare on international flights (although excursion and other discount fares may be even less expensive). Depending on the airline, children under 2 may travel free or at 10% of the adult fare if they sit on an adult's lap. The fare for a second infant without a second adult would be the same as the fare applicable to children ages 2 through 11.

Although some airlines will, on request, supply bassinets for infants, most carriers encourage parents to bring their own safety seat on board, which then is strapped into the airline seat with a regular seat belt. This is much safer — and certainly more comfortable — than holding the child in your lap. If you do not purchase a seat for your baby, you have the option of bringing the infant restraint along on the off-chance that there might be an empty seat next to yours — in which case some airlines will let you use that seat at no charge for your baby and infant seat. However, if there is no empty seat available, the infant seat no doubt will have to be checked as baggage (and you may have to pay an additional charge), since it generally does not fit under the seat or in the overhead racks. The safest bet is to pay for a seat.

Be forewarned: Some safety seats designed primarily for use in cars do not fit into plane seats properly. Most seats carry labels indicating whether they meet federal standards for use aboard planes, but actual seat sizes may vary from carrier to carrier. At the time of this writing, the FAA was in the process of reviewing and revising the federal regulations regarding infant travel and safety devices — it was still to be determined if children should be *required* to sit in safety seats and whether the airlines will have to provide them.

If using one of these infant restraints, you should try to get bulkhead seats, which will provide extra room to care for your child during the flight. You also should request a bulkhead seat when using a bassinet — again, this is not as safe as strapping the child in. On some planes bassinets hook into a bulkhead wall; on others it is placed on the floor in front of you. (Note that bulkhead seats often are reserved for families traveling with children.) As a general rule, babies should be held during takeoff and landing.

Request seats on the aisle if you have a toddler or if you think you will need to use the bathroom frequently. Carry onto the plane all you will need to care for and occupy your children during the flight. Dress your baby simply, because the only place you may have to change a diaper is at your seat or in a small lavatory.

You also can ask for a hot dog or hamburger instead of the airline's regular dinner if you give at least 24 hours' notice. Some, but not all, airlines have baby food aboard. While you should bring along toys from home, also ask about children's diversions. Some carriers have terrific free packages of games, coloring books, and puzzles.

When the plane takes off and lands, make sure your baby is nursing or has a bottle, pacifier, or thumb in its mouth. This sucking will make the child swallow and help to clear stopped ears. A piece of hard candy will do the same thing for an older child.

Parents traveling by plane with toddlers, children, or teenagers may want to consult *When Kids Fly,* a free booklet published by Massport (Public Affairs Dept., 10 Park Plaza, Boston, MA 02116-3971; phone: 617-973-5600), which includes helpful information on airfares for children, infant seats, what to do in the event of overbooked or canceled flights, and so on.

■ **Note:** Newborn babies, whose lungs may not be able to adjust to the altitude, should not be taken aboard an airplane. And some airlines may refuse to allow a pregnant woman in her 8th or 9th month aboard, for fear that something could go wrong with an in-flight birth. Check with the airline ahead of time and carry a letter from your doctor stating that you are fit to travel — and indicating the estimated date of birth.

Ship – Some shipping lines offer cruises that feature special activities for children, particularly during periods that coincide with major school holidays like *Christmas, Easter,* and the summer months. On such cruises, children may be charged special cut-rate fares, and there are youth counselors to organize activities. Occasionally, a shipping line even offers free passage during the summer months for children under the age of 16 occupying a stateroom with two (full-fare) adult passengers. In this case, again, there are special activities for children. Your travel agent should know which cruise lines offer such programs.

Car – Traveling by car allows greater flexibility in traveling and packing. You may want to stock the car with a variety of favorite snacks, and if you pack an ice chest and a grill, you can stop for picnics (most beaches are public and free in Mexico). You may want to bring dry ice, since ice isn't so easy to come by in rural areas. Near the larger cities, ice cubes are sold at gasoline service stations and ice blocks are available from the local beer distributors. However, use this ice only for keeping food chilled in coolers — *never* put it in drinks, as you can't count on the quality of the water from which it was made.

ACCOMMODATIONS AND MEALS: Often a cot will be placed in a hotel room at little or no extra charge. If you wish to sleep in separate rooms, special rates sometimes are available for families; some places do not charge for children under a certain age. Cabins, bungalows, condominiums, and other rental options offer families privacy, flexibility, some kitchen facilities, and often low costs.

It is difficult to find adequate baby-sitting services in most Mexican cities, but most better hotels will try to arrange for a sitter. Whether the sitter is hired directly or through an agency, ask for and check references and keep in mind that the candidates may not speak much, if any, English.

At mealtime, don't deny yourself or your children the delights of a new style of cooking. Children like to know what kind of food to expect, so it will be interesting to look up Mexican dishes before leaving. Encourage your children to try new things; however, even though simple tacos, burritos, and cheese-filled tortillas are similar to hamburgers and grilled cheese sandwiches, they may not fill the bill for some children. In resort areas such as Cancún and Cozumel, you should be able to find American-style food.

Things to Remember

1. If you are spending your vacation touring, pace the days with children in mind. Break the trip into half-day segments, with running around or "doing" time built in.
2. Don't forget that a child's attention span is far shorter than an adult's. Children don't have to see every sight or all of any sight to learn something from their trip; watching, playing with, and talking to other children can be equally enlightening.
3. Let your children lead the way sometimes; their perspective is different from yours, and they may lead you to things you would never have noticed on your own.
4. Remember the places that children love to visit: aquariums, zoos, beaches, nature trails, and so on. Among activities that may pique their interest are bicycling, snorkeling, boat trips, visiting planetariums and children's museums, exploring pyramids and ruins, and viewing natural habitat exhibits.

Staying Healthy

The surest way to return home in good health is to be prepared for medical problems that might occur on vacation. Below we've outlined some things you need to think about before you go.

Typically, tourists suffer two kinds of health problems in Mexico, but neither is inevitable. The first is the stomach upset known the world over as the scourge of travelers: Cairo Crud, Delhi Belly, *la turista,* and in Mexico, Montezuma's Revenge. The second is even more familiar: sunburn. And as a number of diseases are contracted through bug bites (see below), some precaution against biting insects is strongly advised.

Older travelers or anyone suffering from a chronic medical condition, such as diabetes, high blood pressure, cardiopulmonary disease, asthma, or ear, eye, or sinus trouble, should consult a physician before leaving home. Those with conditions requiring special consideration when traveling should consider seeing, in addition to their regular physician, a specialist in travel medicine. For a referral in a particular community, contact the nearest medical school or ask a local doctor to recommend such a specialist. Dr. Leonard Marcus, a member of the *American Committee on Clinical Tropical Medicine and Travelers' Health,* provides a directory of more than 100 travel doctors across the US. For a copy, send a 9-by-12-inch self-addressed, stamped envelope, plus postage, to Dr. Marcus at 148 Highland Ave., Newton, MA 02165 (phone: 617-527-4003).

FIRST AID: Put together a compact, personal medical kit including Band-Aids, first-aid cream, antiseptic, nose drops, insect repellent, aspirin or non-aspirin tablets, an extra pair of prescription glasses or contact lenses (and a copy of your prescription for glasses or contact lenses), sunglasses, over-the-counter remedies for diarrhea, indigestion, and motion sickness, a thermometer, and a supply of those prescription medicines you take regularly.

In a corner of your kit, keep a list of all the drugs you have brought and their purpose, as well as duplicate copies of your doctor's prescriptions (or a note from your doctor). As brand names may vary in different countries, it's a good idea to ask your doctor for the generic name of any drugs you use so that you can ask for their equivalent should you need a refill. Unless it is an emergency, however, some prescriptions may require the signature of a Mexican physician. (In recent years the Mexican Health Ministry has developed a list of restricted drugs and medicines, which includes certain seasickness tablets, that require a written prescription from a local doctor.)

It also is a good idea to ask your doctor to prepare a medical identification card that includes such information as your blood type, any allergies or chronic health problems you have, and any special information that may aid diagnosis of an emergency condition — for instance, if you have heart problems, a copy of your most recent electrocardiogram. This kit also should include your doctor's name, address, and telephone number, as well as your social security number and information on your medical insurance. Considering the essential contents of this kit, keep it with you, rather than in your checked luggage.

■**Note:** A word of warning is necessary about injections (given by doctors or by pharmacists): The needles may be used more than once, and sterilization is not as dependable as it is in the US. Improperly disinfected needles can be a source of AIDS (Acquired Immune Deficiency Syndrome), hepatitis, and other infectious diseases, so insist that the doctor or pharmacist use disposable syringes. (If you have a condition that may need occasional injections, bring your own supply; disposable syringes also are available in Mexico.) Also be aware that some over-the-counter remedies sold in Mexico contain antibiotics sold only by prescription in the US, which may cause allergic reactions or other side effects.

DIARRHEA AND STOMACH UPSETS: Without a doubt, a traveler's most serious complaint traveling in Mexico is dysentery or diarrhea, accompanied by severe intestinal pain and a foul taste in the mouth.

It is very important to take the first few days easy, especially if you land in Mexico City, where the high altitude will be tiring and exacerbate the effect of any alcohol on your system; so drink and eat lightly on arrival.

Fortunately, the vast majority of intestinal disorders encountered during travel represent only a temporary inconvenience, which will go away with rest and time. Serious intestinal trouble almost invariably is the product of drinking water contaminated by a particular strain of *E. coli* bacteria. These bacteria inhabit the human intestinal tract and are transmitted through fecal matter, and from there into plumbing and any unpurified water system. The result most often is called Montezuma's Revenge.

There is a very simple way to avoid it: Don't drink the water. Brush your teeth with bottled water (be sure you're not getting a used bottle refilled with tap water). Wash fruit with purified water, and don't drink iced drinks where the ice has been made from tap water. If you are staying in a first class hotel in a major tourist area, you will be in no danger. Elsewhere, and as a matter of course, it is wise to stick to bottled water (ask for *agua purificada* or *agua mineral*) or substitute wine or beer at meals. You also might carry standard GI water purification tablets (tetraglycine hydroperiodide). Just drop one of these tablets in a carafe of water and let it stand for half an hour.

We also recommend that you eat only those fruits that have been peeled (oranges, bananas, and so on), and cooked vegetables. Garnishes of fresh vegetables (even a small amount of shredded lettuce and tomatoes) and salads (especially those with creamy or mayonnaise-based dressings that have been out on serving tables for any period of time) can wreak havoc with your gastrointestinal system the morning after. Stay away from unfamiliar dishes that are hard to identify, and those tempting-looking alcoholic concoctions served in coconuts or pineapples, as well as fruit juices — even in the better hotels, these may be diluted with tap water. Do not drink or eat raw milk, unpasteurized or uncooked dairy products, and, above all, stay away from food vendors on streets and beaches.

Be sure to carry along an anti-diarrhea medication and recommended antibiotic in case you do develop symptoms. Before you go, pick up a mild over-the-counter preparation, such as Kaopectate, which if used according to directions, should have you back on your feet within 12 to 14 hours (although this comes in a bulky bottle). Many find Pepto-Bismol equally effective, and it comes in a handier tablet form. You also may want to ask your doctor to recommend one of the stronger medications containing an antibiotic. If you are stricken with diarrhea and have no medication with you, have your hotel call a doctor or visit the nearest pharmacy.

INFECTIOUS HEPATITIS OR JAUNDICE: The most serious potential threat to a good vacation, hepatitis (nicknamed the Big H by gringos) frequently is caused by dirty hypodermic needles, a risk even in hospitals. If you are a diabetic or require regular injections for any other condition, carry disposable plastic hypodermic syringes (available in pharmacies). It also may be contracted from contaminated drinking water or food.

MALARIA: If you intend to travel into the jungle, where malaria is prevalent, pick up some antimalarial tablets in a pharmacy in a city before you fly into the bush. These very inexpensive tablets are available everywhere. (Malaria is called *paludismo* in Spanish; ask for *medicina contra paludismo* in Mexico.) Presently, a yellow fever inoculation and prophylactic medication against malaria are recommended and, in many areas, mandatory for travel in many of the tropical and subtropical regions of Mexico, particularly for visitors making extensive trips to the Yucatán Peninsula. As malaria usually is contacted through mosquito bites, precautions against these irritating and potentially harmful bites should be taken (see "Insects and Other Pests," below*).*

■ **Note:** Before you leave for Mexico, check specifically with your local county or state health department, or call the US State Department's *Citizens' Emergency Center* at 202-647-5225 for the most up-to-date information on health conditions and other vital information.

SUNBURN: The burning power of the sun can quickly cause severe sunburn or sunstroke. To protect yourself against these ills, wear sunglasses, take along a broad-brimmed hat and cover-up, and use a sunscreen lotion.

INSECTS AND OTHER PESTS: Insects in parts of Mexico — including the Yucatán Peninsula — can be not only a nuisance but also a real threat. To avoid contact in areas of infestation, do not sleep in on the ground and, if possible, sleep under mosquito netting.

It is a good idea to use some form of topical insect repellent — those containing DEET (N,N-diethyl-m-toluamide) are among the most common and effective. The US Environmental Protection Agency (EPA) stresses that you should not use any pesticide that has not been approved by the EPA (check the label) and that all such preparations should be used in moderation. If picnicking, burn mosquito coils or candles containing allethrin, pyrethrin, or citronella, or use a pyrethrum-containing flying-insect spray. For further information about active ingredients in repellents, call the National Pesticide Telecommunications Network's 24-hour hotline number: 800-858-7378.

If you do get bitten — by mosquitoes or other bugs — the itching can be relieved with baking soda, topical first-aid creams, or antihistamine tablets. Should a bite become infected, treat it with a disinfectant or antibiotic cream.

Though rarer, bites from scorpions, snakes, or spiders can be serious. If possible, always try to catch the villain for identification purposes. If bitten, the best course of action may be to head directly to the nearest emergency ward or outpatient clinic of a hospital. Cockroaches and termites thrive in warm climates, but pose no serious health threat.

PREVENTION AND IMMUNIZATION: Specific information on the health status of any area in Mexico can be secured from its consular services in the US. The Centers for Disease Control publishes a comprehensive booklet, *Health Information for International Travel,* which lists vaccination requirements and other health information for Mexico. To order, send a check or money order for $5 to the Superintendent of Documents (US Government Printing Office, Washington, DC 20402), or charge it to your credit card by calling 202-783-3238. For information on vaccination requirements, disease outbreaks, and other health information pertaining to traveling abroad, you also can call the Centers for Disease Control's 24-hour International Health Requirements and Recommendations Information Hotline: 404-332-4559.

Another useful publication, *Health Hints for the Tropics,* offers tips on immunization and other preventive measures. It is available for $4 postpaid from Dr. Karl A. Western, *American Society of Tropical Medicine and Hygiene,* 6436 31st St. NW, Washington, DC 20015-2342 (phone: 301-496-6721).

If you live in or near New York City, you can take advantage of the *International Health Care Service* set up by New York Hospital–Cornell Medical Center (440 E. 69th St., New York, NY 10021; phone: 212-746-1601) "to encourage and facilitate proper preventive health measures." It offers pre-trip counseling, post-trip, and immunization at per-shot rates. By appointment only, from 4 to 8 PM Mondays through Thursdays (24-hour coverage for urgent travel-related problems). In addition, sending $4.50 (with a self-addressed envelope) to the address above will procure the service's publication, *International Health Care Travelers Guide.*

WATER SAFETY: Mexico's beaches are so beautiful, with sands so caressing and waters so crystalline, that it's hard to remember that the waters also can be treacherous. A few precautions are necessary. Beware of the undertow, that current of water running back down the beach after a wave has washed ashore; it can knock you off your feet and into the surf. Even more dangerous is the riptide, a strong current of water running against the tide, which can pull you out toward the sea. If you get caught offshore, don't panic or try to fight the current, because it will only exhaust you; instead, ride it out while waiting for it to subside, which usually happens not too far from shore, or try swimming away parallel to the beach.

Sharks are sometimes sighted, but they usually don't come in close to shore, and they are well fed on fish. Should you meet up with one, just swim away as quietly and smoothly as you can, without shouting or splashing.

The tentacled Portuguese man-of-war and other jellyfish drift in quiet salt waters and often wash up onto the beach; the long tentacles of these creatures sting whatever they touch. Specialists recommend carrying a small bottle of household vinegar and a container of unseasoned meat tenderizer in your beach bag. If stung, pour vinegar over the irritation to neutralize the effect of the sting and then apply a paste made of vinegar and meat tenderizer to break down the residual venom.

Mexico's coral reefs are extensive and razor sharp. Treat all coral cuts with an antiseptic, and then watch carefully since coral is a living organism with bacteria on the coral surface, which may cause an infection. If you step on a sea urchin, you'll find that the spines are very sharp, pierce the skin, and break off easily. Like splinters, the tips left embedded in the skin are difficult to remove, but they will dissolve in a week or two; rinsing with vinegar may help to dissolve them more quickly. To avoid these hazards, keep your feet covered whenever possible.

Following all these precautions will not guarantee an illness-free trip, but should minimize the risk. As a final hedge against economic if not physical problems, make sure your health insurance will cover all eventualities while you are away. If not, there are policies designed specifically for travel. Many are worth investigating. As with all insurance, they seem like a waste of money until you need them. For more information, also see *Insurance* and *Medical and Legal Aid and Consular Services,* both in this section.

HELPFUL PUBLICATIONS: Practically every phase of health care — before, during, and after a trip — is covered in *The New Traveler's Health Guide,* by Drs. Patrick J. Doyle and James E. Banta. It is available for $4.95, plus postage and handling, from Acropolis Books Ltd., 13950 Park Center Rd., Herndon, VA 22071 (phone: 800-451-7771 or 703-709-0006).

The *Traveling Healthy Newsletter,* which is published six times a year, also is brimming with health-related travel tips. For an annual subscription, which costs $24, contact Dr. Karl Neumann (108-48 70th Rd., Forest Hills, NY 11375; phone: 718-268-7290). Dr. Neumann also is the editor of the useful free booklet *Traveling Healthy,* which is available by writing to the Travel Healthy Program (PO Box 10208, New Brunswick, NJ 08906-9910; phone: 215-732-4100).

For more information regarding preventive health care for travelers, contact the *International Association for Medical Assistance to Travelers (IAMAT;* 417 Center St., Lewiston, NY 14092; phone: 716-754-4883).

On the Road

Credit and Currency

 It may seem hard to believe, but one of the greatest (and least understood) costs of travel is money itself. So your one single objective in relation to the care and retention of your travel funds is to make them stretch as far as possible. This requires more than merely ferreting out the best airfare or the most charming budget hotel. It means being canny about the management of money itself. Herewith, a primer on making money go as far as possible while traveling.

CURRENCY: The basic medium of exchange in Mexico is the peso, which, like the dollar, is based on a decimal system and subdivides into 100 units called centavos. Used only as a basis for translating dollars into pesos, the centavo has been taken out of circulation. Paper bills *(billetes)* are found in denominations of 1,000, 2,000, 5,000, 10,000, 20,000 and 50,000 pesos. Coins *(monedas)* are found in 1-peso, 5-peso, 10-peso, 20-peso, 50-peso, 100-peso, 200-peso, 500-peso, 1,000-peso, and 5,000-peso denominations.

Although US dollars may be accepted in Mexico (particularly at points of entry), you certainly will lose a percentage of your dollar's buying power if you do not take the time to convert it into the local legal tender. By paying for goods and services in the local currency, you save money by not negotiating invariably unfavorable exchange rates for every small purchase, and avoid difficulty where US currency is not readily — or happily — accepted. *Throughout this book, unless specifically stated otherwise, prices are given in US dollars.*

There is no limit to the amount of US currency that can be brought into Mexico. To avoid problems anywhere along the line, it's advisable to fill out any customs forms provided when leaving the US on which you can declare all money you are taking with you — cash, traveler's checks, and so on. If taking over $10,000 out of the US, you must report this to US Customs *before* leaving the US, and if returning with such an amount you should include this information on your customs declaration when you return. Although travelers usually are not questioned by customs officials about currency when they enter or leave, the sensible course is to observe all regulations just to be on the safe side.

FOREIGN EXCHANGE: Because of the volatility of exchange rates, be sure to check the current value of the peso before finalizing any travel budget. And before you actually depart on your trip, shop around carefully for the most advantageous exchange rate offered by various financial institutions — US banks, currency exchange firms (at home or abroad), or foreign banks.

For the best sense of current trends, follow the rates posted in the financial section of your local newspaper or in such international newspapers as the *International Herald Tribune.* It also is possible to check with your own bank. *Harold Reuter and Company,* a currency exchange service in New York City (200 Park Ave., Suite 332 E., New York, NY 10166; phone: 212-661-0826), also is very helpful in determining current trends in exchange rates; or check with *Thomas Cook Foreign Exchange* (for the nearest location, call 800-972-2192 in Illinois; 800-621-0666 elsewhere in the US). *Ruesch International* also offers up-to-date foreign-currency information and currency-related services (such as converting foreign-currency checks into US dollars). *Ruesch* also offers a pocket-size *Foreign Currency Guide* (good for estimating general equivalents while planning) and a helpful brochure, *6 Foreign Exchange Tips for the Traveler*. Contact *Ruesch International* at one of the following addresses: 3 First National Plaza, Suite 2020, Chicago, IL 60602 (phone: 312-332-5900); 1925 Century Park E., Suite 240, Los Angeles, CA 90067 (phone: 213-277-7800); 608 Fifth Ave., "Swiss Center," New York, NY 10020 (phone: 212-977-2700); or 1350 Eye St. NW, 10th Floor and street level, Washington, DC 20005 (phone: 800-424-2923 or 202-408-1200).

In Mexico, you will find the official rate of exchange posted in banks, airports, money exchange houses, hotels, and some shops. As a general rule, expect to get more pesos for your US dollar at banks than at any other commercial establishment. Exchange rates do change from day to day, and most banks offer the same (or very similar) exchange rates. (In a pinch, the convenience of cashing money in your hotel — sometimes on a 24-hour basis — may make up for the difference in the exchange rate.) Don't try to bargain in banks (or hotels) — no one will alter the rates for you.

If banks are closed, you may want to try the money exchanges *(casas de cambio)* located throughout Cancún and Cozumel. Money exchanges are financial institutions that charge a fee for the service of exchanging dollars into pesos. Note that the rates of exchange offered by these establishments usually are less favorable than the terms offered at nearby banks — don't be surprised if you get fewer pesos for your dollar than the rate published in the papers.

That said, however, the following rules of thumb are worth remembering:

Rule number one: Never (repeat: *never*) voluntarily exchange dollars for foreign currency at hotels, restaurants, or retail shops. If you do, you are sure to lose a significant amount of your dollar's buying power. If you do come across a storefront exchange counter offering what appears to be an incredible bargain, there's too much counterfeit specie in circulation to take the chance (see Rule number three, below).

Rule number two: Estimate your needs carefully; if you overbuy, you lose twice — buying and selling back. Every time you exchange money, someone is making a profit, and rest assured it isn't you. Use up foreign notes before leaving, saving just enough for airport departure taxes (which often must be paid in local currency), other last-minute incidentals, and tips.

Rule number three: Don't buy money on the black market. The exchange rate may be better, but it is a common practice to pass off counterfeit bills to unsuspecting foreigners who aren't familiar with the local currency. It's usually a sucker's game, and you almost always are the sucker; it also can land you in jail.

Rule number four: Learn the local currency quickly and keep abreast of daily fluctuations in the exchange rate. Rates change to some degree every day. For rough calculations, it is quick and safe to use round figures, but for purchases and actual currency exchanges, carry a small pocket calculator to help you compute the exact rate. Inexpensive calculators specifically designed to convert currency amounts quickly for travelers are widely available.

When changing money, don't be afraid to ask how much commission you're being charged, and the exact amount of the prevailing exchange rate. In fact, in any exchange of money for goods or services, you should work out the rate before making any payment.

TIP PACKS: It's not a bad idea to buy a *small* amount of foreign coins and banknotes before your departure. The advantage of tip packs are threefold:

1. You become familiar with the currency (really the only way to guard against making mistakes or being cheated during your first few hours in a new country).

2. You are guaranteed some money should you arrive when a bank or exchange counter isn't open or available.

3. You don't have to depend on hotel desks, porters, or taxi drivers to change your money.

TRAVELER'S CHECKS: It's wise to carry traveler's checks on the road instead of (or in addition to) cash, since it's possible to replace traveler's checks if they are stolen or lost; you usually can receive partial or full replacement funds the same day if you have your purchase receipt and proper identification. With adequate proof of identification (credit cards, driver's license, passport), traveler's checks are as good as cash in most hotels, restaurants, stores, and banks. Traveler's checks are issued in both US and Mexican currencies. However, the exchange rates offered by banks generally are better than those offered by the issuing companies, so plan on carrying the bulk of your funds abroad in US dollar denomination traveler's checks.

You will be able to cash traveler's checks fairly easily in major resort areas like Cancún and Cozumel, but don't expect to meander into a one-burro town and be able to get instant cash. Also note that more and more establishments are beginning to restrict the amount of traveler's checks they will accept or cash, so it is wise to purchase at least some of your checks in small denominations — say, $10 and $20.

Every type of traveler's check is legal tender in banks around the world, and each company guarantees full replacement if checks are lost or stolen. After that the similarity ends. Some charge a fee for purchase, others are free; you can buy traveler's checks at almost any bank, and some are available by mail. Most important, each traveler's check issuer differs slightly in its refund policy — the amount refunded immediately, the accessibility of refund locations, the availability of a 24-hour toll-free emergency hotline and refund service, and the time it will take for you to receive replacement checks. For instance, *American Express* guarantees replacement of lost or stolen traveler's checks in under 3 hours at any *American Express* office — other companies may not be as prompt. (Note that *American Express*'s 3-hour policy is based on a traveler's being able to provide the serial numbers of the lost checks — without these numbers, refunds can take much longer.)

We cannot overemphasize the importance of knowing how to replace lost or stolen checks. Be sure to make a photocopy of the refund instructions that will be given to you by the issuing institution at the time of purchase. To avoid complications should you need to redeem lost checks (and to speed up the replacement process), keep the purchase receipt and an accurate list, by serial number, of the checks that have been spent or cashed. You may want to incorporate this information in an "emergency packet," also including the numbers of the credit cards you are carrying and any other bits of information you shouldn't be without. Always keep these records separate from the checks and the original records themselves (you may want to give them to a traveling companion to hold).

Although most people understand the necessity of carrying funds in the form of traveler's checks as protection against loss or theft, an equally good reason is that traveler's checks may get a better rate of exchange than cash does — usually by at least 1%. The reasons for this are technical, and less prevalent in Mexico than elsewhere — the official rate of exchange posted by Mexican banks usually is the rate used to exchange *any* form of US currency — but potential savings still exist, and it's a fact of travel life that should not be ignored.

That 1% bonus won't do you much good, however, if you have already have spent it *buying* your traveler's checks. Several of the major traveler's check companies charge 1% for the acquisition of their checks; others don't. To receive fee-free travelers checks you may have to meet certain qualifications — for instance, *Thomas Cook* checks issued in US currency are free if you make your travel arrangements through its travel agency; *American Express* traveler's checks are available without charge to members of the *American Automobile Association (AAA)*. Holders of some credit cards (such as the *American Express Platinum* card) also may be entitled to free traveler's checks. The issuing institution (e.g., the particular bank at which you purchase them) may itself charge a fee. If you purchase traveler's checks at a bank in which you or your company maintains significant accounts (especially commercial accounts of some size),.the bank may absorb the 1% fee as a courtesy.

American Express, Bank of America, Citicorp, Thomas Cook, MasterCard, and *Visa* all offer traveler's checks. Here is a list of the major companies issuing traveler's checks and the numbers to call in the event that loss or theft makes replacement necessary:

American Express: To report lost or stolen checks in the US and Canada, call 800-221-7282; in Mexico, call the nearest *American Express* office, or the Mexican regional center at 905-661-3266 during business hours; 905-598-8133, collect, after 6 PM (Eastern Standard Time).

Bank of America: To report lost or stolen checks throughout the US, call 800-227-3460; in Mexico, call 415-624-5400 collect.

Citicorp: To report lost or stolen checks throughout the US, call 800-645-6556; in Mexico, call 813-623-1709, collect.

MasterCard: To report lost or stolen checks throughout the US, call 800-223-9920; in Mexico, call 212-974-5696, collect.

Thomas Cook MasterCard: To report lost or stolen checks.throughout the US, call 800-223-9920; in Mexico, call 609-987-7300, collect.

Visa: To report lost or stolen checks throughout the US, call 800-227-6811; in Mexico, call 415-574-7111, collect.

CREDIT CARDS: Some establishments you may encounter during the course of your travels may not honor any credit cards and some may not honor all cards, so there is a practical reason to carry more than one. The following is a list of credit cards that enjoy wide domestic and international acceptance:

American Express: Cardholders can cash personal checks for traveler's checks and cash at *American Express* or representatives offices in the US up to the following limits (within any 21-day period): up to $1,000 for *Green* and *Optima* cardholders; $5,000 for *Gold* cardholders, and $10,000 for *Platinum* cardholders. Check cashing also is available to cardholders who are guests at participating hotels in the US and Canada (up to $250) and at participating hotels abroad (up to $100), and for holders of airline tickets, at participating airlines (up to $50). Free travel accident, baggage, and car rental insurance if ticket or rental is charged to card; additional insurance also is available for additional cost. For further information or to report a lost or stolen *American Express* card, call 800-528-4800 throughout the continental US; elsewhere in the US and in Mexico, call 212-477-5700, collect.

Carte Blanche: Free travel accident, baggage, and car rental insurance if ticket or rental is charged to card; additional insurance also is available at additional cost. For medical, legal, and travel assistance available worldwide call 800-356-3448 throughout the US; elsewhere, call 214-680-6480, collect. For further information or to report a lost or stolen *Carte Blanche* card, call 800-525-9135 throughout the US; in Mexico, call 303-790-2433, collect.

Diners Club: Emergency personal check cashing for cardholders staying at participating hotels and motels in the US and abroad (up to $250 per stay). Free travel accident, baggage, and car rental insurance if ticket or rental is charged to card; additional insurance also is available for an additional fee. For medical, legal, and travel assistance available worldwide, call 800-356-3448 throughout the US;

elsewhere, call 214-680-6480, collect. For further information or to report a lost or stolen *Diners Club* card, call 800-525-9135 throughout the US; 303-790-2433, collect, in Mexico.

Discover Card: Offered by a subsidiary of Sears, Roebuck & Co., it provides cardholders with cash advances at numerous automatic teller machines and Sears stores throughout the US. Please note that *Discover* is *not* accepted in Mexico. For further information or to report a lost or stolen *Discover* card, call 800-DISCOVER.

MasterCard: Cash advances are available at participating banks worldwide. Check with your issuing bank for information. *MasterCard* also offers a 24-hour emergency lost card service; call 800-826-2181 throughout the US; in Mexico, call 314-275-6690, collect.

Visa: Cash advances are available at participating banks worldwide. Check with your issuing bank for information. *Visa* also offers a 24-hour emergency lost card service; call 800-336-8472 throughout the US; elsewhere, call 415-574-7700, collect.

One of the thorniest problems relating to the use of credit cards abroad concerns the rate of exchange at which a purchase is charged. Be aware that the exchange rate in effect on the date that you make a foreign purchase or pay for a foreign service has nothing at all to do with the rate of exchange at which your purchase is billed to you when you get the invoice (sometimes months later) in the US. The amount that the credit card company charges is either a function of the exchange rate at which the establishment's bank processed it or the rate in effect on the day your charge is received at the credit service center. (There is 1-year limit on the time a business can take to forward its charge slips.) If the dollar gets stronger in the time between purchase and billing, your purchase actually costs you less than you anticipated. If the dollar drops in value during the interim, you pay more than you thought you would. There isn't much you can do about these vagaries except to follow one very broad, very clumsy rule of thumb: If the dollar is doing well at the time of purchase, its value increasing against the local currency, use your credit card on the assumption that it still will be doing well when billing takes place. If the dollar is doing badly, assume it will continue to do badly and pay with traveler's checks or cash. If you get too badly stuck, the best recourse is to complain, loudly. Be aware, too, that most credit card companies charge an unannounced, un-itemized 1% fee for converting foreign currency charges to US dollars.

SENDING MONEY TO MEXICO: If you have used up your traveler's checks, cashed as many emergency personal checks as your credit card allows, drawn on your cash advance line to the fullest, and still need money, it is possible to have it sent to you via the following services:

American Express (phone: 800-543-4080) offers a service called "Moneygram," completing money transfers in anywhere from 15 minutes to 5 days. The sender can go to any *American Express* office in the US and can transfer money by presenting cash, a personal check, money order, or credit card — *Discover, MasterCard, Visa,* or *American Express Optima* (no other *American Express* or other credit cards are accepted). *American Express Optima* cardholders also can arrange for this transfer over the phone. The minimum transfer charge is $25, which rises with the amount of the transaction; the sender can forward funds of up to $10,000 (credit card users are limited to the amount of pre-established credit line). To collect at the other end, the receiver must go to an *American Express* branch office and show identification (driver's license or other picture ID).

Western Union Telegraph Company (phone: 800-325-4176). A friend or relative can go, cash in hand, to any *Western Union* office in the US, where, for a *minimum* charge of $13 (it rises with the amount of the transaction), the funds will be transferred to a centralized *Western Union* account. When the transaction is fully processed — in the case of Cancún and Cozumel from 2 to 3 business days — you can go to any *Western Union* branch office or correspondent bank to pick up the transferred funds. For a higher fee, the US party to this transaction may call *Western Union* with a *MasterCard* or *Visa* number to send up to $2,000, although larger transfers will be sent to a predesignated location.

If you are literally down to your last cent and have no other way to obtain cash, the US consular agent on Cancún (phone: 988-42411) or the nearest US consulate (see *Medical and Legal Aid and Consular Services*, in this section) will let you call home to set these matters in motion.

CASH MACHINES: Automatic teller machines (ATMs) are increasingly common worldwide. Some banks provide ATM service only for their own customers at bank branches. If, however, your bank participates in one of the international ATM networks (most do), you can use the "cash card" and your personal identification code or number (also called a PIC or PIN) provided by the bank at any ATM in the same electronic network for financial transactions, including withdrawing cash.

At the time of this writing, ATMs that *are* connected generally belong to either the *Cirrus* (phone: 800-4-CIRRUS) or *Plus Systém* (phone: 800-THE-PLUS) network. Both networks maintain thousands of ATM locations worldwide, including hundreds of locations throughout Mexico and one set of machines in Cancún City (at 19 Av. Tulum). *MasterCard* holders may use their cards to draw cash against their credit lines on either system, and *Visa* cardholders can use their cards to draw cash from the *Plus Systém* machines. (Note that as we went to press, there was an agreement pending between these two companies to join their networks.)

Accommodations

 The best Mexican hotels combine the modern, standardized style of American chains with the continental elegance of European service and a lush, tropical charm unique to Mexico. The enormous growth of tourism in Mexico in recent years has been marked by a corresponding growth in accommodations of all kinds and styles. The popular beach resort areas, such as Cancún, Cozumel, and Isla Mujeres, offer some of the world's most luxurious hotels and resorts in splendid settings.

A number of properties on Cancún and Cozumel are part of well-known international hotel chains. The most elegant of these offer a broad range of facilities and amenities, as well as competent, attentive service. These hotels are modern and comfortable, often include fine restaurants, and the prices, as you would expect, are relatively high. Comparable independent establishments in this area often are even more elegant than the chains. Medium-size hotels can be equally modern, or at least modernized, but are more likely to offer local ambience and charm; in general, they're also more reasonably priced. Some establishments offer the added allure of stunning views, snow white beaches, various sports facilities, and spas. In many hotels, you can splurge and enjoy a life of luxury and leisure, sipping exotic drinks beneath a bougainvillea on your own terrace, at a relatively low cost compared to that of the equivalent degree of decadence in the US.

At the other end of the spectrum are hotels that offer moderate to inexpensive accommodations. These include numerous clean and inexpensive hosteleries of every type — modern or colonial, secluded, centrally located, or on the road — that offer basic amenities, which may or may not include a private bath, air conditioning, TV sets, in-room telephones, bar and/or meal service, and swimming pools. Here the charm consists of a genuine welcome, personal hospitality, often striking scenery, and privacy.

Since room prices in all Mexican hotels are controlled and regulated by the Mexican Ministry of Tourism, they remain stable within basic categories — reflected in this book in the categories expensive, moderate, and inexpensive. For information on specific properties, see THE ISLANDS, DIRECTIONS, and DIVERSIONS.

RENTAL OPTIONS: An attractive accommodations alternative for the visitor content to stay in one spot for a week or more is to rent one of the numerous properties available throughout the Yucatán Peninsula. These offer a wide range of luxury and convenience, depending on the price you want to pay. One of the charms of staying in a house, apartment, condominium, cottage, villa or other rented vacation home is that you will feel much more like a visitor than a tourist.

A vacation in a furnished rental has both the advantages and disadvantages of living "at home" abroad. It can be less expensive than staying in a first class hotel, although very luxurious and expensive rentals are available, too. It has the comforts of home, including a kitchen, which means saving on food. On the other hand, a certain amount of housework is involved because if you don't eat out, you have to cook, and though some rentals, especially the luxury ones, come with maid service, most don't. (If the rental doesn't include domestic help, arrangements often can be made with a nearby service for far less than in the US.)

For a family, two or more couples, or a group of friends, the per-person cost — even for a more luxurious rental — can be quite reasonable. Weekly and monthly rates are available to reduce costs still more. But best of all is the amount of space, which no conventional hotel room can equal. As with hotels, the rates for properties in some areas are seasonal, rising during the peak travel season, while for others they remain the same year-round. To have your pick of the properties available, you should begin to make arrangement for a rental at least 6 months in advance.

Rental Property Agents and Discounts – There are several ways of finding a suitable rental property. They are listed along with other accommodations in publications of local tourist boards, and it also is possible to find them through a travel agent. Many tour operators regularly include rental packages among their more conventional offerings. In addition, a number of companies specialize in rental vacation packages that typically include rental of the property (or several properties, but usually for a minimum 2- or 3-day stay per location), a rental car, and airfare.

The companies listed below rent a variety of properties in Mexico. They handle the booking and confirmation paperwork, and can be expected to provide more information about the properties they handle than that which might ordinarily be gleaned from a listing in an accommodations guide.

Creative Leisure (951 Transport Way, Petaluma, CA 94954; phone: 800-4-CONDOS in the US and Canada). Rents moderate condominiums to deluxe beachfront villas on Cancún and Cozumel.

Hideaways International (PO Box 1270, Littleton, MA 01460; phone: 508-486-8955 or 800-843-4433 throughout the US). Rents luxury beachfront villas, private houses, and condominiums on Cancún and Cozumel. For $75 subscribers receive two issues per year of their guide to current listings, as well as a quarterly newsletter and discounts on a variety of travel services.

Rent a Home International (7200 34th Ave. NW, Seattle, WA 98117; phone: 206-789-9377). Rents private villas on Cancún and Cozumel.

Rent a Vacation Everywhere (*RAVE;* 328 Main St. E., Suite 526, Rochester, NY

14604; phone: 716-454-6440). Handles moderate condominiums and villas throughout Mexico, including Cancún and Cozumel.

Travel Resources (PO Box 935, Coconut Grove, FL 33133; phone: 305-444-8583 or 800-327-5039 throughout the US). Rents condominiums and villas on Cancún.

VHR, Worldwide (235 Kensington Ave., Norwood, NJ 07648; phone: 800-NEED-A-VILLA or 201-767-9393). Handles estates, condominiums, and villas on Cozumel.

Villas International (71 W. 23rd St., New York, NY 10010; phone: 212-929-7585 in New York State; 800-221-2260 elsewhere in the US). Their offerings range from simple to luxurious houses, as well as apartments. Rentals are offered in a number of locations throughout Mexico, including Cancún and Cozumel.

In addition, a useful publication, the *Worldwide Home Rental Guide,* lists private villas and cottages throughout Mexico, as well as the managing agencies. Issued twice annually, single copies may be available at newsstands for $10 an issue. For a year's subscription (two issues), send $18 to *Worldwide Home Rental Guide,* PO Box 2842, Sante Fe, NM 87504 (phone: 505-988-5188).

When considering a particular vacation rental property, look for answers to the following questions:

- How do you get from the airport to the condominium?
- If the property is on the shore, how far is the nearest beach? Is it sandy or rocky, and is it safe for swimming?
- What size and number of beds are provided?
- How far is the property from whatever else is important to you, such as a golf course or nightlife?
- If there is no grocery store on the premises (which may be comparatively expensive, anyway), how far is the nearest market?
- Are baby-sitters, cribs, bicycles, or anything else you may need for your children available?
- Is maid service provided daily?
- Is air conditioning and/or a phone provided?
- Is a car rental part of the package? Is a car necessary?

Before deciding which rental is for you, make sure you have satisfactory answers to all your questions. Ask your travel agent to find out or call the company involved directly.

Accommodation Discounts – Several organizations provide a substantial savings on rental (and some hotel) accommodations in Mexico. Reservations are handled by the central office of the organization, or members may deal directly with the rental agencies or individual property owners. To take advantage of the full selection of properties, these organizations often require that reservations be made as much as 6 months in advance — particularly for stays during the holidays or peak travel periods.

Concierge (1600 Wynkoop St., Suite 102, Denver, CO 80202; phone: 303-623-6775 in Colorado; 800-346-1022 elsewhere in the US). Offers up to 50% discounts on rentals on Cancún. Annual membership fee is $69.95 per couple.

Entry Unlimited (6404 Nancy Ridge Rd., San Diego, CA 92121; phone: 800-843-0265 or 619-558-5838). Up to 50% discounts offered on rentals on Cancún. Annual membership fee $39.95 is per family.

Hotel Express (3052 El Cajon Blvd., San Diego, CA 92104; phone: 800-634-6526 or 619-284-1135). Offers up to 50% off on rentals on Cancún and Cozumel. Annual membership fee is $49.95 per family provides discounts on other travel services, but membership is not required for bargains on rental accommodations.

Privilege Card (3473 Satellite Blvd., Suite 200, Duluth, GA 30136; phone: 800-359-0066 or 404-623-0066). Up to 50% discounts available on condominium and apartment rentals on Cancún and Cozumel. Annual membership fee is $49.95 per family.

Time Zones, Business Hours, and Bank Holidays

 TIME ZONES: The Yucatán Peninsula operates on Central Standard Time. In winter, if it is 9 AM on Cancún (Central Standard Time), it is 7 AM in Los Angeles (Pacific Standard Time), 8 AM in Denver (Mountain Standard Time), and 10 AM in New York (Eastern Standard Time). As Mexico does not observe Daylight Saving Time, during the summer when this time change is in effect in the US, add 1 hour to each of the equivalent US times.

Mexican timetables use a 24-hour clock to denote arrival and departure times, which means that hours are expressed sequentially from 1 AM. By this method, 9 AM is recorded as 0900, noon as 1200, 1 PM as 1300, 6 PM as 1800, midnight as 2400, and so on. For example, the departure of a train at 7 AM will be announced as "0700"; one leaving at 7 PM will be noted as "1900."

One further confusion may arise when you're keeping an appointment with a Mexican acquaintance. Although you may be certain that you have already adjusted your watch and that it is working correctly, your companion may not show up until an hour or more after the agreed time. This is neither unusual nor considered impolite. It is simply a different regard for time than is common in the US. And your trip to Mexico may be even more delightful if you relax and adopt this south-of-the-border attitude.

BUSINESS HOURS: While working hours number about the same as those in the US, the times differ considerably. Executives usually begin working at 10 AM and stop for a leisurely, 2-hour lunch around 2 or 3 PM. The afternoon shift runs from about 4 to 7 PM. Mexican stores are generally open from 10 AM to 7 PM.

Most banks are open from 9AM to 1:30 PM Mondays through Fridays. Key branches of some major banks also may offer additional hours, opening from 4 to 6 PM on weekdays. A few banks may keep even longer hours — staying open from 8:30 AM through 5 PM. Some even may have weekend hours — staying open from 10 AM to 1:30 PM and from 4 to 6 PM on Saturdays, and 10 AM to 1:30 PM on Sundays.

If you are unable to get to the bank, you usually can cash your traveler's checks at money exchanges, which are open Mondays through Fridays until 5 PM and Saturdays until 2 PM. The airport money exchanges are open Sundays as well. (For further information, see *Credit and Currency*, in this section.)

BANK HOLIDAYS: Government offices, banks, and stores are closed on national holidays and often on the days just before and after as well. Many offices (but not banks) close between *Christmas* and *New Year's*. Following are Mexican national holidays and the dates they will be observed this year:

January 1: *New Year's Day (Año Nuevo).*
February 5: *Constitution Day* marks the signing of the constitutions of 1857 and 1915.

March 21: *Birthday of Benito Juárez* honors the man often called the "Abraham Lincoln of Mexico."

April 16: *Holy Thursday.*

April 17: *Good Friday.*

May 1: *Labor Day,* celebrated with parades.

May 5: Anniversary of Mexico's victory over the French at Puebla in 1862.

September 1: The president's state of the union report *(Informe)* and the opening of Congress.

September 16: *Independence Day.*

October 12: *Columbus Day (Día de la Raza).*

November 2: *All Souls' Day* (known in Mexico as the *Day of the Dead*).

November 20: Anniversary of the Mexican Revolution of 1910.

December 12: *Feast of Our Lady of Guadalupe.*

December 25: *Christmas.*

December 31: Banks closed for annual balance.

Mail, Telephone, and Electricity

MAIL: Almost every town throughout the country has a post office, and while there are not many street mailboxes *(buzónes)* on street corners, there are drops in most large hotels, office buildings, and in front of or in every post office.

All foreign postal service is now airmail. The real problem is how long it takes your letter to get from the post office to the plane: Service in Mexico is known as "Burro Express," and can take up several weeks. The good news, however, is that due to the efforts of the Mexican postal authorities, this system is gradually improving.

If you are planning to send packages to destinations either within or outside the country, be sure to have them registered. The procedure is the same as in the US. If your correspondence is important, you may want to send it via one of the special courier services; *Federal Express, DHL,* and other international services are widely available in Mexico. The cost is considerably higher than sending something via the postal service — but the assurance of its timely arrival is worth it.

Several places will receive and hold mail for travelers in Mexico. Mail sent to you at a hotel and clearly marked "Guest Mail, Hold for Arrival" is a safe approach. If you do not know what your address will be, have your mail addressed to the nearest post office in care of the local equivalent of General Delivery: *a/c Lista de Correos.* Note that you are expected to specify the branch, district, postal code *(codigo postal)* and city — and, under the best of conditions, this is very risky. To claim this mail, you must go in person to the post office, ask for General Delivery, and present identification (driver's license, credit card, birth certificate, or passport).

In sending mail to Mexico, avoid using middle names. Mexicans use the paternal and maternal surnames — the paternal is in the middle — and using a middle name could lead to confusion. When inquiring about mail addressed to you, should there be nothing under the first letter of your last name, ask the post office clerk to look for it under the first letter of your first or middle name. If you plan to remain in one place for more than a month, consider renting a post office box *(apartado postal)* in the central post office to eliminate the chance of mail getting lost in local delivery.

If you are an *American Express* customer (a cardholder, a carrier of *American Express* traveler's checks, or on an *American Express Travel Related Services* tour), you can have mail sent to an *American Express* branch office (there are three on Cancún and one on Cozumel). Letters are held free of charge — registered mail and packages are not accepted. You must be able to show an *American Express* card, traveler's checks, or a voucher proving you are on one of the company's tours to avoid paying for mail privileges. Those who aren't clients must pay a nominal charge each time they inquire if they have received mail, whether or not they actually have a letter. There also is a forwarding fee, for clients and non-clients alike. Mail should be addressed to you, care of *American Express,* and should be marked "Client Mail Service." Additional information on this mail service is listed in the pamphlet *Services and Offices,* available from any US branch of *American Express.*

TELEPHONE: Most large Mexican cities and resort areas — including Cancún and Cozumel — have direct dialing to the US. Telephones from which this is not possible require the assistance of the international operator, who can connect you. If you are staying in a small town or in a hotel with no phone, use the phones in local stores or larger hotels. And here again, the operator can tell you the charges.

The procedure for calling Mexico from the US is as follows: dial 011 (the international access code) + 52 (the country code) + the city code + the local number. (The city code for Cancún and Isla Mujeres is 988; Cozumel is 987. For city codes of other areas, check the front of a telephone book or ask an international operator.) For example, to place a call from anywhere in the US to Cancún, dial 011 + 52 + 988 + the local number.

To call the US from anywhere in Mexico, dial 95 + the US area code + the local number. For instance, to call a number in New York City, dial 95 + 212 + the local number.

To make a call from one city in Mexico to another, dial 91 + the city code + the local number. To call a number within the same city code, just dial the local number.

Note that the number of digits in phone numbers is not standardized throughout Mexico and may vary. As making connections in Mexico for either local or international calls sometimes can be hit-or-miss, those who have to make an important call — to make a hotel reservation in another city, for instance — should start to do so as far in advance as possible.

Some important phone numbers throughout Mexico include the following:

> **Emergency assistance:** 915-250-0123 and 915-250-0151.
> **Long-distance operator:** 02 (within Mexico)
> **International operator:** 09 (English-speaking)
> **Local information:** 04
> **Countrywide information:** 01

Hotel Surcharges – Avoiding operator-assisted calls can cut international calling costs considerably and bring rates into a somewhat more reasonable range — except for calls made through hotel switchboards. One of the most unpleasant surprises travelers encounter in many foreign countries is the amount they find tacked onto their hotel bill for telephone calls, because foreign hotels routinely add on astronomical surcharges. (It's not at all uncommon to find 300% to 400% added to the actual telephone charges.)

Until recently, the only recourse against this unconscionable overcharging was to call collect when phoning from abroad or to use a telephone credit card — available through a simple procedure from any local US phone company. Now *American Telephone and Telegraph (AT&T)* offers *USA Direct,* a service that connects users, via a toll-free number, with an *AT&T* operator in the US, who then will put a call through at the standard international rate. A new feature of this service is that travelers abroad can reach US toll-free (800) numbers by calling a *USA Direct* operator, who will connect them. Charges for all calls made through *USA Direct* appear on the caller's regular US phone bill. Note that as we went to press, this service was offered only in a few areas of Mexico, including Cancún. For a brochure and wallet card listing toll-free numbers by country, contact International Information Service, *AT&T Communications,* 635 Grand St., Pittsburgh, PA 15219 (phone: 800-874-4000).

Until such services become universal, it's wise to ask about surcharges *before* calling from a hotel. If the rate is high, it's best to use a telephone credit card (although some hotels still may charge a fee for line usage); make a collect call; or place the call and ask the party to call right back. If none of these choices is possible, make international calls from the local post office or special telephone center to avoid surcharges. Another way to keep down the cost of telephoning from Mexico is to leave a copy of your itinerary and telephone numbers with people in the US so that they can call you instead.

■ **Note:** For quick reference, you might want to get a copy of the helpful pamphlet *The Phone Booklet,* which lists the nationwide, toll-free (800) numbers of travel information sources and suppliers — such as major airlines, hotel and motel chains, car rental companies, and tourist information offices. Send $2 for postage and handling to *Scott American Corporation,* Box 88, West Redding, CT 06896.

ELECTRICITY: Mexico's electrical current is the same as that used in the US, so American tourists can bring their own electrical appliances from home. If you want to be fully prepared, bring along an extension cord (the electrical outlet may be farther from the sink than the cord on your razor or hair dryer can reach), and a wall socket adapter with a full selection of plugs to ensure that you'll be able to plug in anywhere. In some areas and establishments, the current may be weak; your electrical equipment still should work, but not up to maximum capacity. So if you use an electric razor, it is wise to pack a manual safety razor, too, just in case.

One good source for sets of plugs and adapters for use worldwide is the *Franzus Company* (PO Box 142, Beacon Falls, CT 06403; phone: 203-723-6664). *Franzus* also publishes a useful brochure, *Foreign Electricity is No Deep Dark Secret,* which provides information about converters and adapter plugs for electrical appliances to be used abroad but manufactured for use in the US. To obtain a free copy, send a self-addressed, stamped envelope to *Franzus;* a catalogue of other travel accessories is available on request.

Medical and Legal Aid and Consular Services

MEDICAL AID: Nothing ruins a vacation or business trip more effectively than sudden injury or illness. As always is the case with both diseases and accidents, prevention is the best cure. And in Mexico this adage applies not only to diarrhea or dysentery, but to more serious diseases like hepatitis and typhoid fever.

Before you go, be sure to check with your insurance company about the applicability of your hospitalization and major medical policies while you're away (see *Insurance,* in this section). Also make sure you get the most up-to-date information available about health conditions in Mexico. Consult your personal physician or contact your county or state health departments, which generally also can administer necessary or recommended inoculations. (For information on specific health problems, recommended immunizations, and other precautions, see *Staying Healthy,* in this section.)

If you fall victim to any accident or malady that seems serious, do not hesitate to go to a doctor. The medical care available in Mexico is not very different from that offered in the US. There are private doctors, every kind of specialist, clinics, both private and government hospitals, dentists, optometrists, pharmacies, drugstores, and most medications found in the US. The quality of health care and the sophistication of medical facilities are less certain in rural and remote areas, and for specialized treatment it often is best to arrange for transportation to the nearest metropolitan center.

If a bona fide emergency occurs, the fastest way to get attention may be to take a taxi to the emergency room of the nearest hospital. An alternative is to dial one of the following numbers for emergency assistance: to summon the police, fire trucks, and ambulances: 915-250-0123 or 915-250-0151. When calling these numbers, state immediately that you are a foreign tourist and then the nature of your problem and your location. Note that ambulance dispatchers may not be bilingual, so travelers with little or no Spanish language ability should try to get someone else to make the call. You also can dial for the operator and ask for someone who speaks English, although you may need an international operator to place a call to the local emergency service and stay on the line as an interpreter. Most emergency services send out well-equipped and well-staffed ambulances, although ambulances in some areas of Mexico may not be equipped with the advanced EMS technology found in the US and may provide only basic medical attention and be used mainly for transportation.

If a doctor is needed for something less than an emergency, there are several ways to find one. If you are staying in a hotel or resort, ask for help in reaching a doctor or other emergency services, or for the house physician, who may visit you in your room or ask you to visit an office. (This service is apt to be expensive, especially if the doctor makes a "house" call to your room.) Travelers staying at a hotel of any size probably will find that the doctor on call speaks at least a modicum of English — if not, request one who does. When you register at a hotel, it's not a bad idea to include your home address and telephone number; this will facilitate the process of notifying friends, relatives, or your own doctor in case of an emergency.

Any US consul also can provide a list of English-speaking doctors and dentists in the area the consulate serves. (For a list of US consuls in Mexico, see "American Consulates in Mexico," below.) Dialing the emergency numbers (listed below) may also be of help.

Pharmacies *(farmacias)* are a slight variation on the theme to which you are accustomed. While they're owned and operated by licensed pharmacists, diagnoses, prescription filling, and even drug administration often are done by pharmacists or their assistants. In some areas, pharmacies may take turns staying open for 24 hours. If none is open after normal business hours, you may be able to have one open in an emergency situation — such as for a diabetic needing insulin — for a fee. Contact a local hospital or medical clinic for information on on-call pharmacists. If your complaint is not serious and you wish to avoid the hassle or expense of consulting a physician, the local *farmacia* will be happy to recommend a drug, administer it either in bulk or in single doses, and even give or recommend a doctor to give injections.

Emergency assistance also is available from the various medical programs designed for travelers who have chronic ailments or whose illness requires them to return home:

International Association of Medical Assistance to Travelers *(IAMAT;* 417 Center St., Lewiston, NY 14092; phone: 716-754-4883). Entitles members to the services of participating English-speaking doctors around the world, as well as clinics and hospitals in various locations. Participating physicians agree to adhere to a basic charge of around $40 to see a patient referred by *IAMAT.* To join, simply write to *IAMAT;* in about 3 weeks you will receive a membership card, the booklet of members, and an inoculation chart. A nonprofit organization, *IAMAT* appreciates donations; with a donation of $25 or more, you will receive a set of worldwide climate charts detailing weather and sanitary conditions. (Delivery can take up to 5 weeks, so plan ahead.)

International Health Care Service (New York Hospital–Cornell Medical Center, 525 E. 68th St., Box 210, New York, NY 10021; phone: 212-746-1601). This service provides a variety of travel-related health services. A pre-travel counseling and immunization package costs $255 for the first family member and $195 for each additional member; a post-travel screening is $175 to $275, plus lab work. Appointments are required for all services. The *International Health Care Traveler's Guide,* a compendium of facts and advice on health care and diseases around the world, can be obtained by sending $4.50 and a self-addressed, stamped envelope to the service.

International SOS Assistance (PO Box 11568, Philadelphia, PA 19116; phone: 800-523-8930 or 215-244-1500). Subscribers are provided with telephone access — 24 hours a day, 365 days a year — to a worldwide, monitored, multilingual network of medical centers. A phone call brings assistance ranging from a telephone consultation to transportation home by ambulance or aircraft, or, in some cases, transportation of a family member to wherever you are hospitalized. Individual rates are $35 for 2 weeks of coverage ($3.50 for each additional day), $70 for 1 month, or $240 for 1 year; couple and family rates also are available.

Medic Alert Foundation (2323 N. Colorado, Turlock, CA 95380; phone: 800-ID-ALERT or 209-668-3333). If you have a health condition that may not be readily available to the casual observer — one that might result in a tragic error in an emergency situation — this organization offers identification emblems specifying such conditions. The foundation also maintains a computerized central file from which your complete medical history is available 24 hours a day by phone (the telephone number is clearly inscribed on the emblem). The onetime membership fee, between $25 and $45, is based on the type of metal from which the emblem is made — the choices ranging from stainless steel to 10K gold-filled.

TravMed (PO Box 10623, Baltimore, MD 21204; phone: 800-732-5309 or 301-296-5225). For $3 per day, subscribers receive comprehensive medical assistance while abroad. Major medical expenses are covered up to $100,000, and special transportation home or of a family member to wherever you are hospitalized is provided at no additional cost.

■**Note:** Those who are unable to take a reserved flight due to personal illness or must fly home unexpectedly due to a family emergency should be aware that airlines may offer a discounted airfare (or arrange a partial refund) if the traveler can demonstrate that his or her situation is indeed a legitimate emergency. Your inability to fly or the illness or death of an immediate family member usually must be substantiated by a doctor's note or the name, relationship, and funeral home where the deceased will be buried. In such cases, airlines often will waive certain advance purchase restrictions or you may receive a refund check or voucher for future travel at a later date. Be aware, however, that this bereavement fare may not necessarily be the least expensive fare available and, if possible, it is best to have a travel agent check all possible flights through a computer reservations system (CRS).

LEGAL AID AND CONSULAR SERVICES: There is one crucial place to keep in mind when outside the US, namely, the American Services section of the United States Consulate. If you are injured or become seriously ill, the consulate will direct you to medical assistance and notify your relatives. If, while abroad, you become involved in a dispute that could lead to legal action, or if you are stranded abroad without funds, the consulate, once again, is the place to turn. And in the case of natural disasters or civil unrest, consulates around the world handle the evacuation of US citizens if it becomes necessary.

It usually is far more alarming to be arrested abroad than at home. Not only are you alone among strangers, but the punishment can be worse. Granted, the US Consulate can advise you of your rights and provide a list of English-speaking lawyers, but it cannot interfere with the local legal process.

The best advice is to be honest and law-abiding. If you get a traffic ticket, pay it. If you are approached by drug hawkers, ignore them. The penalties for possession of hashish, marijuana, cocaine, and other narcotics are even more severe abroad than in the US. (If you are picked up for any drug-related offense, do not expect US Foreign Service officials to be sympathetic. Chances are they will notify a lawyer and your family and that's about all. See "Drugs," below.)

In the case of minor traffic accidents, it often is most expedient to settle the matter before the police get involved. If the police do get involved in minor accidents or violations, try to establish a fine on the spot and pay it quickly. If you speak the language and feel competent, try to bargain the fine, but wisdom decrees that you do what is necessary to get the matter settled on the spot.

If, however, you are involved in a serious accident, where an injury or fatality results, the first step is to contact the US Consulate in Cancún and ask the consul to locate a lawyer to assist you. The US Department of State in Washington, DC, insists that any US citizen who is arrested abroad has the right to contact the US embassy or consulate "immediately," but it may be a while before you are given permission to use a phone. Do not labor under the illusion, however, that in a scrape with foreign officialdom, the consulate can act as an arbitrator or ombudsman on an American citizen's behalf. Nothing could be farther from the truth. Consuls have no power, authorized or otherwise, to subvert, alter, or contravene the legal processes, however unfair, of the foreign country in which they serve. Nor can a consul oil the machinery of a foreign bureaucracy or provide legal advice. The consul's responsibilities do encompass "welfare duties" including providing a list of lawyers and information on local sources of legal aid, informing relatives in the US, and organizing and administrating any defense money sent from home. If a case is tried unfairly or the punishment seems unusually severe, the consul can make a formal complaint to the authorities.

The consulate is not occupied solely with emergencies and is certainly not there to aid in trivial situations, such as canceled reservations or lost baggage, no matter how important these matters may seem to the victimized tourist. The main duties of any consulate are administering statutory services, such as the issuance of passports and visas; providing notarial services; distributing VA, social security, and civil service benefits to resident Americans; taking depositions; handling extradition cases; and reporting to Washington the births, deaths, and marriages of US citizens living within the consulate's domain.

We hope that none of the information in this section will be necessary during your stay in Mexico. If you can avoid legal hassles altogether, you will have a much more pleasant trip. If you run into a confrontation that might lead to legal complications developing with a citizen or with local authorities, the best tactic is to apologize and try to leave as gracefully as possible. In a foreign country where machismo is part of the national character, some things are best left unsettled.

American Consulates in Mexico – The US Embassy is located in Mexico City (305 Paseo de la Reforma, México, DF 06500; phone: 5-211-0042). The US government also maintains consulates general in nine other cities of Mexico; consular agents operate in ten additional cities.

In the Yucatán Peninsula, there is a consulate general in Mérida (453 Paseo Montejo, Apdo. 130, Mérida, Yucatán; phone: 99-255409) and a consular agent on Cancún (40 Av. Nader, Marruecos Bldg., Rm. 31, Cancún, Yucatán; phone: 988-42411).

You also can obtain a booklet with addresses of most US embassies and consulates around the world by writing to the Superintendent of Documents (US Government Printing Office, Washington, DC 20402) and asking for publication #78-77, *Key Offices of Foreign Service Posts.*

The US State Department operates a *Citizens' Emergency Center,* which offers a number of services to US citizens traveling abroad and their families at home. In addition to giving callers up-to-date information on trouble spots, the center will contact authorities abroad in an attempt to locate a traveler or deliver an urgent message. In case of illness, death, arrest, destitution, or repatriation of an American citizen on foreign soil, it will relay information to relatives at home if the consulate is unable to do so. Travel advisory information is available 24 hours a day to people with Touch-Tone phones (phone: 202-647-5225). Callers with rotary phones can get information at this number from 8:15 AM to 10 PM (Eastern Standard Time) on weekdays, 9 AM to 3 PM Saturdays. In the event of an emergency, this number also may be called during these hours. For emergency calls only, at all other times, call 202-634-3600 and ask for the Duty Officer.

Drinking and Drugs

DRINKING: There are no laws restricting drinking in Mexico — there is not even a minimum drinking age. In fact, the manufacture of alcoholic beverages is one of Mexico's most important industries. Mexican beer is so good that much of it is now being exported to the US, where in some areas it holds its own with American beers — depite its higher imported price. While you're in Mexico, try native brews like Bohemia, Carta Blanca, Corona, Dos Equis, Indio, Negro Modelo, Superior, and Tecate at the source.

Tequila, the national drink, is distilled from the juice of the agave plant, and is the beverage US visitors are most eager to sample. Take it straight, with salt and lime, or in a margarita cocktail, with lime juice and ice, but take it easy. Popular brands include Herradura, Hornitos, José Cuervo, Sauza, Viuda de Romero, and Xalisco.

Mescal is another hard liquor made from the agave cactus, although the taste is quite different from that of tequila; try Gusano de Oro, Gusano Rojo, or Monte Albán. Brandy also is one of Mexico's most popular drinks, and, strangely enough, it often is mixed with Coca-Cola, 7-Up, or mineral water. (Some institutional receptions only serve a choice of brandy and Coke or brandy and soda.) Rum, enjoyed straight, in a daiquiri, or with cola remains a favorite of tourists and residents alike; Bacardi, Castillo, and Potosí all are well regarded.

If you're a wine buff, don't neglect Mexico's wines — they're continually improving. There is a big price difference between Mexican and imported wines in most restaurants. Among the better-known Mexican vintages are Calafia, La Cetto, Domecq, Don Angel, Hammerhaus, Hildago, Padre Kino, Pinson, Los Reyes, San Lorenzo, San Marcos, Santo Tomás, and Urbiñon.

As in the US, national taxes on alcohol affect the prices of liquor in Mexico, and as a general rule, mixed drinks made from imported liquors (such as whiskey and gin) are more expensive than at home. If you like a toddy before dinner, a good way to save money is to buy a bottle of your favorite brand at the airport before leaving the US and enjoy it in your hotel before setting forth. Or stick to locally produced beverages.

If you are buying any quantity of alcohol (such as a case of tequila) in Mexico, be aware that whether you are bringing it with you or having it shipped, you will have to pay US import duties on any quantity over the allowed 1 liter (see *Customs and Returning to the US,* in this section.)

DRUGS: Another way to avoid legal trouble in Mexico is to avoid the drug scene — completely. Illegal narcotics are as prevalent in Mexico as in the US, but the moderate legal penalties and vague social acceptance that marijuana has gained in the US have no equivalents in Mexico. Due to the international war on drugs, enforcement of drug laws is becoming increasingly strict throughout the world. Local Mexican narcotics officers and customs officials are renowned for their absence of understanding and lack of a sense of humor — especially where Americans are involved.

Despite the government's campaign against it, marijuana still is grown in abundance throughout Mexico and is widely available. It is, however, just as illegal in Mexico as it is in the US, and penalties for selling, growing, and smoking it are just as severe. Opiates and barbiturates and other increasingly popular drugs — "white powder" substances like heroin and cocaine, and "crack" (the cocaine derivative) — also are a problem in Mexico, as elsewhere.

The concerted effort by Mexican and other foreign authorities to stamp out drug traffic, with the support and encouragement of the United States, has now become a real war on buyers and sellers in the country — a war that has been — and continues to be — deadly.

It is important to bear in mind that the quantity of drugs involved is of very minor importance. Persons arrested are subject to the laws of the country they are visiting, and in Mexico these laws and their procedures often are very harsh. Once you are in jail, the best lawyers in the country won't be able to get you out — and neither will the US government. Eventually, at the whim of the authorities, you will be tried and, upon conviction, given a stiff sentence. The best advice we can offer is: Don't carry, use, buy, or sell illegal drugs.

Those who carry medicines that contain a controlled drug should be sure to have a current doctor's prescription with them. Ironically, travelers can get into almost as much trouble coming through US customs with over-the-counter drugs picked up abroad that contain substances that are controlled in the US. Cold medicines, pain relievers, and the like often have codeine or codeine derivatives that are illegal, except by prescription, in the US. Throw them out before leaving for home.

■ **Be forewarned:** US narcotics agents warn travelers of the increasingly common ploy of drug dealers asking travelers to transport a "gift" or other package back to the US. Don't be fooled into thinking that the protection of US law applies abroad — if accused of illegal drug trafficking you will be considered guilty until you prove your innocence. In other words, do not, under any circumstances, agree to take anything across the border for a stranger.

Tipping

TIPPING: Many waiters, waitresses, porters, and bellhops in Mexico depend upon tips for their livelihood. The salaries they receive, if they do receive salaries, are far below the equivalent paid in the US (even with the lower Mexican standards of living taken into consideration). There also are situations in which you wouldn't tip in the US but should in Mexico.

In restaurants, tip between 10% and 20% of the bill. For average service in an average restaurant, a 15% tip to the waiter is reasonable, although one should never hesitate to penalize poor service or reward excellent and efficient attention by leaving less or more. (If you notice a 6% or 15% addition to your bill, this usually is a standard tax, called IVA, not a service charge, and a tip still is in order — if you suspect that a gratuity might already be included, ask.)

Although it's not necessary to tip the maître d' of most restaurants — unless he or she has been especially helpful in arranging a special party or providing a table (a few extra dollars *may,* however, get you seated sooner or procure a preferred table) — when tipping is desirable or appropriate, the least amount should be the local equivalent of $5. In the finest restaurants, where a multiplicity of servers are present, plan to tip 5% to the captain. The sommelier (wine waiter) is entitled to a gratuity of approximately 10% of the price of the bottle of wine.

In allocating gratuities at a restaurant, pay particular attention to what has become the standard credit card charge form, which now includes separate places for gratuities for waiters and/or captains. If these separate boxes are not on the charge slip, simply ask the waiter or captain how these separate tips should be indicated. In some establishments, tips indicated on credit card receipts may not be given to the help, so you may want to leave tips in cash.

If you arrive by air, you probably will find a porter with a cart ready to roll your baggage from customs to the cabstand. He should be paid the current equivalent of about $1 to $2 in pesos, depending on how much luggage you have. If you are traveling by train, porters *expect* a tip of about 25¢ to 35¢ per bag — you might want to go higher. Bellhops, doormen, and porters at hotels generally are tipped at the rate of 50¢ to $1 per piece of luggage, along with a small additional amount if a doorman helps with a cab. If you arrive without the right denominations in pesos, tip in US money. (When in doubt, it is preferable to tip — in any denomination or currency — than not to tip.)

In a large hotel or resort, where it is difficult to determine just who out of a horde of attendants actually performed particular services, it is perfectly proper for guests to ask to have an extra 10% to 15% added to their bill. If you prefer to distribute tips yourself, leave the hotel maid at least $1 per day. Tip the concierge and hall porter for specific services only, with the amount of such gratuities dependent on the level of service provided. For any special service you receive in a hotel, a tip is expected — $1 being the minimum for a small service.

Authorized taxi rates are set either by kilometers traveled or by zone, depending on the city or town; in metered cabs current fares are often posted (especially if there has been an increase in fares and the meter has not yet been adjusted). Many cab drivers set their own unofficial fares, and it is a good idea to ask what it will cost to get to a destination before entering the cab and letting the driver take over. Like so many fees in Mexico, this fare is likely to be negotiable. Cab drivers do not expect tips unless they perform some special service. Cabs that you call by phone are slightly more expensive than those that have meters and you hail in the streets.

In Mexico, tourists often are offered services by young children such as watching your car while you shop and sightsee or cleaning your windshield while you stop at a light. You must be firm with them immediately if you don't want their services; otherwise, when the service is complete give your helper a couple of hundred pesos. Arriving and departing from airline terminals also can turn into a battle royal with youngsters over carrying your luggage.

You also may come across uniformed adult car watchers who earn their livelihoods this way. If you find one near your car, give him the current equivalent of $1 in pesos when you return — once you've unlocked the car and made sure everything is still there. If you park your car in a garage or lot, the parking attendant who returns it to you will expect a comparable tip. Unlike in the US, gas station attendants in Mexico expect a tip, even if they don't clean your windshield or check your oil (you should request these services if you want them); 500 to 1,000 pesos is adequate.

Miscellaneous tips: Ushers in theaters should be given about 50¢ after leading you to a seat and giving you a program. Sightseeing tour guides should be tipped. If you are traveling in a group, decide together what you want to give the guide and present it from the group at the end of the tour. If you have been individually escorted, 10% or more of the total tour price is appropriate. Museum and monument guides also are usually tipped a few dollars. Coat checks are worth about 50¢ to $1 a coat, and washroom attendants are tipped — there usually is a little plate with a coin already in it suggesting the expected amount. In barbershops and beauty parlors, tips also are expected, but the percentages vary according to the type of establishment — 10% in the most expensive salons; 15% to 20% in less expensive establishments. (As a general rule, the person who washes your hair should get a small additional tip.)

Tipping aboard ships: Although some cruise lines do have a no-tipping-required policy and you are not penalized by the crew for not tipping, naturally, you aren't penalized for tipping either. Never, however, make the mistake of not tipping on the majority of ships, where it is a common, expected practice. Tips should be paid by and for each individual in a cabin, and the general rule of thumb (or palm) is to expect to pay from 10% to 20% of the total cost of the cruise for gratuities — the actual amount within this range is based on the length of the cruise and the extent of personalized services provided. Allow at least $2 to $5 a day for each cabin and dining room steward. Others who may merit tips are deck and wine stewards, porters, and any others who provide personal service. On some ships you can charge your bar tab to your cabin; throw in the tip when you pay it at the end of the cruise. Smart travelers tip twice during a cruise: about midway through the cruise and at the end; even wiser travelers tip a bit at the start of the trip to ensure better service throughout.

Tipping always is a matter of personal preference. In the situations covered above, as well as in any others that arise where you feel a tip is expected or due, feel free to express your pleasure or displeasure. Again, never hesitate to reward excellent and efficient attention and to penalize poor service. Give an extra gratuity and a word of thanks when someone has gone out of his or her way for you. Either way, the more personal the act of tipping, the more appropriate it seems. And if you didn't like the service — or the attitude — don't tip.

Duty-Free Shopping

Duty-free shops are located in all the major international airports throughout Mexico, including Cancún and Cozumel. If common sense says that it is always less expensive to buy goods in an airport duty-free shop than to buy them at home or in the streets of a foreign city, travelers should best be aware of some basic facts. Duty-free, first of all, does not mean that the goods travelers buy will be free of duty when they return to the US. Rather, it means that the shop has paid no import tax acquiring goods of foreign make because the goods are not to be used in the country where the shop is located. This is why duty-free goods are available only in the restricted, passengers-only area of international airports or are delivered to departing passengers on the plane. In a duty-free store, travelers save money only on goods of foreign make because they are the only items on which an import tax would be charged in any other store.

There is little reason to delay buying locally made merchandise and/or souvenirs until reaching the airport. In fact, because airport duty-free shops usually pay high rents, the locally made goods sold in them may well be more expensive than they would be in downtown stores. The real bargains are foreign goods, but — let the buyer beware — not all foreign goods are automatically less expensive in an airport duty-free shop. You can get a good deal on even small amounts of perfume, costing less than the usually required minimum purchase, tax-free. Other fairly standard bargains include spirits, smoking materials, cameras, clothing, watches, chocolates, and other food and luxury items — but first be sure to know what these items cost elsewhere. Terrific savings do exist (they are the reason for such shops, after all), but so do overpriced items that an unwary shopper might find equally tempting. In addition, if you wait to do your shopping at airport duty-free shops, you will be taking the chance that the desired item is out of stock or unavailable.

Customs and Returning to the US

 Whether you return to the United States by air or land, you must declare to the US Customs official before departing everything you have bought or acquired while in Mexico. The customs check can go smoothly, lasting only a few minutes, or can take hours, depending on the officer's instinct. To speed up the process, keep all your receipts handy and try to pack your purchases together in an accessible part of your suitcase. It might save you from unpacking all your belongings.

DUTY-FREE ARTICLES: In general the duty-free allowance for US citizens returning from abroad is $400. This limit includes items used or worn while abroad, souvenirs for friends, and gifts received during the trip. A flat 10% duty based on the "fair retail value in country of acquisition" is assessed on the next $1,000 worth of merchandise brought in for personal use or gifts. Amounts over $1,400 are dutiable at a variety of rates. The average rate for typical tourist purchases is about 12%, but you can find out rates on specific items by consulting *Tariff Schedules of the United States* in a library or at any US Customs Service office.

Families traveling together may make a joint declaration to US Customs, which permits one member to exceed his or her duty-free exemption to the extent that another falls short. Families also may pool purchases dutiable under the flat rate. A family of three, for example, would be eligible for up to a total of $3,000 at the 10% flat duty rate (after each member had used up his or her $400 duty-free exemption) rather than three separate $1,000 allowances.

There are certain articles, however, that are duty-free only up to certain limits. Individuals are allowed 1 carton of cigarettes (200), 100 cigars, and 1 liter of liquor or wine if over 21. Alcohol above this allowance is liable for both duty and an Internal Revenue tax. Antiques, if they are 100 or more years old and you have proof from the seller of that fact, are duty-free, as are paintings and drawings if done entirely by hand. Gold, gold medals, bullion, and up to $10,000 in currency or negotiable instruments may be brought into the US without being declared; sums over $10,000 must be declared in writing. And to avoid paying duty twice, register the serial numbers of computer, watches, and expensive electronic equipment with the nearest US Customs bureau.

Personal exemptions can be used once every 30 days; in order to be eligible, an individual must have been out of the country for more than 48 hours. If any portion of the exemption has been used once within any 30-day period or if your trip is less than 48 hours long, the duty-free allowance is cut to $25.

The allotment for individual "unsolicited" gifts mailed from abroad (no more than one per day per recipient) is $50 retail value per gift. These gifts do not have to be declared and are not included in your duty-free exemption (see below). The package should be clearly marked "Not for Sale," and you should include a receipt for purchases with each package. The US Customs examiner usually will accept this as indicative of the articles' fair retail value, but he or she is empowered to impose a duty if he or she feels the goods have been undervalued. The duty owed is collected by the US Postal Service when the package is delivered.

It is a good idea, if you have accumulated too much while abroad, to mail home any personal effects (made and bought in the US) that you no longer need rather than your foreign purchases. These personal effects pass through US Customs as "American goods returned" and are not subject to duty. More information on mailing packages home from abroad is contained in the US Customs Service pamphlet *Buyer Beware, International Mail Imports* (see below for where to write for this and other useful brochures).

DUTY-FREE CRAFT ITEMS: In January 1976, the United States passed a Generalized System of Preferences (GSP) to help developing nations improve their economies through exports. The GSP, which recognizes dozens of developing nations, including Mexico, allows Americans to bring certain kinds of goods into the US duty-free, and has designated some 2,800 items as eligible for duty-free treatment.

This system entitles you to exceed your $400 duty-free exemption as long as the purchases are eligible for GSP status. The extensive list of eligible goods includes a wide range of categories. A useful pamphlet, which identifies GSP beneficiary nations and goods included in the program, is *GSP and the Traveler;* order "US Customs Publication No. 515" from the US Customs Service (Customs Information, 6 World Trade Ctr., Rm. 201, New York, NY 10048; phone: 212-466-5550). When in Mexico, information about the GSP status of particular items is available from any US Customs office or at the nearest US consulate (see *Medical and Legal Aid and Consular Services,* above, for addresses).

CLEARING CUSTOMS: This is a simple procedure. Forms are distributed by airline or ship personnel before arrival. (Note that a $5-per-person service charge — called a user fee — is collected by airline and cruise lines to help cover the cost of customs checks, but this is included in the ticket price.) If your purchases total no more than the duty-free $400 limit, you need only fill out the identification part of the form and make an oral declaration to the customs inspector. If entering the US with more than $400 worth of goods, you must submit a written declaration.

Customs agents are businesslike, efficient, and not unkind. During the peak season, clearance can take time, but this generally is because of the strain imposed by a number of jumbo jets simultaneously discharging their passengers, not because of unwarranted zeal on the part of the customs people.

Efforts to streamline procedures used to include the so-called Citizens' Bypass Program, which allowed US citizens whose purchases were within their duty-free allowance to go to the "green line," where they simply showed their passports to the customs inspector. Although at the time of this writing this procedure still is being followed at some international airports in the US, most airports have returned to an earlier system. Americans arriving from abroad now have to go through a passport check by the Immigration & Naturalization Service (INS) prior to recovering their baggage and proceeding to customs. (US citizens will not be on the same line as foreign visitors, however, though this additional wait does delay clearance on re-entry into the US.) Although all passengers have to go through this obligatory passport inspection, those entering with purchases within the duty-free limit may be spared a thorough customs inspection, although inspectors still retain the right to search any luggage they choose — so don't do anything foolish.

It is illegal not to declare dutiable items; not to do so, in fact, constitutes smuggling, and the penalty can be anything from stiff fines and seizure of the goods to prison sentences. It simply isn't worth doing. There is a basic rule to buying goods abroad, and it should never be broken: *If you can't afford the duty on something, don't buy it.*

FORBIDDEN IMPORTS: Narcotics, plants, and many types of food are not allowed into the US. Drugs are totally illegal, with the exception of medication prescribed by a physician. It's a good idea to travel with no more than you actually need of any medication and to have the prescription on hand in case any question arises either abroad or when re-entering the US.

Any authentic archaeological find, Spanish colonial art, and other original artifacts cannot be exported from Mexico. They will be confiscated upon departure, and the violator runs the risk of being fined or imprisoned. Mexico also restricts export of gold and silver coins; people interested in such items should check with Mexican Customs. For further information, contact the *Museo National de Antropología (National Institute of History and Anthropology)* Paseo de la Reforma, Bosque de Chapultepec, México, DF 11580 (phone: 905-553-1902).

Tourists have long been forbidden to bring into the United States foreign-made, US trademarked articles purchased abroad (if the trademark is recorded with US Customs) without written permission. It is now possible to enter with one such item in your possession as long as it's for personal use.

The US Customs Service implements the rigorous Department of Agriculture regulations concerning the importation of vegetable matter, seeds, bulbs, and the like. Living vegetable matter may not be imported without a permit, and everything must be inspected, permit or not. Approved items (which do not require a permit) include dried bamboo; beads made of most seeds (but not jequirity beans — the poisonous scarlet and black seed of the rosary pea), Mexican jumping beans, and some viable seeds; coconut shells (unhusked and empty); cones of pine and other trees; roasted coffee beans; most flower bulbs; flowers (without roots); dried or canned fruits, jellies, or jams; polished rice, dried beans, and teas; herb plants (not witchweed); nuts (but not acorns, chestnuts, or nuts with outer husks); dried lichens, mushrooms, and seaweed; most dried spices; and woven items made of straw.

Other processed foods and baked goods usually are okay. Regulations on meat products generally depend on the country of origin and manner of processing. As a rule, commercially canned meat, hermetically sealed and cooked in the can so that it can be stored without refrigeration, is permitted, but not all canned meat fulfills this requirement. Be careful in buying canned chili, for instance. Chili made with peppers, beans, and meat in itself is acceptable, but the pork fat that often is part of it may not be. (The imported brands you see in US stores have been prepared and packaged according to US regulations.) So before stocking up on a newfound favorite, it pays to check in advance — otherwise you might have to leave it behind.

The US Customs Service also enforces federal laws that prohibit the entry of articles made from the furs or hides of animals on the endangered species list. Don't be tempted by sweaters and other garments made from the fine hair of the vicuña (a relative of the domestic llama and alpaca), which is an endangered species. Also beware of shoes, bags, and belts made of crocodile and certain kinds of lizard, and anything made from tortoiseshell; this also applies to preserved crocodiles, lizards, and turtles sometimes sold in gift shops. Some protected species of coral — particularly large chunks of fresh coral and black coral in any form — are restricted (although most jewelry and other items made of coral usually are permitted). And if you're shopping for big-ticket items, beware of fur coats made from the skins of spotted cats. They are sold abroad, but they will be confiscated upon your return to the US, and there will be no refund. For information about other animals on the endangered species list, contact the Department of the Interior, US Fish and Wildlife Service (Publications Unit, 4401 N. Fairfax Dr.,

Rm. 130, Arlington, VA 22203; phone: 703-358-1711), and ask for the free publication *Facts About Federal Wildlife Laws.*

Also note that some foreign governments prohibit the export of items made from certain species of wildlife, and the US honors any such restrictions. Before you go shopping in any foreign country, check with the US Department of Agriculture (G110 Federal Bldg., Hyattsville, MD 20782; phone: 301-436-8413) and find out what items are prohibited from the country you will be visiting.

The US Customs Service publishes a series of free pamphlets with customs information. It includes *Know Before You Go,* a basic discussion of customs requirements pertaining to all travelers; *Buyer Beware, International Mail Imports; Travelers' Tips on Bringing Food, Plant, and Animal Products into the United States; Importing a Car; GSP and the Traveler; Pocket Hints; Currency Reporting; Pets, Wildlife, US Customs; Customs Hints for Visitors* (*Nonresidents*); and *Trademark Information for Travelers.* For the entire series or individual pamphlets, write to the US Customs Service (PO Box 7407, Washington, DC 20044) or contact any of the seven regional offices — in Boston, Chicago, Houston, Long Beach (California), Miami, New Orleans, and New York. The US Customs Service has a taped message whereby callers using Touch-Tone phones can get more information on various topics; the number is 202-566-8195. These pamphlets provide great briefing material, but if you still have questions when you're in Mexico you can contact the US Customs representative at the nearest US consulate.

Sources and Resources

Mexican Consulates and Tourist Offices in the US

 The Mexican government tourist offices and consulates in the US all are sources of general travel information and provide free maps and useful travel literature. You can request information on specific areas, as well as publications relating to your particular areas of interest: accommodations, restaurants, special events, guided tours, and facilities for specific sports. There is no need to send a self-addressed stamped envelope with your request, unless specified.

Where required, the consulates also issue tourist cards and are empowered to sign other official documents — such as commercial and residence visas — and to notarize copies or translations of American documents, which often is necessary for those papers to be considered legal in Mexico.

The Mexican Embassy is located in Washington, DC (1019 19th St. NW, Suite 810, Washington, DC 20036; phone: 202-293-1710). In most cases, however, visitors to Mexico should direct their inquiries and requests to one of the consulates or tourist offices listed below. Below is a complete list of Mexican consulates general, consulates, and Mexican government tourist offices in the US:

Consuls

Albuquerque: Consulate General, Western Bank Bldg., 401 Fifth St. NW, Albuquerque, NM 87102 (phone: 505-247-2139).

Atlanta: Consulate General, 410 S. Tower, CNN Center, Atlanta, GA 30303-2705 (phone: 404-688-3258).

Austin: Consulate General, 200 E. Sixth St., Suite 200, Austin, TX 78701 (phone: 512-478-2866).

Boston: Consulate General, Statler Bldg., 20 Park Plaza, Suite 1212, Boston, MA 02116 (phone: 617-426-4942).

Brownsville: Consulate General, 724 E. Elizabeth St., PO Box 1711, Brownsville, TX 78520 (phone: 512-542-4431).

Buffalo: Consulate, 1875 Harlem Rd., Buffalo, NY 14212 (phone: 716-895-9800).

Calexico: Consulate, 231 W. 2nd St., Calexico, CA 92231 (phone: 619-357-3863).

Chicago: Consulate General, 300 N. Michigan Ave., 2nd Floor, Chicago, IL 60601 (phone: 312-855-1380).

Corpus Christi: Consulate General, 800 N. Shoreline Blvd., N. Tower, 4th Floor, Corpus Christi, TX 78410 (phone: 512-882-3375).

Dallas: Consulate General, 1349 Empire Center, Suite 100, Dallas, TX 75347 (phone: 214-630-7341).

Del Rio: Consulate General, 1010 S. Main St., Del Rio, TX 78840 (phone: 512-774-5031).

Denver: Consulate General, 707 Washington St., Suite A, Denver, CO 80203 (phone: 303-830-0523).

Detroit: Consulate General, 1515 Book Bldg., Washington Blvd., Detroit, MI 48226 (phone: 313-965-1868).

Eagle Pass: Consulate General, 140 Adams St., Eagle Pass, TX 78852 (phone: 512-773-9255).

El Paso: Consulate General, 910 E. San Antonio St., PO Box 812, El Paso, TX 79901 (phone: 915-533-3645).

Fresno: Consulate General, 905 N. Fulton St., Fresno, CA 93728 (phone: 209-233-3065).

Green Bay: Consulate, 901 Howard St., Green Bay, WI 54303 (phone: 414-435-0710).

Honolulu: Consulate, Control Data Bldg., 2828 Paa St., Suite 2115, Honolulu, HI 96819 (phone: 808-833-6331).

Houston: Consulate General, 3015 Richmond Ave., Suite 100, Houston, TX 77098 (phone: 713-524-2300).

Laredo: Consulate General, 1612 Farragut St., PO Box 659, Laredo, TX 78040 (phone: 512-723-6360).

Los Angeles: Consulate General, 2401 W. Sixth St., Los Angeles, CA 90057 (phone: 213-351-6800).

Madison: Consulate, 312 Newcastle Way, Madison, WI 53704 (phone: 608-249-5201).

McAllen: Consulate General, 1418 Beech St., Suite 102, McAllen, TX 78501 (phone: 512-686-0243).

Miami: Consulate General, 780 W. 42nd Ave., Suite 525, Miami, FL 33126 (phone: 305-441-8780).

Nashville: Consulate, 226 Capitol Blvd., Suite 212, Nashville, TN 37219 (phone: 615-244-7430).

New Orleans: Consulate General, World Trade Center, 2 Canal St., Suite 1140, New Orleans, LA 70130 (phone: 504-522-3596).

New York: Consulate General, 8 E. 41st St., New York, NY 10017 (phone: 212-689-0456).

Nogales: Consulate General, 137 Terrace Ave., Nogales, AZ 85621 (phone: 602-287-4850

Norfolk: Consulate, 5121 E. Virginia Beach Blvd., Suite EZ, Norfolk, VA 23502 (phone: 804-461-4553).

Philadelphia: Consulate General, Bourse Bldg., 215 Fifth St., Suite 575, Philadelphia, PA 19106 (phone: 215-922-4262).

Phoenix: Consulate General, 1190 W. Camelback, Suite 110, Phoenix, AZ 85015 (phone: 602-242-7398).

Portland: Consulate, 545 NE 47th Ave., Portland, OR 97213 (phone: 503-233-5662).

Richmond: Consulate, 2420 Pemberton Rd., Richmond, VA 23233 (phone: 804-747-1961).

Rochester: Consulate, World Travel Bureau, 3 First Ave. SW, Rochester, MN 55901 (phone: 507-288-3130).

Sacramento: Consulate, 9845 Horn Rd., Sacramento, CA 95827 (phone: 916-363-3885).

St. Louis: Consulate General, 1015 Locust St., St. Louis, MO 63101 (phone: 314-436-3233).

Salt Lake City: Consulate General, 182 S. 600 East, Suite 202, Salt Lake City, UT 84102 (phone: 801-521-8502).

San Antonio: Consulate General, 127 Navarro St., San Antonio, TX 78205 (phone: 512-227-9145).

San Bernardino: Consulate General, 588 W. 6th St., San Bernardino, CA 92401 (phone: 714-889-9836).

San Diego: Consulate General, 610 A St., Suite 200, San Diego, CA 92101 (phone: 619-231-8414).

San Francisco: Consulate General, 870 Market St., Suite 528, San Francisco, CA 94102 (phone: 415-392-5554).

San Jose: Consulate General, 380 N. First St., Suite 100, San Jose, CA 95112 (phone: 408-294-3413).

Seattle: Consulate General, 2132 Third Ave., Seattle, WA 98121 (phone: 206-448-3526).

Spokane: Consulate, 12005 E. Sprague Ave., Spokane, WA 99214 (phone: 509-926-9531).

Tampa: Consulate, General Shipping Co., 315 Madison St., Tampa, FL 33602 (phone: 813-223-1481).

Tucson: Consulate General, 553 South Stone Ave., Tucson, AZ 85701 (phone: 602-882-5595).

Ministry of Tourism Offices

Chicago: 70 E. Lake St., Suite 1413, Chicago, IL 60601 (phone: 312-565-2786).

Houston: 2707 N. Loop W, Suite 450, Houston, TX 77008 (phone: 713-880-5153).

Los Angeles: 10100 Santa Monica Blvd., Suite 224, Los Angeles, CA 90067 (phone: 213-203-8191).

New York: 405 Park Ave., Suite 1002, New York, NY 10022 (phone: 212-838-2949).

Washington, DC: 1615 L St. NW, Suite 430, Washington, DC 20036 (phone: 202-293-1710).

Cameras and Equipment

Vacations are everybody's favorite time for taking pictures and home movies. After all, most of us want to remember the places we visit — and show them off to others. Here are a few suggestions to help you get the best results from your travel photography or videography.

BEFORE THE TRIP

If you're taking your camera or camcorder out after a long period in mothballs — or have just bought a new one — check it thoroughly before you leave to prevent unexpected breakdowns or disappointing pictures.

1. Still cameras should be cleaned carefully and thoroughly, inside and out. If using a camcorder, run a head cleaner through it. Always use filters to protect your lenses while traveling.

2. Check the batteries for your camera's light meter and flash, and take along extras just in case yours wear out during the trip. For camcorders, bring along extra Nickel-Cadmium (Ni-Cad) batteries; if you use rechargeable batteries, a recharger will cut down on the extras.

3. Using all the settings and features, shoot at least one test roll of film or one videocassette, using the type you plan to take along with you.

EQUIPMENT TO TAKE ALONG

Keep your gear light and compact. Items that are too heavy or bulky to be carried comfortably on a full-day excursion will likely stay in your hotel room, so leave them at home.

1. Invest in a broad camera or camcorder strap if you now have a thin one. It will make carrying the equipment much more comfortable.
2. A sturdy canvas, vinyl, or leather camera or camcorder bag, preferably with padded pockets (not an airline bag), will keep your equipment organized and easy to find. If you will be doing much shooting around the water, a waterproof case is best.
3. For cleaning, bring along a camel's hair brush that retracts into a rubber squeeze bulb. Also take plenty of lens tissue, soft cloths, and plastic bags to protect equipment from dust and moisture.

FILM AND TAPES: If you are concerned about airport security X-rays damaging rolls of undeveloped still film (X-rays do not affect processed film) or tapes, store them in one of the lead-lined bags sold in camera shops. This possibility is not as much of a threat as it used to be, however. In the US, incidents of X-ray damage to unprocessed film (exposed or unexposed) are few because low-dosage X-ray equipment is used virtually everywhere. While the international trend also is toward equipment that delivers less and less radiation, equipment in Mexico tends to be less up-to-date than in some other foreign countries, and is, therefore, less predictable.

If you're traveling without a protective bag, you may want to ask to have your photo equipment inspected by hand. One type of film that should never be subjected to X-rays is the new, very-high-speed ASA 1000 film. The walk-through metal detector devices at airports do not affect film, though the film cartridges may set them off.

You should have no problem finding film or tapes throughout Mexico, particularly in metropolitan and major resort areas. When buying film, tapes, or photo accessories abroad, the best rule of thumb is to stick to name brands with which you are familiar. The availability of film processing labs and equipment repair shops will vary from area to area.

■ **A note about courtesy and caution:** When photographing in Mexico (and anywhere else in the world), ask first. In many of the smaller towns, and even some of the cities, the Indians have superstitions or religious beliefs that photographing them is an insult at best, and at worst, a violation. Furthermore, some governments have security regulations regarding the use of cameras and will not permit the photographing of certain subjects. When in doubt, look for an official who can tell you if your chosen subject is on the restricted list.

USEFUL WORDS
AND PHRASES

Useful Words and Phrases

Unlike the French, who tend to be a bit brusque if you don't speak their language perfectly, the Mexicans do not expect you to speak Spanish — but are very flattered when you try. In many circumstances, you won't have to because the staffs at most hotels, museums, and tourist attractions, as w as at a fair number of restaurants, speak serviceable English, or at least a versio it, which they are usually eager to try — and that means practicing with you. Pa larly when you get off the beaten path, however, you will find at least a rudim knowledge of Spanish very helpful. Don't be afraid of misplaced accents or m gated verbs. Mexicans appreciate your efforts to speak their language and wi best to understand you. They will also make an effort to be understood.

Mexican Spanish has a number of regional dialects, but the dialect of edu in Mexico City is regarded as standard, is used on national television, and by almost everybody, even though their local speech may be quite differe can communicate in what is considered "standard" Spanish, and the dard Mexican Spanish is a very reliable guide to pronunciation.

The list below is a selection of commonly used words and phr your way. Note that in Spanish all nouns are either masculine o singular and plural, and that the adjectives that modify them m and number. Most nouns ending in *o* are masculine (the corr and *uno* or *un*); most nouns ending in *a* are feminine (the fe *una*). Plurals are formed by adding *s* (the articles are Adjectives almost always follow nouns in Spanish. Otherv as in English.

The following pronunciation rules may also be hel

The vowel before the last consonant in a word (exce is an accent mark on another vowel. When the last c the preceding consonant is accented. In addition

   a is pronounced as in *father*
   e is pronounced as in *red*
   i is pronounced as in *machine*
   o is pronounced as in *note*
   u is pronounced as in *rude*
   ei/ey are pronounced as in *vein*
   oi/oy are pronounced as in *joy* _e, ia, and so on), each letter is pro-
   ai/ay are pronounced like *y* in _nounced as in English, with these excep-
   au is pronounced like *ou* in *h*

In general, in vowel letter seq nounced.

Mexican Spanish consonan tions:

The consonants *b, d,* and *g* are pronounced with the air passage slightly open, producing a softer sound. The consonants *p, t,* and *c/k* are pronounced without the aspiration (the strong puff of breath) that characterizes them in English.

b within words is pronounced like the English *v*

d within words is pronounced like *th* in *other*

g before *e* or *i* is pronounced like a strongly aspirated English *h* or German *ch;* otherwise, as above

h is silent

j is pronounced like a strongly aspirated *h*

ll is pronounced like *y* in *youth*

ñ is pronounced like *ny* in *canyon*

is pronounced *k* before *e* or *i: quilo* is pronounced as the English *kilo*

nounced like the casual English *d* in *pedal*

as in the Scottish *farm*

ounced *z* within words preceding a voiced consonant (*b, d, g, m,*
they are pronounced as the English *s*

pressions
uenos días

enas tardes
nas noches

está usted?
gusto en conocerle

I beego!
(Ex
(I'm s
It doesn't
I don't speak
Do you speak
I don't understan
Do you understand
My name is . . .
What is your name?
miss
(younger unmarried
woman)
madame
(mature married
woman)
(mature unmarried
woman)
mister

és?

nde?

señora

doña

señor

open	*abierto/a*
closed	*cerrado/a*
entrance	*entrada*
exit	*salida*
push	*empujar*
pull	*tirar*
today	*hoy*
tomorrow	*mañana*
yesterday	*ayer*

Checking In

I have a reservation.	*He hecho una reserva.*
I would like . . .	*Quisiera . . .*
a single room	*una habitación sencilla*
a double room	*una habitación doble*
a quiet room	*una habitación tranquila*
with bath	*con baño*
with shower	*con ducha*
with a sea view	*con vista asi el mar*
with air conditioning	*con aire acondicionado*
with balcony	*con balcón*
overnight only	*sólo una noche*
a few days	*unos cuantos días*
a week (at least)	*una semana (por los menos)*
with full board	*con pensión completa*
with half board	*con media pensión*
Does that price include . . .	*Esta incluído en el precio . . .*
breakfast?	*el desayuno?*
taxes?	*los impuestos?*
Do you accept traveler's checks?	*Acepta usted cheques de viajero?*
Do you accept credit cards?	*Acepta tarjetas de credito?*
It doesn't work.	*No funcióna.*

Eating Out

ashtray	*un cenicero*
(extra) chair	*una silla (adicional)*
table	*una mesa*
bottle	*una botella*
cup	*una taza*
plate	*un plato*
fork	*un tenedor*
knife	*un cuchillo*
spoon	*una cuchara*
napkin	*una servilleta*

hot chocolate (cocoa)	*un chocolate caliente*
black coffee	*un café negro*
coffee with milk	*café con leche*
cream	*crema*
milk	*leche*
tea	*un té*
fruit juice	*un jugo de fruta*
lemonade	*una limonada*
water	*agua*
mineral water	*agua mineral*
carbonated	* con gas*
noncarbonated	* sin gas*
orangeade	*una naranjada*
beer	*una cerveza*
port	*oporto*
sherry	*jerez*
red wine	*vino tinto*
white wine	*vino blanco*
cold	*frío/a*
hot	*caliente*
sweet	*dulce*
(very) dry	*(muy) seco/a*
bread	*pan*
butter	*mantequilla*
bacon	*tocino*
eggs	*huevos*
hard-boiled	* un huevo cocido*
fried	* huevos fritos*
omelette	* torta de huevos*
soft-boiled	* un huevo cocido*
	* pasado por agua*
scrambled	* huevos revueltos*
honey	*miel*
jam, marmalade	*mermelada*
orange juice	*jugo de naranja*
pepper	*pimienta*
salt	*sal*
sugar	*azúcar*
Waiter!	*Camarero!/Mesero!*
I would like	*Quisiera*
a glass of	* un vaso de*
a bottle of	* una botella de*
a half bottle of	* una media botella de*
a carafe of	* una garrafa de, una*
	* jarra de*
a liter of	* un litro de*
The check, please.	*La cuenta, por favor.*

| Is a service charge included? | *Está el servicio incluído?* |
| I think there is a mistake in the bill. | *Creo que hay un error en la cuenta.* |

Shopping

bakery	*la panadería*
bookstore	*la librería*
butcher shop	*la carnicería*
camera shop	*la tienda de fotografía*
delicatessen	*la tienda de comestibles preparados*
department store	*el almacén grande*
grocery	*la tienda de comestibles*
jewelry store	*la joyería*
newsstand	*el puesto de periódicos*
pastry shop	*la pastelería*
perfume (and cosmetics) store	*perfumería*
pharmacy/drugstore	*las farmacia*
shoestore	*la zapatería*
supermarket	*el supermercado*
tobacconist	*el estanquero*

inexpensive	*barato/a*
expensive	*caro/a*
large	*grande*
larger	*más grande*
too large	*demasiado grande*
small	*pequeño/a*
smaller	*más pequeño/a*
too small	*demasiado pequeño/a*
long	*largo/a*
short	*corto/a*
old	*viejo/a*
new	*nuevo/a*
used	*usado/a*
handmade	*hecho/a a mano*

Is it machine washable?	*Es lavable a máquina?*
How much does it cost?	*Cuánto cuesta esto?*
What is it made of?	*De qué está hecho?*
camel's hair	*pelo de camello*
cotton	*algodón*
corduroy	*pana*
filigree	*filigrana*
lace	*encaje*
leather	*cuero*
linen	*lino*
suede	*ante*
synthetic	*sintético/a*
tile	*baldosa*

| wood | *madera* |
| wool | *lana* |

brass	*latón*
copper	*cobre*
gold	*oro*
gold plated	*dorado*
silver	*plata*
silver plated	*plateado*
stainless steel	*acero inoxidable*

Colors

beige	*beige*
black	*negro/a*
blue	*azul*
brown	*café*
green	*verde*
gray	*gris*
orange	*naranjo/a*
pink	*rosa*
purple	*morado/a*
red	*rojo/a*
white	*blanco/a*
yellow	*amarillo/a*
dark	*obscuro/a*
light	*claro/a*

Getting Around

north	*norte*
south	*sur*
east	*este*
west	*oeste*
right	*derecho/a*
left	*izquierdo/a*

Go straight ahead	*Siga todo derecho*
far	*lejos*
near	*cerca*

gas station	*la gasolinería*
train station	*la estación de ferrocarril*
bus stop	*la parada de autobúses*
subway station	*estación de metro*
airport	*el aeropuerto*
tourist information	*información turística*
map	*el mapa*

one-way ticket	*un billete de ida*
round-trip ticket	*un billete de ida y vuelta*
track	*el andén*
first class	*primera clase*
second class	*segunda clase*

smoking	*fumar*
no smoking	*no fumar*
gasoline	*gasolina*
regular	*nova*
premium	*extra*
leaded	*con plomo*
unleaded	*sin plomo*
diesel	*diesel*
Fill it up, please	*Llénelo, por favor*
oil	*el aceite*
tires	*las llantas*
Where is . . . ?	*Dónde está . . . ?*
Where are . . . ?	*Dónde estan . . . ?*
How far is it from here to . . . ?	*Qué distancia hay desdeaquí hasta . . . ?*
Does this train go to . . . ?	*Va este ferrocarril a . . . ?*
Does this bus go to . . . ?	*Va este autobús a . . . ?*
What time does it leave?	*A qué hora sale?*
Danger	*Peligro*
Caution	*Precaución*
Detour	*Desvio*
Do Not Enter	*Paso Prohibido*
No Parking	*Estacionamiento Prohibido*
No Passing	*Prohibido Pasar*
One Way	*Dirección Unica*
Pay Toll	*Peaje*
Pedestrian Zone	*Zona Peatonal*
Reduce Speed	*Despacio*
Steep Incline	*Fuerte Declive*
Stop	*Alto*
Use Headlights	*Encender los faros*
Yield	*Ceda el Paso*

Personal Items and Services

aspirins	*aspirinas*
Band-Aids	*curitas*
barbershop	*la barbería*
beauty shop	*el salón de belleza*
condom	*condón*
dry cleaner	*la tintorería*
hairdresser's	*la peluquería*
laundromat	*la lavandería*
post office	*el correo*
postage stamps	*estampillas*

sanitary napkins	*unos paños higiénicos*
shampoo	*un champú*
shaving cream	*espuma de afeitar*
soap	*el jabón*
tampons	*unos tampones higiénicos*
tissues	*Kleenex*
toilet paper	*papel higiénico*
toothpaste	*pasta de dientes*
Where is the bathroom?	*Dónde está el baño?*
toilet?	*excusado?*
MEN	*Caballeros*
WOMEN	*Señoras*

Days of the Week

Monday	*Lunes*
Tuesday	*Martes*
Wednesday	*Miércoles*
Thursday	*Jueves*
Friday	*Viernes*
Saturday	*Sábado*
Sunday	*Domingo*

Months

January	*Enero*
February	*Febrero*
March	*Marzo*
April	*Abril*
May	*Mayo*
June	*Junio*
July	*Julio*
August	*Agosto*
September	*Septiembre*
October	*Octubre*
November	*Noviembre*
December	*Diciembre*

Numbers

zero	*cero*
one	*uno*
two	*dos*
three	*tres*
four	*cuatro*
five	*cinco*
six	*seis*
seven	*siete*
eight	*ocho*
nine	*nueve*
ten	*diez*
eleven	*once*
twelve	*doce*
thirteen	*trece*
fourteen	*catorce*
fifteen	*quince*

sixteen	*dieciséis*
seventeen	*diecisiete*
eighteen	*dieciocho*
nineteen	*diecinueve*
twenty	*veinte*
thirty	*treinta*
forty	*cuarenta*
fifty	*cincuenta*
sixty	*sesenta*
seventy	*setenta*
eighty	*ochenta*
ninety	*noventa*
one hundred	*cien*
one thousand	*mil*

THE ISLANDS

CANCÚN

(pronounced Cahn-*koon*)

For many years, small groups of divers and determined sun worshipers had the lagoons, beaches, and islands of Mexico's Caribbean Coast along the Yucatán Peninsula almost to themselves. People planning a trip to the Yucatán had to choose among the Maya ruins at Chichén Itzá, Uxmal, and Tulum; sun and sea sports along the coast of Quintana Roo, including Xel-Ha (pronounced Shell-*ha*) and Akumal; or the islands of Isla Mujeres, Cancún, or Cozumel. Transportation was too difficult to make all sides of the vacation coin easily accessible. About the only visitors who had enough time to do it all were the wealthy divers who belonged to private clubs tucked away in silent lagoons along the coast and who flew private planes into the Yucatán for stays of 3 weeks or more.

In those days, Mexico's largest island, Cozumel, was the preferred Caribbean destination of less well heeled travelers. They flew into Mérida, grabbed a plane to Cozumel, and flopped there on the sand for several days of swimming, diving, fishing, and lots and lots of lazing. Cancún was an undeveloped spit of land off the coast to the north.

No more. All that changed when FONATUR, the government agency charged with improving Mexico's tourist facilities, chose Cancún as its first multimillion-dollar experiment in resort development. It was discovered that Cancún had all the natural attributes of a resort area — beautiful sea and some of the best diving in the world, adequate space and facilities, proximity to the ruins — and FONATUR proceeded without hesitation. So new it wasn't even marked on road maps in 1970, Cancún has blossomed into one of the world's most bustling — and some feel overdeveloped — young resorts.

In reality Cancún is a Caribbean island — more a sandbar shaped like an emaciated sea horse — 14 miles long and a quarter mile wide, connected by a causeway at its nosepoint to Cancún City, the support city on the mainland where over 200,000 people now live. For most of the island's length, island and peninsula are separated by unruffled Nichupté Lagoon. Most of the island's resort hotels are scattered along the skinny east–west sand spit that forms the seahorse's head. Along its back, the Caribbean surf rolls in along a 12-mile length of shore with intermittent stretches of powdery white beach. There are a couple of commercial hotels in Cancún City, catering mostly to business travelers, but good for budget travelers as well, and there are some pleasant hotels with pools that offer free transportation to and from the beach.

One of the major dividends of the development at Cancún is that travelers no longer have to choose between culture and carousal. Part of the Cancún master plan — a 15-year program of development — is a system of roads, transportation, and communications that connects the resort area to the major ruins and Mérida. Both Cancún and Cozumel benefit from a beeline road from the sea to Chichén Itzá, along which tour buses roll daily. And both are helped by the improvement of the shoreline road to Xel-Ha and the small but interesting ruins at Tulum and Cobá.

But the sea is still the major attraction. The crystalline Caribbean offers visibility to 100 feet, and the stretch of sea along the peninsula and into Belize is world-famous as an area rich in fish, wrecks, and coral. Nichupté Lagoon is protected from the open sea. But the government poured some $80 million into the area to assure a complete resort infrastructure — recreational facilities like the 18-hole Robert Trent Jones, Sr. golf course, a panoply of hotels, ships for touring and boats for sailing — to augment the area's Caribbean attributes.

What the people of Cancún, Cozumel, and Isla Mujeres never imagined, however, was Hurricane Gilbert, which in September 1988 sent huge waves and torrential wind-driven rain over the three islands, seemingly determined to destroy everything in its path. Indeed, on tiny Isla Mujeres just across the bay, all traces of the remains of a centuries-old Maya temple were literally blown out to sea. However, "Gilberto" was no match for the resilience of the Mexican people. With an outpouring of assistance from the rest of the country — and indeed the world — palms were replanted, windows replaced, and rubbish removed. Within a few months, it was just a question of waiting for the sea to return the beach sand and for the new palm trees to take root. Many of the beaches on Cancún's Caribbean side, however, are still not as wide as they once were, while others on the Bahía Mujeres side are wider than before Gilbert hit.

Paseo Kukulcán, the boulevard running from one end of Cancún to the other, has been expanded from two lanes to four to accommodate the anticipated crowds descending to see the "new Cancún." For in addition to the construction attendant to the hurricane-related repairs, many new hotels and support facilities are also being built. Visitors joke that the official bird of Cancún should be the construction crane. There are close to 50 hotels now in operation, plus condominium buildings, shopping centers, restaurants and marinas scattered along Kukulcán. Cancún's weather and facilities are an authentic lure, but this is not the place for those who prize peace and privacy.

COZUMEL

(pronounced Co-zoo-*mehl*)

Although it was the first island to be developed in the area, Cozumel has grown at a much slower pace than Cancún, and tends to attract visitors who are more interested in skin diving and fishing than in the glamour and nightlife of its glitzier neighbor. Plans for several new hotels were dropped because of potential threats to the island's ecological system — not to mention its tranquillity.

Everything moves at a slower pace in Cozumel. Whether strolling, cycling, or touring the island in a rented jeep, you can relax and take in the scenery without the distrations of Cancún's big-city milieu.

Eleven miles off the mainland coast, Cozumel is Mexico's largest island. A favorite haunt of undersea explorer Jacques Cousteau, the island's guest registry also boasts the names of Queen Elizabeth II of England and King Gustav of Sweden. According to local accounts, Charles A. Lindbergh flew Anne Morrow to the island during their courtship in the late 1920s.

The name Cozumel comes from the Mayan phrase *cuzam huzil,* which means "land of the swallows." For over 12 centuries, Cozumel was the exclusive domain of the Maya. As early as AD 300, this 29-mile-long island was the site of a shrine to the lunar goddess Ix-chel, who benevolently watched over weavers and pregnant women but, when angered, released her wrath through violent hurricanes and torrential rains.

Spanish sea captain Gonzalo Guerrero is credited with having been the first European to set foot on Cozumel, when he drifted ashore after being shipwrecked in 1511. Legend has it that Guerrero married the daughter of a local chieftain and introduced the Maya to Western culture. Seven years later, Hernán Cortés and Juan de Grijalva claimed Cozumel for the Spanish crown, bringing with them the plague of smallpox, which essentially eradicated the island's population.

For the next 300 years, Cozumel remained almost uninhabited, except for the occasional pirate ship or adventure seeker who stumbled ashore in hopes of finding lost treasures. It was not until the mid-1800s that Cozumel was finally repopulated by Maya refugees fleeing persecution during the brutal Castes War.

During World War II, the US government used Cozumel as a military airfield and supply base. GIs stationed on the island during that time were, perhaps, the first Americans to discover its underwater attractions.

Cozumel is a scuba diver's paradise, with underwater visibility commonly reaching 250 feet and subaquatic scenery that includes black coral and hundreds of species of tropical fish. Palancar, its main coral reef, is the second-largest natural coral formation in the world. To preserve their beauty, all the reefs surrounding the island have been declared national parks by the Mexican government.

Fishermen are also drawn to Cozumel, where the channel between the mainland and the island — populated with marlin, sailfish, grouper, and mackerel — runs as deep as 600 feet. With catches of up to 120 pounds, several world sailfish records have been set on Cozumel.

With a total population of just over 30,000, the island has only one town, San Miguel, which serves simultaneously as the main seaport, commercial center and restaurant zone. Most of Cozumel's hotels are spread to the left and right of town along the main road, which loops around the southern coastline. There are also 32 registered archaeological sites on the island, although most are unrestored and inaccessible.

ISLA MUJERES

(pronounced *Ees*-lah Moo-*hair*-ehs)

Words like "quaint," "casual," and "easygoing" may never be applied to a super-resort like Cancún, but just across the bay from this island is Isla Mujeres, just 5 miles long and a half-mile wide, and situated 6 miles off Puerto Juárez on the Yucatán Peninsula. Unlike Cancún, Isla Mujeres — with its few charming, but fairly simple, hotels and wide expanses of beach — is an unpretentious little fishing village where things move at a turtle's pace and informality is the order of the day. Most places have phones and there are a few paved roads, but its tiny town, lagoons, reefs, and transparent waters make it a pleasant retreat for snorkelers, skin divers, and loafers.

The name Isla Mujeres (Isle of Women) was coined by the first Spaniards who set foot on this easternmost corner of Mexico. It seems that the ancient Maya had used the island for ceremonial purposes and had left these life-size statues of their goddesses to ward off hurricanes from the sea. While the deities may have been successful in protecting the island from inclement weather, their powers did not save Isla Mujeres from falling into European hands. By 1520, the island was owned and controlled by the conquistadores.

Isla Mujeres, then known as "Dolores," was a vital lookout point for the Spanish, but offered little economically. It did, however, become a favorite haunt for pirates and criminals alike. One of the island's most notorious pirates was Fermín Mundaca, a slave trader, who fell in love with a native girl; in an effort to win her favor the buccaneer presented her with a magnificent mansion on beautifully landscaped grounds. The girl rejected him, fleeing instead with a younger man, and the old pirate mourned his unrequited love to his death. Today, the crumbling ruins of Mundaca's mansion have been reclaimed by the Mexican government, which plans to convert the grounds into an ecological reserve.

Isla Mujeres is a long strip of rocky beach that was once connected to the country's mainland but broke away millions of years ago. Mujeres Bay, a pale green gauntlet that runs between Puerto Juárez and Isla Mujeres, is actually a large sea canal. Once scarcely populated, the island today has 14,000 inhabitants, who live in the tiny village of Isla at the northern tip. This growth has been a direct result of the rise in tourism during the past 5 years. The rest of Isla Mujeres is nothing more than open spaces with an occasional fishing hut or a resort restaurant operated by one of the many cruisers that carry visitors from Cancún each day.

The island's most famous attraction is El Garrafón, an underwater national park located at the southern end and renowned for its coral reef and tropical fish. It's a great place to snorkel or dive, but it can't compete with Palancar Reef.

CANCÚN, COZUMEL, AND ISLA MUJERES AT-A-GLANCE

SEEING THE ISLANDS: The best way to get a bird's-eye view of all three islands is from *Pelican Pier Avioturismo*'s ultra-light seaplane that takes off from Cancún's lagoon for a 15-minute flight over the hotel zone (phone: 30315 or 31935). Kukulcán Boulevard is the only street on Cancún. In mainland Cancún City, Avenida Tulum is the main drag, but Avenida Yaxchilan is shaping up as the address of the more fashionable shops and restaurants. The village of San Miguel on Cozumel is about 10 blocks long and a few blocks wide; with many shops, restaurants, and boutiques, it offers much to see and savor. Isla Mujeres has plenty of choice seafood restaurants, and some of the finest handicrafts for sale, along the streets near the main plaza.

SPECIAL PLACES: Cancún is spread out, but there are lots of ways to get around. Taxis are plentiful, city bus service is good, and cars, motor scooters, and bicycles are available for rent. There are regular bus and boat tours to several areas along with scheduled air service to more distant points and charters from *Pelican Pier Avioturismo* (phone: 30315 or 31935). You can easily tour the little village of San Miguel on foot or drive around the rest of Cozumel. The best way to get around Isla Mujeres is simply to walk. If you prefer, rent a bike or moped to wisk you to the nearest secluded beach or the beautiful national park, El Garrafón.

CANCÚN

Beaches – Many of the hotels on the island are on the beach; the beaches themselves, however, are federal property, so anyone can use them. The most popular public beach on the island is called Chac-Mool, and it is lovely. The "back side" of the island faces out on calm, lovely lagoons, favorite spots for divers and novice swimmers.

Cruises – Any number of voyages may be made from Cancún or nearby points. Ferries (passengers only) leave Punta Sam and Puerto Juárez several times each day for Isla Mujeres. If you wish to take your car, take the ferry from Puerto Morelos. There are also daily ferries (one has room for cars) from Playa del Carmen for Cozumel. The glass-bottom *Fiesta Maya,* with continental breakfast, lunch, an open bar, a show, and orchestra on board, sails to Isla Mujeres every morning, and costs about $30. Many hotel travel desks offer day cruises to Isla Mujeres that include lunch and snorkeling equipment for about $30. Catamarans sail from the *Cancún Yacht Club* through the Lagoon of Love to the ruins at El Rey, said to have been the harem of Maya kings. The *Corsario,* a 50-foot replica of an 18th-century pirate ship, sails daily to Isla Mujeres for snorkeling at El Garrafón, with a seafood lunch included. The *México,* billed as the world's largest water jet, makes the round trip daily to Cozumel. *Aviomar* offers the Escape to Cozumel tour, which leaves Playa Linda Pier daily at 9 AM via bus and water jet to Cozumel; the day includes sightseeing, swimming, refreshments, and lunch on the beach — all for $76 (phone: 46433). There are also 7 daily round trips from Cozumel to Playa del Carmen (phone: 20847 on Cozumel; 46656 on Cancún). The trimaran *Aqua Quinn* (phone: 31883 or 30100) sails daily to Isla Mujeres from Cancún for snorkeling at El Garrafón, with lunch and open bar included. It leaves at 11 AM and returns around 5 PM. The *El Corsario,* a motorized galleon for snorkeling, provides guests with a visit to the giant sea turtle pen, and a buffet lunch (phone: 30200).

Dr. Alfredo Barrera Marín Botanical Gardens – Close to Cancún City, in the direction of Tulum, is this 150-acre nature preserve. Trails wind through the semi-evergreen tropical forests that border a mangrove swamp. Closed Mondays. Admission charge (no phone).

El Castillo – A small replica of El Castillo Pyramid (the original is in Chichén Itzá) sits at the head of Plaza Caracol. Every night, except Tuesdays, the phenomenon of the spring and fall equinoxes is re-created with a spectacular light show. The lights actually produce illusionary shadows of a serpent's body leading from the temple on top to the carved head on the bottom. The show in Spanish begins at 7 PM; in English, at 8 and 9 PM. Admission charge.

COZUMEL

Cozumel Museum – Impressive 3-D models of underwater caves in the offshore reefs; historical and ethnographical exhibits. There's also a library, temporary exhibits, a restaurant, and crafts shop. Closed Saturdays. Admission charge (phone: 21277).

Plaza – The heart of Cozumel is a wide plaza near where the ferry docks, a spot everyone manages to find. Most of the shops and restaurants are here. Motor scooter renters must be careful not to park on the plaza; parking is forbidden and "motos" may be hauled off to scooter prison — and you'll be inconvenienced by having to pay the fine and arrange for their release.

Chankanab Lagoon and Botanical Gardens – About 5 miles (8 km) south of town, it's something of a natural aquarium filled with multicolored tropical fish. However, since suntan lotion collects in the water and harms the fish, swimming and snorkeling are not permitted in the lagoon (but are allowed at the nearby beach).

San Francisco Beach – On the southern tip of Cozumel, the island's best beach now can be reached by paved road. If you're not on a cruise providing lunch, either of the two seafood restaurants here is a good choice.

Punta Morena – At this beach on the open Caribbean side of the island, the surf is rougher and swimming can be dangerous. There's a thatch-hut restaurant out this way, a good place to try grilled fish and a beer.

ISLA MUJERES

El Garrafón – This underwater national park is the island's most famous attraction, and is located at the southern end. Renowned for its coral reef and tropical fish, it's a great place to snorkel or dive; but it can't compete with Palancar Reef (see DIVERSIONS). There's also a sea museum with an aquarium and pieces of wrecked historic galleons. In the middle of Isla Mujeres is a turtle pen, where you can catch a ride on a giant turtle, if you're so inclined.

Caves of the Sleeping Sharks – Those with a thirst for danger will be drawn here. It's about the only place on earth where these man-eating beasts will sit still for human caresses. If you prefer something less risky, you might want to visit some of the locals' pet sea turtles and, if you can catch one, hitch a free ride on its back.

EXCURSIONS

Contoy Island – A national park, completely undeveloped, Contoy is a coral island populated by sea gulls, pelicans, petrels, cormorants, herons, and other sea birds whose numbers are, unfortunately, diminishing. It is especially popular with divers, fishermen, picnickers, and bird watchers. Boats make daily 19-mile (30-km) excursions from Isla Mujeres, which include a fresh fish lunch.

Akumal – One of the best snorkeling and scuba diving spots along Mexico's Caribbean Coast, Akumal is 63 miles (101 km) south of Cancún — and 22 miles (35 km) south of Playa del Carmen, the port closest to Cozumel — on Route 307. Once headquarters of a private club run by undersea explorers in search of treasure from the Spanish Main, Akumal now has an underwater museum where anchors and guns encrusted in coral lie among the rocks, much the way they originally were discovered.

Stops along Route 307 on the way to Akumal include Crococún, Mexico's only crocodile farm, and a biological research center, 19 miles (30 km) south of Cancún; the charming beach of Punta Bete (15 miles/24 km south of Crococún), where thousands of sea turtles lay their eggs every spring — as they do in Pamul, about 22 miles (35 km) farther south; and the sun-kissed beach, cenote, and ruins of Xcaret (16 miles/26 km south of Punta Bete, between Playa del Carmen and Pamul). Also along the route is the rapidly growing high-priced resort of Puerto Aventuras (just 3 miles/5 km south of Pamul and the same distance north of Akumal), which already features the largest marina in Mexico, a 9-hole golf course (with 9 more holes scheduled for completion this year), tennis courts, and a marine archaeology center whose collection includes relics salvaged from a Spanish ship that sank off the coast in 1741. There is also a luxury complex with villa-like suites, a pool, and a restaurant.

If you continue 5 miles (8 km) south of Akumal, a sign welcomes you to Chemuyil, "The most beautiful beach in the world." Also nearby is Xel-Ha, a lagoon that is a natural aquarium.

■ **EXTRA SPECIAL:** Tulum, a once thriving Maya center — built on a cliff above the sea and thought to be a major trading post — remains a place of mystery. Apparently inhabited at the time of the Spanish conquest, when other ceremonial cities had been abandoned, it was fortified and surrounded by a great wall. Tulum reached its apogee between AD 1000 and 1600, during the decline of the Maya civilization, and lacks the magnitude of such earlier cities as Chichén Itzá and Uxmal. The buildings found at Tulum are comparatively small in scale. However, the setting of Tulum — overlooking the fine white beaches and crystalline blue waters of the Caribbean — is magnificent and the trip should not be missed. The ruins are about 80 miles (128 km) from Cancún, with which it is connected by daily bus service. Admission charge.

Discovered in 1840, with excavations begun in 1974, Cobá was one of the largest cities in the Yucatán, covering about 80 square miles. Like Tulum, it is thought to have been a trade center with a population of 50,000 and was connected by a network of highways with other major Maya cities such as Chichén Itzá and Uxmal. About a half-mile south of Tulum is a road that heads 26 miles (41 km) inland to this fascinating jungle-bound site on the banks of an island lagoon.

Extending south of Tulum to Punta Alticub is Sian Ka'an, a 1.2-million-acre biosphere reserve, containing tropical forests, mangrove swamps, salt marshes, palm-rimmed beaches, archaeological ruins, and coral reefs, which combines the protection of wildlife with the balanced use of its resources. It's a paradise for bird watchers and crocodile and butterfly lovers. If you venture far enough into the jungle (not recommended as a solo journey), you're likely to come across a jaguar or some other member of the large cat species. There are two fine hotels on the reserve, where you also are likely to run into some millionaire yachtsmen cruising the Caribbean: the pricey *Club de Pesca Boca Paila* (represented by *Carltony Tours,* A.P. 59, Cozumel, Q.R.; phone: 21176; 800-245-1950 in the US) and the *Pez Maya* (phone: 20072 on Cozumel). Considerably more rustic accommodations are available at *El Retiro* at Punta Xamach (clean cabins, but no private baths), or at *Posada Cuzam* at Punta Allen (thatch palm tepees). In Punta Allen, Sonia Lopez will provide a good meal, but only if you ask nicely, and arrangements can be made with one of the fishermen to visit *los cayos* (the keys). For guided visits, contact the *Association of Friends of Sian Ka'an* (Plaza Américas, Suite 48, Cancún, Q.R.; phone: 42201). For further information on Cobá and Sian Ka'an, see *The Yucatán Peninsula: Cancún to Chetumal, and Belize,* DIRECTIONS.

SOURCES AND RESOURCES

 TOURIST INFORMATION: The best sources of information on Cancún are a pocket-size, biannual magazine, *Cancún Tips,* and the monthly periodical *Cancún Scene,* both available in many hotel rooms or on sale around town. Two similar publications, *Cozumel: What to Do and Where to Go* and *Cozumel Today,* provide up-to-date information about that island. On Isla Mujeres, the *Islander* tells you what's going on. Hotel travel desks are other good sources. The Cancún Tourist Office is in the FONATUR building at Cobá and Nader (phone: 43238), and there's an information booth on Avenida Tulum and Tulipanes, near the *Ki-Huic Market* (phone: 48073). Hotel personnel are also very helpful. On Cozumel, the tourist office (phone: 20972) is in the Plaza del Sol building, and there is an information booth on the main square and at the tourist dock. The Isla Mujeres Tourist Office is at 18 Francisco I. Madero (phone: 20164).

Local Coverage – The *News,* an English-language daily, is flown in from Mexico City; its Sunday travel supplement, *Vistas,* usually carries reports on Cancún and Cozumel.

GETTING AROUND: Bus – Cancún probably has the best municipal bus service in Mexico. Routes follow a straight line, and the vehicles are seldom crowded. Transfers between the airport and hotels are handled by a fleet of minibuses that depart promptly, handle all luggage, and charge about $3 per person. From 6 AM until midnight, another bus flock covers the distance between Cancún City and the Tourist Zone's hotels and shopping area; fare is about 25¢, and it's a popular way to get around. Buses run along the island, passing all the hotels, and go on into the city. Buses also go out to Puerto Juárez, where the ferries leave for Isla Mujeres. Intercity buses, *Aerotransportes del Caribe (ADC;* phone: 988-41365) and *Autotransportes del Oriente (ADO;* phone: 43301) offer four departures daily for Akumal, Tulum, and Chetumal. There are ten departures each day for Chichén Itzá and Mérida.

Taxi – Small green-and-white cabs are available at reasonable fares, according to zone, in Cancún City (fare from the city to the farthest hotel is about $6). Usually taxis are available at all the hotels on the island. If not, a doorman or bellman will call one quickly. In Cancún City there is a taxi stand on Avenida Tulum.

Car Rental – In Cancún City, several agencies offer rental cars and jeeps for about $35 up to $165 a day, including mileage: *Avis* (phone: 42147, 42328), *Dollar* (phone: 41709), *Econo-Rent* (phone: 48482), *Thrifty* (phone: 30373), and *Rent-autos Kankun* (phone: 41175). On Cozumel, *Rentadora Cozumel* (phone: 21120) has jeeps — the best bet for local roads — for about $60 a day, including insurance, tax, and mileage. There are no rental agencies on Isla Mujeres.

Mopeds – Small motorbikes are an easy way to get around and are available at many Cancún hotels. The *Casa Maya* (phone: 30138 or 30354) and *Frankie's* at the *Krystal* (phone: 32033) are two that rent mopeds for about $35 a day. On Cozumel, *Rentadora Cozumel* (phone: 21120 or 21530) charges $25 for a 24-hour rental. They also rent bicycles for $3 a day. On Isla Mujeres, motorbikes — available about 50 paces from the ferry dock, also for about $20 a day — are the only way to go.

Tours – There are dozens of tour operators on Cancún, all of them with hotel offices on the island. Guests at smaller hotels can arrange for tours with any of these operators. Both bus and automobile tours are available.

SPECIAL EVENTS: Held in April or May, the annual spring *Regata del Sol al Sol,* organized by the *Isla Mujeres Yacht Club,* begins in St. Petersburg, Florida and finishes at Isla Mujeres. The annual *Cancún Fair* takes place in November, with bullfights, cockfights, dances, and shows. The annual billfish tournament held on Cozumel each May brings in sportsmen from all over, especially Florida, which sends a virtual fleet. Very much worth seeing on the first day of spring or fall is the Chichén Itzá phenomenon, when light and shadow strike the Castillo Pyramid in such a manner that the snake god Kukulcán (also known as Quetzalcóatl) appears to be crawling down the side of the monument.

 SHOPPING: In addition to such regional items as *guayabera* shirts (dressy-casual with a tucked — sometimes embroidered — front), *huipil* dresses, and Panama hats, goods and handicrafts from all over Mexico (and the world) are sold on Cancún. The big and bustling *Ki-Huic* (Av. Tulum near Cobá) is the city-sponsored crafts market, featuring some 44 stalls with an occasional find, but generally not the best prices in town. In the hotel zone, or Zona Turística, some of the most elegant shops can be found at the *El Parián, Plaza Caracol, Mayfair, La Mansión–Costa Blanca, Flamingo Plaza, Plaza Nautilus,* and *Plaza Terramar* shopping centers.

On Cozumel, the works of some 200 first-rate Mexican artists are displayed at *Bazar Cozumel* (Av. Juárez), which features silver tapestries with modern art motifs, weavings, pottery, and much more at fair prices. Also worth visiting is *Plaza del Sol,* a nest of nearly a dozen art, crafts, jewelry, and import boutiques, including *Los Cinco Soles,* which carries papier-mâché, carved wood, onyx items, and coral jewelry.

Shops on all three islands generally are open from 10 AM to 2 PM and from 4 to 7 PM; although stores post these hours, they may not always open on time.

CANCÚN

Artland – Rubbings, batiks, paintings, and jewelry, all inspired by Maya designs. Hotel zone, *Flamingo Plaza* (phone: 32663).

Caroli – Jewelry and art objects crafted from sterling silver and semi-precious stones. Hotel zone, *Flamingo Plaza* (phone: 50985).

La Casita – Arts, crafts, decorative items, leather, jewelry, and Mexican-inspired clothing. Downtown, 114 Tulum (no phone).

Los Castillo and Lily Castillo – Both are branches of one of Taxco's finest silversmith's, and both carry fine hand-crafted jewelry and art objects. Known for its "wedded" metals, a union of silver, copper, and brass; also designs in stoneware with silver inlays. Hotel zone, *Plaza Caracol* (phone: 31084).

Dominique Imports – French perfume, jewelry, and fashions. Downtown at 33 and 45 Tulum, and *Plaza Caracol* on the island (no phones).

Don Cotton – Wonderful T-shirts in vivid colors with rain forest, Caribbean, and Cancún motifs. The owners also run *Tango* (see below). Hotel zone, *Plaza Caracol* (no phone).

Enea – One-of-a-kind designs for women and a unique selection of handicrafts that use unusual combinations of materials, such as pottery and straw. Downtown, 79 Tulum (phone: 41729).

Galerías Colonial – Tableware with beautifully painted patterns, carved marble knickknacks, and chess sets. Hotel zone, *Plaza Caracol* (no phone).

Galería Maty Roca – Paintings, sculptures, and lithographs by some of Mexico's best contemporary artists. Maty Roca is a friendly woman who is a good source of information, not only on art but on Cancún as well. Hotel zone, *Mayfair Shopping Center* (no phone).

Georgia – Women's fashions by Georgia Charukas, whose romantic designs were inspired by the traditional Mexican wedding dress. Hotel zone, *Mayfair Shopping Center* (no phone).

Gucci – *Not* the real thing, it carries copies of the famous designer leatherwear at very good prices. Hotel zone, *Plaza Caracol.*

Las Mariposas – Super Mexican clothes — muslin caftans, batik shirts, tunics, tops, and shirts — all at reasonable prices. If they don't have your size, ask; they often can fill your request in a day or two. Silver and coral jewelry is sold here, too. *Plaza América* (no phone).

Pali – An unusual and varied selection of some of the very best of Mexico's handicrafts — ceramics, textiles, papier-mâché — at reasonable prices. Hotel zone, *Flamingo Plaza* (phone: 33256).

Ronay – One of Mexico's most prestigious jewelers, specializing in gold and coral designs. Hotel zone, *Plaza Caracol* (phone: 31261).

Tane – Silver and vermeil jewelry, tableware, and art objects — many with traditional pre-Hispanic designs. Others are antique reproductions. In the *Camino Real* (phone: 30100) and *Hyatt Regency* (phone: 30966) hotels.

Tango – In *Plaza Caracol,* more of the same T-shirts that *Don Cotton* (see above) carries in the same plaza (phone: 30114).

COZUMEL

La Casita – The parent of the Cancún store and the source of more smashing Mexican resort clothes, as well as Sergio Bustamante's imaginative animal and bird sculptures. Av. Rafael E. Melgar (phone: 20198).

Plaza del Sol – A nest of nearly a dozen art, crafts, jewelry and import boutiques including *Orbi,* purveyor of imported perfumes, jewelry, and specialty foods. Av. Rafael E. Melgar (phone: 20685).

ISLA MUJERES

La Bahía – Near the ferry dock, this shop carries an upscale selection of beachwear, and rents diving gear (no phone).

Rachat and Romé – Outstanding jewelry designed and crafted by the friendly Cuban who owns this place. In the flamingo-colored building just a few steps from the ferry dock (no phone).

■**Beach (and Street) Vendors:** Although "legally" outlawed in this part of Mexico, these ambulant salespeople manage to materialize on almost every beach. They can be persistent, so don't be afraid of offending them by a lack of courtesy. Unless you are interested in their wares, simply make your feelings understood with a firm "no."

SPORTS: On the islands, sports tend to be for participants, not spectators. The most convenient place to get the latest information is in the lobbies of most hotels.

Boating – Craft large and small, power and sail, crewed and uncrewed, are available on Cancún. Make arrangements at any hotel travel desk, or at *Marina Stouffer Presidente* (phone: 30330), *Club Lagoon* (phone: 31111), *Aqua-Quinn* (phone: 31883 or 988-30100), *Marina Camino Real* (phone: 30100), and *Royal Yacht Club* (phone: 50391). The *Regata del Sol al Sol,* from St. Petersburg, Florida, ends at Isla Mujeres. It's held yearly in April or May, and is followed by the *Amigos* regatta around the island.

Bullfights – Cancún now has its own small bullring, which occasionally attracts major matadors. Corridas are held on Wednesdays at the *Plaza de Toros* in Cancún City. This modern 3-tiered arena has a seating capacity of 6,000, and provides ample parking for bullfight aficionados.

Fishing – White marlin, bluefin tuna, and sailfish lure strong men and women to do battle on the deep sea. Sailfish are in season from March to mid-July; bonito and dolphin, May to early July; wahoo and kingfish, May to September; and plenty of barracuda, red snapper, bluefin, grouper, mackerel, and white marlin year-round. Closer to shore, light-tackle anglers attempt to hook the elusive permit. Boats, both large and small, are available on Cancún at *Club Lagoon, Wild Goat Marina* (phone: 31111), *Avioturismo* (phone: 30315), *Royal Yacht Club* (phone: 50391), and *Aqua Tours* (phone: 30227 or 30400). On Cozumel, try *Aquarius Travel* (2 Calle 3 Sur; no phone), a good place to charter a boat. Here again, hotels can make all the arrangements. Firms charge about $65 per person per day or $240 to $310 for a half day for groups. On Isla Mujeres, *Cooperativa Isla Mujeres* (Av. Rueda Medina; phone: 20274) and *México Divers* (near the dock; phone: 20131) arrange trips for 4 for about $350 a day.

Golf – On Cancún, *Pok-Ta-Pok* (phone: 30871), the Robert Trent Jones, Sr. golf course, offers gently rolling fairways bordered by palms, with the Caribbean breeze making play comfortable throughout the day. Clubs and carts may be rented; open daily. The greens fee is $30; carts, $20. There is also a restaurant.

Horseback Riding – *Hacienda San José de las Vegas* has escorted horseback tours from Cancún through the jungle, four times a day, Mondays through Saturdays. On Sundays, they rent horses by the hour. At Km 11.5 on the road to Tulum (phone: 40373).

Jet Skiing – The lagoon is great for this water sport, which requires a minimum of learning time. The skis slow down and stay with you should you fall off. Available on Cancún at the *Royal Yacht Club* (phone: 50391) and *Marina Jet Ski* (phone: 30766).

Scuba and Snorkeling – Cancún's best scuba diving and snorkeling place is in the reef-filled waters off its southern point. Dive trips and equipment rental can be arranged through your hotel. A 5-hour dive trip including pool checkout and an ocean dive costs about $40, including equipment. Snorkel gear rents for about $5 per person for the day. Guided scuba trips by boat cost about $50 including equipment. The variety of the reefs and the clarity of the water (average undersea visibility, year-round, is 100 feet, but you can often see much farther) make Mexico's Caribbean a top area for underwater exploring. Cozumel takes the diving honors. Its prime attractions are the reefs 500 yards off the island's leeward shore, along El Cantil (The Drop-off), the edge of the shelf that borders the Yucatán Channel to the south. Famous 6-mile-long Palancar Reef has — in addition to forests of black, staghorn, and other species of live coral and friendly swarms of Day-Glo–colored fish — a number of antique wrecks in which to poke around. Besides diving to look and take pictures, you can try your skill at capturing (by hand) giant lobsters, crab, and conch. Spearfishing is forbidden in the waters around Cozumel and Cancún.

Several dive shops on Cozumel — including *Del Mar Aquatics* (in *La Ceiba;* phone: 20816), *Casa del Mar* (phone: 21944), *Aqua Safari* (phone: 20101), *Viajes y Deportes de Cozumel* (in the *Stouffer Presidente;* phone: 20923), *Neptuno Divers* (phone: 20999), and *Discover Cozumel* (phone: 20280) — offer rental equipment, instruction, and dive trips. Most hotels also offer diving facilities at somewhat higher rates, but the convenience is worth it. Scuba pool instruction (about 3 hours) costs about $50 per person. A 4- or 5-day seminar with a certified instructor that includes theory, shallow shore dives, a boat dive to a shallow reef, and a full boat dive to Palancar Reef is about $300 per person (less in the off-season). A full day's guided diving tour from Cozumel to Palancar, including equipment and lunch, is about $40. Equipment rentals run about $6 for a tank and weights; $6 to $12 for a regulator; $5 for fins, mask, and snorkel. Underwater camera rental is about $30 per day at *Cozumel Images* at the *Casa del Mar* hotel (phone: 21900).

For an area that offers scuba divers so much, Cozumel seems short on good snorkeling spots; best are the shallow reefs to the south, where depths range from 5 to 35 feet. Chankanab Lagoon, midway down the leeward coast, with its underwater grottoes and fairly large fish population, is a good place for beginners to get their fins wet. The snorkeling on Isla Mujeres is excellent. Scuba equipment and dive trips are available through *Cooperativa Gustavo Orozco* (phone: 20274) and *Buzos de México* (no phone).

Swimming and Sunning – Cancún's beaches on its surf-pounded Caribbean side still are not as wide as they were before Hurricane Gilbert, but its more serene Bahía de Mujeres and lagoon shores are even wider in some areas. The texture and whiteness of its sand are so distinctive they inspired special studies by geologists, who found that many of the sand's individual grains contain microscopic, star-shape fossils of an organism called discoaster, extinct for 70 million years. Through the ages, the sea has ground and polished these grains till they've become brilliant and powder soft. What's more, their limestone composition has an air conditioning effect that makes the island's sand — even under the noonday sun — feel comfortable to bare feet or bodies in bikinis. Except right in Cancún City, chances are your hotel will have its own beach as well as a pool, but the master plan has provided several public strands as well.

Cozumel's beaches — mostly on the island's leeward side, north and south of San Miguel — are shaped into distinctive coves. The majority of hotels are there, too, and you'll probably spend most of your sun and sea time beside your own hotel or on nearby sands. You can visit others, including the lengthy one about 10 miles (16 km) south of San Miguel at San Francisco (a bit crowded these days, particularly on weekends); the more secluded shore of Passion Island, cupped in its north coast bay; and Punta Morena, on the rough side with a sheltered lagoon nearby. Because the undertow can be tricky, it's a good idea to observe the currents before you take the plunge (plan to enter the water at one point, exit at another), and never swim alone.

On Isla Mujeres, the lazy, unspoiled beaches and El Garrafón, with its undersea formations and colorful fish, are why most visitors come.

■**Playa Tortuga:** This is hands down the dirtiest, smelliest, most polluted beach in all Cancún. Trash and litter clutter the beach and open-air food stands assault your nostrils with some of the most extremely malodorous aromas you may ever encounter. With so many nice beaches to choose from, why waste your time here?

Tennis – On Cancún there are courts at the *Calinda Cancún Beach* (phone: 31600); *Camino Real* (phone: 30100); *Cancún Sheraton* (phone: 31988); *Casa Maya* (phone: 30555); *Aristos* (phone: 30011); *Fiesta Americana Condesa* (phone: 51000); *Fiesta Americana Coral Beach* (phone: 32900); *Hyatt Cancún Caribe* (phone: 30044); *Krystal Cancún* (phone: 31133); *Marriott Casa Magna* (phone: 52000); *Meliá Cancún* (phone: 51160); and the *Pok-Ta-Pok Golf Club* (phone: 30871). On Cozumel there are tennis courts at *La Ceiba* (phone: 20379 or 20844); *Club Cozumel Caribe* (phone: 20100); the *Fiesta Americana Sol-Caribe* (phone: 20700); the *Fiesta Inn* (phone: 22900); the *Meliá Mayan Cozumel* (phone: 20072); the *Stouffer Presidente* (phone: 20322); and the *Villablanca* (phone: 20730). There are no courts available on Isla Mujeres.

Water Skiing – The lagoon behind the island of Cancún is the ideal place to learn or perfect this exhilarating sport. Make arrangements at any island hotel, at *Las Velitas Marina* on the beach at *Club Caribe* (phone: 30311), *Marina Jet Ski* (phone: 30766), or at the *Club Lagoon* (phone: 30222). Boat time costs about $50 an hour.

Windsurfing – Once you've learned to stand on a surfboard, 2 or 3 hours of instruction are all you need. On Cancún lessons are available at several hotels, including the *Club Lagoon*. Boards rent for about $10 an hour. Lessons cost $25, and several places offer weekly rates that include lessons. There are regattas Sundays at *Club Cancún*.

NIGHTCLUBS AND NIGHTLIFE: After-dark activity in Cancún City and the hotel zone has picked up considerably in the past few years. Reigning disco favorites are easily discernible by the crowds gathering outside before opening time (around 10 PM). Current hot spots are *Christine's* (at the *Krystal*); *La Boom* (on Kukulcán Blvd.); the chic *Aquarius* (at the *Camino Real*); *Daddy 'O* (near the *Convention Center*); and the *Hard Rock Café* (at *Plaza Lagunas*). *Note:* If ever a place lived up to its name, *Risky Business* (downtown on Av. Tulum) is it. Renowned for its decibel-deafening music that resembles a distorted brand of 1970s disco, its drinks are watered and its waiters have a nasty way of forgetting to bring you your change. Geared to the college freshmen set in town for spring break, this club is about as refined as a downgraded hog farm. If you decide that this sort of party atmosphere is your cup of tequila, be sure to watch your billfold. *Carlos 'n' Charlie's Cancún* (on the marina) is a good place for food, drink, dancing, and meeting people; it's open until midnight. *Daphny's* (at the *Cancún Sheraton*) is a popular video bar with live and taped music for dancing. *Sixties* (in the *Marriott*) plays dance music from the 1950s, 1960s, and 1970s.

For lots of silly fun, there's the Pirate's Night Adventure cruise, available on both Cancún and Cozumel; for more information call the Cancún Visitor's Bureau (phone: 31021). Not to be missed is the *Ballet Folklórico* at the *Hyatt Regency*, presented Mondays, Tuesdays, Thursdays, and Fridays. Tickets include buffet dinner and drinks (phone: 30966). A torchlit beach, a delicious buffet, and exotic drinks make for a romantic evening at the *Hyatt Cancún Caribe*'s Mexican Night, Mondays, Wednesdays, Fridays, and Saturdays at 7 PM. The *Sheraton* hosts a similar event on Wednesdays at 7:30 PM, and *Plaza las Glorias* hosts one on Tuesdays.

On Cozumel, *Scaramouche* (downtown) is lively and attempts sophistication. *Neptuno* (next to *El Acuario* restaurant on the *malecón*) is also popular. No matter where you go, the crowds tend to be young.

On Isla Mujeres, there are *Buho's Disco Bar, Calypso, Tequila Video Disco,* and *Casablanca,* as well as beach parties and night cruises.

■**Coscorrónes:** Also known as "muppets," this concoction of half-tequila, half-Sprite, blended in a covered shot glass by a couple of strong raps on the imbiber's table or head (depending on how many he or she has already had), is the quickest route to a Mexican hangover. Usually offered as a come-on to attract *turistas,* the *coscorrón* — literally head-knocker — is almost always produced with the lowest-grade tequila on the market. No self-respecting *Mexicano* would fall for it. If you want to try tequila, do it in style, with a slice of lime and a lick of salt, and make sure you choose a decent brand name. A good name in tequila is Sauza; Conmemorativo is the cognac of Sauza.

■**La Zona de Tolerancia:** Nearly every city in Mexico — with the exception of Mexico City — has one: Cancún's "zone of tolerance," or red-light district, is just north of the city, and it's a very enterprising place. The most obvious deterrent for sampling the wares of the ladies of the evening these days is the threat of AIDS and other social diseases. If this is not enough of a deterrent, consider the fact that many of these charming young girls are in fact charming young men in drag, and their main objective is to liberate a visitor of cash and valuables.

BEST IN TOWN

 CHECKING IN: All the hotels on Cancún are relatively new — some are newer than others — aspire to be lavish, and boast some of the highest prices in Mexico. Travelers on a budget, however, can find less costly accommodations away from the major beaches. During high season (December to May), expect to pay $180 to $270 per day for a double room in those places we call very expensive (the highest price would be for a 2-bedroom villa); about $175 in expensive places; $75 to $100, moderate; and $60 or less, inexpensive. Prices drop as much as 50% during the summer months. Even with close to 6,000 hotel rooms (and more added every month), Cancún really does not have enough hotel space to meet the demand during the winter months, so it is best to go only with a confirmed reservation.

The more luxurious Cozumel hotels are in either the North Zone or the South Zone, above and below the town. The in-town hotels (which have neither beach nor pool) appeal most to budget travelers. Hotel prices on Cozumel are similar to those on Cancún, and it is also best to arrive here with a prepaid reservation. Hotel rates on Isla Mujeres tend to be moderate to inexpensive. All telephone numbers on Cancún and Isla Mujeres are in the 988 area code; on Cozumel, 987 unless otherwise indicated.

■**Note:** Parking can be a problem at some hotels.

■**Motels:** There is a very different connotation given to the word *motel* in Mexico. While a Mexican *hotel* is generally comparable to the US version, a *motel* is a whole other story; it serves one purpose, and that is to rent by the hour. These *auto-hoteles*, as they are also advertised, have curtained garages to insure the privacy of any "guests" who might not like their license plates seen. Many an unsuspecting tourist and his family have pulled into a *motel* hoping to enjoy a relaxing evening, only to discover that there is no furniture (other than one rather predominant bed), no closet, and no phone in the room.

CANCÚN

Camino Real – Virtually surrounded by water, Westin Hotels' magnificent 381-room pleasure palace has an enclosed saltwater swimming lagoon, a bar in the pool, 3 tennis courts, 3 restaurants, *Aquarius* disco — the works. On the island (phone: 30100; 800-228-3000 in the US; FAX: 31730). Very expensive.

Fiesta Americana – Its appearance is unique, with a Mexican pink façade and a fountain-filled lobby. Each of the 280 rooms has rattan furnishings and a balcony overlooking the water. The pool area is very nicely laid out with thatch-roofed, open-air restaurant and bars, beyond which is the aqua blue bay. Snorkeling gear is available poolside. The lobby is a pretty place for before-dinner cocktails, with a strolling mariachi band. On the island (phone: 31400; 800-FIESTA-1 in the US; FAX: 31495). Very expensive.

Fiesta Americana Condesa – A Grand Tourism hotel (Mexico's 5-star rating), it has three towers, each with its own atrium lounge covered by a glass, *palapa*-shape roof. The decor is mostly rattan complemented by fresh, vivid colors. There are 500 rooms — including 27 suites with Jacuzzis on private terraces — plus a split-level pool with a 66-foot waterfall, 5 restaurants, 3 lighted tennis courts, a jogging track, spa, and a lobby bar where live music is played in the evenings. The beach, most of which was swept away by Hurricane Gilbert, had only partially returned as we went to press. Kukulcán Blvd. (phone: 51000; 800-FIESTA-1 in the US; FAX: 51650). Very expensive.

Fiesta Americana Coral Beach – Two rather overwhelming, modern, peach-colored towers are the setting for this all-suite hotel. There are 3 restaurants, 3 bars, a nightclub, a coffee shop, huge pool, 3 lighted artificial grass tennis courts, and a gym. Hotel zone (phone: 32900; 800-FIESTA-1 in the US; FAX: 32905). Very expensive.

Hyatt Cancún Caribe – A graceful white arc a short walk from the *Convention Center*, this 200-room resort has 60 villas, 4 restaurants, 3 lighted tennis courts, 3 pools, a Jacuzzi, water sports, and an art gallery in the lobby. On the island, Km 8.5 of Kukulcán Blvd. (phone: 30044; 800-288-9000 in the US; FAX: 31514). Very expensive.

Hyatt Regency – Beautifully housed under a glass atrium, all 300 rooms have ocean views. It has a pool, 3 bars, and 3 restaurants. On the island (phone: 30966; 800-233-1234 in the US; FAX: 73369). Very expensive.

Krystal Cancún – With lush, thick greenery outside and in, it offers 318 rooms, tennis, and 5 fine restaurants, including a good breakfast buffet. On the island (phone: 31133; 619-792-1443 in the US; FAX: 31205). Very expensive.

Marriott Casa Magna – A 6-story hostelry of contemporary design, it is stunningly decorated with Mexican textures and colors. All rooms have balconies providing a view of either the Caribbean or the lagoon. Four restaurants — including a Japanese steakhouse — nightclub, pool, Jacuzzi, and 2 lighted tennis courts. Hotel zone (phone: 52000; 800-228-9290 in the US). Very expensive.

Meliá Cancún – With a waterfall that cascades over part of its entrance, this marble and glass complex has a huge, central atrium that looks and, unfortunately, *feels* like a tropical jungle. It's all beautifully decorated with bright tiles, bentwood, and wicker. Four restaurants, 5 bars, 3 tennis courts, and an 18-hole golf course. Hotel zone (phone: 51160; 800-336-3542 in the US; FAX: 51085). Very expensive.

Meliá Turquesa – A giant white pyramid that slopes down to the beach, it offers 446 rooms decorated in soft colors and equipped with satellite TV, mini-bars, and safe-deposit boxes. Two restaurants, 3 bars, a coffee shop, pool, and 2 lighted tennis courts. Hotel zone (phone: 32544; 800-336-3542 in the US; FAX: 51029). Very expensive.

Stouffer Presidente – On the golf links and boasting 1 tennis court, fishing, and water skiing, this stately, 295-room hostelry is a favorite of sports enthusiasts. Its beach and location are among the best on Cancún. On the island (phone: 30200; 800-HOTELS-1 in the US; FAX: 21360). Very expensive.

Villas Tacul – A colony of 23 Spanish-style villas with gardens, patios, and kitchens, where guests can set up luxurious housekeeping, eat out at the *palapa*, cook for themselves or arrange for someone to come in — or all of the above. With 2 to 5 bedrooms per house, on a narrow but pleasant beach. Good for families and congenial 2- or 3-couple groups. Km 5.5 on Kukulcán Blvd. (phone: 30000; 800-842-0193 in the US; FAX: 30349). Very expensive.

Calinda Cancún Beach – Situated on the best beach on the island, between the Nichupté Lagoon and Bahía Mujeres, this hostelry isn't as lavish as many of its neighbors; very popular, it boasts a loyal following of return guests. Facilities include a restaurant, bars, a pool, tennis, and a gym (phone: 31600; 800-228-5151 in the US; FAX: 31857). Expensive.

Cancún Sheraton – This 748-room gem — self-contained and as big as a village — is set apart on its own beach, which it shares with a small Maya temple. Facilities include 6 tennis courts, 6 pools, and *Daphny's* video bar with live music; there are also aerobics classes and scuba lessons. On the island (phone: 31988). Expensive.

Casa Maya – Originally built as condominiums, the 350 rooms and suites here are large, to say the least, with immense walk-in closets, sinks the size of bathtubs, and tubs the size of swimming pools. Among the amenities are moped rental, 2 lighted tennis courts, a swimming pool, restaurant, and cordial service. The place seems to be especially popular with families. On the island (phone: 30555; 800-899-6383 in the US; FAX: 31188). Expensive.

Club Med – Completely rebuilt after Hurricane Gilbert and boasting one of the widest beaches in the island, it's now one of the prime places to stay on Cancún. The 410 rooms, each with 2 European single beds and traditional Mexican decor, are set in 3-story bungalows facing either the ocean or the lagoon. Windsurfing, sailing, snorkeling, and scuba diving (including scuba instruction) are included in the basic rate, as are all meals. Lunch and dinner include complimentary wine. There's entertainment nightly. At Punta Nizuc (phone: 42409 or 800-CLUB-MED). Expensive.

Conrad – Opened in the spring of 1991, this new complex features 385 rooms, including 94 in the Tower, which offers special facilities for guests, such as a private pool and cocktail lounge, and complimentary continental breakfast. The decor is typically tropical, and all rooms provide an ocean or lagoon view; tower rooms have private balconies (as do some in the low-rise building). Facilities include 5 outdoor swimming pools, 2 lighted tennis courts, a health club and recreation center, water sports center, and a boat dock for access to scuba diving, snorkeling, small boating in the large bay, water skiing, board sailing, and evening cruises. There are 2 restaurants and 2 lounges. Kukulcán Blvd., at Punta Nizuc on the southern end of the island (phone: 50086 or 50537; 800-HILTONS in the US; FAX: 50074). Expensive.

Miramar Misión – This 189-room hostelry has several bars, 3 restaurants, and nightly entertainment. On the island (phone: 31755; FAX: 31136). Expensive.

Omni – All of the 285 rooms have large terraces; there also are 35 suites and 27 villas. Facilities include 2 lighted tennis courts, 8 restaurants, bars, a gameroom, and a health center. Its beautiful beach was all but washed away by Hurricane Gilbert, but hammocks have been strung up on the grounds for lounging and sipping tropical drinks by the sea. Four of the rooms are specially equipped for handicapped guests, and there are access ramps to all public areas. Km 16.5 on Kukulcán Blvd. (phone: 50714; 212-517-7998 in the US; FAX: 50184). Expensive.

Royal Solaris Super Club – A Maya pyramid–like structure, it has 223 rooms, including 3 suites), an Olympic-size pool, health club, and social programs. The beach, narrower since Hurricane Gilbert hit, is in fairly good shape. Km. 23 on Kukulcán Blvd. (phone: 50100; FAX: 50354). Expensive.

America – There are 180 large rooms, each with its own terrace, at this pleasant place. It is not right on the beach, but does provide free shuttle service to its own beach club. Pool, restaurant, bar, coffee shop. Av. Tulum (phone: 41500; 800-899-6283 in the US; FAX: 41953). Moderate.

Aristos Cancún – The friendly scale and Mexican hospitality make for easy comfort here. There are 244 smallish but pleasant rooms. Inviting pool area, beach, 2 lighted tennis courts, and restaurant. Km 9.5 on Kukulcán Blvd. (phone: 30011; FAX: 30078). Moderate.

Club Lagoon – This secluded collection of adobe-type dwellings on quiet Laguna Nichupté, including rooms and 2-level suites, is a real find. One picturesque courtyard opens onto another, with flowers playing colorfully against the white cottages; the best face the lagoon. It also has 2 restaurants, 2 bars, and a nautical center. On the island (phone: 31111; FAX: 31326). Moderate.

Fiesta Inn – Decorated in shades of soft pastels, the 120 rooms here are set right at the edge of the *Pok-Ta-Pok* golf course. Guests receive a 50% discount on greens fees, and they are allowed use of the facilities and services of other Fiesta Americana hotels on the island (charges are automatically billed to rooms). There is no beach, but free transportation is provided to the hotel's beach club. On the island (phone: 32200; 800-FIESTA-1 in the US; FAX: 32532). Moderate.

Playa Blanca – A pioneer among the Cancún hotels, it opened in 1974 on a small beachfront and is now part of the Best Western chain. It has 161 rooms, a pool, and every water sport imaginable. Since it's next door to the marina, the boating facilities are excellent. On the island (phone: 30344; 212-517-7770 in the US; FAX: 30904). Moderate.

La Posada del Capitán Lafitte – In Punta Bete, this delightful beachfront bungalow complex is set in an area especially good for hanging out in a hammock or exploring one of the patch reefs that lie just a few yards offshore. There is a restaurant. Twenty miles (32 km) south of the Cancún airport. For information and reservations, contact *Turquoise Reef Resorts,* Box 2664, Evergreen, CO 80439 (phone: 230485 or 216114; 800-538-6802). Moderate.

Antillano – Amid the bustle of Avenida Tulum, this 48-room, modern white structure is a pleasant, economical place to stay. Cancún City (phone: 41532; FAX: 41878). Inexpensive.

Kailuum – Next door to *La Posada del Capitán Lafitte* bungalows (see above), it shares the same tranquil surroundings. The 40 tents have comfortable mattresses, maid service, 2 centrally located bathhouses with flush toilets, and hot and cold running water. No electricity, telephones, or children allowed. About 20 miles (32 km) south of the Cancún airport. For reservations and information, contact *Turquoise Reef Resorts,* Box 2664, Evergreen, CO 80439 (phone: 800-538-6802). Inexpensive.

Plaza Caribe – A good bet downtown, across from the bus station. The air conditioned rooms fill up fast. Cancún City (phone: 41377; 800-334-7234 in the US; FAX: 46352). Inexpensive.

Plaza del Sol – Half-moon–shape, with two stylized canoes over its portals, it has 87 rooms, a pool, restaurant, bar, and free transportation to the beach. Cancún City (phone: 43888; FAX: 44393). Inexpensive.

COZUMEL

Club Cozumel Caribe – A twisting, palm-canopied drive leads to this expansive 280-room property with attractive grounds. It offers tennis, a small pool, and a restaurant. Rate includes all meals, drinks, water sports, sightseeing, and a moonlight cruise. San Juan Beach (phone: 20100; 800-327-2254 in the US; FAX: 20288). Very expensive.

Fiesta Americana Sol-Caribe – A beautiful 322-room resort (102 rooms are in a new tower) 'twixt beach and jungle, it has 3 tennis courts, good diving facilities, and a fine dining room. South Zone (phone: 20700; 800-FIESTA-1 in the US,; FAX: 21301). Expensive.

Stouffer Presidente Cozumel – The original luxury establishment on the island and still one of the best. Pleasant beach, nice pool, tennis, and an excellent dining room. South Zone (phone: 20322; 800-HOTELS-1 in the US; FAX: 21360). Expensive.

Meliá Mayan Cozumel – Set on the isolated north end of the coast, this 12-story high-rise on the beach has 188 rooms and suites, an abundance of terraces, 2 tennis courts, a *Fiesta Mexicana* on Thursdays, and a *Caribbean Fiesta* on Fridays. Playa Santa Pilar (phone: 20072; 800-336-3542 in the US; FAX: 21599). Expensive to moderate.

Barracuda – Near the shopping area, this small place has in-room bars. Breakfast is served on the beach. No pool. Rate includes continental breakfast. Av. Rafael E. Melgar, south of town (phone: 20002; FAX: 20884). Moderate.

Cabañas del Caribe – A semitropical hideaway on one of the island's best beaches, it has a small pool, 39 rooms, and 9 cabañas. Informal, friendly. North Zone (phone: 20017; 800-336-3542 in the US; FAX: 21599). Moderate.

La Ceiba – The best equipped and located for scuba divers, this 115-room hostelry has satellite TV, spa, tennis, a restaurant, and cocktail lounge. Paradise Point (phone: 20815 or 20816; 800-621-6830 in the US; FAX: 800-235-5892). Moderate.

El Cozumeleño – This property has 104 large rooms, 3 restaurants, a bar, tennis court, and a free-form pool. Santa Pilar (phone: 20050; FAX: 20381). Moderate.

Fiesta Inn – Part of the Fiesta chain, the 3-story, colonial-style hostelry is surrounded by beautiful gardens and connected to the beach by a tunnel. The 178 rooms and 2 suites have satellite TV. Facilities include a large pool, tennis court, motorcycle rental, dive shop, restaurant, bar, and coffee shop. Km 1.7 Costera Sur (phone: 22900; 800-FIESTA-1 in the US; FAX: 22154). Moderate.

Mara – Most of the 48 rooms face the lovely beach. Pleasant pool, restaurant, and dive shop. North Zone (phone: 20300; 800-221-6509 in the US; FAX in Mérida: 239290). Moderate.

La Perla – Right on the beach, this 4-story hotel has its own swimming cove and a pier with diesel, light, and water connections for private yachts. Also a pool, deli-bar, dive packages, and a quiet, comfortable, unpretentious atmosphere. 2 Av. Francisco I. Madero, PO Box 309 (phone: 20188). Moderate.

Playa Azul – A family favorite, it has 60 rooms and suites, a restaurant, bar, and water sports. North of San Miguel, at Km 4 on Carr. San Juan (phone: 20033; FAX: 21793). Moderate.

Aguilar – It has a pool (but no beach), gardens, and glass-bottom boat and motorcycle rentals. In town (phone: 20307). Inexpensive.

Villablanca – Though its facilities resemble those of a resort hotel — tennis court, pool, dive shop, boat for up to 60 divers, classes in all water sports — this property has only 30 rooms and suites, some with Roman baths and all with air conditioning and fans. Across the street, on the water's edge, is its restaurant–bar–beach club, *Amadeus*. Playa Paraíso, Km 2.9 (phone: 20730; 306-891-3949 in the US). Inexpensive.

ISLA MUJERES

Cabañas María del Mar – At the north end of the island, it has 35 units (including 10 cabañas), a restaurant, and a full-service 20-slip marina. The proprietors, the Limas, make everyone feel at home. Av. Carlos Lazo (phone: 20179). Moderate.

Perlas del Caribe – Formerly the *Rocas del Caribe*, it's been expanded and remodeled into a 3-story hotel with 97 rooms, all with balconies; there is a restaurant and pool. 2 Av. Madero (phone: 20444; FAX: 20011). Moderate.

Berny – A downtown hostelry, with 37 rooms, pool, and restaurant. Av. Juárez (phone: 20025; FAX: 20026). Inexpensive.

Kan Kin – It's also known as *María's,* after the popular restaurant (see *Eating Out*), which now has expanded to include several colorful, air conditioned rooms. The setting is gorgeous, and El Garrafón Beach is a short walk away. Five miles (8 km) south of town, at Km 5 (phone: 20015; FAX: 20395). Inexpensive.

Posada del Mar – This pleasant 42-room hostelry is one of the best on the island, with palm-shaded grounds, restaurant, bar, pool, laundromat, and air conditioning. Across from the beach. 15 Av. Rueda Medina (phone: 20300). Inexpensive.

Rocamar – Thirty-four basic but pleasant rooms, all with a view. Av. Nicolás Bravo y Garero (phone: 20101). Inexpensive.

EATING OUT: Food on the Yucatán Peninsula has been influenced by the cuisines of Cuba, Europe, and Asia, and is distinctively different from that of the rest of the country. Here, tacos, called *papadzul,* are made with regular tortillas but filled with diced hard-boiled eggs and covered with a sauce made from puréed squash seeds, tomato, and mild chili. A lot of pickling is done in this region, including everything from pigs' feet, beef, and chicken to pork. This pickled meat is then used as filling for tacos and enchiladas. In several rural areas meats are wrapped in banana leaves to conserve the moisture and baked in outdoor ovens. Very little chili is used in preparing Yucatán dishes, but meals are almost always accompanied by a sauce made from the *habanero* chili, the hottest in all of Mexico.

Hotel food on Cancún is better than average, because the hoteliers want to keep the money spent on food in the house, which means that the non-hotel restaurants must work extra hard to lure customers. There is a sampling of ethnic cooking, and by all means try Yucatecan specialties, which are quite different from standard Mexican fare. Start the day with eggs *moltuleños* — fried eggs on a tortilla — black beans, and a spicy sauce. And don't miss delicious and filling Yucatán lime soup, which also contains chicken, vegetables, and tortillas.

Expect to pay $40 to $60 for two in restaurants we list as expensive; about $30 at moderate places; and $20 in inexpensive ones. Prices do not include wine, tips, or drinks. Almost all the restaurants on Cozumel are in town, although a few, open only for lunch, are out on the beaches. Restaurant prices on Cozumel and Isla Mujeres are somewhat more moderate than those on Cancún. All restaurants listed below accept MasterCard and Visa; a few also accept American Express and Diners Club. Unless noted otherwise, restaurants listed below are open daily. All telephone numbers on Cancún and Isla Mujeres are in the 988 area code; on Cozumel, 987 unless otherwised indicated.

CANCÚN

Blue Bayou – Cajun and creole fare and specialty drinks are served in a multilevel dining area suspended among waterfalls and lush tropical greenery. Live jazz. Dinner only. Reservations necessary. *Hyatt Cancún Caribe* (phone: 30044, ext. 54). Expensive.

Bogart's – International dishes served with quiet elegance in exotic Moroccan surroundings. Seatings at 7 and 9:30 PM. No shorts or T-shirts. Open daily. Reservations advised. At the *Krystal Cancún* (phone: 31333). Expensive.

Carlos 'n' Charlie's – Fun 'n' games are the strong points at this branch of Mexico's well-known restaurant chain, where good spareribs and shrimp are served. There's also a small dockside disco where diners can dance the night away. Open daily. No reservations. On the island (phone: 31304). Expensive.

Chac-Mool – The menu is continental, sprinkled with seafood specialties and home-made pasta. Classical music adds to the atmosphere. Reservations advised. Km 10 on Kukulcán Blvd., next to the *Aristos Cancún* hotel (phone: 31107). Expensive.

La Dolce Vita – Modern decor is the backdrop to intimate dining, where the sweet life is manifested in tasty pasta and seafood dishes. Open daily. Reservations advised. 87 Cobá in Cancún City (phone: 41384). Expensive.

La Habichuela – The place local folk go for a night out and for *mar y tierra,* alias surf and turf. Open daily. Reservations advised. 25 Margaritas in Cancún City (phone: 43158). Expensive.

Hacienda el Mortero – An authentic copy of a Mexican hacienda in Súchil, Durango, it specializes in steak and Mexican haute cuisine. Open daily. Reservations advised. In the *Krystal Cancún,* Km 9 on Kukulcán Blvd. (phone: 31133). Expensive.

Maxime – Formerly the mayor's home, this elegant dining place has European furniture, Oriental rugs, English china, and French crystal — not to mention 4 sitting rooms, 1 dining room, and an upstairs piano bar. The French chef recommends the breast of chicken in red wine or the shrimp in puff pastry. Jackets are not required; shorts and sandals are not permitted. Open daily. Reservations advised. On the island (phone: 30438). Expensive.

El Pescador – Perhaps the best seafood eatery in Cancún, it serves fresh lobster, shrimp, and red snapper on Mexican pottery. Don't miss the Yucatecan lime soup or the hot rolls, and try for a table outside, on the fan-cooled terrace. Closed Mondays. Reservations unnecessary. 5 Tulipanes, Cancún City (phone: 42673). Expensive.

Scampi – Superb Northern Italian fare — delicious pasta, meat, and seafood — is served in a beautiful setting. The service is impeccable. *Hyatt Regency* (phone: 30966). Expensive.

Señor Frog's – Under the same ownership as *Carlos 'n' Charlie's,* it offers a similar menu (see above). Open for breakfast, lunch, and dinner. At Km 5.5 on Kukulcán Blvd. (phone: 32931). Expensive.

Seryna – Japanese specialties such as sushi, teppanyaki, sukiyaki, yosenabe, shabu-shabu, tempura, and other traditional dishes are served in a pretty setting. Open daily. Reservations advised. *Flamingo Plaza* (phone: 51155 or 32995). Expensive.

Augustus Caesar – Seafood and traditional Italian dishes are served with flair in pretty surroundings. Live music is featured from 8:30 PM to midnight. No shorts or T-shirts. Open daily. Reservations advised. At *La Mansión–Costa Blanca Shopping Center* (phone: 33384). Expensive to moderate.

Bombay Bicycle Club – Casual and comfortable, this spot offers fare from the States — good hamburgers, barbecued ribs, and calorie-filled desserts. Excellent, friendly service. Open 7 AM to midnight. No reservations. Kukulcán Blvd., across from Playa Tortuga (no phone). Moderate.

La Mamá de Tarzan – Another link in the ubiquitous Anderson's chain, this one is a cafeteria-style eatery with good salad, a lively bar, nightly fiesta, and dancing on the pier. Open daily. Reservations advised. Opposite Chac-Mool Beach (phone: 31092). Moderate.

Pop – Gringo-style breakfast, lunch, and dinner, and cheerful service. Open daily. No reservations. 26 Tulum (phone: 41991). Moderate.

Torremolinos – Paella, crayfish, and crab done the Spanish way. Closed Tuesdays. No reservations. Tulum and Xcaret (phone: 43639). Moderate.

Pizza Rolandi – All kinds of Italian dishes are served in an informal, outdoor setting. Open daily. Reservations unnecessary. 12 Av. Cobá, Cancún City (phone: 44047). Moderate to inexpensive.

Los Alemendros – Authentic Yucatecan food and the same management as its famous Mérida namesake. Open daily. Reservations unnecessary. Av. Bonampak and Sayíl in Cancún City (phone: 40807). Inexpensive.

Augustus Pizza – Popular with kids, it's an Italian pizza parlor in the great US tradition. Open daily. Reservations unnecessary. *Convention Center,* on the island (phone: 30530). Inexpensive.

Café Amsterdam – Reasonably priced European dishes are served in this intimate bistro. The delicious bread is baked on the premises, and there is a huge salad and fresh fruit bar. Open daily, except Mondays, from 7 AM to 11 PM. 70 Av. Yaxchilan (phone: 44098). Inexpensive.

100% Natural – The place to go for fresh fruit drinks, salads, sandwiches, and fruit and vegetable platters. Live jazz music nightly. No reservations. 6 Sunyaxchen (no phone). Inexpensive.

COZUMEL

El Acuario – Once a real aquarium, it's now an elegant seafood restaurant, with entertainment provided by an immense tankful of exotic tropical fish in the middle of the room. Open daily. Reservations advised. On the *malecón* (phone: 21097). Expensive.

Carlos 'n' Charlie's and Jimmy – The Cozumel branch of Mexico's favorite restaurant chain, where people come for ribs and good times. Open daily. Reservations advised. On the *malecón* (phone: 20191). Expensive.

Morgan's – Lobster thermidor and special coffees are favorites at this very comfortable, popular wood cabin serving good steaks and seafood on the main plaza. Open daily. Reservations advised (phone: 20584). Expensive.

Pepe's Grill – This romantic spot by the waterfront has excellent seafood and steak. A variety of live music is featured nightly. Open daily. Reservations advised. Av. Rafael E. Melgar (phone: 20213). Expensive.

Casa Denis – The menu varies at this cozy spot where Yucatecan dishes are served under a tropical fruit tree. Reservations advised. Just off the south side of the main square in San Miguel (phone: 20067). Moderate.

Mezcalito's – Set on the surf-pounded Caribbean side of the island, this large open-air *palapa* serves up some of the tastiest grilled shrimp and fish on the island. The atmosphere — white sand, ocean breezes, and friendly chatter — is unbeatable. A good spot, too, just to stop for a cold beer or a piña colada. Punta Morena (no phone). Moderate.

Las Palmeras – Just opposite the ferry dock, it's a great meeting place offering a varied menu for every meal. The homemade biscuits and French toast are a treat for breakfast. Open daily. Reservations unnecessary. On the *malecón* (phone: 20532). Moderate.

Plaza Leza – A sidewalk café serving good Mexican snacks, charcoal-broiled steaks, and seafood. Open daily. Reservations advised. On the main plaza (phone: 21041). Moderate.

La Laguna – A big *palapa* at Chankanab where nachos, hamburgers, and the like are served from 10 AM to 4 PM. Open daily. No reservations (no phone). Inexpensive.

El Portal – This is a favorite for breakfast. Open daily. Reservations unnecessary. On the *malecón* (no phone). Inexpensive.

San Francisco – The fare — what else? — is seafood (try the snail ceviche), and a band plays in the afternoons. Open daily for lunch only. Reservations unnecessary. A quarter mile from San Francisco Beach and about 9 miles (14 km) from town (no phone). Inexpensive.

Las Tortugas – Simple but good Mexican fare is served here, along with good, cold beer. Don't be put off by the nondescript surroundings. Open daily. Reservations unnecessary. 82 Av. 10 Norte, in the heart of town (no phone). Inexpensive.

ISLA MUJERES

Ciro's Lobster House – A wide selection of Mexican wines accompanies the lobster and red snapper served here. Open daily. Reservations advised. 11 Matamoros, in town (phone: 20102). Expensive.

Gomar – Lobster and fresh fish are best enjoyed on the romantic terrace, where tables sport bright, striped Mexican cloths during the day, white at night. You can also dine indoors. Open daily. Reservations unnecessary. Hidalgo and Madero (phone: 20142). Moderate.

Hacienda Gomar – In addition to a good seafood buffet and exotic drinks, there is a natural aquarium where one can swim among giant, 100-year-old turtles — and even ride them. Open daily. No reservations. On the west side of the island on the road to El Garrafón (no phone). Moderate.

María's Kan Kin – Travel the 5 miles (8 km) south of town to this delightful villa with its unassuming façade and a knockout view. As if open-air dining on fresh seafood, generous, tasty tropical cocktails, and the seductive surroundings weren't enough, the menu itself is a work of art: hand-done in colors on woven straw. A meal that's less than leisurely is unthinkable here. Open daily. Reservations advised. Near El Garrafón (phone: 20015). Moderate.

Los Pájaros – Facing the beach on the north end of town, this *palapa*-style eatery serves good Mexican fare. Reservations unnecessary. *Posada del Mar* hotel (phone: 20044). Moderate.

Buho's Paradise – Great for late snacks. Open daily. Reservations unnecessary. Next to *Cabañas María del Mar* (phone: 20179). Inexpensive.

Pizza Rolandi – Pizza cooked in a wood-burning oven, and other Italian dishes. Open daily. Reservations unnecessary. Hidalgo between Madero and Abasolo (phone: 20429). Inexpensive.

■**Mobile Food Stands:** One international public health specialist we know refers to these movable feasts as "epidemics on wheels looking for a place to happen." Food at these less-than-sanitary open-air stands is usually left unrefrigerated for long periods of time, exposed to the street soot, gasoline fumes, and heat. Do yourself and your health insurance company a favor and eat only in clean, good-quality restaurants or at your hotel.

DIVERSIONS

For the Experience

QUINTESSENTIAL CANCÚN, COZUMEL, AND THE YUCATÁN

Among other things, traveling south of the border doubtless has taught you that the real spirit of Mexico lies somewhere between the Maya and *mañana.* If you've tried on the requisite number of sombreros, admired the azure waters of Cancún, and haggled over a colorful serape, you've certainly scratched the surface. You may even have gone parasailing, mixed it up with a marlin, eaten an enchilada, and finally learned how to pronounce Xel-Ha. But, amigos, until you savor the places and pleasures listed below, you haven't experienced the true meaning of "Viva Mexico!"

BALLET FOLKLÓRICO DE MÉXICO: In every Mexican town and village, music and dance express the soul of the people. Pre-Hispanic Mexican music, simple and almost hypnotic, was dominated by percussion and wind instruments, and was designed to accompany dances and religious rites; each of the many Indian cultures had its own dances and costumes. In spite of very forceful efforts by the conquistadores to stamp out all traces of indigenous cultures, music and dance survived, mainly because the Spanish clergy realized that these arts could be used as tools for recruiting the heathens into the church. The dances and music didn't really change; what changed was the name of the god to whom they were dedicated. Slowly, Spanish, French, and other European traditions found expression as part of this multicultural heritage. Even today, a church festival isn't considered complete without the performance of brilliantly clad folk dancers.

Although the main *Ballet Folklórico* school is in Mexico City, there are numerous smaller troupes across the nation that faithfully re-create the country's dance in the style and tradition of their ancestors. On Cancún, you can enjoy a whirlwind tour of the entire Mexican republic through one of the *Fiesta Mexicanas* offered at several of the larger hotels. The *Hyatt Regency* on Cancún (in the hotel zone; phone: 988-30966, or 800-228-9000 in the US) boasts the best and most complete folklore ballet in town, presented Mondays, Tuesdays, Thursdays, and Fridays. Tickets include domestic drinks and a dinner buffet.

CAVES OF THE SLEEPING SHARKS: In the late 1960s, oceanographer Ramón Bravo — Mexico's answer to Jacques Cousteau — discovered an incredible phenomenon just off the shores of his native Isla Mujeres. Deep below the surface of the island's coastal plateau lay an intricate network of wide caverns, which has since gained international fame under the misnomer Caves of the Sleeping Sharks.

Normally beasts of perpetual motion, the man-eating sharks that congregate in these caves become almost totally still and give the appearance of being asleep. In fact, this particular species is incapable of sleeping. A living fossil, the shark is one of the few surviving sea creatures void of the sophisticated breathing system that allows other fish to inhale through their mouth and gills. Instead, the lowly shark must remain in constant motion in order to breathe, thus creating a current of water that carries fresh air through its cavities.

The underwater caves at Isla Mujeres contain constant currents which offer the shark a welcome rest, allowing the ocean do his breathing exercise for him while he remains stationary. And because of the fossilized fish and coral deposits that surround the caves, the water that passes through them is saturated with concentrated calcium, which produce an almost narcotic effect on the sharks, tranquilizing them into a near stupor. Consequently, divers are able to approach and even *pet* these grim reapers of the ocean floor without fear of attack.

It is an experience that can be had only in the Mexican Caribbean. Warning: Unlike Rip Van Winkle, the sharks don't "sleep" for years on end. They have been known to awaken at very inopportune moments, and become extremely aggressive toward divers. But if your heart is strong, your life insurance paid up, and your nerves intact, you may want to venture below the ocean's surface and meet these real-life *Jaws* firsthand.

CENOTES: Geographically speaking, the Yucatán Peninsula is one massive, porous, limestone shelf, suspended over an ocean plateau and pitted by cenotes, sinkholes created by a combination of erosive rains and underground caverns. The limestone is slowly worn away in certain areas until it becomes so thin that it collapses into the water bed below. The result is a deep, usually circular cavity that acts as a natural cistern to collect rainwater.

Because the peninsula has very few lakes and rivers, the cenotes were — and still are — a vital source of fresh water for the natives. The ancient Maya selected the locales of their cities based on the proximity of these sinkholes, and the village cenote came to have a crucial significance for their survival. To appease the sinkhole gods, particularly in times of drought, sacrifices had to be made. Gold necklaces, jade figurines, and even humans (usually young virgins, but sometimes mighty warriors, depending on the personal preferences of the specific cenote deity) were cast into the bottom of the holes to entice the gods to produce rain.

Today, most of the Yucatán's cenotes have been dredged of their early treasures — including the skeletons — and are now popular swimming holes for the native *yucatecos*. The water in the cenotes is frequently crystal clear and extremely refreshing — a perfect place for those who like to plunge themselves into a country's history.

Cenotes come in all shapes and sizes throughout the peninsula. One of the most famous — and inviting — is *Cenote Azul* (Blue Sinkhole) just south of Bacalar. There is also a very beautiful cenote at Xcaret, near Playa del Carmen, which has the added attraction of being connected to a series of underground caverns.

CEVICHE: You've tried sashimi and sushi at Japanese restaurants, but did you know that Mexico has its own rendition of raw fish? Delicate morsels of red snapper, tuna, shrimp, crab, or sea snails (a Cozumel specialty) are marinated overnight in lime juice with finely diced tomatoes, onions and chilies, olives, slivers of avocado, and a generous pinch of coriander to produce one of Mexico's most delectable appetizers, ceviche. Be sure to sample the superb sea snail ceviche at the *San Francisco* restaurant on Cozumel.

CHICHÉN ITZÁ, Yucatán: When someone says that you haven't seen Mexico until you've been to the Yucatán, this is what it's all about. The most famous and complete of the ancient Maya cities, this site is a testament to their engineering genius. Here are temples, sacrificial wells, sacred ball courts, reclining idols, and the great El Castillo Pyramid. Stand and face El Castillo, which is topped by a temple to the feathered snake god, Kukulcán (also known as Quetzalcóatl); giant carved heads are at the base of the balustrade. Believe it or not, on the first day of spring and the first day of autumn, the undulating shadows form a serpent's body leading from the temple on top to the carved head on the bottom. It's worth planning your trip around the equinoxes!

DIA DE LOS MUERTOS (DAY OF THE DEAD): Although Mexicans fear and respect death as much as any other peoples, they face it, defy it, mock it, and even toy with it more than most cultures. Never is this more apparent than on November 1,

All Souls' Day — known in Mexico as the *Day of the Dead* — an eminently Mexican holiday perpetuating a tradition of death and rebirth.

By mid-October, bakeries and markets throughout Mexico are filled with sweets and toys created with death as their theme. Bake shops are piled high with *pan de muerto,* a coffee cake decorated with meringues fashioned into the shape of bones. Children, friends, and relatives are given colorful sugar skulls with their names inscribed on them; death figures shaped from marzipan are on sale at most sweets shops. Verses, called *calaveras,* containing witty allusions or epitaphs, are written about living friends, relatives, and public figures, and by the end of October, shop windows take on a macabre air, with shrouded marionettes and other ghoulish-looking figurines heralding the holiday.

On the actual date, families gather in graveyards to picnic and spend the day with their departed, bringing along their loved ones' favorite foods and drink. Graves are decorated with bring orange *zempasuchil* (marigolds), the flower of the dead; *copal,* an incense that dates back to pre-Hispanic cultures, is burned. The celebration begins with prayers and chants for the dead, and usually ends with drinks to the health of the departed. Homes are decorated in much the same way, with tables filled with marigolds and objects of which the deceased was especially fond.

DIVING OFF COZUMEL: For those who can't resist crystal-clear water and being near the second-longest reef in the world (Palancar Reef), Cozumel is just the spot. Schools of tropical fish and a rainbow of coral deposits prove irresistible to diving enthusiasts — particularly from May through August. Those who are less daring can also enjoy the beauty of the reef without donning scuba gear. A face mask, snorkel, and set of fins are all you really need to get a ringside view of this undersea splendor.

GUM FRUIT: Although Quintana Roo's main industry today is tourism, the region was once renowned for its chicle, or gum, production. In fact, it was during his travels through the Yucatán Peninsula in the late 19th century that Thomas Adams (Adams Chiclet Gum) first noticed that the native Maya Indians customarily chewed on sticks of dried resin from the sapodilla spruces that flourish in the state's tropical jungles. It occurred to him that this practice might prove popular in the US, and Adams ordered a 2-ton shipment of the resin to be sent to his office back home. Within a decade, Adams had built an entire empire on chicle latex.

The introduction of artificial gum substitutes in the mid-1940s resulted in a collapse of the world chicle market, but even today, Quintana Roo still exports an estimated 500 tons of the sticky resin each year.

The chicle tree also produces a fragrant and fleshy fruit known as the *chicozapote,* which is commonly available throughout Mexico. At first glance, the dark, leathery-skinned gum fruit looks a bit like an overripe eggplant, but under its homely peel lies a sumptuous rosy marrow with an indescribably subtle sweetness. *Chicozapote* does not appear on most menus — particularly those in English — but if you ask your waiter, he can usually produce a sample from the chef's personal larder. If not, you can find *chicozapote* in local fruit markets.

MARIACHI MUSIC: The melodies pervade all of Mexico. Groups of musicians roam the streets of cities large and small, serenading under the windows of apartment buildings and in the doorways of restaurants and shops. Students, carrying guitars and flutes on subways and buses, often play for their fellow passengers in hope of earning a few pesos on the way to and from school. Although every region of Mexico has its own special music, none is more associated with the country as a whole than mariachi (the word comes from the French for "marriage").

During Emperor Maximilian's reign, wealthy Guadalajara families, trying to imitate the customs of the court, hired musicians to entertain their guests. Today, mariachis — made up of at least one vocalist, a guitar, bass, violin, and a trumpet or two — are usually hired to serenade girlfriends or to play at special events (weddings, birthdays, anniversaries). Their vast repertoire consists of such sentimental love songs as "Si Estás

Dormida," "Las Mañanitas" (the Mexican equivalent of "Happy Birthday," but sung for almost any occasion), "Guadalajara," "La Bamba," or "Cucurrucucu Paloma." The traditional Mexican fiestas frequently held at large resort hotels normally include at least one group of mariachis, and any sizable town will have a few restaurants and bars where they provide the entertainment. On weekends, a mariachi band can be heard carousing along the sidewalks of Avenida Tulum in downtown Cancún City in the late evenings. And despite the heat, they will be dressed to the nines in their close-fitting pants, a pistol hanging from each belt; bolero-type jackets, decorated with silver; and wide-brimmed hats.

MOLE: To an uninformed gringo reading a Mexican menu, an entrée of turkey mole conjures up visions of a drumstick topped with hot fudge. Nothing could be further from reality. The word mole comes from the Nahuatl *mulli,* which means sauce — and this one is made of more than 30 ingredients, only one of which is unsweetened chocolate. Most Mexican housewives pride themselves on preparing the sauce from scratch, a time-consuming recipe that involves at least four kinds of chilies (which have to be seeded, deveined, and roasted), sesame seeds, almonds, peanuts, raisins, prunes, plaintains, onions, garlic, coriander, anise, cinnamon, and an infinitesimal amount of the aforementioned chocolate.

Traditionally, it is served with chicken or turkey, as a filling for tamales, or as a sauce for enchiladas. If you are served mole in a Mexican household, you know you're an honored guest (remember, in pre-Columbian times, cacao seeds were the accepted currency, so quite literally, eating mole in those days was eating money). If a private invitation isn't forthcoming during your stay in the Yucatán, you can order it at the *Hacienda el Mortero,* next to the *Krystal* hotel on Cancún.

XTABENTÚN: One of the most popular after-dinner drinks in the region, Xtabentún is touted as being the nectar of the pre-Columbian gods. According to a local legend, this delicious anise-scented liqueur was born of a great Maya romance. Long before the Spaniards ever set foot on the Yucatán Peninsula, the story goes, a beautiful maiden by the name of Sak-Nicte (White Flower) fell in love with Tolhal, a young warrior of her tribe. Unfortunately, Sak-Nicte's beauty also attracted the interest of the village's cruel chieftain, who demanded the girl for himself. A few nights before Sak-Nicte was to be wed to the evil chief, the young lovers fled their homes and took refuge in the Maya jungle. Lost and hungry, they came across a beehive, from which they took the honeycomb and hid it in a basket made from anise branches. That evening, the gods sent a heavy rain to flood their camp. During the deluge, the rainwater mixed with the honey in the basket, giving it an unusual licorice flavor. The following day, the angry chieftain found the lovers and was about to condemn them to death when Sak-Nicte offered him a drink of the honey-anise mixture. The liquid calmed the chieftain's fury and he promised to let Sak-Nicte marry Tolhal in exchange for the beverage's secret recipe.

Xtabetún is still touted as an aphrodisiac. If you want to savor this delicate bouquet for yourself, it can be ordered in most restaurants and bars straight up or on the rocks with a dash of mineral water. It just might lead to romance.

The Yucatán's Best Resort Hotels

Whether your idea of a resort is a place to bake elegantly under the tropical sun, with no greater exertion than raising your wrist to sip a tall, cool drink (remember that the now-famous "swim-up" bar was invented in Mexico, at Acapulco's *Villa Vera*), or you prefer a haven that inspires you to play tennis and golf in the morning, go boating or riding in the afternoon, and dance all night, the Yucatán has a spot that's absolutely perfect.

The region's major resort areas are Cancún and Cozumel, but there are a lot of new up-and-coming spots that offer natural beauty and quality services at a discounted price. Far less populated than the bigger resorts, these towns are frequently enveloped in Maya ruins, uninhabited beaches, and pristine cenotes.

Prices vary significantly according to the location within the area (in town or on the beach), reputation, season, and meal plan, but first class Mexican resorts are almost always less expensive than their West Indies or Hawaiian counterparts. Cancún usually offers (often requires) that hotel guests agree to the Modified American Plan (MAP); especially during the high season, breakfast and lunch or dinner are eaten at the hotel every day — or at least paid for. During the off-season, guests can usually choose between different meal plans or rent rooms without any requirement to take meals at the hotel.

The peak season for all of the Yucatán's coastal resorts is from December 15 through April 15. Those who travel during the off-season (approximately April 15 through December 15) normally can save from 40 to 80% on accommodations. The temperature may be a bit hotter and the crowd a bit less chic, but there will be fewer people, and the lower rates may permit an increase in the level of hotel luxury and the length of stay.

CANCÚN

CAMINO REAL: A dramatic beachfront hotel with 381 air conditioned rooms and suites, all with Caribbean views, private lanais, and hammocks. There is a freshwater pool and a saltwater lagoon as well. There are tennis courts and all water sports. A big, beautiful place that's run by the Westin chain and clearly one of the best around. Hotel zone (phone: 988-30100; 800-228-3000, Westin Hotels; 800-223-6800, Leading Hotels of the World; or 212-838-3110 in New York City).

FIESTA AMERICAN CORAL BEACH: Designed in Mediterranean style with a definite calypso accent, this super-luxury, massive flamingo-pink complex is a considered by many to be a true Mexican masterpiece. And though it may be a bit too rococo for some gringo tastes, it's where all of Cancún's elite hold their social events. A self-contained beachside wonderland, it offers deluxe suites, restaurants, bars, a swimming pool, tennis courts, satellite TV, and its own gym. Hotel zone (phone: 988-32900; 800-FIESTA-1 in the US).

HYATT CANCÚN CARIBE: Those who like all the comforts of home, but with an elegant, modern touch, select this hillside paradise as their base in Cancún. The grounds seem to go on forever, with serried terraces, gardens, and verandahs giving an air of spaciousness — and offering spectacular views. Located close to all the best shopping as well as one of the choicest strips of beach on the island, this elegant 200-unit resort boasts several restaurants — including the *Blue Bayou*, specializing in superb Cajun cooking. Tennis courts, 3 swimming pools, and a Jacuzzi are an enticement to work off the extra calories. Hotel zone (phone: 988-30044; 800-288-9000 in the US).

MARRIOTT CASA MAGNA: A new 120-unit complex that combines European style with Mexican motifs in a splendid Maya setting — complete with a prolific tropical jungle — this resort offers Old World charm and service — with attention to even the minutest detail. There are several restaurants, a bar, a nightclub, a swimming pool, tennis courts, satellite TV, a Jacuzzi, and plenty of pampering. Hotel zone (phone: 988-5200; 800-228-9290 in the US).

MELIÁ CANCÚN: If you never want to step outside of your hotel, this is the place for you. The self-contained property is modeled on a safari theme — everything from rattan furniture to potted palms — with a dramatic entrance reminiscent of a Tarzan movie set, replete with toucans, palm trees, and waterfalls. The tropical motif is maintained throughout the complex, from the bamboo closets in the guestrooms to the jungle decor in the restaurants and bars. There are also 2 large (Tarzan-size) swimming pools, satellite TV, tennis courts, and an 18-hole golf course that is quite challenging. Hotel zone (phone: 988-51160; 800-336-3542 in the US).

COZUMEL

CLUB COZUMEL CARIBE: Off the beaten path and surrounded by gardens that would make Scarlet O'Hara forget Tara, this spacious, air conditioned, 280-room resort is the height of elegance in Cozumel. That's the good news. The bad news is that it's so far removed from everything else on the island that you may have trouble getting a taxi to and from snorkeling at Palancar Reef or shopping in San Miguel. But then, when in paradise, why hurry to leave? Also offered here are satellite TV, a restaurant, a bar, a swimming pool, and tennis courts. San José Beach (phone: 987-20100; 800-327-2254 in the US; FAX 987-20288).

STOUFFER PRESIDENTE COZUMEL: Convenient to the peninsula's many intriguing archaeological sites, beaches, and lagoons, this is one of the best hotels in the sophisticated, lively resort area. It has a pool, private beach, 2 bars, shops, tennis, golf, and 189 rooms and 9 suites. On Costa Residencial, south of San Miguel, the only major town on the island, near the Chankanab Lagoon and Palancar Reef (both fine places to skin dive). Carr. Chankanab Km 6.5 (phone: 987-20322; 800-HOTELS-1 in the US).

ISLA MUJERES

POSADA DEL MAR: It may not be as luxurious as one of its competitors on Cancún, but this 42-unit bungalow-hotel on the *malecón* is as swank as the laid-back living gets on this unpretentious little island in the sun. If you want to go fishing, you can usually find a master angler hanging around the lobby who will take you out and show the ropes (or lines, as the case might be) on his own boat for a nominal fee. The tropical gardens that surround the individual cottages harmonize perfectly with the rustic mood of the architecture. Air conditioning, swimming pools, color TV sets, restaurant and bar. 15 Av. Rueda Medina (phone: 988-20300).

ELSEWHERE

LA POSADA DEL CAPITÁN LAFITTE, Punta Bete, Quintana Roo: Built for sun-loving, well-heeled Europeans who want to get away from it all, this is about as far from civilization as you can get and still enjoy a fair degree of luxury. The German-operated complex is one of the oldest resorts in the area (over 25 years old) and is run in an informal one-for-all-and-all-for-one fashion that is something of a cross between a summer camp and an Israeli kibbutz. Still, those who don't want to "play" holiday campers can find their own place on the tropical beach, bury themselves beneath a straw hat, and soak up the tropical sunshine. It has 24 bungalows, a swimming pool, a great restaurant, and a bar. It is also one of the best places to watch giant sea turtles deposit their eggs in the sand. Km 60, Carr. Cancún–Tulum, Punte Bete, Quintana Roo (phone: 99-230485 or 99-216114; 800-538-6802 in the US).

FIESTA INN, Progreso, State of Yucatán: A supermodern, oceanfront beauty (more like a luxury US resort than an island one), there's little Mexican about this place except its spectacular setting: It sits on the best beach in Progreso. There are 38 rooms, a restaurant, bar, air conditioning, and cable TV. Malecón Progreso, Progreso, Yucatán (phone: 993-25072).

PUERTA DEL MAR, Puerto Aventuras, Quintana Roo: The "in" place for Mexican and US yachtsmen alike, this 68-unit complex is built on the largest marina in Mexico. Originally designed as a time-share property (now owned by Holiday Inn), this is probably one of this area's best bargains: For about the price of a room in any other hotel, guests get an entire apartment with everything from fully equipped kitchens (complete with microwave), giant closets, and in-room safety boxes to air conditioning and cable TV. The property also has a swimming pool and 2 first-rate restaurants. Puerto Aventuras, Quintana Roo (phone: 5-208-1628 or 5-208-7156 in Mexico City).

RANCHO ENCANTADO, Bacalar, Quintana Roo: A small, intimate resort with a lakeside view that exudes good taste. Every cottage is personally appointed with authentic pre-Columbian artifacts and handwoven tapestries. The gardens — where almost every tree is dripping with orchids in full bloom — are meticulously maintained. And for diners with a conscience, the French fare served in its excellent restaurant is carefully prepared to keep calories and cholesterol down. You can rent a sailboat for the day if you feel like exploring the lagoon. Space is limited, so book well in advance. Carr. 307, Bacalar, Quintana Roo (phone: 800-748-1756 in the US; FAX 983-20920).

VILLA MARINA, Puerto Morelos, Quintana Roo: Strictly a fisherman's resort; you won't find any discos at this place. The manager-owner is a bit of a cranky ol' cuss who has the heart of a fisherman and the vocabulary to go with it — which might discourage you from bringing the kids. In fact, if you asked him, he would probably advise you to leave the Mrs. at home as well. But the beer is always cold and there is generally a good game of poker going in the lobby. Built by an American with Americans in mind, this 38-apartment complex offers all the comforts of home with the benefits of a good hotel. The list of amenities include air conditioning, a swimming pool, a restaurant, and 2 bars. Puerto Morelos, Quintana Roo (phone: 800-322-6286 in the US).

The Yucatán's Natural Wonderlands

One of the last frontiers in Mexico's industrial and economic development program, the Yucatán was, until relatively recently, largely unclaimed by man, a free domain of feral jungles and wild fauna. With modern highways and the sudden surge in tourism along the Caribbean Coast, much of the peninsula's savage rain forests and natural wonders have become the victims of modern man's manifest destiny. But while large parcels of the natural landscape have been plowed away to make room for industrial plants or luxury resorts, and many plant and animal species that previously flourished in the lush jungles are now in danger of becoming extinct, the Mexican government has begun to take serious steps to preserve the country's ecological heritage. In the last few years, several wildlife and nature reserves have been established across the region, bringing new hope for many endangered species and calming the doomsday jitters of many an international environmentalist.

For the eco-tourist, the Yucatán is a Disney-like parade of tropical plants, fish, birds, reptiles, and mammals. It is a natural laboratory where flamingos come to nest and manatees and dolphins frolic along the coastal waters without the dangers of being netted by fishermen or slashed by propellers of passing motorboats.

Getting a front-row seat to view all of this unadulterated beauty can mean having to trek for several hours through dense jungles or plowing through sand marshes in a four-wheel-drive vehicle, but for the committed nature-lover, the experience is well worth the effort.

The parks and wildlife reserves listed below are open to the public. No hunting or fishing is permitted in these areas, nor are plants or other organic materials allowed to be removed without explicit written authorization from the appropriate agencies. Be sure to pack your insect repellent.

PALANCAR REEF: The absolute best for snorkeling or diving. Off the coast of Cozumel, this spectacular series of coral atolls is teeming with spotted moray, snake eels, trumpet fish, bigeye, copper sweepers, grunt, and angelfish. Between the columns of red, yellow, and violet coral are white-sand passageways and intricate caverns.

The entire area has been declared a national park, and it is illegal to touch any of the coral. You can, however, take a bag of bread crumbs to feed the fish; they'll actually come up and eat out of your hand.

Almost any scuba or snorkeling boat in Cozumel will take visitors to Palancar.

EL GARRAFÓN: Not nearly as impressive as the massive atolls along Cozumel, El Garrafón does provide visitors an interesting variety of fish and several coral formations to explore.

El Garrafón is on the northeastern tip of Isla Mujeres.

CONTOY: This federal bird sanctuary is 11 miles (18 km) northeast of the Quintana Roo coast. About 70% of the island's surface is covered with mangrove thickets, 20% is tropical palms, and 10% is rough grass. More than 300 species of migratory and sea birds nest here each year, including the pelican, which has been negatively affected by the use of pesticides and threatened with extinction in other parts of the world.

To get to Contoy, hire a boat on either Cancún or Isla Mujeres. It's at least a 2-hour ride (depending on the craft and the wind factor), much in unsheltered waters, so if you tend to become queasy at sea, don't make this reserve your first choice.

SIAN KA'AN: A massive 1.2-million-acre biosphere of jungle, swamp, and coral beach, with a tepid bay tucked away in its center where dolphins and manatees play tranquilly with any human who happens to pass their way. This is the largest nature reserve in the country, and it contains just about every species the peninsula has to offer, from giant boa constrictors and man-eating crocodiles to docile honey bears and risible spider monkeys.

Sian Ka'an lies just south of Tulum on the continuation of Route 307 from Cancún and Playa del Carmen.

XEL-HA: Although not nearly as crystal clear as it once was, this natural aquarium is a good place to test your snorkeling mask and fins before heading into the deeper waters at Palancar.

Xel-ha is just north of Tulum on Route 307 to Chetumal.

RÍO LAGARTOS: One of the only three known nesting sites in the world for the salmon-toned flamingo, this marshy reserve is 81 miles (130 km) north of Valladolid in the state of Yucatán.

Shopping at the Source

Browsing through Cancún's mammoth *Plaza Caracol* or *Flamingo Plaza* shopping centers, you will come across almost every conceivable Mexican regional craft, from handwoven serapes and baskets to stylish stoneware dinner sets and fine silver jewelry. But the Yucatán has its own brand of native arts and handicrafts which you can buy in the local shops, perhaps even from the artisan who made them. In many places, shoppers are expected to bargain for a purchase; to do this, a buyer really should know some basic Spanish, even if it's just a few numbers. (When absolutely necessary, however, body language will suffice.) There are several approaches to bargaining, depending on the place, the item you are after, and your personality. One way to shop is simply to look carefully, decide upon a fair price, and make a firm offer. Or you can offer half to two-thirds of the requested price and argue firmly from there.

Although bargaining is fun, very often the amount in question is so small that it is easier for most tourists to be generous. Bargaining is an art, and you also should know when *not* to practice it. Don't bargain in shops that have the sign *"precios figos"* (fixed prices), in government shops (often called *Artes Populares*), or in hotel shops.

Mexican native crafts are usually less expensive in local markets than in shops. It is better to buy more expensive items — jewelry or gems — in reputable shops.

And if someone offers to sell an archaeological relic from a Mexican ruin, turn him down flat. In most cases these "relics" are manufactured by the truckload, and if by some wild chance you are being offered a genuine artifact, the sale is illegal, and the item cannot be exported from Mexico without breaking the law. Even if you unknowingly obtain an authentic pre-Columbian item thinking it is a reproduction, you can be held responsible for possession of it when you try to leave the country (ignorance of the law — or the crime — is no excuse, and more than a few well-intentioned tourists have ended up on the wrong end of a Mexican jail for just such an error).

Check carefully the quality of any merchandise you are considering. Goods often presented as hand-crafted are usually machine-made — although if the price is right and the item attracts you, this is certainly no reason to refrain from buying it. But be sure you are paying what you feel the item is worth.

There are a lot of good buys in Mexico, spanning the merchandise spectrum from leatherwork to copper pots, but since most of them are produced in regions outside the Yucatán (which means they have to be transported over a difficult terrain), they are slightly higher in price on Cancún or Cozumel then they would be in, say, Mexico City or Guadalajara.

What local crafts do exist are exceptional. Some, in fact, such as black coral jewelry, are hard to find anywhere else. Discovered on Cozumel and Isla Mujeres in the early 1960s, it is fashioned into a broad selection of earrings, bracelets, and necklaces, plus key chains and other small items. That's the good news. But be warned: Some species of coral — including all black coral and large chunks of coral fresh from the sea — are protected and cannot be imported into the US. Check with the US Fish and Wildlife Service (phone: 718-917-1707) before purchasing such items.

In Mérida, the city that henequen (sisal) built, are the world's most comfortable hammocks at bargain basement prices. The best types are always hand-tied and made of sturdy sisal hemp. They come in single and "matrimonial" widths (comparable to twin and double beds) and are generally a set length.

The Yucatán's capital city is also the best place to find *guayaberas,* short- or long-sleeve cotton men's shirts with a tucked — sometimes embroidered — front. Usually white, but also available in pastels, *guayaberas* are the last word in elegant dressing for men on the Yucatán Peninsula; they're also extremely comfortable in the tropical heat.

Panama hats — a misnomer if ever there was one — actually originated in Equador. (It was because they were so popular among the Europeans and Amercians who built the Panama Canal in the early 1900s that they were given the appellation of that country.) You can bend, fold, or squash a Panama hat in a suitcase and it will still keep its shape. The secret: The hats are made from a special palm plant known as *jilijapa,* which grows only in the Yucatán. There are not a lot of styles to choose from, but you will find that your Panama hat not only will keep the sun out of your face but can be molded when wet to any Bogart-like look you might want to create.

Locally designed sportswear and evening clothes can also be a good buy. The items are seldom hand-stitched, but the quality is generally high and the prices are reasonable.

Besides native crafts, Cancún and Cozumel have bargains on items produced outside the country. Because they are duty-free zones, there is an abundance of international discounted items, ranging from French perfume and Chinese silks to Cuban cigars and tins of Danish butter. *Warning:* Some expensive items carrying the name Gucci and other top European designers, and sold in shops of the same name, are *not* the real thing, no matter what you're told; they are imitations made in Mexico and sold through a quirk in Mexican laws. Also, don't try to bring any goods of Cuban origin back to the US; they will be confiscated by customs officials. So if you are planning to savor that hand-rolled Monte Cristo, do so before you board the plane for home.

Silver has been plentiful in Mexico since the Spanish conquest. Silver items should be marked *sterling* or .925 so that you know that there are not less than 925 grams of pure silver for every 1,000 grams of weight. If you are told that the silver in the jewelry came from local mines, be skeptical. Nowadays, all silver from Mexican mines goes to the central Bank of Mexico, where it is melted into bars and then resold around the country to craftspeople.

Pottery is one of the major crafts of Mexico. There's a lot of it — some of high artistic value — and it's usually inexpensive, but *don't* buy it to cook in and *never* store acidic foods in it, since lead compounds are often used in glazing. Even when ceramics are labeled as stoneware, they frequently have not been fired at a high enough temperature to seal in any traces of lead. If you are bound and determined to use that quaint little ceramic pitcher you found in the market to serve lemonade, have it checked for lead content by a specialist first.

Serapes, rebozos, blankets, and other woven articles, such as the beautiful bulky Toluca sweaters that were the height of fashion back in the early 1970s, are usually great bargains. They should be handloomed from wool; examine the weave to make sure that other yarns weren't used.

Examine leather goods, also, to make sure that they are pure rawhide, not leather glued to cardboard or plastic. Other native crafts are huaraches (braided sandals), *huipiles* (embroidered dresses), all sizes and shapes of baskets, woodcarvings, and piñatas (papier-mâché figures to be filled with toys and candy).

Copper and tin goods can be found all over Mexico. Copper was once the most popular metal of the Mixtec and Aztec Indians. Kettles, pots, pans, and pitchers are sold in markets as well as in the more expensive shops. Again, check for quality — some articles are actually made of iron sprayed with copper-toned paint.

Be wary of gems that are sold as bargains. Jade has not been found in Mexico since the Spanish conquest. Turquoise, like all other stones, should be bought only in reputable stores; gold is not much less expensive in Mexico than in the US. Mexico does, however, have high-quality amethysts and opals and some lovely onyx and black obsidian.

Mexico is the home of many working artists and craftspeople, some of whom combine new materials and designs with the art of the past to produce original art, sculpture, weaving, jewelry, and much more. In many ways, Mexico is a perfect place for an artist to live: Life moves slowly and is relatively inexpensive outside the resort areas; also, the country's great natural beauty and breathtaking land and seascapes are inspiring. You can see the work of these artists in galleries in the better shopping centers of Cancún and Cozumel.

You are allowed to bring most Mexican crafts into the US duty-free under the Generalized System of Preferences (GSP) program. (For complete details about customs regulations in the US, see *Customs and Returning to the US,* GETTING READY TO GO.)

Below, we offer a survey of the best areas in which to shop on the Yucatán Peninsula. See also *Shopping,* THE ISLANDS.

CANCÚN

The most elegant shopping is in the hotel zone, in such posh shopping arcades as *Plaza Caracol, Plaza Nautilus, El Parián,* and *Flamingo Plaza.* But, as might be expected, prices are higher in these stylish quarters than they are in the less chic stores downtown. Best bets are usually larger stores, because the boutiques sometimes up their prices to cover their overhead. Most large hotels also have boutiques, but the selection is generally limited and prices are as high as double what they would be at a shopping center.

For good-quality gold and coral jewelry, check out *Ronay* in *Plaza Caracol.* You will also find a lot of first-rate designer wear in small shops at many of the malls. It's just a question of exploring and finding a store that is suited to your particular tastes. For good Mexican handicrafts from around the nation, try browsing in the *Plaza La Fiesta* across from the *Convention Center.* Good buys can also be found in the *Ki-Huic* crafts market downtown at the Tulum and Cobá intersection, but be sure to check for quality. These stands are often fly-by-night, and their merchandise is not the best. Don't think that just because you bought in a flea market, you didn't get fleeced. These scheming merchants will triple the price if they figure they can get it. Here is an ideal spot to practice your bargaining skills.

COZUMEL

Almost all the major shops are on the main boulevard in San Miguel, but there are a few interesting stores tucked into the side streets or a block or two away from the *malecón* (beachfront). One place in particular that merits a visit is the *Bazar Cozumel* (on Av. Juárez). Over 200 artisans display their work here, and the prices are reasonable enough (if you know how to barter, they can even be bargains). For good coral jewelry (and Cozumel is *the* place to buy coral), try *Los Cinco Soles* at *Plaza del Sol.*

ISLA MUJERES

In a place as tiny as Isla Mujeres, it's hard not to hit every stall or stand that has something of interest to sell. Unless you are looking for seashell necklaces or hand-dyed T-shirts, it's probably better to make the trek to Cancún, where the selection is bigger and the prices (although sometimes inflated by US standards) are better. The one major exception is probably *Rachat and Romé*'s beautifully crafted jewelry across from the ferry dock.

ELSEWHERE

While Cancún may be the best place to shop-till-you-drop, Mérida has quite a few interesting places for the "shop-oholic" to reconnoiter. There is a good public market near Calles 56 and 67. Mérida is the best place to buy hammocks (check the weave — the more threads, the better the hammock). It's also known for its Panama hats, *huipiles* (the embroidered dresses worn by the native Maya), the sandals called huaraches, mosquito netting, *guayabera* shirts, silver and gold filigree.

For import goods — particularly French perfume and Italian cosmetics — try the main drag in Chetumal. There are also lots of novelty food items from different parts of the world, including Dutch cheeses, Israeli chocolates, New Zealand butter, and Norwegian smoked salmon.

If you get down to Belize, be sure to pick up a bottle of the local rum. Some people say it's better than Jamaican, and the price is an incredibly low $5 (US dollars) per liter.

Bullfights: The Kings of the Rings

 If you're truly interested in Mexican culture, you should experience at least one bullfight. The bullfight, a spectacle rather than a sport, dates from before the Christian era. Modern bullfighting originated on the Iberian Peninsula during the 12th century. (Cretans were known to have hand-wrestled bulls long before the Moors introduced bullfighting to Spain.) The Spanish brought bullfighting to Mexico just 8 years after the conquest, and the first official bullfight in the New World took place in 1529.

Do not attend a fight with the idea of rooting for the bull as though it were the home team, because the bull never wins. Some people find the spectacle of an animal being killed before a cheering crowd thoroughly repugnant. If the idea offends you, don't go. Others consider the bullfight an art form, as much a part of Mexican culture as weaving, pottery work, or onyx sculpture. In any case, the bullfight is certainly a colorful event. Matadors, picadors on horseback, banderilleros, and helpers parade into the plaza accompanied by stirring *pasadoble* music. If the matadors make graceful, artistic passes with their capes or muletas (the red kerchief they wear at the hip when they enter the ring), yell "Olé!" with the rest of the crowd. Should they succeed and make a clean kill with a single sword thrust, wave your handkerchief — you may be rewarded by seeing the judge grant the matador one bull's ear, a pair of ears, or possibly a tail.

The *Plaza de Toros* in Cancún City was built in 1987, and is the most successful bullring in the world in economic terms. In fact, it is the only ring that has for over 4 years running held weekly corridas, and the bullfighting season shows no sign of coming to an end. Founded by a *yucateco* (a native of the Yucatán) with a deep-seated love for the ring, Cancún's plaza adds an extra element of struggle: the stifling tropical heat. Decked in a sequined velvet cape and tight-fitting satin pants, the matador must battle the bull in temperatures that sometimes surpass 100F. The challenge of enduring both the heat and the bull has attracted quite a few master *matadores* to Cancún, which means that there are frequently world class corridas for tourists to enjoy. The events are held every Wednesday at 3:30 PM.

Cancún's modern, 3-tiered ring has a seating capacity of 6,000. Downstairs, there are 40 commercial establishments cubbyholed into the circular plaza. There is also ample parking, and over 20 different food stands, vending everything from hot dogs to tacos, located at convenient intervals around the ring.

Many smaller towns hold bullfights (or at least matches with aspiring bullfighters practicing on whatever bovine opponent is at hand); the local tourist offices can provide information.

For The Body

Amazing Beaches

 Mexico's Caribbean coast has white, soft beaches and fine resorts along all three of its resort islands. Because of their geography, these islands enjoy warm weather almost year-round — although they are susceptible to tropical storms and strong currents. The beach season peaks from December through *Easter Week,* after which the rains and winds tend to increase.

Since all beaches in Mexico are open to the public, visitors can swim and use all the facilities, including those near luxurious hotels (though access to these resort strips may prove awkward or difficult). Beaches that are designated "public recreational areas" are maintained (at least in theory) by the government and are much used by resident Mexicans. For those who prefer privacy and seclusion, there are miles and miles of undeveloped, largely untouched beaches along the Quintana Roo coast.

CANCÚN

The Acapulco of the Caribbean, this computer-spawned resort city is among the most recent triumphs of Mexico's booming tourist trade. It is a l4-mile sandbar fringed with palms and gilded with plush hotels and a variety of recreational facilities. Primarily a spot for the sporty and socially oriented vacationer, many major hotels have beaches (although a good number of beaches are still narrower than they were before Hurricane Gilbert hit in 1988), and there are public beaches along Kukulcún Boulevard, such as *Playa Tortuga* (although we don't recommend it) and *Chac-Mool.* There's a restaurant specializing in local seafood dishes. Dressing rooms and showers are available (open from 10 AM to 11 PM).

COZUMEL

Off the coast of Quintana Roo, 45 miles (72 km) south of Cancún, this island is edged by powder-white beaches, hidden coves, and azure-blue waters. The mainland side of the island has the more popular beaches, including *San Francisco* and *San Juan.* Beautiful, nearly deserted beaches can be found by following dirt paths on either side of the island. *Chen Río Beach,* on the southern end of the Caribbean side, is protected from unpredictable, turbulent Caribbean currents by a ledge of coral that juts into the sea. *Punta Molas Beach,* on the northern end of the island, is accessible by boat or jeep and offers a pleasant day's journey.

ISLA MUJERES

Off Puerto Juárez, this small island has several white, uncrowded beaches. *North Beach* is the main one, covering the entire northern end of the island; the beach, on the Caribbean side, is good for sunbathing but dangerous for swimming. *El Garrafón Beach,* on the southern end of the island, is known for its crystal-clear waters and skin diving. The journey from the mainland (usually Cancún) to El Garrafón by boat is an adventure in itself — crew members catch fresh fish en route while passengers view schools of astonishingly "tame" tropical fish and turtles. About midway on the island is a research center studying lobsters, shrimp, and giant turtles. Visitors can ride one of the turtles — if they can catch one.

ELSEWHERE

Although it may seem from a mid-Cancún hotel zone vantage point that every conceivable square inch of available white-sanded coast has been landscaped, developed, and topped with a five-star resort, there are still plenty of virgin beaches in Quintana Roo. Route 307 from Cancún to Tulum is chock-full of undeveloped oceanfront with vacant sun-kissed beaches right out of *The Blue Lagoon*. The best beaches are those that have no signposts. Just follow any dirt path that detours toward the ocean and you may find a secluded strip of sand to call your own for a few hours or even a few days — if you're willing to play Robinson Crusoe for a while. (One favorite hidden cove is Xcalacoco, 30 miles/48 km south of Cancún. There's no sign, but look for a large cement pillar along the roadside and turn off when you get there.)

   Those who want the peace and quiet of a private beach with all the modern conveniences of electricity, running water, and a waiter to bring them their daily quota of piña coladas will prefer the more beaten paths that lead to Punta Bete, Playa del Carmen, Pamul, or the slowly developing luxury of Puerto Aventuras. Akumal, headquarters for all Mexican divers, deserves a special mention because it is everything that Cancún could be with about 95% fewer tourists. Chemuyil and Xcacel, both just before Tulum, are little-known bights with tranquil waters and plenty of fringed coconut palms. The beaches along the Gulf of Mexico in the state of Yucatán, such as Progeso, are also great sunning centers, but don't expect to find the turquoise waters of the Caribbean. Instead, the ocean is a deep green. To really get away from it all, try the coasts of Belize, which offer coral atolls, Caribbean waters, and the uncompromising quality of European-style service.

Scuba and Skin Diving: Best Depths

 Mexico's Caribbean boasts some of the finest skin and scuba diving spots in the world. The clear, warm lagoons of Cancún, Cozumel, and Isla Mujeres teem with tropical fish, invertebrates, and incredible coral deposits of intricate formations and colorful hues. Palancar Reef, the second-largest coral atoll in the world and the largest in the western hemisphere, is one of the most spectacular and popular dived regions in the world.

   Every major beach resort on the Yucatán Peninsula rents equipment and offers instruction and organized diving tours. Make sure to bring your diver's certificate with you because you will have to show it when you rent tanks or charter a boat. For those who haven't tried skin or scuba diving before, any of the spots listed below would be a good place to start. There are a number of good schools available to provide training — and even a certificate upon completion of a basic course. Needless to say, only persons in good physical health should attempt diving. If you prefer to view the underwater magic from the surface, try donning a snorkel, mask, and fins. The water is so clear that the vista is almost as good as from below.

CANCÚN

The island (which is linked to the mainland by a causeway) is perfectly situated for swimming and diving amid coral reefs, fish, turtles, and waters whose colors changes from turquoise to indigo to emerald to tourmaline. Operators, such as *Aqua Tours* (phone: 988-30227 or 988-30400), and all the larger hotels maintain boat centers with all equipment for rent and also provide skin and scuba diving tours, which run about $40 to $50 per person. Excellent diving instruction is also available. Items recovered from shipwrecks are on display at the *CEDAM Museum* (at Bahía de Mujeres and Kukulcán Blvd.). Xcaret inlet, surrounded by jungle and the site of caverns and Maya ruins, is outstanding for skin diving (rental equipment available).

COZUMEL

This island 12 miles off the Caribbean coast is world-famous for its exquisitely clear water and its proximity to Palancar Reef, the second-largest reef in the world, where underwater visibility can be 200 feet or more. Diving is particularly good from May through August. Daily (except Sunday) trips to Palancar, which include organized diving tours, lunch, drinks, and a guide, leave *Aqua Safari* (near the pier at Av. Rafael Melgar between Calles 5 and 7; phone: 987-20101) every morning at 9:30 AM.

Chankanab Lagoon is another good spot — it swarms with reef fish. About one-quarter of a mile to the north and south of the lagoon, elkhorn coral and a variety of tropical fish are visible. Off the beach at *La Ceiba* hotel (phone: 987-20815/20816) — probably the best equipped for divers — lies the hulk of a C-46 aircraft that "crashed" here in the movie *Cyclone*. Moonlight diving escapades through the fuselage of this wrecked plane, which settled amid clusters of coral, are a celebrated nocturnal event on the island.

Since currents are strong on Cozumel, don't dive without a guide. The tourist office (in the municipal palace on the main square) or any hotel desk can provide detailed information about scuba and skin diving lessons and equipment.

ISLA MUJERES

Small and remote, this island off Puerto Juárez, at the tip of the Yucatán Peninsula, has transparent waters, coral reefs, and lagoons that are renowned among skin divers around the world. Ferries leave for the island from Puerto Juárez (on the mainland, just north of Cancún) seven times daily (people and baggage only), and from Punta Sam, just north of Puerto Juárez, seven times daily (people, cars, campers, and so on). The *Cooperativa* (at Av. Rueda Medina; phone: 988-20274) rents boats and equipment. El Garrafón Beach, at the southern end of the 5-mile-long, half-mile-wide island, has crystal-clear waters and lovely coral gardens teeming with brightly colored, seemingly tame fish.

ELSEWHERE

Akumal, a 10-mile-long palm-fringed beach west of Cozumel and south of Cancún, is framed by a large barrier reef. The best diving spots are at *Club Akumal Caribe* and *Akumal Cancún* (both on the Tulum Hwy.), and the *Capitán Lafitte* hotel (at Punta Bete, about 6 miles/10 km past Playa del Carmen). The waters have 200-foot visibility and stay at about body temperature all year. At 80 to 100 feet, divers can observe magnificent coral gardens, fish, and remnants of 15th-century shipwrecks. The teaching staff at *Club Akumal* offers excellent instruction, and the club rents all kinds of diving equipment. At Xel-Ha Lagoon, a wildlife refuge just south of Akumal, there is a deep, rock-surrounded inlet of crystal water where snorkelers can view an endless array of colorful fish (rental equipment available). Skin diving is not permitted.

Sailing: Mexico's Caribbean Afloat

With the Yucatán's phenomenal coasts, it is not surprising that sailboat races and regattas are held here throughout the year. Sailing is a sport Mexicans enjoy from one end of the peninsula to the other, as well as on inland lakes. Most of the resort hotels in the Mexican Caribbean will rent small sailboats to guests, and windsurfing is becoming increasingly popular, especially at the *Club Med* enclave in south Cancún. For exact dates of regattas and competitions, as well as general information, write to the *Mexican Sailing Federation,* 42 Córdoba at Puebla, México, DF (phone: 5-533-3412 or 5-533-4664).

CANCÚN

The calm, clear water of the Cancún lagoon offers pleasant sailing protected from Caribbean currents and wind. Boats can be rented at *Club Lagoon* (phone: 988-31111) or *Aqua-Quinn* (phone 988-31883 or 988-30100).

COZUMEL

The two yacht basins on the mainland side of Cozumel, *Caleta Marina* and *Puerto de Brigo* (a full-service marina), offer protection from tropical storms. They are the only protected harbors for sailboats along Mexico's Caribbean coast.

ISLA MUJERES

This tiny island welcomes the annual *Regata del Sol al Sol* boat race in April or May, followed by the *Amigos Regatta* around the island. The biennial *Regata del Golfo al Caribe Mexicana* (sailing again in 1993) starts in Galveston. Most participants come from Mexico or the US.

ELSEWHERE

Puerto Aventuras, site of the largest marina in all of Mexico, boasts 240 slips for yachts and sailboats up to 100 feet long. This is the "in" place for the elite yachtsman to dock his craft. There are also several idyllic places to sail on the Gulf of Mexico off Progreso in the state of Yucatán. You can rent sailing (and fishing) craft at either Puerto de Abrigo (just west of town) or in front of the *Playa Linda* hotel (on the main street). Those who prefer inland boating will find the seven-hued lagoon at Bacalar delightfully calm with just enough wind to bellow their sails. Small boats are available for rental at all three locations.

Tennis

As with golf, the popularity of tennis is growing by leaps and bounds on Mexico's Caribbean Coast. Both Cancún and Cozumel have luxury resorts with tennis facilities, although the heat does tend to discourage many foreigners from taking to the courts. (If you aren't used to it, try playing in the early morning or late afternoon.)

In addition to the hotel courts listed below, the *Pok-Ta-Pok Golf Club* on Cancún will open its courts to the public for a fee, as does the *Puerto Aventuras Golf Club.*

CANCÚN

ARISTOS: 2 lighted cement courts (phone: 988-30011).
CAMINO REAL: 3 lighted cement courts (phone: 988-30100).
CASA MAYA: 2 lighted asphalt courts (phone: 988-30555).
FIESTA AMERICANA CONDESA: 3 indoor courts (phone: 988-51000).
FIESTA AMERICANA CORAL BEACH: 3 lighted, synthetic-surface courts (phone: 988-32900).
HYATT CANCÚN CARIBE: 3 lighted courts (phone: 988-30044).
KRYSTAL CANCÚN: 2 cement courts (phone: 988-31133).
MARRIOTT CASA MAGNA: 2 lighted, hard-surface courts (phone: 988-52000).
MELIÁ CANCÚN: 3 lighted, hard-surface courts (phone: 988-51160).
POK-TA-POK GOLF CLUB: 2 lighted, synthetic-surface courts (phone: 988-30871).
SHERATON: 6 lighted courts (phone: 988-31988).
STOUFFER PRESIDENTE: 2 lighted cement courts (phone: 988-30200).
VILLAS TACUL: 2 well-maintained hard-surface courts (phone: 988-30000).

COZUMEL

LA CEIBA: 1 cement court (phone: 987-20379 or 987-20844).
CLUB COZUMEL CARIBE (on San Juan Beach): 1 cement court (phone: 987-20100).
FIESTA AMERICANA SOL-CARIBE (on Paraíso Beach): 3 lighted cement courts (phone: 987-20700).
FIESTA INN: 1 lighted court (phone: 987-22900).
MELIÁ MAYAN COZUMEL: 2 cement courts (phone: 987-20072).
STOUFFER PRESIDENTE COZUMEL: 2 lighted cement courts (phone: 987-20322).
VILLABLANCA: 1 hard-surface court (phone: 987-20730).

Good Golf

 There are two 18-hole golf courses on the Yucatán Peninsula (a third course, at *Puerto Aventuras,* currently has 9 holes with an additional 9 scheduled to open this year), and while the choices may be few, they are top-rate. The popularity of these three courses is due to the excellent maintenance, the challenge, and their unsurpassed locales.

Two of the courses, *Pok-Ta-Pok* on Cancún and the *Puerto Aventuras Golf Club* at the new resort of the same name, are in the state of Quintana Roo and were constructed with the tourist in mind. Access to these two clubs is fairly easy. Almost every major hotel in the respective cities is connected with the corresponding golf course and will openly offer to secure greens privileges for their guests; clubs can even be rented in case you left yours at home.

La Ceiba golf course just north of Mérida, on the other hand, is part of a private country club and visitors must obtain special invitations through members, or the state tourist board, in order to gain access. This may sound complicated, but because the state of Yucatán government is eager to promote its tourism on every front, the formalities of an official invitation are often little more than an obligatory pile of forms filled out in triplicate and left at the Tourism Office in Mérida. For further information contact the Tourist Information Center in the *Peón Contreras Theater* (open daily from 8 AM to 8 PM; phone: 99-249290).

CANCÚN

POK-TA-POK: This 18-hole, 72-par, Robert Trent Jones, Sr. course is renowned for its fast greens and wide fairways. *Pok-Ta-Pok* (Maya for stroke-by-stroke) is a very playable course with a sensational view of both the Caribbean Sea and the Nichupté Lagoon, but watch out for the ocean wind factor. The sand traps and water hazards are deadly, so most golfers carry about double their usual quota of balls. The course has a bar and restaurant, as well as putting greens. Golf clubs, shoes, and electric carts can be rented in the pro shop. The club is open from 6 AM daily, but reservations are a near must. The pro is Felipe Galindo (phone: 988-30871).

MÉRIDA

LA CEIBA: Francisco Mier y Terán designed this 18-hole course. The sloping hills around the course make judging distances more difficult than on flatter terrains. The greens always look closer than they really are, and even the best golfers have had to readjust their sights after missing a sure shot. Par is 72, but it's hard to make on this course. The manager is Gustavo Ponce; the pro, Javier Chi. Km 14.5 of Rte. 261 toward Progreso (phone: 99-240070).

Fishing Mexico's Rich Caribbean Waters

 The Mexican Caribbean coast offers some of the best deep-sea and fly fishing in the world, and American and European fishermen travel thousands of miles up and down the Yucatán coast to hook snook, bass, dorado, striped marlin, sailfish, red snapper, billfish, and shark. Many an experienced angler will come to Mexico just to be able to compete in one of the area's numerous fishing competitions held each year. There is no problem bringing any kind of fishing gear into the country, and every major port has charter boats and fishing gear for hire (figure an average of $275 a day, gear and bait included). Even the smallest fishing village is likely to have at least one fishing boat that can be rented for half a day or more.

Visiting anglers can readily obtain a Mexican fishing permit from the *Secretaría de Pesca* (269 Av. Alvaro Obregón, México, DF 06700) or from any one of its more than 140 offices throughout the country. Licenses are free for fishing from the shore. There is a charge of $3 a day to $70 for 6 months, for fishing from a small vessel. There are also weekly and monthly rates. Temporary permits are issued for boats and trailers entering Mexico. Anglers who bring a boat will be asked at the border to pay a small fee based on the weight of the vehicle, will be required to register the boat with the port captain, and must obtain a license (for a small fee), which is good for 1 year.

More information on fishing in Mexico, including guides, regulations, fishing seasons, and tournaments, can be obtained by writing to the *Dirección General de Administración de Pesca,* 269 Av. Alvaro Obregón, Mexico City, Mexico 06700 (phone: 5-511-1881).

Recently, more and more sport fishing areas have adopted policies of catch and release in order to eliminate the possibility of "fishing the waters dry." Be sure to check the current regulations for the area and for the specific types of fish you will be after.

CANCÚN

This super-resort in the Caribbean is a haven for deep-sea and lagoon fishing. Sailfish and dolphin run from March through July; bluefin tuna in May; blue and white marlin in April and May; kingfish and wahoo from May through September. Boat rates are set by the *Boat and Yacht Association.* Deep-sea charters (for up to 6 people), including crew, tackle, and lunch, cost approximately $65 per day per person, or $240 to $310 per half day, full boat charter; small outboards cost about $30 an hour. For information, go to the Chac-Mool pier or the *Playa Blanca* hotel pier. *Aqua Tours* has a fleet of 30- and 36-foot boats (phone: 988-30227 or 988-30400).

COZUMEL

The best fishing from this island off the Yucatán Peninsula occurs from March to July for sailfish, bonito, and dolphin, and from May to September for wahoo and kingfish. Marlin, barracuda, and red snapper can also be found in the Caribbean here. Fishing boats cost from $275 to $550 per day, including crew, tackle and lunch, and hold up to 6 passengers. *Aquarius Travel* (2 Calle 3 Sur, next to the *Bahía* hotel) is a reliable place to charter a boat.

ISLA MUJERES

A casting-off spot for deep-sea fishermen, this island is most popular with anglers during the months of April and May, when the sailfish and marlin are biting. There are always plenty of boats available to take a paying customer to what locals hail as "the absolute best fishing spot in the Caribbean."

ELSEWHERE

Fly fishers prefer the waters around Sian Ka'an, where the waters are teeming with barracuda, tarpin, red drum, snook, wahoo, and even pompano. Since this area is part of a national wildlife reserve, there's no taking home your trophy to mount on the wall. Chetumal, which used to be a fashionable starting point for fishing expeditions, is still frequented by local anglers, but has very little appeal for the international set. For the best fishing near Progreso head out east toward Chicxulub, where you'll also view several typical fishing villages. If you make it the 18 miles/29 km to Chicxulub, stop off at the shipyards. This is where the pirate-style ships seen in Cancún are constructed by hand. To the east is Chelem and Chuburna, both renowned for their tranquil abandoned beaches and natural wildlife. This is also a great place to sample grilled duck (in season).

The Yucatán on Horseback

Along with the Catholic church, the lust for gold, and a host of Spanish traditions that were to take root in Mexico and wreak various degrees of havoc for the next 3 centuries, Hernán Cortés reintroduced one thing to Mexico that proved to be an outright blessing: the horse. There were no horses in Mexico when Cortés arrived, but recently discovered cave paintings in northern Mexico indicate that a smaller species once existed — and apparently became extinct. Mexicans are enthusiastic and skilled equestrians, and the tradition of horsemanship is a perfect marriage between the riding heritage of Spain and the workaday requirements of ranches and farms throughout the country.

Sport riding along Mexico's Caribbean coast is a relatively new idea, but it is catching on fast. *Hacienda San José de las Vegas* (on Rte. 307 to Tulum) offers escorted horseback tours four times a day, Mondays through Saturdays. On Sundays, you can rent horses by the hour and explore on your own, but be careful where you go. Except for a few privately owned estates, horses are banned on the beaches, and the fines for littering — no matter how organic it might be — are very steep.

There also are a few small ranches in the states of Yucatán and Campeche where horses (not thoroughbreds by any means) can be rented for a few hours or a few days to explore the surrounding areas. Look for signs along the highway that say "*se aquilla caballos*" (horses for rent). The going rate is whatever the market will bear, and most Mexicans automatically assume that the rich tourist market can bear quite a lot, so bargain.

Not for amateur cowboys, but yielding great rewards for those riders who venture in, the Yucatán is a region not tamed by highways; it has jungles, plains, and beaches yet to be discovered even by the most enterprising visitor.

Camping along Mexico's Caribbean Coast

 Perhaps because of its isolation from the rest of the country, the Yucatán Peninsula has been lagging in its development of camping services and facilities. Driving an RV all the way to Cancún or anywhere else on the peninsula is quite an ambitious task in itself. There are a few trailer parks, mostly in Mérida or as a secondary service at a so-so beach hotel, but don't expect them to include playgrounds, washing machines, or any of the other conveniences you may have come to expect.

If, on the other hand, your idea of camping is a sleeping bag under the stars, you will find the Mexican Caribbean far more accommodating. There are many free beaches, and the absence of laws prohibiting camping on public land opens thousands of miles of secluded grounds to hoist a tent. *Beware:* There are *bandidos* who prey on unwary campers.

Also, many of the national parks and wildlife reserves allow campers to spend a night or two, but check first to make sure that no formal permits must first be obtained. The administrators of Contoy, for example, allow only overnight stays for organized ornithology groups with prior documentation and authorization from the Secretariat of Ecology (SEDUE), proof of immunization against tetanus, a notarized letter of intent as to the reasons for wanting to camp there, and medical certification by a local physician stating that you are in good general health — a considerable exercise in bureaucracy even by Mexican standards.

Still, there is a special appeal associated with touring an area with your own self-contained accommodations that can be picked up and moved from one day to the next, regardless of whether they consist of an army surplus pup tent or a fully equipped, 3-bedroom Blue Bird.

Hunting

 The Yucatán is a hunter's paradise; game is plentiful from the Quintana Roo jungles to the plains of Campeche. With the proper papers, hunters can go after wild turkey, most kinds of duck, geese, quail, wild boar, deer, grouse, doves, agoutis, peccaries, and armadillo. A special permit is required to hunt white-tailed deer, puma, and gray fox.

Different parts of the peninsula have different types of game. Deer (*venado*), particularly the princely white-tailed deer, are most heavily concentrated in the state of Quintana Roo. Campeche and the state of Yucatán also have deer, but they tend to be *temazate*, a small jungle deer. Quail (*cordonizes*), doves (*palomas*), duck (*patos*) — especially teal, pintail, and mallard — geese (*gansos*), and wild turkey are found almost everywhere in the region. Big-game hunters will have to go as far as Campeche to find fox, but you can still hunt *tepezcuintles* (small wild pigs) in the early winter on the island of Tamalcab in southern Quintana Roo. (*Important:* Check an updated list of endangered species before you decide what game to go after. Right now, jaguar, ocelot, puma, and crocodiles are on the endangered list. Your local zoo will be able to help.)

Hunting in Mexico is relatively easy once you've gotten across the border, but there is quite a bit of red tape involved in bringing guns into the country and taking them out again. Moreover, there are a lot more restrictions in Mexico as to the type of weapons allowed. Some arms that are classified as sport rifles in the US are considered lethal weapons in Mexico and can be used and owned only by the military. Not only are arms subject to strict limitations, but so are the number of rounds permitted for each gun. Plan a hunting trip well in advance in order to obtain the necessary papers. If you enter the country without the proper documentation, your rifles may be confiscated and you may even end up in a Mexican jail.

Hunting seasons and bag limits vary according to the state and the abundance of game each year. For general information in English or Spanish, or for answers to specific questions, permit information, and the official hunting season calendar (*calendario cinegetico*), write to the *Subsecretaría de Ecología, Dirección General de Conservación Ecológica de los Recursos Naturales* (20 Río Elba, 8th Floor, México, DF 06500; phone: 5-553-9535 or 5-553-5545). It will supply a current hunting season calendar and an application for hunting licenses or special permits for any game that require them. In order to obtain a special permit, state the game you are after and the season and region in which you will be hunting. (*Note:* Because of the timing, you will probably have to write to the Hunting Bureau *twice:* once to obtain the calendar and list of game requiring special permits, and then again stating which animal you will be hunting, and when and where. It's realistic to start the process at least 3 months before your scheduled arrival in Mexico.)

Every hunter in Mexico must be accompanied by a registered Mexican hunting guide, and each hunter must have a hunting license — a document completely separate from the special permit, which is required only for those going after particular species. But first you must obtain a permit to transport arms temporarily into Mexico. To get this permit, you must present — to the Mexican consulate nearest your American address — a valid passport, a letter from your sheriff or police department stating that you have no criminal record, five passport photos, and a letter asking to take firearms temporarily into Mexico. The letter must state the brand name, caliber, and serial numbers of the arms you intend to take into the country. Hunters are allowed only one high-powered rifle of any caliber, or two shotguns of any gauge. Automatic weapons are prohibited. The Mexican consulate will issue a permit for firearms and a certificate of identity with a description of your weapons. The fee for this service is around $50. To facilitate re-entry into the US, you should, before departure, register firearms and ammunition with US Customs. No more than three nonautomatic firearms and 1,000 cartridges will be registered for one person.

There's more, however. Actual hunting licenses, good only in the state for which they are issued, can be obtained from the *Dirección de Area de Flora y Fauna Silvestre* (Wildlife Bureau; *Dirección General de Conservación Ecológica de los Recursos Naturales,* 20 Río Elba, 8th Floor, México, DF 06500), or from the state delegations of the Ministry of Urban Development and Ecology (SEDUE). To obtain a license for hunting birds or small mammals, you must fill out and sign an application, show proof that you have hired a local hunting organizer, pay the fee, and, most important, present your permit to transport arms temporarily into Mexico. "Special permits" are issued only through the Mexico City office of the Wildlife Bureau, and two passport-size photos again are required. Hunting licenses for birds or small animals cost about $20 per state. You will also be asked to register your weapons with the office of the commander of the local military garrison. Costs of licenses for other species vary. A license for hunting bighorn sheep, for example, costs about $3,200! Along with a licensed guide, hunters are required to have a medical certificate of good health in order to obtain the permit to hunt certain species, such as black bear.

Once you've made it into the country, obtained your license and permits, tramped through the jungles, and bagged your game, your final task is to get your game out of the country and into the US. First, check bag limits with the Mexico hunting department *and* with US Customs — they're different and they change. Game mammals and migratory game birds require a Mexican export permit or the permission of a Mexican game official. US law requires that a permit be issued from the Fish and Wildlife Service for wild game birds, wild fowl, or wild game animals. Animals may be protected by international law, by US law, or by both. The regulations covering them change periodically, so before going to Mexico, consult the *Division of Law Enforcement* (PO Box 3247, Arlington, VA 22203-3247) and the *Office of Management Authority* (PO Box 3507, Arlington, VA 22203-3507) — both part of *The Fish and Wildlife Service, US Department of the Interior* — about the specific laws and regulations involved in bringing game back into the US.

All of the above deals only with ground transportation. If you enter Mexico by air, and your license and permit are in order, you shouldn't have any trouble with customs.

Some of the red tape can be avoided if you join a hunting expedition to Mexico from the US, or engage a Mexican hunting guide before leaving the US. You can do this through *Mexico's Ministry of Tourism Branches* (see *Mexican Consulates and Tourist Offices in the US* in GETTING READY TO GO), or through local tourist offices throughout the Yucatán.

Below is a survey of the peninsula's best hunting spots listed by state, a general guideline as to what game can be hunted during which seasons, and data as to where to contract guides in each capital city.

QUINTANA ROO: Most birds, including ducks, geese, guinea hens, garganeys, quail, and doves, can be hunted during the winter months, from about mid-November through early March. The pin-tailed sandgrouse and chachalaca (*ortalis vetula macalli*), on the other hand, nest in the early winter and can be hunted only during the autumn months. Agoutis, armadillo, rabbit, raccoon, badger, and possum are usually open game in November through January. The *tepezcuintle* season is only about 1 month long, starting sometime in mid-November. You will probably need a special permit to hunt wild boar (November through December) or deer (October through April), and you will be restricted to killing only adult males of these species.

Because Quintana Roo is now pushing its eco-tourism rather than hunting, game limitations are becoming stricter by the day. Make sure you have the latest information on regulations before setting out. Just because you were told 2 months ago that a particular species was fair game does not mean the same rules apply today.

Unfortunately for the visitor to Cancún, Cozumel, or Isla Mujeres, all paperwork must go through the capital city of Chetumal, in the extreme south of the state. On the up side, the south is where the best hunting is found, so it is not that far out of your way to visit the appropriate offices. The offices (at Prolongación Venustiano Carranza, Av. Napoles, Chetumal, 77039 Mexico; phone: 983-22865 or 983-21742) are open from 10 AM to 2 PM and from 6 to 9 PM, Mondays through Fridays.

STATE OF YUCATÁN: Duck-hunting season runs from about mid-December to early March, and the hunting is best on the north and west coasts (especially between

Sisal and Celestún). Bobwhite and quail can also be found in the flatlands near Mérida. Trips into the jungle for wild boar and a species of 2-foot-tall jungle deer can be arranged during the month of December.

Local permits can all be arranged in the capital city of Mérida through the local bureau of the *Desarrollo Urbano y Ecología* (Urban Development and Ecology; 70 Calle 27, 3rd Floor, Col. México-Oriente, Mérida, Yucatán 97137, Mexico; phone: 992-63414 or 992-63503), open from 9 AM to 3 PM Mondays through Fridays. There are a lot of hunting lodges and clubs in Mérida, which the representative from the ecology bureau will be able to recommend in accordance with the type of game you are after.

CAMPECHE: Although the ocelot and the jaguar are protected against hunters under current national law, visitors can still bag big game in Campeche. Puma can be stalked during March and April. Gray fox is permissible game during November and December. Most birds can be hunted during the fall and winter months, and small mammals are allowed to be hunted from November through February. Deer season runs from November through April, depending on the species.

The address for the local bureau of ecology is Av. de las Palmas, Col. San Francisco, Campeche, 24010 Mexico (phone: 981-66619 or 981-66433).

For The Mind

The Yucatán's Magnificent Archaeological Heritage

Astonishing ruins of ancient Indian civilizations are peppered across the entire Yucatán Peninsula. Archaeological excavations and restoration have opened up some of the sites where the ancient Maya — and even cultures that preceded them — flourished. These restorations have permitted visitors to take a closer look at the region's extraordinary past. Through extensive research, archaeologists have been able to partially decode the complex glyphs that conceal the secrets of these great cultures and to give some insight as to what life must have been like before the Spanish landed on Mexican soil.

Recent evidence has shown that as early as 18,000 BC, there were indigenous people living on the Yucatán Peninsula, although very little is known about who they were and where they came from. These people, while basically hunters and gatherers, also left their mark on the Yucatán landscape, constructing primitive mounds and stone structures. Eventually, they were replaced by the Maya, one of the greatest pre-Columbian civilizations and masters of engineering, architecture, and astronomy.

The Maya were heir to the Olmec culture, the first Mesoamerican civilization. The Olmec mysteriously appeared around 1200 BC, along the Gulf of Mexico. Known for their ability to move giant 10-ton stones over long distances of water, they built giant temples, were sculptors of great facility — carving giant basalt heads as well as intricate jade miniatures — and had a written language. Before they disappeared as mysteriously as they had emerged, around the time of Jesus Christ, their civilization streched from the Valley of Mexico in the north (surrounding what is today Mexico City), to the land that is now Guatemala and El Salvador.

The Maya culture spanned the centuries between the disappearance of the Olmec and the coming of the Spanish, reaching its peak between AD 300 and 900. They are considered to have been the most advanced of the ancient Mexican civilizations, with a highly developed social structure, a vast knowledge of astronomy and mathematics, and a system of hieroglyphics. Their amazing accomplishments include the erection of immense, terraced pyramids and other places of worship, whose walls, portals, and stairways were embellished with frescoes and stone carvings. By the 8th century, the Maya controlled the entire Yucatán Peninsula.

Their culture flourished until the 10th century, when the Toltec, a militaristic branch of the Nahuatl Indians, seized control of the peninsula. The aggressive brutality of the Toltec was expressed in their art as well as their warfare. At Chichén Itzá there is dramatic evidence of this fierce stylistic influence in the sculptures with jaguar motifs, feathered serpents, birds of prey holding human hearts in their claws, and frescoes depicting human sacrifice. The invaders and inhabitants of the area around Mérida became more integrated between the 10th and 13th centuries, however, and a new culture emerged: the Maya-Toltec. The excavations of Chichén Itzá that began in 1923 have yielded a great deal of information on the merging of the two cultures. After 3 centuries of serving as the temple for the Maya-Toltec, Chichén Itzá was abandoned. Within the next 100 years, the Maya-Toltec civilization declined.

The following is a description of the architectural and cultural features of the Yucatán's major archaeological zones.

QUINTANA ROO

TULUM: Perched on the edge of a cliff, this small, strange Maya site towers above sparkling white beaches on the Caribbean and is enclosed by a stone wall. This late post-classic city is often referred to as "decadent"; that is, it dates from the time of the waning of the Maya civilization. The architecture, although built by the Maya, lacks their refinement of style; it shows squarish Toltec influence and is crudely designed and constructed.

The principal structure is El Castillo, a pyramid topped by a small temple with simple columns marking the entrance. In the *Temple of the Frescoes* are well-preserved, brightly colored murals and sculptured decorations.

Reached by day-long tours from Cancún, 80 miles (128 km) north, or boat trips from Cozumel; by car via Route 180 east to Puerto Juárez, then south, along Route 307.

COBÁ: This Maya city, not far from Tulum and Cancún, is slowly being reclaimed from the jungle. Already uncovered are a 130-foot pyramid, a 9-tiered castle, and remnants of a ball court. A *Club Med Villa Arqueológica* is at the site. On Route 307, about 26 miles (41 km) from Tulum.

KOHUNLICH: This poorly restored site (36 miles/58 km west of Chetumal on Rte. 186) includes the only two Maya pyramids known to have been used for human burials. Most of the structures are still covered in jungle and brush, but you can still appreciate the vast size of this city from a vantage-point view atop its Pyramid of the Masks.

STATE OF YUCATÁN

CHICHÉN ITZÁ: This site is easily reached from Cancún. Chichén Itzá was an insignificant Maya site until the Toltec conquered it, built their structures on top of existing Maya ones, and dominated the area until they abandoned it in AD 1224. (An evening sound-and-light show in English explains the site's history, though performances are frequently canceled because of power failures.)

The Toltec built structures in their own style, exemplified at Tula; good examples here are the Temple of the Warriors, the Group of a Thousand Columns, the Temple of Kukulcán, the Temple of the Chac-Mool, and the ball court.

The Toltec initiated rites of human sacrifice at Chichén Itzá. The *zompantli* (a platform on which human skulls were exhibited) is decorated with carved stone skulls, and the ball court displays carved relief figures depicting the traditional sacrificial deaths of the losing team. The bottom of the cenote, or natural well, nearby was littered with human skeletons and valuables; live victims were drowned here to appease the gods.

The *Temple of Kukulcán* displays a mixture of architectural features — Toltec warrior reliefs as well as Maya corbeled vaults. At the topmost altar, reached by an interior stairway, is a stone statue of a jaguar, painted red with jade eyes and spots and white flint fangs still in place.

The *Group of a Thousand Columns* was probably the marketplace of the great center. Several acres in size, the area is completely surrounded by colonnades.

Sculptures of Toltec warriors are carved on the columns of the *Temple of the Warriors.* Chac-Mools, feathered serpents, and small Atlantean figures recall the style of Tula. Mula recount the story of battles between this tribe and surrounding groups. In the *Temple of the Chac-Mool,* paintings on the benches show Toltec seated on jaguar thrones and Maya rulers on jaguar skin–covered stools.

The observatory is outside the Toltec compound. A spiral stairway leads to a small tower where openings in the structure were used to observe the equinoxes.

Chichén Itzá is 125 miles (200 km) west of Cancún on Route 180.

UXMAL: This site, the name of which means "three times built," was the major site of the Maya classic period (AD 600–1000), and during this time it underwent several periods of transition. Uxmal, which was abandoned in the early post-classic period, when the neighboring Maya center, Chichén Itzá, fell to the Toltec, is generally considered the best example of the fine, classic Maya architecture: The temples and other buildings are beautifully proportioned and designed. There is a sound-and-light show in English.

The two largest pyramids, the *Temples of the Dwarf and Magician,* contain intricate masks, panels, and mosaics. The *Governor's Palace,* a majestic structure 322 feet long and 40 feet wide, is built on multiple levels with vaulted passages and lateral wings containing exquisite latticework and mosaics. The *House of Turtles* is a well-proportioned and simply adorned structure northeast of the *Governor's Palace.*

Uxmal is 48 miles (77 km) south of Mérida along Route 180.

OXKINTÓK: Opened for public viewing since 1991, this exceptional Maya city, believed to be the largest on the Yucatán Peninsula, was constructed during the 5th century. The most impressive structure of this massive complex is a 3-story labyrinth, which can take days to explore. There is also a large ball court and several Olmec-like heads that suggest a cultural link between the two civilizations.

Oxkintók is located 31 miles (50 km) to the south of Mérida on Route 180.

CAMPECHE

EDZNÁ: A shining example of classic Maya architecture, this site is recognized as a pre-Hispanic masterpiece in hydraulic engineering. The name Edzná (which means "House of the Grimaces") refers to two grim masks encrusted in one of the main structures.

Edzná lies 38 miles (61 km) to the southeast of Campeche on Route 180.

The Yucatán's Museums

The Yucatán Peninsula has several fascinating museums that showcase its ancient and rich history, as well as its broad cultural diversity. The major museums are concentrated in Mérida, but there are others scattered throughout the region with displays of pre-Hispanic artifacts and relics dating back 10,000 years. The museums described below have the most extensive and interesting collections in the area, and although they may not be as impressive and massive as their larger counterparts in Mexico City or Guadalajara, they are definitely worth visiting.

COZUMEL MUSEUM, Cozumel: The next best thing to donning a snorkeling mask and discovering the underwater world of Palancar Reef firsthand. The 3-dimensional figures of tropical fish, coral atolls, and man-eating sharks on display at this museum of marine life are extremely lifelike and can provide a good background on undersea life around the island. Closed Saturdays. Admission charge. On the main avenue across from the ferry dock (phone: 987-21277).

CANTÓN PALACE (Museum of Anthropology and History), Mérida: Recently refurbished and expanded, this is one of the finest provincial museums in Mexico. It depicts the lifestyle of the Maya, and a visit prior to touring the ruins helps bring Maya history into focus. The museum is housed in the *Palacio Cantón,* the largest and perhaps loveliest of the splendid mansions on the Paseo Montejo. This building was formerly the official residence of the governor of the state of Yucatán. Closed Mondays. Admission charge. Entry is on Calle 43 (no phone).

MUSEO NACIONAL DE ARTE POPULAR (National Museum of Popular Art), Mérida: A bit of a hike from downtown Mérida, this small museum is worth it. On display are masks, pottery, clothing, and other examples of *yucateco* arts and crafts. Upstairs there is an excellent — though completely unorganized — collection of folk art from all over the country. There is also a shop on the first floor, with items for sale at incredibly reasonable prices. Open Tuesdays through Saturdays from 8 AM to 8 PM. No admission charge. On Calle 59 between Calles 48 and 50 (phone: 99-280078).

PAYO OBISPO ZOO, Chetumal: Most of Chetumal's historical records were destroyed in 1955 by Hurricane Janet, but the city does combine a small museum of its insurgent past with an intriguing sampling of the region's natural heritage. Specimens of indigenous wildlife — from the playful manatee to the illusive kinkajou — are on display in the brackish waters, replicating their natural jungle setting. There is also a building that houses a scanty synopsis of the city's tormented history and a few artifacts from Kohunlich. Admission charge. Open daily. Av. Insurgentes on the corner of Andrés Quintana Roo (no phone).

CAMPECHE REGIONAL MUSEUM, Campeche: This small museum is, in many ways, more impressive from the outside than from the inside. Once the private home of a military leader, Lieutenant Alfonso del Rey, it now houses a compact collection of Maya artifacts, including a stunning jade mask, necklace, and arm bands retrieved from a nearby tomb. Closed Mondays. Across from the main square and City Hall on the *malecón*. Admission charge (phone: 981-46878).

FUERTE SAN MIGUEL (San Miguel Fort), Campeche: Pirate fans will find this museum exciting. There are swords, maps, and various items of gold and silver that were looted from Spanish and English vessels. There is also a scale model of Campeche when the city was a major, bustling seaport. Open daily. Admission charge. Calle 59 (no phone).

PABLO BUSH ROMERO CEDAM MUSEUM, Puerto Aventuras: This small, privately owned museum displays various items recovered from sunken galleons, including the famed *Mantanceros,* which sank off the coast of Akumal in 1741. There are also several Maya figurines that were found at the bottom of surrounding cenotes (sinkholes) used for sacrificial purposes. Open daily from 11 AM to 5 PM. No admission charge. Eastern end of Malecón del la Marina (no phone).

DIRECTIONS

Introduction

Until quite recently, the possibilities of travel along Mexico's Caribbean Coast and through the Yucatán Peninsula were extremely limited. Even for Mexicans, just getting there represented an ambitious trek through marshy, corkscrew jungle roads which often were so consumed with wild underbrush that every few miles the growth had to be slashed with machetes in order to clear a path for a vehicle. Within a matter of days, the tropical jungles would reclaim the territory and hardly a sign would remain that man or woman had even penetrated that region.

Fortunately, this is no longer the case. In the late 1960s, when the Mexican government decided to commercialize the remotest province in the republic (until about 20 years ago, most of the Yucatán Peninsula was still considered a national territory without state status), "Phase One," an all-out development plan backed by public funding, was put into motion. The region's first international airport — and the first runway of any kind in the state of Quintana Roo — was constructed on an obscure tip on the eastern coast, a tiny fishing village and island called Cancún. Roads were cleared and infrastructure facilities, such as electrical generators, phone lines, and water purification plants, were installed. The government also built Cancún's first resort hotels, *Villas Tacul* and *Playa Blanca*. Fast on their heels followed private-sector complexes, with a massive *Club Med* absorbing the island's southernmost tip. Suddenly, Cancún was an international tourist destination and almost-daily charter flights from the US, Canada, Europe, and even Asia were transporting hundreds of visitors to its powdery shores.

But to keep the tourists' interest and to convince them to stay longer, the Mexican government knew that the Yucatán had to offer more than surf, sun, and sand. Convinced that the region's rich archaeological heritage and virgin jungle could give Quintana Roo's fledgling tourist industry the cutting-edge advantage it needed to be able to compete successfully with well-established and better-known destinations such as Jamaica or Hawaii, Mexican officials opted to inaugurate "Phase Two" of its Yucatán promotion program in the mid-1970s. Once again, massive quantities of state capital were funneled into development, this time for clearing roads, restoring Maya vestiges, and building marinas. It didn't take long for private investors to figure out that if Cancún could skyrocket from an unknown fishing village to a major international resort area in less than 10 years, so could other parts of the peninsula. To get US tourists (and their mighty US dollars) to these new "me-too" resorts, highway communication had to be improved, and no small amount of private capital went into leveling, grading, and paving roads.

The big winner, of course, was the tourist, who now could easily journey from one end of the Yucatán to the other, admiring all the mysteries and magic that this remarkable peninsula has to offer — secluded beaches, Maya ruins, flamingo nesting grounds, colonial haciendas, and picturesque villages.

What follows is a general description of the Yucatán Peninsula plus the prime driving routes through the region, including day trips from Cancún to Cozumel, Isla Mujeres, Akumal, and Tulum; and exploration of the Yucatán, from Cancún to Campeche, and from Cancún to Chetumal, near the Mexico-Belize border. Entries describe the highlights of each route, including useful suggestions for sightseeing and dining, plus descriptions of the driving conditions and approximate timetables for coming and going. *Best en Route* lists suggested accommodations at the best available hotels and inns along the way. Detailed maps introduce each itinerary and note the major reference points along the route.

We've made route selections based on our opinions of the most memorable Yucatán sites and sights, and it's certainly possible to string two or all three of these itineraries together for more extensive roaming. For those with less time, following any single itinerary will help you to see the most notable points of interest (and the most attractive accommodations) in any given area.

Driving from Cancún is not difficult. Your best bet is to rent a car in Cancún City (not at the airport, where the price is considerably higher). In fact, arrange to have a rental car delivered to your hotel the morning of your departure. Several international rental firms, as well as some smaller, regional ones, have offices in the city (see *Sources and Resources* in THE ISLANDS). It's best to reserve a car in advance through a travel agent; specify very clearly what kind of vehicle you require. If you are planning to drive as far as Belize (see *The Yucatán Peninsula: Cancún to Chetumal,* in this section), you will need a special letter from the rental company granting you permission for the temporary export of the vehicle. Budget travelers can find VW Beetles and Nissans within their price range. Those planning a trek through the jungles of Sian Ka'an down to Punta Allen should seriously consider a four-wheel-drive vehicle. For pure indulgence, try a big, air conditioned, automatic Ford, Dodge, or Chevrolet. These are the biggest autos available in Mexico, and they are constantly in demand, which is why advance reservations are so important. Without a reservation, a car that has these creature comforts may not be available, which can make things sticky for drivers who never learned to shift gears. When you get right down to it, air conditioning, too, is more of a necessity than a luxury for most visitors. The Yucatán is hot all the time.

One word of caution about traveling by car anywhere in Mexico: It's always wise for travelers who will be driving on remote country roads (and the Yucatán has more than its fair share of these) to allow sufficient time to reach their destinations well before dark. Few of the roads covered in the driving itineraries that follow are superhighways, meaning it's inevitable that it will take you considerably longer to cover a given segment of ground here than to drive a similar stretch back home. Driving secondary roads in Mexico after dark is not something we recommend; as a matter of fact, it's a risk we earnestly advise travelers to avoid.

Finally, as anywhere in the world, picking up strangers, camping on a lonely beach, or sleeping in a car in some isolated area can invite serious trouble. It takes only a little common sense, and some very basic planning, to make a driving tour of the Yucatán Peninsula both a safe and an especially memorable travel adventure.

Mexico's Caribbean Coast: Cancún to Tulum

Although Route 307 stretches south from Cancún to Chetumal, many of the points of interest along the way are within easy reach of Cancún and can be seen in a series of individual day trips. The trips outlined below are for those who have had their fill of basking on the beach on Cancún (temporarily, at least), but prefer to pack and unpack only once during a vacation. Though these day trips presuppose a hotel base in Cancún, we offer both hotel and restaurant suggestions for those who opt to continue on to some of the longer routes (see *The Yucatán Peninsula: Cancún to Chetumal* and *Cancún to Campeche* in this section).

DAY TRIP 1: COZUMEL

Despite the fact that many people tend to mentally clump Cancún and Cozumel together as a single tourist destination, they are *not* twin cities. In fact, there is a considerable distance between them — 53 miles (85 km) to be exact (there is a causeway that connects the island of Cancún to Cancún City on the mainland). Distance is not the only thing that lies between Cancún and Cozumel. There is also an immense wonderland of semi-undeveloped beaches, fishing villages, and sleepy sea coves which are well worth a look. Most commercial tour buses will zip you from Cancún to Playa del Carmen (the town where you catch the ferry to Cozumel) and back again.

However, if you choose to drive, you can enjoy a leisurely tour through small villages — such as Puerto Morelos — and excellent beaches — among them, Punta Bete and Playa del Carmen — and explore this extraordinary stretch of Caribbean Coast. Moreover, there are plenty of unnamed beaches just a few miles off the highway, with no markings other than a well-worn dirt path. With a four-wheel-drive vehicle, you can discover your own "Paradise Found" in the midst of the Yucatán jungles. In the springtime, the area offers yet another bonus for biology buffs: At this time of year, thousands of sea turtles come ashore at night to lay their eggs at Punta Bete, just north of Cozumel — it's a truly impressive sight.

En route from Cancún – Going from Cancún to Cozumel is easy. Route 307, a two-lane highway, runs from the south of Cancún (Cancún City) 41 miles (66 km) to Playa del Carmen.

As you head out south from Cancún's hotel zone toward the airport on Kukulcán Boulevard, there is a fork in the highway. The road on the right doubles back to downtown Cancún, while the road on the left continues toward the airport. Take the road on the left; within a few hundred feet the highway will divide again.

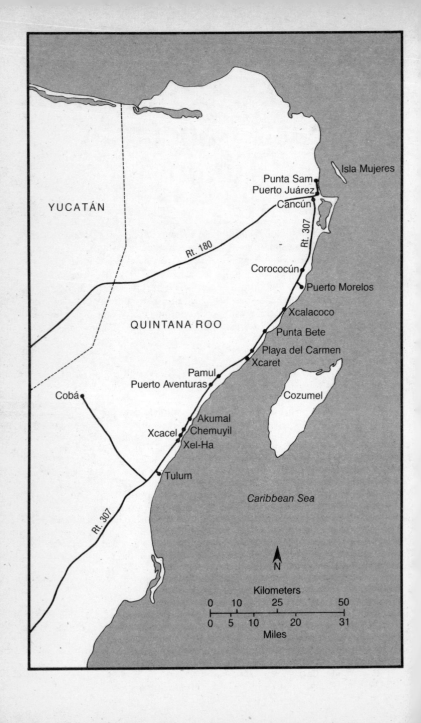

YUCATÁN

Punta Sam
Puerto Juárez
Cancún

Isla Mujeres

Rt. 180

Rt. 307

Corococún

Puerto Morelos

QUINTANA ROO

Xcalacoco

Punta Bete

Playa del Carmen

Xcaret

Pamul
Puerto Aventuras

Cozumel

Cobá

Akumal
Chemuyil
Xcacel
Xel-Ha

Tulum

Caribbean Sea

Rt. 307

N

Kilometers

0   10   25   50
0   5   10   20   31
Miles

There will be two signs, one pointing right to the airport and the other, on the left, marked "Tulum." Take the Tulum Highway. This will put you on Route 307, and from here on it's straight going to Playa del Carmen.

CROCOCÚN: Mexico's only crocodile farm, Crococún is 19 miles (30 km) south of Cancún on Route 307; this should be your first stop on the way to Cozumel. A privately run enterprise operated under the strict watch and auspices of SEDUE (the National Ecology Secretariat), this 60,000-square-foot farm was first opened in 1986. SEDUE's intention was to have it serve as a natural reserve and as a breeding center for the endangered Yucatán crocodile. As recently as 20 years ago, the peninsula was infested with over 10,000 swamp-loving morelete crocodiles, but today poachers and indiscriminate hunters have nearly annihilated the species. Hence, Crococún was founded to replenish the mangrove marshes with specimens of one of the oldest surviving creatures on earth. Eventually, the owners plan to commercialize the crocodile skins, which are internationally prized for their subtle, even-grained belly hides. However, because the reproduction process is so slow (only about 50 eggs are hatched each year and a crocodile does not reach sexual maturity until it is about 25 years old), this is definitely a long-term marketing objective. Currently, the ranch has fewer than 500 crocodiles, and SEDUE will not grant a marketing permit until the population reaches at least 10,000.

One of the more interesting aspects of Crococún is that it is also a biological research center. A few years ago, a local herpetologist discovered that the sex of the moreletes is determined by the degree of humidity and temperature the eggs are exposed to within the nest. Since a slightly lower temperature and dampness will result in the birth of a female crocodile, studies are now under way at Crococún to incubate the eggs under laboratory conditions, thus increasing the female-to-male ratio and speeding up the time it will take to replenish the crocodile stock.

The farm is staffed by veterinary students on a field study from the Yucatán University in Mérida, and for a small fee, they will provide visitors with personalized tours (in English and Spanish) of the grounds. The crocs are kept in large muddy pits according to age. The smaller crocodiles, which may look harmless from a distance, are actually the most dangerous. If you are lucky, your guide will volunteer to mud-wrestle one of the larger reptiles Tarzan-style, and tie its mouth shut so that you can see it up close and caress its tender underbelly. *Don't* try this yourself. Crocodiles can lay totally immobile with their mouths wide open for hours, or even days, but will spring into action as soon as anything that resembles a possible meal approaches.

Also on the farm are white-tailed deer, raccoon (some running wild), spider monkeys, and over 10 species of snakes.

Next door to Crococún is *Acuario Palancar,* a shoddy, aquatic would-be museum which resembles a carnival sideshow trying to cash in on the main event. Inside are 12 aquariums with little more than a miniature turtle, a few goldfish, and a trout or two. Don't waste either time or money on this place. Instead, stop for lunch at the *Iguana Club* (a few hundred yards past Crococún on Rte. 307; no phone). This American-run establishment offers the best Texas-style barbecue south of the Rio Grande. The atmosphere is rustic, but the cooking is definitely down-home and good.

PUERTO MORELOS: About 3 miles (5 km) past Crococún is the turnoff for Puerto Morelos, which is 2 miles (3 km) east of the highway down a dirt path to the coast. Primarily a fishing village, Puerto Morelos is known across the state for its ocean-fresh fish. There is a large coral reef just 500 yards from shore, making it a great place for snorkeling (although not on a par with Cozumel's Palancar National Park). The beaches here usually are empty by Cancún standards, and the dining and accommodations will cost about one-quarter of what they would cost on the resort islands. If seafood is your weakness, here's the place to indulge your taste buds. *Los Pelícanos* (no phone), a casual seaside restaurant on the main drag, has been a favorite dining and watering hole for locals for over a dozen years. *Doña Zenaida* (no phone), a block before you reach the oceanfront, bills itself as "the oldest restaurant in the Mexican Caribbean" and has a good reputation for simple *yucateca* cuisine. For overnight free spirits, visits can include sacking out on the beach near the lighthouse (it's guarded 24 hours a day and is open to the public for camping, but be sure to bring insect repellent and mosquito netting). For those seeking more sybaritic sights, there are deluxe suites at the newly opened *Villa Marina Beach Club,* 2 miles (3 km) south of town (see *Best en Route*).

Continue south on Route 307 for 15 miles (24 km) to Punta Bete. Halfway there (8 miles/13 km), look for a large cement pillar along the roadside; turn off here to reach a favorite hidden cove, Xcalacoco.

PUNTA BETE: Unknown to most Americans, this charming, tranquil beach has been a favorite of well-heeled Europeans for nearly 2 decades. The main attraction, outside the German-run *Capitán Lafitte* hotel (see *Best en Route*), is that every May the shores are inundated with thousands of sea turtles laying eggs in the sand. Like salmon and monarch butterflies, sea turtles instinctively return to the site of their own hatching year after year, to lay up to 200 eggs in a single nest under the light of a full moon. If you are lucky enough to witness this extraordinary event, keep your distance so as not to disturb the turtles and their eggs.

Originally, this area of Quintana Roo was home to the largest colony of sea turtles in the world. Today, their species is in danger of extinction because their eggs have been stalked by culinary pleasure-seekers as an exotic delicacy, and poachers have killed most of the adults for their amber-hued shells. The Mexican government has clamped down on the senseless slaughter of these slow-moving reptiles, but greed have unfortunately kept the tortoiseshell black market alive. (You might be offered turtle cream, tortoiseshell jewelry, or any number of other items made from this sea creature.) Besides the fact that purchasing any of these products will only promote poaching, it is illegal to bring any tortoise-derived products back to the US, and if found by customs officials they will be confiscated.

PLAYA DEL CARMEN: Just 6 miles (10 km) south of Punta Bete, Playa del Carmen is an underestimated tourist destination. For years, it has been thought of almost exclusively as "the place you take the ferry to get to Cozumel." Recently, however, more discerning travelers have discovered that this port city has merits of its own, including *Las Molcas* hotel, a comfortable beach resort, a slew of good restaurants, and some of the most tranquil beaches on the peninsula — all at rates far below their counterparts in better-publicized island destinations.

Playa del Carmen is a good walking town, and it's easy to get around. In fact, it is far easier to get around on foot than by car. The town has a disproportionately high population of police, who make comfortable incomes from fining unsuspecting tourists who leave their vehicles along unmarked, supposedly "illegal" parking zones or drive down one-way streets that suddenly change direction. Since ferries to Cozumel leave every half hour, it's possible to program an itinerary to include a few hours in Playa del Carmen without having to stay long enough to have a personal encounter with one of these ticket-happy officers of the law.

For those here at lunchtime, the *Chicago Connection* in the north of town satisfies the meat-and-potatoes crowd. *Al Bacco* (2 blocks from the ferry dock) offers fine Italian food in a garden setting, and *Las Molcas* (just across from the dock) is the top-rated hotel (see *Best en Route*) and serves the best seafood in town.

From Playa del Carmen, take a ferry (there's one for vehicles as well as passengers) across to Cozumel. Or if you prefer, leave your car in Playa del Carmen (there is a parking lot directly across from the ferry dock which is well lighted and quite secure). Passenger ferries to Cozumel leave from the main dock across the street from *Las*

Molcas hotel in Playa del Carmen every hour on the half hour from 6:30 AM to 7:30 PM. The ride takes about 45 minutes to an hour, depending on water conditions and the quality and swiftness of the craft. Unless you are particularly fond of long, rocky boat rides, opt for one of the modern, jet-propelled catamarans operated by *Aqua-Quinn* and *Aviomar*. Their ticket offices are at the dock on the right side. Just opposite them is the ticket booth for the smaller craft. The cost for the jet-propelled ferries will be slightly higher, but the ride is somewhat smoother, and you'll arrive up to 15 minutes faster, which can be a godsend if you don't have your sea legs. (For those prone to seasickness, be sure to bring Dramamine.)

For those determined not to go to sea, air transport via *Aero Cozumel* is also available; but prices are steep for the quick trip from the mainland. Planes depart Cancún Airport for Cozumel daily at 8 and 10 AM, noon, 2, 4, and 6 PM.

Those travelers who wish to take their cars will have to leave from Puerto Morelos, 22 miles (35 km) south of Cancún on Route 307. Once a day (at no set hour), a large ferry laden with produce and commercial supplies departs on a 3-hour ride to Cozumel. If you are planning to take this tack, be at the dock no later than 6 AM and be ready to wait. For a detailed report on Cozumel, its hotels and restaurants, see THE ISLANDS.

BEST EN ROUTE

The towns and beaches along the route from Cancún to Cozumel are so small that very few have bothered to validate a formal address system. Most of the hotels and restaurants are *conocidos* (known by all). If you are not among the "all" they refer to, ask any local resident to point you in the right direction. For a double room, expect to pay up to $100 at an expensive hotel; $40 to $95 in moderate places; and $35 or under in inexpensive ones.

PUERTO MORELOS

Villa Marina – A modern, 38-unit facility built especially for snorkelers and deep-sea fishermen. The rooms are big, clean, and air conditioned, with kitchens and an ocean view. There is also a swimming pool, a dive shop, a small cafeteria, and 2 bars (phone: 800-322-6286 in the US). Expensive.

Plaza Morelos – Conveniently located on the main plaza, this modest, family-run establishment has 30 rooms with overhead fans, hot showers, and a cafeteria (no phone). Inexpensive.

PUNTA BETE

Capitán Lafitte – A perfect place to get away from it all in style. There are no fans or air conditioning in the 24 bungalows at this German-run resort, but the cool ocean breeze is refreshing enough and the home-cooked dishes are outstanding. In addition to a dining room, there is a pool hall, a swimming pool, a dive shop, a bar — and superb service (phone: 99-230485 or 99-216114; 800-538-6802 in the US). Expensive.

PLAYA DEL CARMEN

Las Molcas – Located directly across from the ferry dock, this modern 40-room complex is enhanced by a garden of tropical flowers. All rooms are big and air conditioned. There is a good restaurant, 3 bars, a swimming pool, and a boutique (phone: 988-46846 or 988-46433). Expensive.

Suites Quintas – Modeled after a typical *Holiday Inn* in the US, this bland-decored, air conditioned, 20-unit inn is nonetheless comfortable and very clean. One major drawback: It's not on the beach (phone: 987-20688). Expensive.

Costa del Mar – This 14-room mom-and-pop establishment is at the northern edge of town along the beach. A swimming pool, homey touches, and a terrific restaurant are pluses (phone: 987-21783). Moderate.

En route from Cozumel – Take the ferry back to Playa del Carmen and pick up Route 307 north to head back to Cancún.

DAY TRIP 2: ISLA MUJERES

Six miles north of Cancún's shore is Isla Mujeres, Quintana Roo's third resort island. At some point, almost everybody staying on Cancún takes a boat over here for lunch and a swim. Passenger ferries to Isla Mujeres leave from the Punta Sam ferry dock (north of Puerto Juárez, approximately 5 miles/8 km north of Cancún City) every hour and a half from 6:30 AM to 8:30 PM. Although the Tranportes Turisticos Magana craft are a bit run-down, they are dependable (if not always prompt) and cost about $2. The crossing takes 20 to 30 minutes and can be rough for even seasoned sailors.

However, a more comfortable way to Isla Mujeres is on one of the escorted tours (some include glass-bottom boats) that depart every morning for full-day trips from the dock at Playa Bonita. Costs vary from about $30 to $40; most offer lunch, drinks, entertainment and a snorkeling jaunt at El Garrafón.

Those who prefer to make their own itinerary can usually find small private craft at Playa Bonita or Playa Langosta that ferry guests across to Isla Mujeres for about $15.

Many people stay overnight on this very small island. The downtown section is a mere 5 blocks wide and 8 blocks long. Most of the streets are unpaved, and there are very few cars. Extremely informal, it's popular with younger folk. Sweatshirts and jeans are about as elegant as anybody gets. Completely relaxed, the island attracts an arty, intellectual crowd who stay on until money runs out.

The island's name in Spanish means "isle of women," but this is not intended to get male hopes up. Those first Spanish explorers found the place crammed with female idols. Apparently, the Maya chose the spot for fertility rites. Nowadays, Isla Mujeres is known mostly for its great swimming and snorkeling. Day-trippers should be sure to get to El Garrafón (the Jug), a spectacular national park and beach sheltered by a long coral reef. Here, the fish are larger, and you can swim through schools containing thousands of them. At the turtle pen, you can ride sea turtles and, if you're up to it, cautiously swim up to a "sleeping" shark. Treat yourself to a fresh seafood lunch at *María's Kan Kin* (5 miles/8 km south of town; phone: 988-20279), *Ciro's Lobster House* (11 Matamoros, in town; phone: 988-20102), or *Hacienda Gomar* (on the west side of the island on the road to El Garrafón; no phone). For a detailed report on the island, its hotels and restaurants, see THE ISLANDS.

En route from Isla Mujeres – Take the ferry to return to Cancún.

DAY TRIP 3: AKUMAL, TÚLUM

This route takes in Akumal, one of the best snorkeling and scuba diving spots along Mexico's Caribbean Coast, and Tulum, with its rich archaeological treasures. The beach at Xcaret and the luxurious Puerto Aventuras resort are also on the route, as are the turtle-breeding grounds at Pamul.

Akumal is a seemingly endless breadth of seductive white-sand beaches, spattered with a medley of sheltered coves, Maya ruins, and resort hotels. Snorkelers will be lured to the crystal-clear waters of Xcaret, and Xel-Ha's natural aquarium. Full-fledged scuba pros will prefer the promise of sunken treasures off the Akumal coast (rental equipment is readily available). The scholarly anthropologist may even be able to ignore the serene call of the Caribbean shore and make a beeline for the magnificent walled ruins of Tulum and the jungle-enshrouded mysteries of Cobá. Whatever your particular fancy, you will no doubt find it realized along this incredible strip of beachfront paradise.

En Route from Cancún – Route 307 follows the coastline for 63 miles (101 km) straight into Akumal. From there, your only dilemma will be deciding which way to continue. To the northwest, 26 miles (42 km) away, lies Cobá, a massive collection of unexplored Maya structures swallowed up in untamed jungles; this is the largest archaeological site in Mexico. The main highway (Route 307) continues down into the controversial no-man's-land, where pirates and rebels have disregarded the voice of authority since early colonial days. If time permits, try to squeeze a glimpse of each of these attractions into your holiday schedule.

XCARET: If you visit only one beach in this area, make it this one. Xcaret (pronounced Shkah-*ret*), 10 miles (16 km) past Playa del Carmen on Route 307, is a happy blend of ancient ruins and sun-kissed beach with an extra helping of cenotes (sinkholes) and underwater caves.

There isn't much academic data available on the ruins at Xcaret because for as long as anyone can remember, they have been in the hands of the Gómezes, a local family that exploits the popularity of the place by charging a token fee to visitors. Although hardly majestic, the ruins are interesting. At the entrance to the grounds is a short base of what must have been a pyramid encrusted with geometric figures and abstract animal motifs. A short distance beyond this structure are two extremely deep cenotes, apparently once used for dumping virgins down to the lustful gods of the underworld in exchange for bumper harvests. There are also 12 steps leading up to an arched doorway barely big enough for a miniature poodle to maneuver through. The Mexican Institute of Anthropology and History contends that there are numerous other unexcavated edifices that help to make up the site, but until someone gets around to excavating them, they remain a matter of conjecture rather than certitude. Because the exposed structures are so close together, the obligatory archaeological rounds can be completed in less than half an hour; then proceed down the dirt trail to the enchanted little limestone cove at the water's edge. Here, even those who are too lazy to don a snorkeling mask can see the schools of golden damselfish that call these waters home.

But a visit to Xcaret doesn't end with the cove. Up the hill past the cove there is the open-air *Xcaret Café,* which serves a tangy sea snail ceviche and fresh-baked banana bread; beyond is a 50-foot cenote enclosed in the mouth of a cavern. Plunge into the cool, sweet water of this natural pool to wash off the salt from the ocean. Intrepid divers can also explore the various grottoes and crevices of the caves which extend underwater for about 1,500 feet (rental equipment is available at the dock in nearby Akumal).

There are no hotels at Xcaret, but if you bring your own sleeping bag, you can camp out near the ruins in exchange for a small contribution to the Gómezes' personal nest egg. There are restrooms and shower facilities on the grounds, which Mrs. Gómez keeps extremely clean.

PAMUL: Nowhere else on the peninsula do so many giant sea turtles come to nest. Every spring thousands of these gawky, slow-moving reptiles waddle ashore to lay their eggs in the soft, powdery sands of Pamul, and within a few weeks, the tiny offspring hatch and scurry into the turquoise ocean waters to begin the process anew. The amazing part of this annual breeding ceremony is that somehow the turtles instinctively return each year to the place of their birth to renew the age-old cycle. Those who want to witness this dramatic event can catch a ringside seat in Pamul between May and July, depending on the species. There are three main types of sea turtles in Quintana Roo — the hawksbill, the *caguama,* and the *blanca* — and all nest at Pamul.

The turtles usually come ashore in the late evening and burrow themselves into the sands headfirst. Once totally submerged, they release their eggs, up to 150 at a time.

The entire process takes about an hour; at the end the turtles quickly return to the sea without a moment's concern for the fate of their progeny. Sadly, most of the eggs will not hatch. Instead, they will be eaten by predator crabs, birds, or insects.

Until recently, turtle eggs were also the unfortunate prey of man — who considered them a delicacy — but under current Mexican regulations all sea turtles and eggs are now protected — at least from humans. Despite these laws, there are still folks who traffic in turtle products ranging from tortoiseshell jewelry to turtle egg soup. The tab for their nefarious merchandising may well be the extinction of the slow-footed beast. Say no to anyone who tries to sell you turtle products.

The overnight accommodations in Pamul are not nearly as swank as in Punta Bete, but there is an 8-unit provincial inn with hot showers, overhead fans, and a restaurant (see *Best en Route*). There is also an RV park with all the basic hookups run by the owners of the hotel.

PUERTO AVENTURAS: Once you've had your fill of roughing it with the sea turtles, bask in pampered luxury at Puerto Aventuras, just 3 miles (5 km) past Pamul and 19 miles (30 km) south of Playa del Carmen on Route 307. This swank, high-priced resort is by far the most exclusive in the Mexican Caribbean. The deluxe facilities at this up-and-coming vacation destination include the largest marina in Mexico, a 9-hole golf course (another 9 holes are scheduled for completion this year) — built around several pre-Columbian structures and a couple of ancient cenotes — a tennis club, and two fashionable waterfront hotels. The best of these is unequivocally the *Puerta del Mar,* a 68-unit, Mediterranean-style complex that opened in early 1991, and includes private villa-like suites replete with everything from microwave ovens to personal valets upon request (see *Best en Route*). The living is easy, but don't expect these select accommodations to be gentle on the pocketbook. Puerto Aventuras was built as a posh oasis for Mexico's well-heeled elite with discerning palates.

The marina, a yachtsman's dream come true, is located on a turquoise cove that is fed by underground springs, keeping the water crystalline fresh, despite the large number of craft docked here. It has a mooring capacity of 240 slips, for yachts up to 100 feet long. Landlubbers will be attracted to Puerto Aventuras' scenic landscaping, which incorporates the natural beauty of the region with transplanted Asian palms, and orchids brought from the Brazilian Amazon. There is also a private museum, the *Pablo Bush Romero CEDAM,* displaying 18th-century silver goblets, gold coins, medallions, cannon, and other relics salvaged from the *Mantanceros,* a Spanish merchant ship that sank off the coast of Akumal in 1741. Open daily from 11 AM to 5 PM.

Because the resort is still under development, there aren't many restaurants from which to choose, but the few that do exist are quite good. For a toothsome casual lunch in a safari-like atmosphere, try the *Papaya Republic,* run by the vagabond son of one of Mexico City's better-known upper-class families. For more formal fare, try *Carlos 'n' Charlie's* (a member of the ubiquitous chain), serving everything from spicy barbecued spareribs to chicken Kiev.

AKUMAL: Akumal is just a few minutes south of Puerto Aventuras, 3 miles (5 km) on Route 307. Originally part of a private copra plantation, Akumal gained international status in 1958, when a diving exploration headed by Pablo Bush, a Mexican philanthropist, stumbled across the sunken remains of the *Mantanceros,* a Spanish galleon that was lost at sea more than 2 centuries ago. Since then, the place has become an unofficial scuba and snorkeling headquarters for the not-so-idle rich called the *Mexican Underwater Explorers' Club.* When the club was first founded, its members flew down in private aircraft to put on wet suits and scuba tanks for expeditions to the sunken wreck of the *Mantanceros;* later they came upon submerged Maya ruins in places where the sea had swallowed up the land.

Today, Akumal is open to the public, and *Club Akumal Caribe* (see *Best en Route*) is a lovely hotel with grounds that contain cannon recovered from the ancient wreckage. There are also several smaller, European Plan hotels in town, mostly geared to hearty meals and no-frills sleeping quarters to accommodate the diving crowd.

For those who want just a taste of adventure, Akumal has an underwater museum where coral-encrusted anchors and guns lie among the rocks much the way they originally were found.

Those who prefer the real thing will want to don their scuba equipment and head into the placid ocean. The Akumal reef with its towering coral buttresses is alive with over 300 types of tropical fish, and every now and again a lucky diver will encounter a tarnished button or sand-encrusted coin that was overlooked by the 1958 Pablo Bush underwater expedition. Inexperienced divers can learn from the best here, since every other person you meet is a scuba pro. However, a diver's certificate card is required to rent tanks or charter a boat.

There are dive shops on virtually every corner and a few convenience stores that stock beer, wine, and snacks. That's just about it. There is no swinging nightlife in Akumal, only a pearly white beach and azure waters where visitors can luxuriate in the tropical sun under a leafy coconut palm.

CHEMUYIL: This relatively unknown beach, 5 miles (8 km) past Akumal on Route 307, is about as close to a Paul Gauguin landscape as you can get in Mexico. Sisal hammocks strung casually between palm trees and exotic drinks served in fresh coconuts make this out-of-the-way little club a whimsical spot where anyone can lounge for a few hours of Robinson Crusoe grandeur. There are also camping facilities, and a charming hotel with 10 suites and 12 tents for campers. For further information, write Don Lalo Román Chemoir Fidercomisco, Xel-Ha, Tulum, Q.R., Mexico.

XCACEL: Another perfect little slice of virgin waterfront 2 miles (3 km) south of Chemuyil along Route 307, Xcacel (pronounced Shka-*sell*) is waiting for someone to build a resort on it and make a fortune. For the moment, visitors lucky enough to discover this secluded stretch of sand can still enjoy its peace and serenity.

Just south of Xcacel on Route 307 is Xel-Ha.

XEL-HA: This lagoon — or series of lagoons — forms a natural aquarium filled with colorful tropical fish and turtles. Xel-Ha (pronounced Shell-*Ha*) used to be a great place for novice snorkelers to test their fins, but daily caravans of commercial tour buses have tended to erode its innate beauty. Too many tourists and too little upkeep have led to the once-transparent waters becoming clouded with murk and debris. This is clearly a case of paradise lost.

While the aquarium may not have much allure anymore, there are several scattered ruins on the grounds of this national park that are interesting, if uninspiring. The main structure, a 10-minute hike over jagged limestone terrain, is the Temple of the Birds, where a faint image of Chac, the rain god, and several plumed flamingos can be discerned in the western wall.

Continue south on Route 307 for 12 miles (20 km) to Tulum.

TULUM: The crowning glory of any coastal drive (82 miles/129 km south on Route 307) from Cancún is Tulum. Although small, the archaeological zone south of Xel-Ha has some superb Maya buildings.

In fact, this was one of the few cities that was still inhabited when the Spanish arrived. Juan de Grijalva described sighting it from his ship in 1518: "A city so large that Seville would not have seemed more considerable." Little of that metropolis remains, but what there is fascinates scholars. Tulum is the only Maya city known to have been encircled by a walled fortification. It is also one of the few Maya sites on the seacoast.

Apparently, the site was founded hundreds of years before the Christian era began, yet it survived long after other Maya cities had been abandoned. To some, this would indicate that the wall and seafront location were a good idea. The formation that the Spaniards called El Castillo (The Castle) is the zone's most curious structure; it does resemble a castle, and for all we know may actually have been one. Walk carefully to the side facing the sea for a stunning view of white, sandy beaches at the bottom of 80-foot limestone cliffs. About 400 yards offshore is a "blue hole," the ocean equivalent of a cenote. The Temple of the Frescoes contains rare Maya paintings, but Tulum's most famous building is the Temple of the Descending God; over its main door is a large cleaved sculpture of a winged deity plummeting headfirst toward the sea. The conventional theory is that it represents the rain god; an alternative theory is that it represents a descending spaceman.

There are a total of 60 structures at the site, and they can all be seen in about 2 hours of walking. In addition to its Maya paintings, the Temple of the Frescoes bears traces of the original paint on carved limestone statues, still detectable by the discerning eye.

Tulum offers some natural amenities as well. The beach just below the site is beautiful. The local waters can be fished year-round, and hunting in the jungle is quite good. Four major duck migrations rendezvous here each year. Wilder game include boar and deer.

En route from Tulum – Head north on Route 307 to return to Cancún.

BEST EN ROUTE

Prices along the Caribbean Coast are often high — especially considering the often rustic (or worse) accommodations available along the way — even outrageous by US standards. Those areas (such as the scuba divers' haven at Akumal) enjoying "favorite resort" status often charge more for less, while other, as yet undiscovered regions, offer elegant accommodations at down-to-earth prices. A double room in Puerto Aventuras, for example, will run at least $120 a night and, depending on the season, may start at $150 a night. You can rent a cabin in Pamul, on the other hand, for about $60 a night. Tulum is a vacationer's bargain, with rustic cabañas going for about $40 a night. Don't be surprised, though, if the electricity runs only part-time.

PAMUL

Cabañas Pamul – An 8-cottage complex with hot showers, overhead fans, and a small restaurant; all of the cabins open onto the beach for a ringside view of the spring turtle parade. Km 85 on Rte. 307 (phone in Mérida: 99-259422). Moderate.

PUERTO AVENTURAS

Club de Playa – The first hotel built at this new 36-room resort, the building is exquisite, but the service is lacking. There is a swimming pool, air conditioning, and a restaurant. Prices are comparable to those at *Puerta del Mar,* but the quality is not nearly so good (phone: 987-22300 or 987-22211). Expensive.

Puerta del Mar – A 68-unit, superluxury complex with fully equipped kitchens, air conditioning, a swimming pool, cable TV, and 2 restaurants. Reservations can be made in advance in Mexico City (phone: 5-208-1628 or 5-208-7156). Expensive.

AKUMAL

Akumal Cancún – Right on the beach, it has 81 air conditioned rooms with terraces, 11 two-bedroom suites with kitchenettes, a pool, 2 lighted tennis courts, all water sports, a dive shop, a disco, 2 restaurants, a video bar, and miniature golf (phone: 988-42272 or 988-42641). Expensive.

Club Akumal Caribe – Formerly a private club for well-heeled divers, this lovely 150-room place is now open to the public. Near Tulum and Xel-Ha, it's also a fine spot for lunch (phone: 988-41975 on Cancún; 987-22532 on Cozumel; 800-351-1622 in the US). Expensive.

TULUM

Ana y José – The most comfortable accommodations in the vicinity, this 15-unit inn has provincial charm and overhead fans. The gardens which surround the red tile buildings are particularly inviting. Km 7 on Rte. 307 to Tulum (phone: 987-41117). Inexpensive.

Cabañas Tulum – If you want to catch a sunrise at Tulum, this collection of 12 small cabins with overhead fans offers a good view of the ruins. No phone and no hot water, but very economical. Inexpensive.

Sian Ka'an Ocho Oasis – At the entrance of Sian Ka'an Wildlife Reserve, this complex of thatch cabañas is an exceptionally clean little spot with a great ocean view and a restaurant that specializes in vegetarian dishes. On the down side, there is no air conditioning and the electricity is on for only a few hours a day. No phone. Inexpensive.

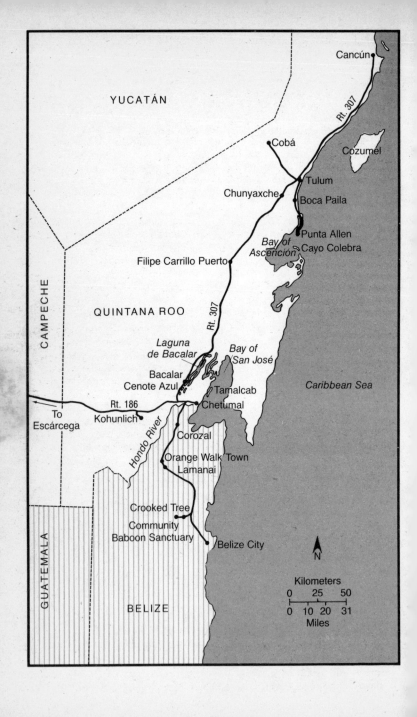

The Yucatán Peninsula: Cancún to Chetumal, and Belize

The southern coast of Quintana Roo — which stretches from Cancún to Chetumal — is a peculiar blend of blissfully tranquil beaches and untamed jungle that served as the backdrop for one of Mexico's bitterest conflicts, the Castes War. The highway that leads to Chetumal, the capital of the state of Quintana Roo, was once a road paved with the blood of Maya Indians and Spanish colonists.

Isolated and largely ignored by the rest of the country, and even the rest of the peninsula, southern Quintana Roo (pronounced Kin-tah-nah *Row*) is nonetheless strategically important from a military standpoint because of its location on the Bay of San José and its proximity to both Guatemala and Belize (both of which have at one time or another tried to lay claim to the region). The Maya also recognized the significance of this remote area and were slow in relinquishing it to the Spanish aggressors. Unlike their brothers in the north, the southern Chetumal Maya refused to submit to the Spanish throne. When Pedro de Alvarado — a conquistador sent by Spain to control the area in 1525 — ordered them to pay tribute, Nachankan, the Chetumal chieftain of the area, sardonically replied that he would pay only "turkeys in the shape of spears and corn in the shape of arrows." In fact, this was the last section of Mexico to fall from Maya hands.

When the Spanish finally had their fill of the insurgent Chetumal Maya, they resorted to a long period of brutal massacres, bordering on genocide, in order to subdue them. Consequently, the region was left almost uninhabited except for a few independent settlers, a military battalion, and a few straggling lumberjacks.

Economically, the region had much in its favor: rich copra orchards, abundant logwood (used for making dye), mahogany forests, and fertile sugarcane fields. There was also enough land for anyone who was willing to work it, and a general sentiment of indifference toward the law. This factor attracted social and political deviants as well as wide-eyed fortune hunters and rough-and-tumble buccaneers.

During the 18th and 19th centuries, with little or no intervention from the local sheriffs and plenty of open seashore to transport undeclared and un-levied goods, many a southern Quintana Rooer found himself engaged in the import and export of unsavory cargoes, including weapons, drugs, and even slaves. This brought prosperity, and with it an onslaught of unsolicited visits by pirates, looters, and carpetbaggers. The bloodletting in this region was so prevalent that at one time the entire population of southern Quintana Roo was reduced by 80% in a single year.

When Quintana Roo gained statehood in 1974, the Mexican government decided to instill a semblance of law and order in the region by clamping down on the transport of contraband, drugs, and other illegal trade. The notorious brothels and opium dens in Chetumal's red-light districts were closed down and an all-out effort to register the local citizenry was launched. Despite an ambitious effort, the undertaking was only partially successful. The brothels moved to new addresses, and those people who did not want to be on the official registries simply took refuge in the jungles during the census taking.

Today Chetumal, Quintana Roo's capital, is a hodgepodge of flashy lights and shady activities, a poor man's New York in the tropical jungle. Despite a veneer of respectability, the city has always managed to keep itself just outside the reach of the long arm of Mexican law. Always isolated, not only from the Mexican mainland but also from the rest of the Yucatán Peninsula, Chetumal is totally exempt from Mexico's protective tariffs, giving it a duty-free status that more than occasionally borders on the illegal. To some extent, the region is a safe harbor for smugglers. Contraband — electronics, drugs, and weapons, not necessarily in that order — is big business in this part of Mexico, although the authorities have tried to curb the trafficking of some of the more notorious merchandise in recent years.

Driving through this area is a stimulating experience. The beaches are less traveled — and less spoiled — than those in northern Quintana Roo. Giant sea turtles, now almost extinct throughout the world, can be seen almost everywhere along the coast laying their eggs in the moonlit sands during early spring. This is a land that still belongs to nature. Man has only brushed the surface of the vast Quintana Roo jungles, where ocelots, crocodiles, and howler monkeys still roam wild in their native habitat. Even the homely, cumbersome (yet somehow endearing) manatee, rarely seen anywhere else on earth, playfully romps in the brackish waters of the Bay of Ascención and Hondo River. Fishermen find this region an angler's paradise, where bonefish, snook, and the succulent pompano almost leap onto their hooks. The two largest Maya archaeological sites in the state, Tulum and Cobá, are also along this route, as is the Sian Ka'an Wildlife Reserve, which occupies a full 1.2 million acres of jungle, marsh, and coral beach.

The roads are surprisingly good, particularly compared to the highway that leads to the Yucatán state border. The 235-mile (376-km) drive from Cancún to Chetumal can take only about 3 to 4 hours, but with so much to see in between, wiser travelers allow several days. If time permits, the British Commonwealth Republic of Belize, just south of Chetumal, offers a delightful change of pace from standard Mexican meanderings. The shuttered wooden clapboard houses and creole accents give this little country a distinctively colonial appeal.

En Route from Cancún – Route 307 follows the coastline for 80 miles (128 km) straight into Tulum. For a detailed report on the route to Tulum, points of interest, and hotels and restaurants along the way, see *Mexico's Caribbean Coast: Cancún to Cozumel, Isla Mujeres, and Tulum* in this section.

The route from Tulum to Chetumal can be covered in about 4 hours. But if time allows, two side trips — each requiring a return to Tulum before continuing on to Chetumal — are well worth considering: a day trip from Tulum 26 miles (42 km) northwest to Cobá, and a day trip (or a possible overnight stay) 36 miles (57 km) south to Punta Allen. There are other options on the way to Chetumal: You may choose to stop off for the night in Bacalar to savor the beauty of its peaceful, multihued lagoon, or, as suggested above, take a side trip overnight to Belize. The Kohunlich archaeological zone 36 miles (58 km) west of Chetumal is also worth viewing, and should take about 2 hours to tour comfortably.

Just past the Tulum exit on Route 307, there is a turnoff on the right for the unnumbered road northwest to Cobá. This 26-mile (42-km) highway is paved and, although not as smooth as Route 307, quite drivable.

COBÁ: Cobá is Quintana Roo's largest archaeological site; to get a reasonably complete survey of it, count on a full-day visit. There is only one hotel near this 81-square-mile Maya site: the rather austere *Villa Arqueológica* run by *Club Med* (see *Best en Route*). But those who decide to spend the night probably will be more interested in playing Indiana Jones, cutting through the unexplored portions of Cobá than worrying about delivery of breakfast from room service.

The formal name of this classic Maya city is Cobá Kinchil, which translates as "Waters Stirred by the Winds at the City of the Sun God" — a rather cumbersome moniker by any standards. The massive city was first noted by American archaeologist John Lloyd Stephens sometime around 1840, but no one bothered to excavate it until the National Geographic Society came up with a grant to research the region in 1974.

Unlike the rest of the peninsula, the Cobá area is endowed with five natural lakes, which apparently allowed the ancient Maya to irrigate their fields and live in relative comfort. Not surprisingly, the city maintained a large population, perhaps as many as 9,000 people. Experts estimate that there are at least 6,500 structures buried in the all-consuming jungles of Cobá, but only a few of them have been charted and restored. Even more impressive than the number of buildings is the complex network of *sacbes*, or roads, that linked the main groupings (6 in all) to one another and extended out to other Maya cities. There was even a 12-foot-wide *sacbe* that led as far as Chichén Itzá, some 56 miles (90 km) to the northwest through the densest rain forests on the peninsula.

The 120-step Nohoch-Mul pyramid, the tallest pre-Columbian structure in the Yucatán, is the highlight of a trek through Cobá, but the august Maxcanxoc stelae are strong contenders for any visitor's attention. The eight 8-foot-high monolith tablets are intricately carved with finely crafted relief figures.

Because it is such a sprawling site, getting from one end of Cobá to the other is a complicated and lengthy process, and possible only on foot — so make sure to wear sensible shoes or, better yet, hiking boots. Insect repellent is also advised. The jungles still govern the park, and mosquitoes, gnats, and ticks are everywhere. Travelers wishing to continue on this route must return to Tulum before setting out for Chetumal. Those opting to take a second side trip to Punta Allen must also return to Tulum.

For a side trip to Punta Allen, take Route 307 south from Tulum. There are signs indicating a turnoff onto an unnumbered road south to Punta Allen. The 36-mile (57-km) drive will become, after a few short miles of pavement, an uneven (sometimes rutted) jungle road. It's well worth it, however, because along the way is Sian Ka'an (pronounced Shahn-*can*), Mexico's prized national wildlife preserve — an ecological wonderland teeming with reptiles, mammals, and a rain forest.

SIAN KA'AN: In January 1986, a 1.2-million-acre biosphere of virgin jungle, swamp, salt marsh, coral beach, and mangrove forest in east Quintana Roo was declared a national wildlife reserve by presidential decree. Mexico's largest federally protected area, Sian Ka'an (which translates as "Place Where the Sky Is Born") is an eco-tourist's paradise, where over 320 species of birds and 68 different types of reptiles and mammals flourish and multiply in their natural habitat. For those who want a taste of the jungle and are willing to endure the harsher side of nature, Sian Ka'an is a delectable adventure into an untamed wonderland. An overland excursion along the jungle path can mean coming face-to-face with a giant boa constrictor, a curious spider monkey, or a glimpse of a sprightly ocelot startled into action by the sound of a car motor. Those who go deep enough into this bewitching rain forest may even have a chance to romp in the Bay of Ascención with a couple of inquisitive manatees or a congenial dolphin. A 2-hour canoe trip through a series of lagoons shrouded by webbed vines can even mean an opportunity to survey unexplored pre-Hispanic ruins dating from up to 20,000 years ago.

But this kind of adventure does not come without paying a hefty physical price. The road into Sian Ka'an is unpaved and generously pitted with potholes. The 36-mile (58 km) drive to Punta Allen, where the road terminates at the Bay of Ascención, takes at least 3 hours to navigate in good weather. Moreover, the jungle literally closes in as you proceed, and there are times when your vehicle will actually have to slice its way through the overhang and palm trees. Sudden thunderstorms are common (they don't call them tropical rain forests for nothing), and there are giant puddles in the road large enough to swallow a VW Beetle. Stop your vehicle frequently and test the terrain ahead on foot to be sure you won't end up in a mass of quicksand or swamp quagmire. Insects are also a problem, and repellent and long sleeves are highly advised. The heat is sometimes stifling in the murky jungles, and the stench of organic decay around the stagnant marshlands often is overwhelming.

That said, for those still determined to undertake an expedition into Sian Ka'an, there are a few basic guidelines to follow. First, gas up at the filling station near the Cobá exit. At the same time, make sure your car's fluid levels are good and let about 5 pounds (more for heavy-traction vehicles) out of the tires so that they will ride more easily over the jungle terrain. Picking up a couple of bottles of drinking water is also a good idea. Almost any vehicle in good condition can endure this journey, but four-wheel-drive jeeps are much more suited to the topography. The adventurous type (a foregone conclusion for the traveler willing to embark on this venture) may even want to purchase some food and soft drinks to stage a jungle cookout and picnic along the ocean shore.

For those with an urge to play Tarzan along the way, there are several rustic cabaña-style cottages with hammocks, running water, and electricity during certain hours of the day (don't try to plug in an electric razor; the light here is battery-powered, 12 volts, direct current). The best of these primitive little makeshift guesthouses is the *Posada Cuzan* in Punta Allen, run by Sonia López, a New York anthropologist turned Sheena (see *Best en Route*). She whips up a delicious potluck dinner (usually lobster tails sautéed to perfection in local herbs) for a pittance, and can offer firsthand information about what to see and how to get there. Two pricey hotels on the reserve, *Club de Pesca Boca Paila* and *Pez Maya* (see *Best en Route*), are frequented by millionaire yachtsmen who come for fishing and sunning, but these places are booked months in advance and don't accept drop-ins.

Unlike many nature reserves, Sian Ka'an combines the protection of wildlife with the balanced use of resources and the cooperation of local inhabitants. This "holistic" approach to the preservation of the nation's natural heritage, without the forced relocation of indigenous populations that have lived on and worked the land for centuries, reflects a relatively new stance in finding a practical equilibrium between ecological concerns and economic realities. The reserve is divided into three sections, each with its own restrictions regarding exploitation by humans. Along the edges of the reserve there is a 10-mile-deep buffer zone where those families who have ancestral ties to the region (about 1,000 people in all) are allowed to continue their traditional vocations as fishermen and hunters. There is also a gathering zone where these people are allowed to collect the plants they use for dietary or medicinal purposes. Only government and private-sector researchers and ecologists are allowed to enter the highly protected core zone of the reserve.

The end result of this experimental policy is that the indigenous inhabitants of the region are working hand in hand with the scientists to find better ways of protecting the local flora and fauna. Rather than trying to stop the commercialization of crocodile hides, for example, the government administrators have devised a program whereby crocodiles are raised in captivity and protected from their natural predators until they are fully grown. About half of each litter is eventually released in the wild, while the other half is sold legally for their skins, with a share of the profits going to the local Maya. Also, the government has enlisted the support of the natives in locating coconut groves infested with yellow palm disease. By cutting down infected trees and substituting more resistant strains, the Sian Ka'an administrators have been able to effectively keep the disease from spreading farther north. With the help of the scientists, local farmers are learning how to better regulate their lobster fishing so as not to deplete the waters of this crustacean, an essential source of income for the community. The friendship between the two groups has also benefited the scientific world, because local shamans are sharing their secrets of herbal medicine with the Sian Ka'an researchers.

The part of Sian Ka'an that is open to tourists is the outer buffer zone. The first 6 miles (10 km) of the drive, as far as Boca Paila, is along the coast and the land is fairly firm. This is jungle, but far less wild than what lies ahead. Boca Paila, a small community that caters to the whims of elite fly fishermen (accommodations here run about $250 a night per person, double occupancy, with no air conditioning; see *Best en Route*), is set on a tranquil lagoon hemmed in by a mangrove forest. From Boca Paila, hire a boat for fishing or bird watching along the Sian Ka'an coast to the south.

From Boca Paila, the road continues to deteriorate as it winds inward toward the marshy swampland to the south. Because this part of the tour is less traveled than the first leg of the road, you are more likely to catch a glimpse of local reptiles and mammals. Keep an eye peeled for an oversize boa wrapped around a palmy vine or a spotted margay scurrying across the roadway. Iguanas are everywhere and the comical basilisk, rather like a miniature *Tyrannosaurus rex,* can be seen flitting from shrub to shrub in search of a grasshopper meal. Stop the car for a few minutes: You will probably be able to hear the wail of the howler monkey calling to his mate, and there may be a pretty kinkajou, or honey bear, hidden in the branches of a mangrove tree curiously studying your four-wheeled beast. Closer to Punta Allen, a hazy mist encircles the forests. The barren tops of dead coconut trees tower above the all-consuming fog like mammoth shafts in a hauntingly beautiful twilight zone landscape. It seems the road will never end, when suddenly Punta Allen appears.

PUNTA ALLEN: After so many miles of wilderness, the modest playground and basketball court at the entrance to Punta Allen are an abrupt, but most welcome, promise of civilization.

There are several guides available for boat trips into the placid Bay of Ascención, home to most of Mexico's manatee and dolphin population. There is also an island called Cayo Colebra, inhabited by several colonies of frigate birds. Also known as man-o'-war birds, the frigates have the longest wingspan of any sea bird. During the winter months, the male frigate displays a bright red gular pouch which balloons to almost 30% of his normal size. It is an astounding vision right out of the pages of *National Geographic* magazine. Fly fishermen will find the waters around the island literally jumping with barracuda, tarpin, red drum, snook, pompano, bluefish, and wahoo. Fishing in and around Sian Ka'an is on a catch-and-release basis only, but a local photographer is always on hand to provide documentation of your angling talents.

For a slightly higher fee, hire a canoe and travel through a series of connecting lagoons to the unexplored Chunyaxche ruins, which date back 20,000 years (for rental information, ask Sonia López, owner of the *Cuzan* guesthouse in Punta Allen).

Almost all the dining facilities are rustic at Punta Allen, and lobster tail is a staple. Those who spend the night will probably wake to a breakfast of scrambled eggs and lobster — pretty fancy fare for roughing it. To resume the route to Chetumal, retrace your steps on the unnumbered road back to Tulum and Route 307.

En Route to Chetumal – From here, the highway south bends westward and inland 152 miles (243 km), until it dead-ends with Route 186 along the Belize border. To the west, Route 186 continues through the jungle for 159 miles (254 km), to meet up eventually with the town of Escárcega and then doubles back north as Route 261, completing the Yucatán loop. This is a lonely, deserted highway with little to offer save steamy vegetation and a generous portion of potholes. To the east, Route 186 leads 12 miles (19 km) straight into Chetumal. There will be plenty of signs indicating which way to turn.

FELIPE CARRILLO PUERTO: The first town of any significant size on the road from Tulum is Felipe Carrillo Puerto, 61 miles (98 km) south of the ancient walled city. This town gets its name from a populist Yucatán governor of the 1920s who loved an American woman. The lady was Alma Reed, a reporter from San Francisco, who could easily have been invented by a romance novelist. Long before the Chicanos were fighting against prejudice, Ms. Reed took up their cause. Her California paper allowed her to probe the murder conviction of a young Mexican, and her article convinced the authorities that the jury had made a mistake. The governor signed a pardon, and the Mexican government, pleased to have found a friend, invited the newswoman to tour the country as its guest.

Those were rough-and-tumble days, when the Mexican revolution had not been quite settled, and people were frequently getting shot. Ms. Reed, undeterred, accepted the government's invitation and in the course of her journey visited Mérida. She interviewed Carrillo Puerto, then Governor of the state of Yucatán. Apparently he was impressed, because later he had a mariachi band drop by her hotel to serenade her, as Mexican swains are fond of doing. He went a step farther and had a tune, "Peregrina" (Pilgrim), written especially for his lady. It's still considered a classic among Mexican love songs. Alma Reed booked passage on a steamer for New York, where she planned to buy her wedding dress. While she was there, political fortunes turned in Mérida, and the other side grabbed the statehouse, took Carrillo Puerto prisoner, and executed him. Ms. Reed never married. She became a promoter of Mexican culture and archaeology. She died in 1966 and is buried in Mérida, very close to her beloved Felipe Carrillo Puerto.

Aside from the tale of the man for whom it was named, the town of Felipe Carrillo Puerto has little to recommend it except for an extraordinary restaurant on the highway called *El Faisán y El Venado* (The Pheasant and the Deer), which serves fresh venison steaks perfectly prepared at extremely reasonable prices. You won't find it on the menu, because technically commercial deer hunting is *verboten* in Quintana Roo, but the restaurant is a town tradition and local authorities turn a blind eye to the sale of venison in exchange for a discount price on a meal. Ask your waiter for *venado* (venison), in a low voice as discreetly as possible.

Continue south on Route 307 about 70 miles (112 km) to Bacalar Lagoon.

LAGUNA DE BACALAR: The crystalline, "Lake of Seven Colors" is the place where the ancient Maya thought the rainbow was born. Those who witness the red, turquoise, blue, and violet tones that this magnificent natural wonder reflects throughout the day can easily understand the reasons for this belief. Surrounded by a wall of gently sloped hills, the lagoon's waters are so still that at times they seem like a mirror of brightly polished glass. This is a perfect setting for boating, swimming, or snorkeling, and there are two very pleasant hotels along the shore, *La Laguna* and *Rancho Encantado* (see *Best en Route*), for those who want to spend the night and watch the sunrise on the lagoon.

Although the main reason for stopping off in Bacalar is the lagoon, the town has a bonus attraction that is often overlooked: San Felipe, a stately stone fort constructed by Spanish colonists during the first half of the 18th century.

Founded in 1528 (14 years before Mérida), Villa Real (Royal Village), as Bacalar was originally called, was the first major Spanish outpost on the Yucatán Peninsula. Unable to subdue the fierce and primitive Maya in Chetumal, conquistador Alfonso Davíla decided to establish a military base along the lagoon to regroup his forces for an attack. The post was poorly protected and could easily have been overpowered by the Maya warriors, but rather than waste his men and energy storming the colonial encampment, the chieftain of Chetumal decided to bide his time and let the elements of nature conquer the conquerors. Within 2 years, disease, mosquitoes, and the stifling heat of the jungle had bested the Spanish army, and Villa Real was abandoned.

Fifteen years later, the Spanish made a second attempt to settle the area, this time under the capable direction of Melchor Pacheco, who repopulated the fort and dubbed it "Nueva Salamanca de Bacalar" (New Salamanca of Bacalar), in honor of his hometown. The new colonists were better prepared for their stay in the wilderness: They transported their ample supplies — brought from the Old World — through a canal they had dug linking the lagoon to the Caribbean Sea. The colonists survived for almost a century in relative peace. But by 1640, Spanish-Maya tensions were aggravated by the brutal murders of four local farmers, and the Chetumal community stormed the settlement in retaliation. For well over 2 years, the bloodletting continued, and almost 75% of the Spanish colonists were killed or fled. Those who stayed became easy prey for pirates and English corsairs, who razed Bacalar in 1652. Exasperated, the Spanish government decided it was high time to gird its interests in the southern Yucatán. In 1725, Antonio Figueroa y Silva, governor of the peninsula, ordered the transportation of the entire Spanish population of the Canary Islands to Bacalar in order to construct a massive fortress to defend the town. The 30-foot-high structure took 25 years to complete, but although its 4-towered walls and 12-foot-deep crocodile-laden moat were impressive to look at, they were militarily weak against attack. Still, the San Felipe fort served its purpose, inhibiting the number of raids by outside intruders. The town prospered from its chicle and coconut plantations, and by 1847 a road was constructed that linked Bacalar to Mérida through the southern jungles.

Had the Castes War not broken out in 1848, the city probably would be the capital of Quintana Roo today. But once again, the Chetumal Maya released their fury on the people of Bacalar, and after a bitter struggle San Felipe fell into Maya hands. The British in Belize, happy to see the Spanish overcome in a region they considered rightfully theirs, actually recognized Venancío Pec, the Maya military head, as the official governor of the city, a move that infuriated the Spanish and led to quick annihilation of Pec and his army. Once the Spanish had regained face, they abandoned the city and the Maya timidly reclaimed it, this time without any vainglorious shows of victory. For 50 years, Bacalar was a Maya city. It was not until 1901 that the Mexican government finally decided to peacefully repossess the fort and its surroundings, in order to use it as a commercial stopover between Felipe Carrillo Puerto and Chetumal.

San Felipe Fort, now a museum, was restored in 1983 by the Governor of Quintana

Roo, and is open to the public from 9 AM to 6 PM daily. A park of well-manicured gardens surrounds the 150-square-foot fortress, which houses old weapons, artifacts, and a magnificent mural. The central watchtower offers a scenic view of the town and lagoon. Admission charge.

CENOTE AZUL: This azure cenote (sinkhole), just 3 miles (5 km) south of Bacalar on Route 307, is a perfect place for a dip in the water, Maya-style. The limestone pool of sweet water is 600 feet wide and almost 280 feet deep and is surrounded by eucalyptus and other shade trees. The small, rustic, open-air *Cenote Azul* restaurant, on the banks, serves fresh fish and other seafood. The house specialty is an excellent dish of giant shrimp stuffed with cheese, wrapped in bacon, and deep-fried. There are also camping facilities nearby for those who want to spend the night under the Caribbean stars; open from 10 AM to 6 PM daily.

Follow Route 307 south 23 miles (37 km) to Chetumal.

CHETUMAL: Originally a Maya city, Chetumal or *Chetemal* ("Place of the Falling Rain") was inhabited in 2000 BC, making it one of the oldest cities on the Yucatán Peninsula. Its strategic location on the Bay of San José and the mouth of the Hondo River has always made it a sought-after military and commercial base. When the Spaniards landed on the peninsula in the early 1500s, they tried to subdue the natives of Chetumal and claim the location for their own, but the Maya had other ideas. After a futile battle that lasted nearly 3 weeks, the Spanish armies packed up their gear and retreated north to Bacalar Lagoon. Thinking they might catch more flies (and land) with honey than with vinegar, the conquistadores tried to sweet-talk the Maya into surrendering Chetumal, this time offering them trinkets, baubles, and other European "riches" in barter; but again the Maya refused to yield. The third attempt by the Spanish was clearly a might-is-right approach: In 1544, storming the Maya city at night with 12 battalions of rifled soldiers and savage attack dogs, the Spaniards finally brought the Maya (at least temporarily) to their knees. This assault was to go down as one of the most barbaric and cruel in the annals of Mexican history. Women and children, even newborn babies, were dismembered or chained to stones and cast into the ocean screaming for mercy. Turning a deaf ear, the Spaniards pillaged the city. There were even accounts of macabre mutilations and cannibalism on the part of the conquerors. The few Maya who did survive either escaped into the jungle or were left to starve to death amid the plundered ruins.

Under Spanish dominion, Chetumal thrived. Copra, cocoa, and banana plantations as well as lumber and sugar mills prospered, and for about 50 years Chetumal was an exemplary colonial city. But the long memory and simmering wrath of the Maya knew no absolution, and in a lightning attack in the summer of 1583, the city fell back into native hands as quickly as it had been lost almost half a century before. The Spanish-Maya struggle to take and hold the coveted city went on for 3 centuries, with the lengthy tally of casualties mounting with every battle. Only in 1898 did the Maya finally lose their tenacious grasp on the region; Chetumal was declared a Spanish municipality and renamed Payo Obispo (The Peasant Bishop), after a well-known Catholic missionary. At long last the tragic fate of the Chetumal Maya had been sealed. No more would their chieftains rally to combat the white intruders. Chetumal and the southern tip of Quintana Roo were now a conquered land. Eventually, Chetumal would reclaim its original appellation, but the city would never again be a Maya domain.

But what the Maya could not accomplish, nature did. In 1955, Hurricane Janet leveled all but 14 buildings of the teeming border town. Chetumal had to be rebuilt from scratch, this time with financial support from the Mexican government. Modern cement and mortar structures replaced the traditional wood-paneled cottages that had become synonymous with the city. The highway linking the city with Campeche and Mérida made the free-port status of Chetumal big business for importers and traders of legal and illegal goods. Cantinas and houses of ill repute abounded, and Chetumal entered a new heyday of commercial activity.

Today, Chetumal resembles the setting for a stereotypical 1940s Hollywood private eye story. Balanced delicately on the Mexican border with Belize (formally British Honduras), it still maintains free-port status, impervious to Mexican import tariffs and quotas. This odd little state capital is aglitter with shops selling Japanese electronic devices, Dutch cheeses, Czech crystal, Italian silk, and French perfume. Mexicans usually have to pay 100% (or more) duty on luxury goods from abroad (if the items are allowed into the country at all); so for the people of cities such as Mérida and Villahermosa, Chetumal is the next best thing to Hong Kong. Chetumal is also a staging point for hunting and fishing expeditions. Just a mile off shore is the small island of Tamalcab, home of the *tepezcuintles,* small pigs that are a favorite with hunters and pork lovers.

Unless you have spent the night in Bacalar, you probably will arrive in Chetumal late in the day, which will give you enough time to stroll around town, have dinner, and get a good night's sleep. Formal, numbered street addresses are rarely used here; like many of the towns in the Yucatán, Chetumal is small and easy to negotiate, and shops, restaurants, and hotels simply don't use addresses. *La Cascada* at the *Continental* hotel serves a good selection of seafood and international dishes. If you prefer Italian food, try *Sergio's Pizza,* just off the main boulevard. Late-night snackers will appreciate *24-Horas,* open around the clock, on the main drag. The hotels in Chetumal are comfortable, but nothing to write home about (see *Best en Route*).

From Chetumal, visitors can make a side trip to the Maya vestiges at Kohunlich, 36 miles (58 km) due west on Route 186, toward the town of Escárcega. Or consider a diversion of a day or two south in Belize, over the natural border provided by the Hondo River.

KOHUNLICH: Officially, Kohunlich was discovered in 1967, when construction workers came upon the ruins while cutting a *trocha,* or path, for Route 186. Like all the other Maya cities, Kohunlich is a former ceremonial center, or temple. Its pyramids were observatories from which the seasons were measured. In the tropics, where winter blends into spring with no robins to herald the change, spotting the equinox was a great problem and of vital importance to the Maya, for it told them when to plant their corn. It is probable that only the high priests, who lived in the temples and performed rites on top of the pyramids, knew how to separate the seasons. Because the area has only recently begun to be excavated, most of Kohunlich is as yet undiscovered. Archaeologists have determined that Kohunlich's Pyramid of the Masks contained tombs; the only other Maya pyramids known to have been used as burial places are at Altun Ha (see below) and at Palenque (in the nearby state of Chiapas).

Four temples stand at Kohunlich, along with a plaza of large stone bas-relief plaques and the ubiquitous ball court, where the Maya played a game that appears to have been a combination of modern-day soccer and basketball. The idea was to get a hard rubber ball through the opposing team's goal, which was a small stone ring. Players were not allowed to use their hands to score. Considering the small circumference of the goal ring, this must have been quite difficult. The teams did their best, however, and according to legend, the winning captain celebrated his victory by lopping off his rival's head, symbolically fertilizing the ground with the blood.

Kohunlich is by no means as well ordered as Uxmal (see *The Yucatán Peninsula: Cancún to Campeche* in this section). Archaeologists continue to look for clues as to how the Maya lived and why the civilization disappeared. Visitors may well get a sense of ongoing exploration and feel as if they actually are in the midst of potentially important discoveries.

Retrace Route 186 back to Chetumal.

En Route to Belize City – Five miles (8 km) west of Chetumal, just before Route 186 meets up with Route 307 back to Tulum, there is a cutoff that leads to the Belizean border. Travelers wishing to cross the Mexican border into Belize will have to temporarily surrender their tourist visas at the Mexican checkpoint.

The contrast between the two countries is immediately apparent. A milieu of choppy Caribbean-English accents and officials decked out in neatly starched khaki uniforms announces that the British influence still prevails in this quaint little Commonwealth country.

Entry visas are not required for citizens of the United States, or of Great Britain or other Commonwealth nations. Those driving a leased car, however, will have to present a letter of authorization from the rental firm granting permission for the temporary export of the vehicle. Also, you must purchase local car insurance, available at a little shack at the edge of the customs house parking lot, for a fee of about $5 US per day (those who stay for 1 week pay a flat fee of $20). Make sure to gas up in Chetumal before crossing the border, because the price per gallon is almost double in Belize. On the other hand, the restrooms at the filling stations in Belize are much cleaner than the so-called *sanitarios* in Mexico.

Belize is tucked into one of those obscure little corners of the world where few seem to have visited; but for those who have, the trip can supply cocktail party conversation for months.

Belize was formerly known as British Honduras, England's last colony on the mainland of the Americas. English pirates, probably members of the same band that raided Campeche, settled Belize during the 17th century. They found shelter behind its protective reefs, and if they had any wounds to lick, this is where they licked them. From here they would sally forth to raid along the Spanish Main. Eventually, perhaps as they grew older, the buccaneers sought a less risky line of work. They found it in logging; harvesting the hardwoods of the Belize forests proved to be more profitable — as well as far safer — than pirating.

The British colonists began importing black slaves to do the heavy work, and the Spanish, who controlled most of the general area at the time, looked with great disfavor on these English settlements. The neighboring Guatemalans were no happier and, when they became independent, claimed the territory as their own. London really wanted nothing to do with the place, but yielded to the pleadings of its colonists, who begged for the protection of the British flag.

As early as 1961, the British government made it plain that Belize could cut its ties to the mother country anytime it wished. However, it took another 20 years before Britain agreed to keep a token military presence in the country (against the threat of a Guatemalan takeover), and then Belize's independence was formally declared.

Though the road down to Belize City, the Northern Highway, is good except within city limits (presumably because the federal government springs only for the paving and upkeep of rural areas), it has no white lines, signposts, or other amenities to recommend it for night driving.

Follow the Northern Highway 92 miles (147 km) to Belize City. The drive will take about 2 hours, not counting excursions to the Maya ruins of Altun Ha or the Baboon Sanctuary on the Belize River.

Only 10 miles (16 km) from the Mexican border, is Corozal, a town that is half-Mexican and half-Belizean. Things move slowly here. This is a sleepy little town that brings new meaning to the phrase "laid-back." Perhaps Corozal's only redeeming attraction, *Tony's Inn* is a charming seaside retreat with good food and spacious accommodations at about half the price you'd pay in Mexico (see *Best en Route*). Outside of this evocative little stopover, there is not much to say about Corozal. With all the non-charm of any border city, it is as about as representative of Belize as Laredo, Texas, would be of the US. Founded by Mexican refugees from the Caste War, Spanish seems to be the lingua franca here. Hand-painted signs in garbled English, hung almost as an afterthought below their Spanish counterparts, serve as the only token acknowledgment that this is Belizean territory. If time doesn't allow for a visit to Belize City, at least continue 24 miles (38 km) farther to Orange Walk Town, which offers a better sense of the country.

ORANGE WALK TOWN: More what one would expect a Belizean city to look like: The clapboard-sided wooden houses built on stilts and horse-drawn carriages driven by denim-clad Mennonites, a nonmilitant Protestant sect, give this town an air of Caribbean island charm. Outside of the occasional 2-ton truck overflowing with chopped sugarcane en route to Belize City for processing, you might feel that you had dropped into a time warp and regressed 100 years in history.

Hikers with a yen for a *Romancing the Stone* adventure can head out to Lamanai, one of the largest Maya cities in Belize, just south of Orange Walk on the Northern Highway. Dating from about 1500 BC, Lamanai (which means "Submerged Crocodile") is considered to be one of the finest examples of pre-classic Maya constructions. Largely abandoned by modern-day man, Lamanai has become a refuge for howler monkeys, iguanas, and even ocelots that stalk the pyramids at night. Be warned: This is mostly archaeologically uncharted territory; a majority of the ruins are still buried beneath mounds of earth and jungle.

Follow the Northern Highway south about 30 miles (48 km) to a dirt road that branches off to the right onto a causeway over a marshy lagoon; this roads leads to the Crooked Tree Wildlife Reserve.

CROOKED TREE WILDLIFE SANCTUARY: About 2 miles (3 km) off the Northern Highway and 64 miles (99 km) south of the Mexican border lies the Crooked Tree Wildlife Sanctuary. Black howler monkeys, crocodiles, coatimundi, and several species of turtles, as well as over 50 species of birds, call Crooked Tree home. The jabiru stork, the largest flying bird in the western hemisphere, with a wingspan of up to 12 feet, also abounds in the sanctuary. Belize has the largest nesting population of these birds in all of Central America. Each November, flocks of the lanky jaribu arrive in pairs to nest in the low pine savannas of Crooked Tree, returning northward in April or May when the heavy rains come and their young have fledged.

The reserve is open to the public, but you might want to hire a local guide to help you find the monkeys.

An excursion through Crooked Tree means giving your hiking boots a healthy workout and being ready to traipse through some pretty rugged terrain, including swamps, grasslands, and even jungles — not recommended for suburban cement-lovers.

COMMUNITY BABOON SANCTUARY: Approximately 4 miles (6 km) west of Crooked Tree is the Community Baboon Sanctuary. This privately owned reserve was established in 1985 to protect one of the last healthy populations of black howler monkeys on the continent. Colloquially known as "baboons" in Belize, howler monkeys are primarily leaf-eaters that occasionally augment their diets with fruits and flowers. Due to deforestation, their numbers have been reduced dramatically, and they are now listed as an endangered species.

Fortunately, with the protection of local farmers and the *Belize Audubon Society,* the howlers are beginning to thrive in this 3,000-acre natural habitat. Visitors to the sanctuary can take a walk on the wild side along winding dirt paths hedged by rose apple, sapodilla, and bay cedar trees to catch a glimpse of these fascinating creatures and hear their unusual raspy howl as they call to one another.

En route to Altun Ha – Retrace your steps back to the Northern Highway (15 miles/24 km before Belize City), where you will turn around and head northeast on the old highway to the Maya ruins of Altun Ha. The going is rough on this 17-mile (27-km) strip of road, but amateur archaeologists will find it well worth the effort.

ALTUN HA: The name means "Limestone Pond," and Altun Ha is practically unique among Maya ruins because of its shaman burial tombs. Moreover, the opulence of the ancient city (the Maya of Altun Ha are believed to have conducted trade on a regular basis with the city-state of Teotihuacán, north of Mexico City) was reflected in a tradition of elaborate offerings of jade and amber sculptures that were smashed to bits and cast into a blazing fire — along with human sacrifices — to appease the gods and keep the lands fertile. The jade head of the sun god Kinich Ahua (now in Belize City), one of Belize's greatest national treasures, was recovered from this site. The best restored of all Belize's Maya ruins, Altun Ha has 13 major structures congregated around 2 large plazas. The largest, the Temple of the Sun, is an imposing canopied pyramid that ascends 60 feet above the jungled surface. Admission charge.

Follow the old highway to the Northern Highway for 28 miles (45 km) south to Belize City.

BELIZE CITY: Besides being hot and humid, Belize City has an interesting mixture of British colonial architecture and small-town ambience. With a population of 45,000, it is the only real city in the country. It is filled with old, mostly wooden buildings and ramshackle houses, the line broken only occasionally by Victorian-style government buildings.

The most colorful things in the city are its street names: Queen's Square is bordered by Antelope, Armadillo, and Seagull Streets; the Mesopotamia area has streets with such Middle Eastern monikers as Euphrates, Cairo, and Tigris; and the Caribbean Shores area relies on church figures for names.

The city's small business and shopping area is centered around the few blocks on either side of the Belize Swing Bridge (most of the buildings do not have addresses). Here are Albert and Queen Streets, which make up the commercial district, and Regent Street, which houses most of the government buildings. At the northeast end of the bridge is the Paslow Building, an interesting bit of architecture that houses the post office. Across the street (91 Front St.) is the Belize Philatelic Bureau, where stamps may be purchased by collectors. The *Baron Bill Institute* (on Southern Shore, near the Swing Bridge) was dedicated to the British multimillionaire who left several million dollars to Belize City in the 1920s; it contains carved stone monuments from the ancient Maya ceremonial center of Caracol, in the Maya Mountains.

Also located on the southern side of the Swing Bridge is Old Fort George, with its Memorial Park; standing along Regent Street are some of the old slave quarters. Also on Regent, across from the *Mopan* hotel, is a bookstore (no name, no address) which has a small selection of Belizean historical publications. St. John's Cathedral, built in 1826, is one of the oldest Anglican cathedrals in Central America.

For a firsthand look at native crafts in the making, drop in at the studio of George Gabb, reputedly Belize's best carver, on the Northern Highway going out of town, just after the Texaco station. The workshop is open every day from 8 AM to 6:30 PM. The genial Gabb, widely known as a cracker-barrel philosopher, will demonstrate how he carves the native ziricote hardwood, which, when cut across the grain, reveals a brown and black "rose" on a white background. Most of his work is exported, and the 12-foot statue *To Be Born Again,* which he donated to the US for its bicentennial, is now at Lansing (Michigan) Community College.

The city has an Old World charm that is reminiscent of the glory days of the British Empire in such remote areas as India, Pakistan, and West Africa. Once-elegant homes with canopied verandahs and attic sun rooms testify to better times for this now somewhat scruffy city. Locals still enjoy their afternoon tea on the front porch with homemade orange-rind marmalade and freshly baked biscuits.

Savor a bit of this decadent luxury for yourself at one of the finer old hotels such as the *Château Caribbean* or *Four Fort Street* (see *Best en Route*). Both are well-appointed inns with fine dining and service. There are also several less stuffy eateries in town, which serve topflight Chinese food and the standard Belizean fare of red beans and rice. Belikin, the local brew, is a major European export success story with a flavor similar to that of the well-known Danish draft from which it borrowed its name.

It is a good idea to stop by the Mexican Consulate (20 N. Park St.; phone: 501-44301) to pick up a tourist card for your return trip, especially if you are planning to extend your stay for longer than a week or so. Mexican border guards can be difficult about granting long-term visas without the incentive of a *mordida* (bribe).

BEST EN ROUTE

The available accommodations along the route are, with few exceptions, far less posh than those found on more traditional tourist trails. The quality of service is also not always up to par with international standards, but for the most part, neither are the prices. Many of the places below are rustic to an extreme — you may end up sleeping in a hammock instead of a bed — but they all are usually clean and as close to topnotch as you can get in this region. Most of them do not have phones or fax machines to handle reservations, but they will almost always manage to accommodate drop-ins. The up side of these slight inconveniences is that there is a homey feeling at most places, and they will often go that extra mile to please their guests. Breakfast is sometimes included in the price, and the wholesome goodness of Mexican cooking can be a welcome relief from industrialized commercial kitchens. If prices inside the confines of Sian Ka'an seem high, the reason is that everything here must be brought in from outside. Also, there is no public electricity in the biosphere, so individual generators must be used to provide light and energy. For a double room, expect to pay up to $250 at an expensive hotel; $40 to $90 in moderate places; and $35 and under in inexpensive ones.

COBÁ

Villa Arqueológica – The only hotel at the ruins in Cobá, it is set in an isolated jungle environment close to many unexplored sites. You actually can get out of bed and hack your way through the jungle. Run by Club Med, it has tennis courts, a swimming pool, and a library on Mesoamerican archaeology (phone: 1-800-CLUB-MED; 5-203-3086 or 5-203-3833 in Mexico City; 800-CLUB-MED in the US). Moderate.

BOCA PAILA

Boca Paila Fishing Lodge – Pricey, unadorned rooms for the fly fishing enthusiast with money to burn. Reservations essential (phone: 529-872-0053 or 529-872-0124). Expensive.

Club de Pesca Boca Paila – This rustic little lodge has 6 cabins with no air conditioning, no TV sets, and no other amenities to speak of. What it does offer is superb saltwater fly fishing. This rusticity doesn't come cheap: $250 per person per night/double occupancy. Don't try to visit without a reservation; the place is booked months in advance, and there is a house policy not to receive drop-ins. (phone: 800-245-1950 in the US). Expensive.

Pez Maya – From the same folks who brought you *Club de Pesca Boca Paila* comes this set of 7 cabins at an even higher price — stripped bare (and we do mean bare!) of the usual necessities and with little else to offer but fly fishing (phone: 987-20072). Expensive.

PUNTA ALLEN

Posada Cuzan – This modest collection of thatch tepees is run by an American who believes that a taste of nature is worth a little discomfort. The rooms are clean, but you may end up having to sleep in a hammock, because there are only a few beds. The dining room, a huge cabaña with a sand floor, serves exceptionally good food (FAX: 983-40383 in Felipe Carrillo Puerto). Inexpensive.

BACALAR

Rancho Encantado – A cozy, lakeside, 5-cottage resort, its restaurant has a continental menu. Lots of personal touches show the interest of the American-born owners. The gardens are wonderful for leisurely strolls under the orchid-laden palms that line Bacalar Lagoon. Worth an extra day's layover. Reservations essential. Rte. 307 just north of Bacalar City (phone: 800-748-1756 in the US; FAX: 983-20920). Expensive.

La Laguna – This is a clean, family-run, 34-unit establishment with air conditioning, a swimming pool, a restaurant — and some of the slowest service on the face of the earth. Notwithstanding, the view of the lagoon is spectacular and there is a small boat dock. 316 Bugambilias (phone: 983-23517). Moderate.

CHETUMAL

Continental Caribe – This first class hotel has air conditioned rooms, a swimming pool, a bar, a restaurant, a garage, and movies (with English subtitles). 171 Av. Héroes (phone: 983-21100). Expensive.

Del Prado – Run by one of Mexico's largest hotel chains, with air conditioned rooms, a swimming pool, a restaurant, and a bar, this is by far the best in town. Héroes del Chapultepec (phone: 983-20544). Expensive.

Jacaranda – Clean and comfortable, this unforgettable bargain glows with outpost-of-empire atmosphere. 201 Alvaro Obregón (phone: 983-21455). Moderate.

Real Azteca – A pleasant hotel, with air conditioned units, parking, a restaurant, and a bar. 186 Belice (phone: 983-20666). Moderate.

COROZAL TOWN, BELIZE

Tony's Inn – A pleasant out-of-the-way 22-unit resort where the dining room offers a continental menu. There is air conditioning, a swimming pool, and a big sandy beach all to itself. South End Corozal (phone: 512-422055 or 512-422829). Expensive.

BELIZE CITY

Fort George – Recently purchased by the US-based Radisson chain, this modern 72-room complex offers all the comforts of home, but not much in the way of ambience. Air conditioning, swimming pool, satellite TV, restaurant, bar, and a gift shop. 2 Marine Parade (phone: 800-44-UTELL). Expensive.

Bellevue – Built on the Southern Shore in the early 1900s, this quaint little inn, complete with air conditioning and cable TV, is run by descendants of the original owners. Amenities also include good, down-home food (be sure to sample their home-baked bread). The only major drawback is that the location is not in the best part of town. 5 Southern Foreshore (phone: 501-277051 or 501-277052). Moderate.

Château Caribbean – Without a doubt, this is the classiest act in town. Large, elegantly appointed rooms, air conditioning, satellite TV, an exquisite dining room offering first-rate fare, and a fantastic view of the ocean, all in an old estate that once served as the local hospital. The service is impeccable. It's the best place to linger over afternoon tea as the sun sets over the verandah. 6 Marine Parade (phone: 501-230800). Moderate.

Four Fort Street – Another place with definite local charm, this 5-room bed and breakfast inn is just off the shore in an old renovated home. Air conditioning and a topnotch restaurant. Reservations necessary. 4 Fort St. (phone: 501-45638). Moderate.

The Yucatán Peninsula: Cancún to Campeche

The Yucatán Peninsula encompasses the three Mexican states — Yucatán, Campeche, and Quintana Roo — that jut into the Gulf of Mexico where it joins the Caribbean Sea. Most famous for the magnificent Maya ruins at Chichén Itzá, the Yucatán also has a walled city that could have come right out of a late-show pirate movie, outposts of an empire that Graham Greene might have invented, and some of the most enchanting resorts in the entire Caribbean, the best known being the islands of Cancún, Cozumel, and Isla Mujeres. While Isla Mujeres and Cozumel, the largest island in all of Mexico, have no land connecting them with the mainland, Cancún is linked to the peninsula by two long, sandy causeways built in the 1970s (see *Mexico's Caribbean Coast: Cancún, Cozumel, Isla Mujeres, and Tulum* in this section).

The state where these islands are located is Quintana Roo (pronounced Kin-tah-nah *Row*), the youngest in the Mexican republic (along with Baja California Sur, it was given full autonomy in 1974). The state — which takes its name from Andrés Quintana Roo, a hero in Mexico's War of Independence — was originally part of the state of Yucatán but was lopped off in reprisal for the Yucatecan's rebellious ways. Until recently, the *yucatecos* considered that no great loss. Once the former federal territory was granted statehood, however, the Yucatán state created a boundary dispute. Considering that the border runs through still unexplored jungle, no one has taken the *yucatecos* challenge very seriously to date, but with the growing development of tourism throughout the region, it seems likely that the issue will come to a political head within the course of the next few years, and formal boundary lines will no doubt be established.

In many ways, the three states on the peninsula constitute a country within a country. While the rest of the mainland is made up of hills, forests, and deserts originally settled by the Aztec, the peninsula consists of the flat jungles of the Maya. About the size of Arizona, the peninsula was isolated from the rest of Mexico for centuries. Mainland Mexicans may joke about the Yucatán as a "sister republic," but several times in the course of its history the peninsula has in fact almost become a separate country. During the 19th century especially, there were more than a few efforts at secession. When these failed, the Yucatecans responded by and large by simply ignoring the government in Mexico City, pretending as best they could that it didn't exist.

The Maya came from Central America to settle in the Yucatán about 500 BC, around the same time that the ancient Greek civilization was flourishing. The Maya, in fact, had more in common with the Greeks than just contemporaneity. Like the Greeks', theirs was a civilization more intellectual than

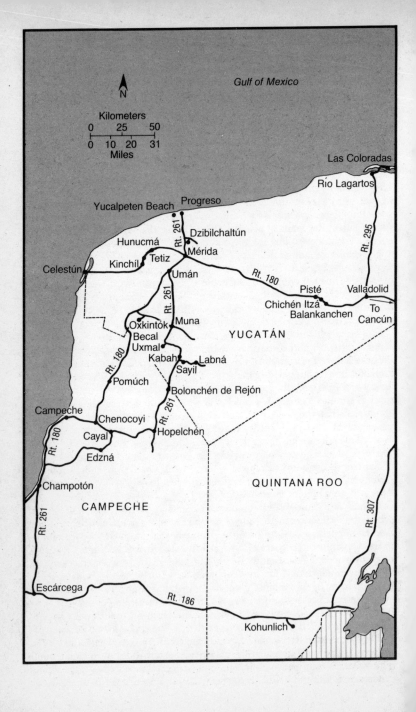

Gulf of Mexico

Kilometers
0   25   50
0 10 20 31
Miles

Las Coloradas

Río Lagartos

Rt. 295

Progreso
Yucalpeten Beach

Rt. 261

Dzibilchaltún

Hunucmá

Mérida

Kinchíl   Tetiz

Celestún

Umán

Rt. 180

Pisté   Valladolid

Chichén Itzá
Balankanchen

To
Cancún

Rt. 261

Oxkintók   Muna

Becal

Uxmal

Kabah   Labná

Sayil

Pomúch

Bolonchén de Rejón

Campeche

Chenocoyi

Rt. 261

Cayal

Hopelchén

Edzná

Rt. 180

Champotón

Rt. 261

CAMPECHE

YUCATÁN

QUINTANA ROO

Rt. 307

Escárcega

Rt. 186

Kohunlich

political; and like the Greeks, they never managed to form any kind of unified national political organization. Each Maya city was a little kingdom unto itself. And for some reason as yet undiscovered, one after another the great cities of the Maya — really ceremonial centers — were abandoned. Though a number of theories have been put forward to try to explain this, no one really knows why. During the 11th century, just about the time the Normans were conquering England, the Toltec conquered the Maya. The Toltec were from central Mexico and had a culture similar in many ways to that of the Aztec, who later became the most successful and powerful tribe in pre-Spanish Mexico.

Two large mysteries remain unexplained about the Maya before the Toltec invasion: why they moved from Central America into the Yucatán Peninsula in the first place, and why they periodically abandoned the magnificent ceremonial cities they built at various sites around the jungle peninsula. The answer to both questions is most likely buried in the glyphs (pictographs etched into stone) found at Chichén Itzá and other ruins, but these have not been fully deciphered. It's thought that the long messages carved into the giant ruins contain information about the Maya god-kings' ancestors, their lives and deaths, rituals and relationships. The spoken language of the Maya, on the other hand, is very much alive. The chatter in any market in the Yucatán is more likely to be in Maya than in Spanish.

The Toltec invaded the Yucatán after they had been driven out of the central highlands near the Valley of Mexico, where the Aztec, that roaming and warlike group of Indians, eventually settled. The Toltec brought to the Yucatán the worship of the plumed serpent, Quetzalcóatl. The serpent was the symbol of a god whose other identities included those of a priest and a king. The founder of the Toltec capital of Tula took Quetzalcóatl's name as his own and assumed the position of high priest to the god. According to legend, Quetzalcóatl populated the world by pouring his blood over the bones of people who had died from an earlier world; this myth of a god nurturing mankind with his own blood became the basis of ritual sacrifice, which the Toltec brought to the Yucatán.

Interestingly, the Maya absorbed the Toltec as much as the Toltec influenced Maya theology and building; many of the ruins show Toltec forms. Essentially the Toltec became latter-day Maya.

Although the Maya lands were occupied, the Maya could claim with some justification that they were never really conquered. The first Europeans to arrive were immediately chased away. The Yucatán was finally breached by Europeans in 1517, with a brief visit by Francisco Fernández de Córdoba. Spanish conquistador Juan de Grijalva renamed the region New Spain in 1518. Hernán Cortés explored the coast, landed in 1519, and soon was greeted by Aztec emissaries from central Mexico, who believed he was the fair-skinned Quetzalcóatl, returning as predicted in legend. Cortés's march to the Aztec capital at Tenochtitlán started in 1519 in Veracruz, which he founded. Twenty years after the Halls of Montezuma had been sledged into rubble, Francisco de Montejo founded Mérida in the western Yucatán. The surrounding area never completely fell under Spanish domination, and Mexico's independence in 1821 did little to change things. The Castes War, in which remnants of the Maya battled outside domination, dragged on through most of the 19th century.

Eventually, economics did what force of arms could not. The production of henequen, a form of sisal used in making rope, changed the economic and social systems in the Yucatán. The US and European nations needed rope for their ships. The Yucatán was a handy source of supply, and the great henequen plantations began to thrive. A feudal system of land ownership developed, and the Yucatán Indians became peons on great Spanish haciendas. The hacienda owners, for their part, discovered wealth beyond their avaricious dreams. Like the rich of many other lands, they turned toward Europe for cultural standards and status. They sent their children to schools on the Continent or, when they could not get to Paris themselves, settled for New Orleans. The owners of the haciendas were very similar to their counterparts in Peru, who allowed Indians to work the land while they partied in Paris rather than journey into the interior of their own country. The Yucatán *hacendados,* the landowners, ignored the rest of Mexico partly because, before the air age, it was difficult to reach and partly because, as far as the aristocracy was concerned, it was not worth the effort.

Only since the 1950s has a paved highway linked the Yucatán with the rest of the country. The rail service has always been painfully slow. Not that long ago, the best route to Mérida was a Pullman to Veracruz and a transfer to a coastal vessel bound for Progreso, the port 33 miles (53 km) away, where taxis could be hired for the hour's drive to the state capital.

Today, a highway system completely circles the peninsula, and driving is the best way to get a feeling for the entirety of this magnificent area — from the resort area of Cancún on the Caribbean to the inland routes to Mérida, passing Chichén Itzá and other major archaeological areas. This route can be completed in 4 easy days of driving, seldom with more than 6 hours spent on a road in any 1 given day. But there's so much to see that for an in-depth look, even a week is sometimes not enough. All in all the roads are good, the countryside flat, and destinations fairly close to each other.

The Yucatán today is still vastly different from the rest of Mexico. The *yucateco* accent is as distinct as a Southern drawl in the US. To this day, henequen remains the major crop and can be seen growing in expansive fields along the highways. In the villages, people still speak Maya, live in white, oval, thatch huts called *chozas,* and wear white garments — embroidered *huipiles* for women, tailored *guayaberas* for the men. Almost nowhere else in Mexico are native costumes seen with such frequency as in the Yucatán. The peninsula has its own cuisine, too. Pork *pibil* is one of the favorite dishes, while venison and pheasant are still basic staples in the local diet. Yucatán beer and ale, particularly the Montejo brand of stout, rare outside the immediate region, are prized throughout Mexico. Teetotalers will want to sample *soldado* (soldier), a local chocolate-flavored soft drink, available across the peninsula.

While the glitzy polish of Cancún and the raw beauty of the Yucatán's untamed jungles have much to offer, they are hardly representative samples of what Mexico is all about. The states of Yucatán and Campeche reflect a colonial heritage of grace and elegance in stately mansions and staid cathedrals. The archaeological ruins in these states are also better restored and far more accessible to the public; its citizens have family roots dating back several centuries, and are proud of their ancestral home. This attitude is clearly echoed in the warmth and hospitality they extend to visitors.

Interestingly, the name "Yucatán" comes from a rather humorous misunderstanding. When the Spaniards first landed in the region in the early 1500s, they asked the indigenous Maya what the area was called. Confused, the Indians replied in their native tongue, *"Ci u than,"* which meant "We don't understand you." Somehow the Spaniards transmogrified the Maya phrase and officially dubbed the territory Yucatán.

Hitting the Yucatán trail inevitably means a trip to Chichén Itzá and at least 1 night's stay in Mérida, but those with more time will want to extend their explorations. To the south lie the stunning ruins of Uxmal and the "forgotten" state of the Yucatán trilogy, Campeche, offering seclusion, sensational seafood, and fortresses from pirate days. To the north is the newly renovated port city of Progreso. To the west, there's the breathtaking flamingo refuge of Celestún. In short, the Yucatán has something for every taste.

En Route from Cancún – The highway from Cancún to Mérida is Route 180, a 198-mile (317-km) trip which will take at least 4 hours to drive, not counting time out to visit the ruins of Chichén Itzá or any of the other sights along the way. Count on spending at least 1 night in Mérida, although with so much to see in the Yucatán, you will probably want to stay as long as your itinerary will allow. To continue on to Campeche, add at least 1 more day to your agenda. A side trip to Celestún or Progreso, or a diversion to Río Lagartos, will mean still another day's drive. Mérida itself is worth spending time in. This colonial city has a traditional charm and distinctive character not found in the flashy resorts of Quintana Roo. The center of colonial Yucatán, Mérida is still the largest city on the peninsula, and the focus of all major business. This is the real Mexico, not a tinsel-town showcase built to appease sun worshipers and party animals. History radiates from every street corner, and the warmth of Yucatecan hospitality is reflected in the smiles of everyone you meet.

The road from Cancún to the border between Quintana Roo and the state of Yucatán is chock-full of enough potholes to make a visitor want to turn around and go back, but take heart: Once you get past the border checkpoint at Pueblo Nuevo, 26 miles (42 km) down the so-called highway, the driving conditions improve 100%. There will still be a bounty of obstacles on the road, but they will be in the form of speed bumps, intentionally placed and adequately marked in advance. Chichén Itzá, the most famous of the Maya ruins, lies 92 miles (147 km) farther, with Valladolid about halfway in between.

VALLADOLID: About 48 miles (77 km) west of Pueblo Nuevo on Route 180 is one of the Yucatán's largest cities. Valladolid doesn't have much to offer; its chief point of interest is a Franciscan monastery on the zocalo in the center of town, completed in 1560. The town was named for the city in Spain where Ferdinand and Isabella, the 15th-century Spanish monarchs, were married. The city also made the history books as the site of a bloody massacre during the Castes War, the 19th-century Maya uprising. At the rejection of the Catholic church by the new Mexican Republic, the long-converted and devout Maya, already distraught from other grievances, rose up against the wealthy landowners. The two sides slaughtered each other from 1848 until the Mexican army claimed victory in 1901.

En route to Río Lagartos – Take Route 295 north from Valladolid for 81 miles (130 km) to Río Lagartos.

RÍO LAGARTOS: Although it is certainly a major deviation from the route to Mérida, a side trip to Río Lagartos is a must for nature lovers. On the northernmost coast of the Yucatán state, this national wildlife reserve is one of only three known nesting grounds for flamingos in the world. Surrounded by dense tropical jungles, this flat, marshy cluster of lagoons is covered every May and June with literally thousands of salmon-hued flamingos that come to lay their eggs and nurture their young. The nesting ground is a peculiar sight to behold. Muddy, cone-shape nests, each accommodating only a single egg, protrude like giant anthills from the marshy waters. The female flamingos stand watch at one end of the nests, gracefully balancing themselves on one leg. Depending on the time of year (although spring is their nesting season), there is usually also a colony of white fledglings (they don't turn pink until they are at least 3 months old). During the spring incubation period, it's hard to get close to the flamingos. Protective of their nests, they startle more easily than usual and if disturbed, panic and often destroy their own eggs. If you do go during the nesting season, your guide will no doubt discourage any attempt to approach the colony any nearer than 100 yards. Throughout the rest of the year, it is possible to get within 70 to 80 yards of the birds without their flying away.

There are several ways to track the flamingos in Río Lagartos, the most practical being on a rented boat captained by a local guide (don't worry about finding a guide; they seem to be everywhere, eager to shepherd visitors through the area). More adventurous flamingo stalkers will want to hike out to the breeding grounds. This can be a tedious and time-consuming experience, but true nature enthusiasts will find it to their liking to explore the abandoned mangrove marshes at the same time that they are hunting the ruby-colored avifauna. Those who opt to go by foot should be sure to wear rubber-soled shoes and take along insect repellent. Though there are several types of water snakes in the area, none are poisonous. Still, it's a good idea to plan to be back in the local town way before dark. It's easy to get lost in the mangroves at night, and although most of the crocodile population that gave the reserve its name (*lagartos* is Spanish for lizards) have been killed off over the years by illegal hunters, you wouldn't want to have a close encounter with one of the few surviving specimens.

Since it will take at least 2 to 3 hours, even by boat, to reach the nesting grounds, you will most likely want to spend the night in the town's only hotel geared for tourists, the *Nefertití* (see *Best en Route*). Don't expect the *Ritz*. The accommodations are spartan to an extreme — no air conditioning or hot water — but the rooms are clean and the food is fair, if somewhat bland.

If time permits, the salt lagoons at Las Coloradas — only 10 miles (16 km) east of Río Lagartos on the same unnumbered road — are a beautiful sight at sunset. The lagoons — where the ocean water is dammed in to evaporate — reflect the light in an incandescent flush of red. Be sure to take a camera. It is also worth noting that these saltworks have been in operation since pre-Columbian times and that the world's largest salt producing company, Exportadora de Sal in Baja California Sur, was modeled after them.

CHICHÉN ITZÁ: About 80 miles (128 km) east of Mérida on the Valladolid–Puerto Juárez Highway is Chichén Itzá. Some of the most dramatic ruins in all of Mexico, these cover 7 square miles. Plumed serpents, carved in stone, appear everywhere in this place, whose name means "at the mouth of the well of the Itzá" (a Maya tribe).

Part of Chichén Itzá, the "new" city, lies on one side of the highway, surrounding El Castillo (The Castle) Pyramid; the ball court (with acoustics so fine a voice scarcely louder than a whisper can be heard 500 feet away); the Temple of the Jaguars, dedicated to an order of warriors; the Temple of the Eagles and the Tigers; and the Thousand Columns, with pillars resembling plumed serpents that at one time, no doubt, supported a roof. Here and there are the Chac-Mools, reclining idols that in spite of their name are no relation to Chac, the rain god. Chac-Mools were the centerpiece on sacrificial altars. They held large bowls in which were placed the still-beating human hearts torn from living victims. Less gory but equally tragic is the sacrificial well, the large cenote lying a short walk from the other ruins. Its depths have been extensively explored, but archaeologists have recovered only a fraction of its contents. The bottom is a bramble of branches and twigs. Recently, divers have brought up the bones of the victims — men, women, and even children. Youngsters were considered most precious; hence, they were the greatest treasure that could be offered to the rain god.

The ruins of Old Chichén across the road are rather less impressive. There is another cenote, or sinkhole well, but it was used for more peaceful purposes, as a water supply. The original Maya, it would seem, were less than enthusiastic about sacrifices. The conquering Toltec were the ones who gloried in killing for their gods. A round observatory, El Caracol (The Snail), in Old Chichén gets its name from the spiral stairway within; its circular structure makes it a rarity among Maya buildings. Some of the observatory's features resemble El Castillo Pyramid. The windows are aligned in such a way as to record the longest and shortest days of the year and are set to permit measurement of astronomical phenomena with precision. On the first day of spring and the first day of autumn, shadows form a serpent's body leading from the temple on top to the carved head on the bottom.

Also in the group of ruins is the ossuary, or bone depository, a 30-foot-high pyramid with stairways on each side and a miniature temple on top. The temple is in the same form as El Castillo Pyramid. This building was used by the Toltec as a burial place. Nearby is the Akad-Dzib, a building of obscure writings and red handprints believed to have something to do with Kabul or Zamná, the god whose name meant "heavenly hand."

There is a smaller group of buildings in Old Chichén that are still overgrown with jungle vegetation. You have to walk along some rough trails to get to them. The structures in this part of Chichén Itzá include the Castillo of Old Chichén, the Temple of the Turtle, the Temple of the Sculptured Jambs, the Temples of the Lintels, and the Temple of the Hieroglyphic Jambs. The paths leading among the different temples are known as *sacbes,* or holy paths, where people often were led to be ultimately sacrificed. There's a sound-and-light show with English narration nightly at 9 PM. Open daily. Admission charge.

In the nearby town of Pisté is *Xaybe,* a large, airy restaurant with leather-strung chairs and a handsome wrought-iron mural; it offers attentive service and a fixed-price (inexpensive) menu that includes good broiled pork chops and baked chicken. There are also buffets for large groups and a generous selection of mixed drinks (phone: 985-71233).

BALANKANCHÉN CAVERNS: Only 5 miles (8 km) from the ruins at Chichén Itzá lie caves sealed for some 500 years. Their beauty is impressive, and entering them today gives one the feeling of stepping into sacred space; in fact, the local descendants of the Maya, who used to hold ceremonies here, thought carefully before opening the caves to the public. The passageways are narrow and steep, and even small children have to stoop sometimes; those prone to claustrophobia stand forewarned. At the end of the caves is a perfectly clear pool that gives the impression of peering into a canyon. Groups are limited to a minimum of 3 and a maximum of 15 (oxygen gets scarce fast). Tours, which last 45 minutes, are given by local guides from 9 AM to 4 PM daily, with a break from noon to 2 PM, or can be arranged through travel agencies in Mérida. Admission charge.

En route to Mérida – Continue about 75 miles (120 km) west on Route 180 to Mérida.

MÉRIDA (pronounced *May*-ree-dah): The capital of the state of Yucatán and, with a population of 900,000, the only city of significant size on the peninsula (the entire state has barely 1.7 million people), Mérida was founded on January 6, 1542, by Spanish nobleman Don Francisco de Montejo. Having razed the nearby Maya city of T'Ho, Montejo salvaged the debris and quarried the local pyramids for stone to construct a "Christian" settlement in its stead, modeled in the Romanesque style of his birthplace, Mérida, Spain.

The Maya, never a people to be easily conquered, responded to the desecration of their city and holy places with a fierce rebellion against the white intruders. On June 20, 1542, 250 Spaniards held off between 40,000 and 60,000 Maya Indians who attempted to lay siege to Mérida, then only 6 months old. This battle marked the end of the Maya era and the beginning of a feudal land-ownership system in which large tracts of property were owned by the Spanish and worked by the Indians, who toiled virtually as slaves. It wasn't until the 1930s that a more equitable system of distribution gave the Indians of the Yucatán a fairer stake in the land their families had lived on for centuries.

Until the middle of this century, the Yucatán Peninsula was so cut off from the rest of Mexico that it was easier to get there from Cuba, the US, or even Europe. It is east of the highlands, and the flat, steamy, tropical jungle peninsula covers about 1,000 square miles of parallelogram-shape land jutting northeast from the Mexican mainland into the Gulf of Mexico. Nowadays, it's possible to drive the 1,000 miles (1,600 km) between Mexico City and Mérida in about 3 days.

Formerly known as the Paris of the West, the White City, and the City of Windmills, Mérida has outgrown all of its old sobriquets. It was called the Paris of the West during the heyday of sisal production, when people were getting rich and importing many luxury products from Europe, particularly from France. With the development of synthetic fiber products, this era was dissolved. It was known as the White City because residents used to wear white and the streets were always spotlessly clean. Today, the streets are still pretty clean, but all colors are now worn. And the windmills that used to pump water from the subterranean rivers have virtually disappeared in favor of more efficient methods.

The Maya sites of Chichén Itzá, Uxmal, Sayíl, and Kabah are all within driving distance of Mérida, and are among the most remarkable testimonies to a historic civilization anywhere on the American continent — or in the world, for that matter. Still others visit with no thoughts of archaeology on their minds. Some of them are said to be marijuana smugglers (although this is mostly myth since the majority of Mexico's illegal drug trade is concentrated along its border towns). Most visitors are nature lovers who come to appreciate the wildlife that inhabit the surrounding natural parks or hunters drawn to the area because of its duck, quail, deer, and wild boar. Indeed, the area has become so popular that some sports enthusiasts make the city the headquarters of their annual or biannual expeditions.

The best source of information about Mérida is your hotel's travel desk or desk clerk, or the tourist information center (in the *Peón Contreras Theater,* Calle 60 near Calle 57; phone: 99-249290); open daily from 8 AM to 8 PM.

Mérida's air conditioned international airport has flights to the US (via Mexico City or Cozumel) and Cuba, but Mérida is also something of a tourist destination in its own right. It has its share of interesting colonial buildings, with several good hotels, restaurants, and a few shops selling local handicrafts. And it has a distinctive-looking population. Look closely: You will probably notice that quite a few residents have broad faces with high cheekbones, and that their eyes are often almond-shape and their noses somewhat hooked. They are also comparatively short. These are the descendants of the ancient Maya, many of whom speak both Maya and Spanish, or sometimes hardly any Spanish at all — a haunting postscript to any tour of the ruins.

The best place to get a sense of the city, flat as a pancake and surrounded by jungle, is from the ground, along any of its main streets. An enjoyable way to sightsee is from a *calesa,* or horse-drawn buggy. There are always several free concerts and regional dance recitals at one of Mérida's many parks every weekday night. Also, during *Mardi Gras* there are parades, dances, bullfights, cockfights, and a king and queen contest.

Except for a few main boulevards, most streets in Mérida are numbered rather than named. It's helpful to remember that all east–west streets have odd numbers; north–south streets have even numbers.

To get a feeling for the city, start at the main plaza, or zocalo, called Plaza de la Independencia. As in all Mexican cities, the main plaza is the center of activity. The most interesting sites, shops, hotels, and restaurants are within 3 blocks of the zocalo; walking is pleasant and easy.

On the south side of the plaza is Casa Montejo, once a lovely Spanish colonial home, built in 1549 as the residence for the Montejo family. Now a bank, it is still impressive. It originally covered an entire block, and even though only a section remains, it's worth a look. The lovely, large rooms were built around two patios and furnished with imported European furniture. Most striking is the stone carving around the entrance door. It's the Montejo coat of arms, flanked on each side by a Spanish conquistador with a foot on the head of a Maya Indian. The figures on top are Adelantado Montejo, his wife Beatriz, and daughter Catalina. Open Mondays through Fridays, 9 AM to 1:30 PM.

Not too far away, on the east side of the zocalo, is the rather majestic, twin-towered cathedral, designed by Juan Miguel de Agüero, the architect who also created Morro Castle in Havana. Above the entrance is the royal coat of arms of Spain; inside, the Chapel of Christ of the Blisters, with a statue reputed to have been carved from the wood of a tree that burned all night but was found untouched the next morning. Open daily, 7 AM to noon and 4 to 8 PM.

Absolutely not to be missed is the Government Palace, on the north side of the plaza at the corner of Calles 60 and 61. Walk into the courtyard and up the back stairs. All the murals lining the walls were painted by Carlos Pacheco, a leading *yucateco* artist. On the second floor of the building is the Hall of History, easily the handsomest room in all of Mérida. Open daily. No admission charge.

Frequently used for fashionable weddings is the Franciscan Church of the Third Order, located on the east side of Calle 60, at the corner of Calle 59. It is considered by many to be the prettiest church in town.

Four blocks from the plaza, between Calles 66 and 64, La Ermita de Santa Isabel is a tiny church notable for its gardens with Maya statuary. Built in 1742, it was originally outside the city's walls and used by travelers as a sanctuary in which they prayed for a safe journey. Nowadays, its small interior botanical garden is a wonderful place just to relax. Open daily to 11 PM.

Originally a Jesuit institution, the University of Yucatán was founded in 1618 as the Colegio de San Pedro. Situated at Calles 57 and 60, it has since expanded considerably to include more than half a dozen separate faculties and several preparatory schools. Open daily.

As you tour the city, you'll no doubt come upon Paseo Montejo, where wealthy 19th-century residents built splendid homes on a wide, tree-lined imitation Parisian boulevard. An 8-block thoroughfare lined with small palaces, chalets, and extravagent monuments, this is truly one of the most amazing sights in Mexico. Be sure to stop at the Monument to the Flag, a giant — flagless — sculpture depicting Mexico's history from the pre-Columbian era to the 20th century.

Refurbished and expanded, *Cantón Palace* (now the *Museum of Anthropology and History*) is one of the finest provincial museums in Mexico. It beautifully depicts the lifestyle of the Maya, and a visit prior to touring the ruins helps bring Maya history into focus. The museum is housed in the largest and perhaps loveliest of the splendid mansions on the Paseo Montejo formerly the official residence of Yucatán's governors; the entrance is on Calle 43. Closed Mondays. Admission charge.

Once a walled city, Mérida had 13 Moorish gates, of which only 3 remain today. One is the Arco de San Juan (Arch of St. John), about 5 blocks south of the plaza on Calle 64 in San Juan Park, which has a statue of Rachel at the well near its central fountain. This arch leads to the hermitage, La Ermita de Santa Isabel (see above). The Dragon Arch is near the Dragónes military regiment's headquarters, at Calles 50 and 61. The third, Bridge Arch, is at Calles 50 and 63.

A bit of a hike from downtown, the *Museo Nacional de Arte Popular* is well worth it. This small museum exhibits masks, pottery, clothing, and other examples of *yucateco* arts and crafts. Upstairs there is an excellent — though completely unorganized — collection of folk art from all over the country. There is also a shop on the first floor, with incredibly reasonable prices. Calle 59 between Calles 48 and 50. Open Tuesdays through Saturdays from 8 AM to 8 PM.. No admission charge.

If you've had your fill (temporarily) of churches, museums, and archaeological tours, Mérida is also a great city for shopping; the public market, or *mercado* (on the corner of Calles 56 and 67), is a good place to find local crafts. It's usually less expensive than anyplace else in town if you have the patience to bargain. Shops (and offices) usually open between 8 and 9 AM, close for lunch and a siesta from 1 to 4 PM (when the sun is at its strongest), then open again at 8 PM. The most popular native crafts are bags and placemats made of sisal, a hemp fiber. Yucatecan hammocks of various sizes, made of fine cotton thread, are a great buy; another is the *jipi,* a fine version of the Panama hat, made by hand near Mérida. The *guayabera,* a tailored men's shirt in solid colors, with or without an embroidered front, is a typical Yucatán product that you can buy in shops throughout Mérida. The average price for a good cotton shirt with long sleeves is less than $20. Most stores also stock a few articles made from tortoiseshell (if purchased, these will be confiscated by US Customs), and there are replicas of the Maya idols. Stores usually have fixed prices, so you can't bargain as in the market. The main shopping streets are Calles 57 and 59 in the 10-block area between Calles 54 and 64. The following are those we consider to be the best shops in town:

Casa de las Artesanías – There is no bargaining at the government-run handicrafts store, but the prices are very reasonable. 503 Calle 63 between Calles 64 and 66 (no phone).

Guayaberas Jack – Theme and variations on the traditional *guayabera* — short and long sleeves, white or pastel, embroidered or plain. The best are 100% cotton. 507 Calle 59 between Calles 60 and 62 (phone: 99-215988).

Marie-Soleil Boutique – Fernando Huertas sells a tasteful selection of crafts, as well as his French-inspired designs in cotton. 511 Calle 59, between Calles 62 and 60 (phone: 99-216035).

Palacio – More of Fernando Huertas's selection, as found at the *Marie-Soleil Boutique.* Calle 62 between Calles 59 and 61 (phone: 99-218550).

For sportspeople — spectators and otherwise — Mérida offers a variety of activities. Bullfights are held on Sundays throughout the year, but the big-name matadors usually perform only from January through March. The *Plaza de Toros Mérida* is on Paseo de la Reforma, a block from Avenida Colón.

This area is excellent for hunting and fishing. Hunting for duck, quail, deer, and wild boar is no problem, so long as you check with the Mexican consulate nearest your home for information on regulations for importing arms. Manuel Cano (147 Calle 33, Progreso; phone: 993-50727) arranges hunting and fishing trips; Victor Vales at *Maya Tours* (425-4 Calle 60; phone: 993-243022) has a hunting club and is also quite reliable. Inquire at your hotel or at the tourist information center. Good angling can be found at Río Lagartos, famous for the pink flamingos that call it home (see *Río Lagartos*). Almost all of Mérida's hotels have small swimming pools, and there are quite a few nice beaches and good water skiing 23 miles (37 km) north, at Progreso.

Though Mérida's after-dark action is on the quiet side, the *Panamericana Calinda* has a Mexican fiesta Friday and Saturday evenings and regional dances other nights. *Los Tulipanes* (462 Calle 42; no phone) is where tour buses take the crowds to see native dancers, while the *Montejo Palace* (phone: 99-247644) has a rooftop supper club, and the *Misión Mérida* (phone: 99-239500) has a nightclub. The *Trovedor Bohemio* (no phone) and *Peregrina Piano Bar* (by Santa Lucia Park; no phone) both offer drinks and relaxed entertainment, including guitar music. *Kalia Rock House* (no phone), about 10 minutes from downtown, and *Excess* disco (no phone) are the current favorites. The *Holiday Inn*'s nightclub (phone: 99-256877) is also popular, as are *Oasis, Charro* (no phones), *El Cocoon* at the *Panamericana Calinda* (phone: 99-23911), and *Bin Bon Bao* (no phone).

EATING OUT: The Yucatán has a distinct cuisine, and Mérida's restaurants offer ample culinary opportunities. Very little chili is used in cooking, although it is served alongside the main dish as a sauce. Many meat and fish dishes are wrapped in banana leaves and then baked in outdoor ovens, a method that originated because of the hot climate. Pickled and charcoal-broiled meats are Yucatecan specialties, too. Try the *cochinita pibil* (pork baked in banana leaves); *papadzul* (hard-boiled eggs chopped into a filling for a tortilla, topped with a sauce of ground pumpkin seeds); *panuchos* (open-faced tortilla topped with chicken and pickled onion); and *pollo pibil* (chicken baked with achiote sauce in banana leaves). Expect to pay up to $40 for a meal for two in the restaurants we've listed as expensive; $25 at those places listed as moderate; and about $15 at inexpensive ones. Prices do not include drinks, wine, or tip. Reservations are advised at midday for all expensive places. In the evening, reservations are unnecessary unless otherwise noted. Most restaurants listed below accept MasterCard and Visa; some also accept American Express and Diners Club. Unless otherwise noted, all restaurants are open daily.

Alberto's Continental Patio – Set in a lovely colonial mansion with outdoor and indoor dining areas; the Lebanese dishes here are first-rate. There are also some continental and local specialties. The service is very friendly. 482 Calle 64 (phone: 99-212298). Expensive.

Amarantus – Decorated with light wood and rattan and lots of plants, this bright, spacious spot serving continental food is cheerful and friendly. There's a video bar with live music. 250 Paseo de Montejo (phone: 99-268752). Expensive.

Carlos 'n' Charlie's – A member of the Anderson group popular throughout Mexico, it features good salads and oysters, and winsome waiters. 447-A Prolongación Montejo (no phone). Expensive.

La Casona – Fifteen tiled tables with caned chairs rim an interior courtyard with a lovely fountain; there's also an inside dining room, sporting unusual antique barber's chairs at the bar. Italian food, including homemade pasta, is the highlight, but the steaks and seafood rate, too. The restaurant's cellar stocks French and Mexican wines. Open for lunch and dinner. 434 Calle 60 at Calle 47 (phone: 99-238348). Expensive.

Château Valentín – Converted from one of Mérida's elegant 18th-century homes, this establishment serves well-prepared regional dishes such as *pollo pibil* as well as international fare. 499-D Calle 58-A at Paseo de Montejo (phone: 99-255690). Expensive.

Le Gourmet – Once an elegant home, it specializes in French and creole cooking and is where the local gentry go to celebrate on big nights out. Closed Sundays. 109-A Av. Pérez Ponce (phone: 99-271970). Expensive.

Muelle 8 – Well-presented, fresh seafood is served in a wharf warehouse setting where you can almost taste the salt air. 142 Calle 21 (phone: 99-274976). Expensive.

Pancho's – In spite of its Mexican name, the owner is Canadian and the menu is continental, with lots of flambéed dishes prepared tableside. With its ancient photos and Victrola, it resembles an old antiques store — kind of like *Carlos 'n' Charlie's,* Maya-style. Live music and dancing are featured Wednesdays through Saturdays. Dinner only. 509 Calle 59, between Calles 60 and 62 (phone: 99-230942). Expensive.

Picadilly's – An elegant English-style pub, but the atmosphere is casual (ties and jackets are not required) and the fine food is strictly gringo: barbecued ribs, onion rings, pasta, and grilled beef, with cherry cheesecake for dessert. Live music and dancing are featured in the evenings. 118 Av. Pérez Ponce (phone: 99-265391). Expensive.

El Pórtico del Peregrino – It consists of romantic courtyards and dining rooms in a chapel-like setting. The low-key atmosphere is enhanced by a menu that includes shrimp grilled in garlic, chicken liver shish kebab, baked eggplant casserole with chicken; also delicious desserts and homemade sangria. On Calle 57 between Calles 60 and 62 (phone: 99-216844). Expensive.

Yannig – Named after its inspired chef, this small, sophisticated spot set in a beautiful old home delivers well-prepared and appetizingly presented dishes, among them crêpes with a mild roquefort sauce, New Orleans–style chicken, and *popiette* (fish and mushrooms in a pastry shell). Open for lunch and dinner. 105 Av. Pérez Ponce (phone: 99-270339). Expensive.

Los Almendros – This is one of the best places to sample the finest in *cochinita pibil, panuchos, pollo pibil,* and other Yucatecan delicacies. Service is slow, so be prepared to spend a long time. 493 Calle 50-A, between Calles 57 and 59, in front of the Plaza de Mejorada (phone: 99-212851). Moderate.

La Prosperidad – The local favorite, hands down, it serve Yucatecan dishes in a large, thatch-roofed dining room. A variety of appetizers accompanies each meal. Entertainment is live and lively, as is the ambience. Good fun. Calle 56, corner of Calle 53 (phone: 99-211898). Moderate.

Dulcería y Sorbetería Colón – A well-known, well-loved ice cream parlor. All the ice cream is made from fresh fruit (coconut is the most popular flavor), and you get a lot of it for a little money. No credit cards accepted. On the plaza and at Paseo de Montejo between Calles 39 and 41 (phone: 99-213304). Inexpensive.

Jugos California – This Art Deco bar serves only juices, but what juices! Luscious tropical fruits line the walls, and all the drinks are made with honey. No credit cards accepted. Calles 62 and 63, on the plaza, and elsewhere around the city (phone: 99-234142). Inexpensive.

Kon Tiki – If you're hungering for Chinese food, here's the local place to go. All the usual dishes, surprisingly well prepared. 194 Colón and Calle 14 (phone: 99-254409). Inexpensive.

Siqueff – An unassuming, cheerful place with hearty fare, its menu includes venison filet (in season). The fruit drinks made with bottled water are quite good. There is also take-out service and, rare among restaurants here, a public phone. 553 Calle 59, corner of Calle 68 (phone: 99-249287). Inexpensive.

Yaxbé – Almost identical to *Xaybe* in Pisté (see *Chichén Itzá*), and run by the same owner, it's conveniently located at the edge of the ruins (no phone). Inexpensive.

Mérida is a good base for those who would like to explore this area but would rather not go through the hassle of packing and unpacking. The following day trips are within easy drives of the city, and the sites can be covered to most travelers' satisfaction within a day's time.

DAY TRIP 1: PROGRESO

Just 23 miles (37 km) to the north of Mérida lies Progreso, the only major seaport on the Yucatán and the peninsula's major commercial link with the outside world since colonial times. Over the course of the last few years, the Yucatán state government has been promoting *maquiladora* (assembly plant) investment to take advantage of the region's cheap labor, low-cost property, and ready access to the US and Caribbean markets, by offering big tax incentives and redeveloping the port facilities in Progreso. The city's 3½-mile pier, the longest in the world, was officially opened for operation in 1990, and business has been booming ever since. Route 261 from Mérida to Progreso is the best highway on the peninsula — a well-lighted, four-lane thoroughfare meticulously maintained to encourage further investment capital to cash in on the Progreso renaissance. The state's only golf course, *La Ceiba,* is also on this highway, just 9 miles (15 km) north of Mérida, on Km 14.5 of Route 261 and if you didn't bring your clubs, a set can be rented for a small fee.

DZIBILCHALTÚN (pronounced Zee-bee-chal-*toon*): About 13½ miles (22 km) north, just off the road to Progeso, this archaeological site can be reached in about 20 minutes from downtown Mérida. To get there, take Route 261 north 9 miles (15 km), until you reach *La Ceiba* golf course. Turn right and continue down a very narrow road (about one and a half lanes for two-way traffic, so watch out for oncoming vehicles) for about 4 miles (6 km). This is the archaeological site closest to Mérida and the place believed to have been inhabited longest by the Maya — from about 1500 BC until the arrival of the conquistadores. The Temple of the Seven Dolls is especially interesting during the spring and autumn equinoxes, when the light is reflected through parts of this series of complex structures, once used by the Maya as a solar observatory. Open daily from 8 AM to 5 PM. Admission charge.

PROGRESO: Back on Route 261, continue north for 14 miles (22 km) beyond *La Ceiba* to Progreso, the hub of the Yucatán's international commercial exchange, where huge crates of honey, cement, sisal rope, fish, steel, and locally assembled lingerie line the docks awaiting dispatch to markets in the US, Canada, and even Europe. There is an electric rail system that transports the cargo to the far end of the pier to be loaded aboard freighters, as well as a wide boulevard open to passenger cars and trucks. It takes a full 5 minutes to drive to the end of the pier, but along the way you can get a feel of the sheer stamina and architectural genius that went into the construction of this engineering feat. The reason the pier is so long is that the Yucatán Peninsula is set on a giant limestone shelf that gradually drops off into the gulf (there are geologic hypotheses that the Yucatán, Cuba, and Florida were once a single expanse of land). For over 3 miles out, the water off the pier is only about 20 feet deep. At the pier's end, there is a visitors' center with a very modern, very clean cafeteria and a small museum which highlights the history of the pier.

In contrast to the turquoise waters of Cancún and Cozumel, the water in the Mexican Gulf is emerald green, and the sand on the beaches is considerably coarser and has a golden hue. The beaches are rarely crowded, and there are water skiing facilities as well as plenty of fishing boats for hire. There is an abundance of open-air fresh seafood restaurants along the shore near the pier, but for a special meal with an Old World flair, drive 10 minutes west along the coastal highway to Yucalpeten Beach and the elegant restaurant at the *Sian-Ka'an* hotel or the equally fine dining place at the *Fiesta Inn* on the *malécon*. These are also ideal spots for an overnight stay for those who want to get away from it all (see *Best en Route*).

After visiting Progreso, take Route 261 south back to Mérida.

DAY TRIP 2: CELESTÚN

Those who didn't get up to Río Lagartos on their way to Mérida still have a chance to view Yucatán flamingos by taking a day trip to Celestún, the state's other major nature reserve. The 58-mile (92-km) drive west on Route 281 is extremely scenic, and the charm of Hunucmá, a quaint little town on the way, is one of the state's best-kept secrets. The drive will take about 2 hours, mainly due to the winding roads, speed bumps, and unexpected obstacles (such as stray cows, lost dogs, and abandoned bicycles) that tend to materialize suddenly in the middle of the highway, so leave early in order to have enough time to see everything. Committed ornithologists may want to spend the night and see these coral-colored birds in the light of dawn. There is a small, very rustic hotel in town which is slightly, albeit *only* slightly, more comfortable than camping out on the beach.

HUNUCMÁ: In addition to its being exceptionally clean, the first thing you will notice about Hunucmá, 12 miles (19 km) west of Mérida, is that all of the houses are fenced by low, whitewashed stone walls. As you follow the meandering road toward the center of town, you will also encounter another distinguishing characteristic of Hunucmá: There are almost no cars, but the streets are teeming with three-wheeled pedicabs busily transporting people, merchandise, and even loads of squeaking piglets from one end of town to the other. These open-air pedaled carriages are an efficient, practical, and inexpensive means of getting around in a town that is spread over 20 square miles of pitted terrain. There is even a central cab rank in the main plaza where pedicabs are ready and waiting to scurry off in any direction a paying passenger may request.

Hunucmá's zocalo, or main square, is also noteworthy. Lined with shady eucalyptus trees, this tranquil plaza, peppered with ice cream carts and *huipil*-clad old women enjoying the afternoon sun, is a scenic vestige of bygone years. On weekends, the plaza comes alive with activity when the local orchestra offers a free concert of Yucatecan music. Across from the plaza stands the 16th-century Church of San Francisco de Asís (the patron saint of the region), the second-largest cathedral in the Yucatán (the largest is in Mérida). While somewhat run-down, this three-doored basilica still maintains an aura of its past glory.

As you leave Hunucmá to continue on to Celestún, the route passes through two smaller towns, Tetiz and Kinchíl. At the far edge of Kinchíl, 9 miles (14 km) beyond Hunucmá, the highway divides into what initially looks like two dirt paths. The only marking (at the time of this writing) is a small, barely decipherable, hand-painted sign that is nailed to one of the buildings. Whether or not you see the sign, turn right for Celestún.

CELESTÚN: From Hunucmá to Celestún, there are 46 miles (74 km) of lonely, flat highway surrounded by jungle. After nearly an hour's drive through this wilderness and almost without warning, a bridge marks the outskirts of Celestún.

Across the bridge, on the right-hand side, is the National Center for the Study of Aquatic Birds. With luck, you may be able to convince one of the ornithology students from the center to give you a personalized tour (in English) of the marshlands, replete with an academic explanation of the breeding, migration, and nesting habits of each of the 230 species that inhabit the refuge. More likely, you will have to hire a boat and guide at the bridge. A 2½-hour tour will run about $20 to $25, depending on the size of the boat, time of year, and availability of guides (the old supply-and-demand factor comes into play). Make sure to check the boat before agreeing on a price. The best bet is a motorized fiberglass craft with a captain who looks at least old enough to have a learner's permit to drive in the States. This is the place to use insect repellent, since mosquitoes and other pests can be a major problem, particularly during the summer. Also, don't forget sunscreen, rubber-soled shoes, and a hat. Most of the trip is in open marsh, where the sun's intensity is multiplied by the still reflections on the water.

It takes about half an hour to get to the flamingos' feeding grounds. Unlike Río Lagartos, Celestún is not a breeding ground for these rosy-plumed birds, but there is usually a small colony of white fledglings feeding to one side of the adult population. As you approach the birds, your guide will shut off the motor to keep from spooking them. Once they notice human visitors, they will take off running in near military formation, charging across the shallow waters until they gather enough speed to take flight. During the mating season (April through May), there can be as many as 100,000 flamingos at any given site. As they flood the air, the birds create an awe-inspiring giant cloud of pink that sails gracefully overhead.

When you've had your fill of flamingos in flight, ask your guide to take you through the *manglares* (mangrove forests) that surround the marsh. There is a hidden pool with an underground spring, which feeds the marsh with sweet water that is ideal for a quick dip to cool off before taking the boat back to your car. Also to be seen at Celestún are colonies of pelican, loon, stork, crane, avocet, and heron. Sea turtles are common as well, as are spider monkeys and ocelots, but chances are you won't catch a glimpse of these creatures unless you are in the marsh either at dawn or at dusk.

Although none of the restaurants in Celestún could be categorized as premier dining establishments, there are a few open-air cafés downtown (all one street of it), along the ocean shore, which offer fresh seafood at extremely reasonable prices. The best (and cleanest) is the *Celestún* (on Calles 11 and 12). A family-run business, this place specializes in seafood dishes. The *Gutiérrez,* a modest, 18-room hotel down the street, has overhead fans and hot-water showers. The rooms are meager, but clean enough (see *Best en Route*). To return to Mérida, retrace your steps, traveling east along the unmarked road.

DAY TRIP 3: UXMAL

The ruins of Uxmal (pronounced Oosh-*mahl*) are about 50 miles (180 km) south of Mérida on the Mérida–Campeche Highway (take the left-hand fork at Umán, 11 miles/18 km beyond Mérida; after another 30 miles/48 km, bear right at the fork, at Muna). Not as large as Chichén Itzá, Uxmal is equally fascinating. The buildings here are purely Maya in style, without later Toltec influences, and are lavishly decorated with masks, cornices, and mosaics. Uxmal means "built three times," but a number of structures appear to have been rebuilt as many as five times. Among the most remarkable sites are the extremely steep and somewhat oval Pyramid of the Magician; the Nunnery Quadrangle, whose façade contains many carved rain god masks, serpents, and figures of warriors; the House of the Doves, so named for the dovecote design in the roof comb; and the huge, ornately carved, 320-foot-long Governor's Palace.

Many of the ruins at Uxmal remain almost unexplored, and there is plenty to see. Archaeologists move slowly among the remote sections of the ruins, sifting through every spoonful of earth as it is removed. This is why Uxmal's large ball courts remain mostly wilderness. The House of the Old Women and the Temple of the Phalli still await further exploration. Guided tours usually take about 4 hours. Many come back after a tour just to wander among the monuments. Uxmal has a sound-and-light show with a recorded English narrative of its history nightly at 9 PM (in Spanish at 7 PM). Open daily. Admission charge.

KABAH: This ceremonial center 12 miles (19 km) south of Uxmal was built in the same architectural style, though smaller. Largely unrestored, Kabah is most notable for its Temple of the Masks, the façade of which is covered with innumerable carved masks of the rain god, Chac. Most impressive, too, is Codz-Pop, a rare spiral-shape pyramid. Also found at Kabah is the great arch, the gateway to the ancient causeway linking this city with Uxmal. Open daily from 8 AM to 5 PM. Admission charge.

SAYÍL AND LABNÁ – A paved road has replaced the old dirt lane that leads to these two Maya ceremonial centers, which previously could be reached only by jeep. Sayíl is 20 miles (32 km) from Uxmal; Labná, 5 miles (8 km) farther. Little of either site has been restored, but it is still possible to appreciate the fine sculpture and carving that decorate the façades of their palaces. Open daily, 8 AM to 5 PM. Admission charge.

Day-trippers should take Route 261 north back to Mérida. However, travelers who are continuing beyond Mérida on this route through the western Yucatán should instead stay on Route 261 south to Campeche, 142 miles (227 km) past Labná (see *En Route to Campeche*).

En Route to Campeche – When leaving Mérida to continue the route through the western Yucatán, drive south on Route 261 toward the port city of Campeche. The entire 228-mile (365-km) trip should take about 5 hours. That leaves plenty of time to poke around the various Maya ruins along the route (see *Day Trip 3: Uxmal*) and still get to Campeche by dusk.

Just beyond Mérida, take the left-hand fork at a town called Umán.

UMÁN: Only 11 miles (18 km) southwest of Mérida, Umán is a thriving suburb of the Yucatán's capital city. In earlier days, however, Umán was a great city in its own right. The majestic domed early-17th-century Cathedral of San Francisco de Asís, which can be seen several miles away from town, is evidence of its past glory. Occupying 2 city blocks, the church constitutes one of the finest examples of Franciscan architecture in all of Mexico.

Continue south on Route 261 for about 30 miles (48 km) to Muna, where the road divides again. Bear right. The road soon goes past the Maya ruins of Uxmal, Kabah, Sayíl, and Labná (see *Day Trip 3: Uxmal*). Continue south on Route 261.

BOLONCHÉN DE REJÓN: This side trip on the way to Campeche is a must for spelunkers. Even for amateurs, these stalactite-studded caverns 200 feet below the earth near the Campeche state line, about 100 miles (160 km) southwest of Uxmal, are worth a look. Bolonchén, which means "nine wells," refers to the nine Maya cisterns once used to supply water to the inhabitants in pre-Columbian times. The de Rejón part of the name comes from Manuel De Rejón, a local hero who drafted the Mexican constitutional amendment that guarantees the right of habeas corpus for all prisoners.

For a small fee, a guide will escort you through the subterranean passages. Don't try to explore these caves on your own. They go on for miles with extremely dangerous reaches, and at present, only the first few chambers have been fitted with lights and handrails.

When you leave Bolonchén de Rejón, you will be entering the state of Campeche (pronounced Com-*pay*-chay), home to over half of Mexico's shrimp boats. The word "Campeche" is actually a Maya acronym for "land of serpents and ticks," but don't let the name throw you. Rich with oil, Campeche is a place where the pace is slow and the living is easy. In fact, if a Mexican wants to say that a person is lazy or tends to put things off, he will call him a *campechano*. A meal, for example, can take up to 3 or even 4 hours in Campeche, where the idea of rushing through anything, especially something as enjoyable as savoring good food in the company of friends and family, is as alien as snow in the tropics. Foreigners, used to the hurried world of fast-food restaurants and a 45-minute lunch hour, sometimes find the leisurely tempo of *campechano* service hard to adjust to; smart visitors will just lean back and enjoy the laissez-faire lifestyle.

HOPELCHÉN: About 21 miles (34 km) south of Bolonchén de Rejón, the road angles sharply to the right at Hopelchén. Founded in 1622, this town's only distinction is that it was once totally surrounded by a military fort constructed on top of Maya ruins during the latter half of the last century. Most of the fort walls have since collapsed, but remnants of the structure, intermingled with hints of small pyramids, can still be discerned by a careful observer. There is also a 17th-century church, dedicated to St. Anthony, with a giant wooden altar composed of ten hand-painted portraits of the patron.

Campeche is 56 miles (90 km) south of Hopelchén on Route 261.

CAMPECHE: One of Mexico's least visited and most picturesque port towns, Campeche has been walled and fortressed from the early days of the Spanish conquest. No one has ever bothered to promote tourism here, but with a couple of fine hotels and some unique monuments, Campeche is waiting to be discovered. Its fortresses and walls resemble a Caribbean city, unique along Mexico's Gulf Coast.

Cortés first landed on Mexican soil at the site of Campeche in 1517; founded in 1540, the city steadily increased in importance. The conquistadores discovered logwood, a rare and costly source of dye, growing in the nearby forests. By the mid-1550s, they were getting rich exporting the precious commodity to Europe. Though remote and isolated, Campeche rapidly grew into one of the most thriving cities of New Spain — and attracted the attention of Caribbean buccaneers. Rich as Campeche was, it was also defenseless. The city was first sacked by William Parck and his band of cutthroats in 1597. Thirty-five years later, in 1632, a pirate known as Diego el Mulato did it again. Then came Peg Leg (yes, there really was a swashbuckler by that name), and Laurent de Graff, a Dutch adventurer whom the locals dubbed Lorencillo. L'Olonois of France, who had a sweetheart in town, was another frequent visitor. This Frenchman earned a reputation as the most sadistic of buccaneers due to his habit of eating his victim's eyeballs! In 1685, when Lewis Scott, another buccaneer, sacked the place once again, the city decided to protect itself. The people began work on the wall and forts in 1686, a task that took 18 years to complete. Parts of the wall have since been removed, evidence of more peaceful times, but the two main gates and seven of the original eight fortresses remain. The wall and the gates now offer endless possibilities to photographers and watercolorists, who may well never want to leave.

The former Fort of San Pedro is now a handicrafts market. The tourist office (in the former Fort of Santa Rosa; phone: 981-67364) is where you can get a guide to show you around town. The rooftop of San Pedro is much as it was in days of old, its fighting deck heavy with now-ancient cannon. How these quaint guns managed to stop marauding men-of-war from taking everything in sight is not easy to understand, but clearly they did. The marksmen must have been remarkable. With a bit of persuasion and a few extra pesos, your guide will take you to the secret passageways beneath the fort. Now mostly sealed off with bricks, these tunnels once linked many houses in the city. Some of the passages were built during the Maya period and were simply expanded by the Spanish. These underground hiding places sheltered women and children when pirate ships came into view.

The *Casa del Teniente del Rey* (Lieutenant del Rey House) has been converted into the *Campeche Regional Museum,* with an interesting collection of Maya objects, including a jade mask and a collection of jewelry discovered in the Colakmul tomb. Closed Mondays. Admission charge. *San Miguel,* the handsomest of all Campeche's fortresses, is now a museum displaying pirate arms and portraits of the worst scoundrels who harried the city. There is also a model of walled Campeche as it looked nearly 3 centuries ago. The guides are quite fond of telling horror stories about how San Miguel's moat was filled with quicklime instead of water, or how the water was stocked with crocodiles. They are somewhat vague about whether any malefactor ever earned his grisly reward by being tumbled into the moat. Open daily. Admission charge. Calle 59.

Church lovers, who will find pickings pretty slim along the Yucatán Peninsula, can score comparatively heavily in Campeche. The cathedral on the main plaza was completed in 1546 — only 6 years after Don Francisco de Montejoy-León ordered construction to begin, on the same day that he founded the city. The San Francisco Monastery, just off the *malecón* (seafront esplanade), is nearly as old. Mass was first said here in 1546. About 20 years later, the grandson of Hernán Cortés was baptized here at a font still in use today.

Campeche has its modern side, too. The brightly colored Government Palace has been dubbed "the jukebox" by irreverent local citizens, and the modern Legislative Palace is known as "the flying saucer." In fact, these modern structures were rather carefully designed to fit in with Campeche's unique native architecture and have completely avoided the glass-box look so prevalent in many high-rise sections of Mexican cities. Nonetheless they have offended the taste of the city's proud and conservative older guard. Other modern additions that have pleased residents more are the city's growing network of wide, handsome boulevards and the futuristic University City — rivaled only by the suburb of the same name in Mexico City.

Campeche is noted for its seafood, especially the shrimp it sells all over the world. Some crab (*cangrejo moro*), pompano, and a black snapper (known as *esmedregal*) are local favorites. Campeche is also known for its intriguing seafood combinations. In addition to shrimp and oyster cocktails, there are *campechanos* in which both are served together. Light beer and dark beer are served half-and-half, too, on request. The restaurant in the *Baluartes* hotel, Campeche's most modern hostelry (see *Best en Route*), serves good seafood and accepts major credit cards. The *Miramar* restaurant, across the street from the Government Palace, is less expensive and more crowded, but serves food that's at least as good as the *Baluartes*'s, in a junky waterfront setting.

EDZNÁ: Archaeology buffs will want to make a side trip to this exceptional Maya site. Only 38 miles (61 km) southeast of Campeche, Edzná is surprisingly easy to reach. Follow Route 180 due south to a town called Cayal, 26 miles (42 km) from Mérida. Turn left and follow a rather bumpy Route 188 for 12 miles (19 km) and you will almost literally run right into this site.

One of the oldest ruins in the Yucatán, Edzná is believed to have been inhabited as early as 600 BC. The name, which translates to "House of the Grimaces," refers to the two grim masks that are encrusted in the base of the Five-Story Temple, the largest construction in the ancient city. Because of the "Puuc" architecture, characterized by elaborately decorated façades, pre-Columbian authorities have linked the builders of this 3-square-mile vestige with the classic Maya who populated Guatemala.

While the pyramids themselves are not particularly impressive (only three of the structures have been restored), Edzná boasts the most advanced hydraulic system in the whole of the Maya world. Because of its geographic position, the area receives little or no rain except during the summer. Consequently, the resourceful engineers who laid out the city designed a complex network of dammed reservoirs and irrigation canals to store and distribute water.

Towering 120 feet high, the Five-Story Temple is clearly the center of attraction in Edzná. The steps are overgrown with weeds and in poor repair, so it's not a very good idea to plan on scaling this edifice. However, in order to get an overview of the main plaza below and the rest of the ruins, you probably can work your way up the temple's first or second story without any major calamities. To the left is a smaller pyramid, Paal U'Na, or the House of the Moon. Just behind this building is a small acropolis, which can barely be distinguished in the underbrush. Opposite Paal U'Na is the Northern Platform, with five chambers that apparently were used for storage of sacred treasures. There is also a ball court and elongated annex that must have served as a living quarters for Edzná's chieftains and shamans, who are buried beneath heavy foliage.

En Route from Campeche – Unlike the winding Ruta Puuc, which snakes its way from ruin to ruin, the coastal road back to Mérida is a straight, smooth shot from Campeche. Route 261 east of the city picks up Route 180 north in Chenocoyi, a tiny village (if a few thatch huts can be called a village) 17 miles (27 km) out of town. From then on, the road heads in only one direction, so it is practically impossible to get lost. Because the road is well paved and adequately maintained, the 121-mile (194-km) drive will take only about 2 hours. The main stop along the way will undoubtedly be Oxkintók, which has only recently been opened to the public. Constructed sometime during the 5th century, this site was excavated during the late 1980s by European archaeologists, through funding provided by the Spanish Ministry of Culture as part of a program to commemorate the 500th anniversary (this year) of the discovery of the Americas. It is believed to have been the largest Maya city in the Yucatán Peninsula. You may also want to stop off in Becal to pick up a Panama hat.

POMÚCH: Located 23 miles (37 km) northeast of Campeche on Route 180, Pomúch is renowned throughout the region for its spongy, sweet bread, purported to be the best in Mexico. As you drive past, you will see a series of roadside stands selling this sugary fare. As long as the bread is sealed in plastic bags, you might want to sample it and find out firsthand why the town has gained such acclaim.

BECAL: If you want to buy a Panama hat, Becal, 32 miles (51 km) farther north on Route 180, is the best place in Mexico to find one. Using only the finest straw from the *jilijapa* palm, the inhabitants of this town have been mass-producing these hats for over a century and exporting them to literally every corner of the globe. As you drive by, you may notice that most of the houses in Becal have large mounds in their courtyards that resemble oversize firing kilns for ceramics. These are in fact manmade caverns which are used to keep the straw moist and flexible during the weaving process. In addition to hats, the Becalans are very adept at fashioning shoes, handbags, necklaces, and other items from the *jilijapa* palm.

OXKINTÓK: Past the Campeche–Yucatán state border, 11 miles (18 km) north of Becal, is the modern-day town of Oxkintók. Turn right on the dirt path marked "Maxcanu" and continue about 4 miles (6 km) to find the archaeological ruins. Don't expect to find a lot of signs indicating how to get to this site. It was virtually unknown until 1986, and has been open to the public only since last year.

Excavated courtesy of a grant from the Spanish government, Oxkintók, constructed in the 5th century, is now considered to be the largest Maya vestige on the peninsula. Although archaeologists are still trying to determine its exact size, experts estimate that the city extended over at least 7 square miles, and during its heyday, in the late 9th century, Oxkintók probably was inhabited by as many as 50,000 Maya. Oxkintók, which means "Three Stone Suns," was in fact the New York City of the Maya world, serving as a merchandising and distribution center for the entire region, as well as a gateway for trade with the Mexican mainland.

The main building, Santunsát, is a giant 3-story labyrinth, the only one of its kind in the Yucatán. This rectangular edifice measures over 20 feet high and includes seven long passageways on the ground floor that intertwine in a complex maze to eventually reach the second floor, which has eight meandering chambers. The third and final level has only four tangled hallways to surmount, leading to a narrow exit on the east side. To date, no one has been able to determine with certainty what function this structure served. The local townsfolk maintain that those who offended the gods were locked in its chambers as punishment for their crimes and could find their way out again only if they repented. Modern scholars, on the other hand, contend that the maze has a more esoteric significance, suggesting that the building's 3 stories represent the 3 levels of the universe — the underworld, the earth, and the heavens. Other theories about Santunsát include that it might have been an observatory or a burial site, a premise supported by the fact that a tomb and small burial urn were discovered nearby during the latest excavations. A word to the wise: Do not attempt to explore this labyrinth without an experienced guide, or you could spend the rest of your vacation trying to solve the mystery of Santunsát from the inside out.

There are also several other less impressive, if less intimidating, structures at Oxkintók. Among these are a mammoth-size ball court, 27 stelae etched with Maya glyphs, a huge stone head of the sun god Kinich Ahua, and two rather ho-hum pyramids.

Exploring this site can take up to 4 hours (or longer — *much* longer — if you get lost in the labyrinth), so amateur archaeologists who want more than a superficial glance should give themselves plenty of time to enjoy it by leaving Campeche early in the morning.

Alternate Route from Campeche – If you want to continue the Yucatán Loop, drive southeast to Chetumal, stopping to take in the ruins of Kohunlich, but this is not a journey for the timid-spirited. Although the trip is only 260 miles (416 km), it is a tedious odyssey that can take up to 7 hours to complete because every few miles the roads are pitted with industrial strength *topes* (road bumps), which can wreak havoc on both your timetable and your shock absorbers. This is wild jungle country, and traveling these parts is similar to roaming around the headwaters of the Amazon. Roads are new in this part of Mexico, and amenities are sparse. It is a good idea to take along a box lunch and fill up whenever a gas station comes into view.

From Campeche, follow Route 180 south for 41 miles (66 km) to Champotón, the last stop on the Gulf of Mexico coast. Champotón is noteworthy because it was here in 1517 that Hernández de Córdoba and his party celebrated the first mass on the American continent. Route 261 leaves Route 180 at Champotón and continues due south to Escárcega. Little more than a collection of huts, Escárcega is where you pick up Route 186 east to Chetumal. From here on, the jungles close in. It is not unusual to see an ocelot or tapir darting across the road. Tarantulas on the asphalt are downright common. The scenery is not particularly beautiful, but neither is it quickly forgotten.

Underscoring the remoteness of the region is the customs shed at the Quintana Roo state line. No one driving in has to stop, but vehicles leaving Quintana Roo are required to submit to a customs inspection at the checkpoint. As a free zone, beyond the reach of Mexico's protective tariffs, Quintana Roo has always been a base for smugglers and gun-runners. A word of warning: If you choose to take this less beaten path, do so with care. The area is notorious for *bandidos* (highway bandits) who prey on unsuspecting motorists by placing sharp rocks in the middle of the road to cause mechanical breakdowns. Should you have a sudden blowout along the way, do not stop immediately. Instead, slow down slightly and continue at least half a mile or so down the highway before pulling over. This will no doubt damage the tire beyond repair, but it could well protect you from the hands of a modern-day pirate. For detailed information on Chetumal and alternate routes back to Cancún, see *The Yucatán Peninsula: Cancún to Chetumal* in this section.

BEST EN ROUTE

This area offers a wide assortment of hotels, some elegant, some downright primitive. With the exception of Mérida, many villages and towns in the Yucatán are simply too small and too informally arranged to require street addresses for hotels and restaurants. Most towns have only one or two streets. Therefore, occasionally a specific address (as we know it) may not exist. For a double room, expect to pay up to $100 at an expensive hotel; $40 to $70 in moderate places; and $35 or under in inexpensive ones.

VALLADOLID

María de la Luz – Pleasantly modern, it's a nice little provincial hotel with a swimming pool, restaurant, and bar with live entertainment. 195 Calle 42 (phone: 985-62071). Moderate.

Mesón del Márquez – Heavy on atmosphere, this old-fashioned colonial inn is one of a dying breed, with 24 rooms and 2 suites, a restaurant-bar, and gardens. 203 Calle 39 (phone: 985-62073). Moderate.

RÍO LAGARTOS

Nefertití – With a nice view of the lagoon, this modest place is clean and comfortable enough, although amenities are sparse. There is a restaurant (which closes early), and overhead fans. There is also hot and cold running water, but no air conditioning. Still, given that the 20-room inn is the only hotel in town with anything even approaching a two-star rating, you haven't got a lot of options. No credit cards accepted. 123 Calle 14 (no phone). Inexpensive.

CHICHÉN ITZÁ

Dolores Alba – Absolutely lovely and a nice change of pace from hotel stays, this country house has only 18 rooms, each with a private terrace. There's also a cozy dining room, pool, and tropical grounds. Km 122, between Chichén Itzá and the Balankanchén Caves (phone: 985-213714; FAX: 985-283163; 99-283163 in Mérida). Expensive.

Hacienda Chichén – Just a century ago this was a private hacienda; today it is a hotel with rooms available in individual bungalows. Facilities include ceiling fans, restaurant, bar, and a pool. Open from November through *Easter*. Chichén Itzá (phone: 985-62777; 99-248722 in Mérida; 800-824-8451 in the US). Expensive.

Mayaland – Overlooking the ruins, this luxury resort has large, old-fashioned rooms, a restaurant, cocktail terrace, swimming pool, and evening entertainment. East Access Road (phone: 985-252122; 99-252133 in Mérida; 305-341-9143 in the US; FAX: 99-62777). Expensive.

Misión Inn Chichén Itzá – This modern hotel has 40 air conditioned rooms, bar, restaurant, pool and lovely grounds. Rates include breakfast and dinner. Pisté, about a mile (1.6 km) from Chichén Itzá (phone: 99-239500 in Mérida; FAX: 99-237665). Moderate.

Villa Arqueológica – This Club Med guesthouse attracts people who love Maya culture and modern comfort (phone: 1-800-CLUB-MED; 99-62830; 5-203-3086 or 5-203-3833 in Mexico City; FAX: 5-203-0621 in Mexico City). Moderate.

Pirámide Inn – So comfortable, it's hard to leave it to explore the ruins. Facilities include a pool, tennis courts, lush gardens, restaurant, bar, even a book exchange. The 47 air conditioned rooms are adequate. Chichén Itzá (phone: Pisté, Exchange No. 5). Inexpensive.

MÉRIDA

Holiday Inn – Built in the colonial manner, with old trees incorporated into the design. There are 213 rooms and suites, a tennis court, pool, nightclub, and a fine specialty restaurant. Air conditioned. Just off Paseo Montejo at Av. Colón and Calle 60 (phone: 99-256877; 800-HOLIDAY in the US; FAX: 99-257755). Expensive.

Los Aluxes – A modern 109-room hostelry, it rises white and impressively spotless between Paseo de Montejo and the zocalo. It has an outdoor pool and poolside bars, dining room, and a cheerful coffee shop whose placemats are the best city map available. 444 Calle 60, between Calles 49 and 51 (phone: 99-242199; 800-782-8395 in the US; FAX: 99-233858). Moderate.

Casa del Balam – Only 2 blocks from the plaza, this neo-colonial establishment has 54 air conditioned rooms, a swimming pool set in an attractive patio, a good dining room, and a bar. At Calles 57 and 60 (phone: 99-248241; 800-624-8451 in the US; FAX: 99-245011). Moderate.

El Castellano – With 170 rooms, it's one of Mérida's largest and sleekest hotels, including a spacious, hacienda-style lobby. Amenities include shops, restaurant, bar, and swimming pool. Air conditioned. 513 Calle 57, between Calles 62 and 64 (phone: 99-230100; FAX: 99-263389). Moderate.

Misión Mérida – Entrance is through a beautiful 19th-century mansion. The 147 rooms are located in a modern tower, and have air conditioning and cable TV. There's a coffee shop, lobby bar, and restaurant. Three blocks from the zocalo at 491 Calle 60 (phone: 99-239500; 800-648-7818; FAX: 800-648-7818). Moderate.

Montejo Palace – Quiet, with 90 air conditioned rooms, all with refrigerators and small balconies. In addition to a dining room and a good coffee shop, *Las Farolas,* there is a cocktail lounge. 483-C Paseo Montejo (phone: 99-247644; 800-221-6509; FAX: 99-280388). Moderate.

Panamérica Calinda Mérida – A Quality Hotels property with a lobby and reception area housed in a turn-of-the-century mansion, it has 110 modern, air conditioned rooms, color TV sets, a restaurant, and a bar. There is a Mexican fiesta Friday and Saturday nights; regional dances from the state of Yucatán are performed other nights. Downtown at Calle 59 between Calles 52 and 53 (phone: 99-239111; 800-228-5151; FAX: 99-248090). Moderate.

Autel 59 – A comfortable, modern property just a few blocks from the main plaza. Its 106 rooms are all air conditioned, and there's a restaurant and pool. 546 Calle 59 at Calle 68 (phone: 99-242100). Inexpensive.

Casa Mexilió – American Roger Lynn took an interesting 150-year-old Mérida home, complete with patios, sun decks, and balconies, and turned it into a bed and breakfast establishment, filled with antiques and crafts that reflect his love of the country. The 5 rooms have private baths, and there is a pool and Jacuzzi on the central patio. Mr. Lynn arranges for transportation from the airport. 495 Calle 68 between Calles 57 and 59 (phone: 99-214032; 800-538-6802 in the US). Inexpensive.

Colón – An old-fashioned, air conditioned gem, a block from the zocalo, it has a pool, sauna, a pleasant restaurant, and breakfast buffet. Twelve of the 53 rooms have steambaths. 483 Calle 62 (phone: 99-234355). Inexpensive.

Del Gobernador – A tidy, tasteful spot, it offers a good restaurant, live music several times a week, and a very small pool. 535 Calle 59 at Calle 66 (phone: 99-237133; 800-458-6888 in the US; FAX: 99-281590). Inexpensive.

Gran – This replica of a turn-of-the-century French hotel has elaborate ceilings, columns, and large, old-fashioned rooms, some air conditioned. The 3-story building centers around a delightful patio. There is a good dining room. Cepeda Peraza Park (phone: 99-247622). Inexpensive.

Paseo de Montejo – A 5-story modern colonial-style establishment, it has 92 air conditioned rooms, color TV sets, restaurant, bar, and pool. 482 Paseo de Montejo (phone: 99-239033). Inexpensive.

Posada Toledo – Only some rooms are air conditioned, but it's set in a gorgeous old house that is furnished with antiques and has a magnificent garden in the patio. The owner speaks English. This is a delightful alternative to larger, more impersonal establishments. Three blocks from the plaza at 487 Calle 58 (phone: 99-232256). Inexpensive.

PROGRESO

Fiesta Inn – The finest in town, this 38-room hostelry opened in late 1990 to accommodate the sudden flood of businesspeople and government officials cashing in on the rebirth of the city's port facilities. It has a lobby bar, restaurant, cafeteria, swimming pool, and gift shop. All rooms are air conditioned and have cable TV. On the *malecón* (phone: 993-25072). Expensive.

Sian-Ka'an – This 6-suite, air conditioned inn is a holdover from earlier days when service was personalized and mass anything was unthinkable. Manager Edgardo Sánchez attends to each guest's needs on a one-on-one basis and the home-style menu changes daily. Definitely a class act. Calle 17 on the Chelem Highway (phone: 993-51243 or 993-273525). Moderate.

Tropical Suites – Another small establishment, this 10-unit place is geared to families and groups that prefer to rough it and do for themselves. Kitchenettes, overhead fans, and big balconies with a view of the ocean. 143 Calle 19 (phone: 993-51263). Moderate.

Posada Juan Carlos – Owned by a Swiss family, this 16-room hotel operates primarily for European tour groups. The rooms are clean, but stripped down to the minimum and devoid of any personal touches. 148 Calle 24 (phone: 993-51076). Inexpensive.

Real del Mar – A 10-unit motel with overhead fans, a restaurant-bar, and a big sandy beach all to itself. Calles 19 and 20 (no phone). Inexpensive.

CELESTÚN

Gutiérrez – The only halfway presentable place in town, this 18-unit facility is a bit reminiscent of a dormitory for seminary students — not much to offer but a cot, hot shower, and overhead fans. 107 Calle 12 (phone: 99-246348). Inexpensive.

UXMAL

Hacienda Uxmal – Elegant and charming, it has large, cool rooms, some air conditioned, that overlook lovely gardens. Restaurant, bar, shops, and 2 pools (phone: 99-23597; 99-252133 in Mérida; FAX: 99-247142). Expensive.

Misión Inn Uxmal – A modern, air conditioned place, with a restaurant and pool (phone: 99-247308; FAX: 99-247308). Moderate.

Villa Arqueológica – Right in front of the ruins, this air conditioned hostelry is equipped with the standard facilities of all Club Med Villas Arqueológicas: a good French restaurant, pool, and tennis (phone: 1-800-CLUB-MED; 99-247053; 5-203-3086 in Mexico City; FAX: 5-203-0681 in Mexico City). Inexpensive.

CAMPECHE

Alhambra – Its 100 rooms are air conditioned, and there is a restaurant, coffee shop, disco, pool, and satellite TV. 85 Av. Resurgimiento (phone: 981-66822 or 981-66092). Expensive.

Ramada Inn – This is a fine hotel with a swimming pool, bar, disco, and restaurant. 51 Av. Ruíz Cortinez (phone: 981-62233). Expensive.

Baluartes – Here is a handsome, well-located, traditional hotel that is near the sea, with a swimming pool and restaurant. 61 Av. Ruíz Cortinez (phone: 981-63911). Moderate.

López – Small and friendly, it is known for its charming bar and restaurant. The air conditioned rooms are furnished quite comfortably. 189 Calle 12 (phone: 981-63021). Moderate.

Siho Playa – If you want to stay around for more than 1 night, this small resort is perfect. With a tennis court, boat rental (about 3 miles/5 km from the hotel), swimming pool, and restaurant, the environment is very relaxing. At Km 40 of the Carr. Campeche–Champotón (phone: 981-62989). Moderate.

INDEX

Index